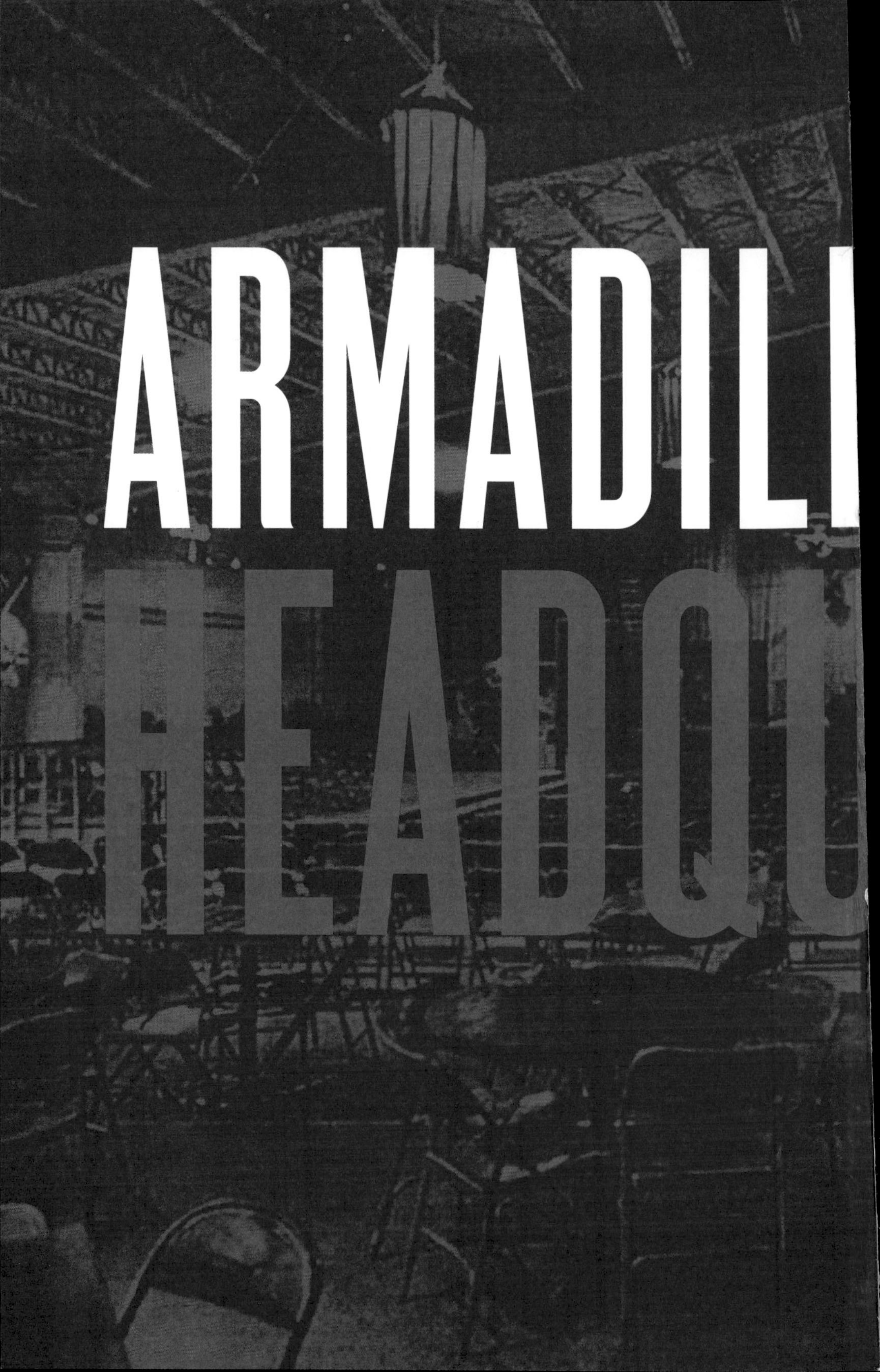
ARMADIL
HEADQU

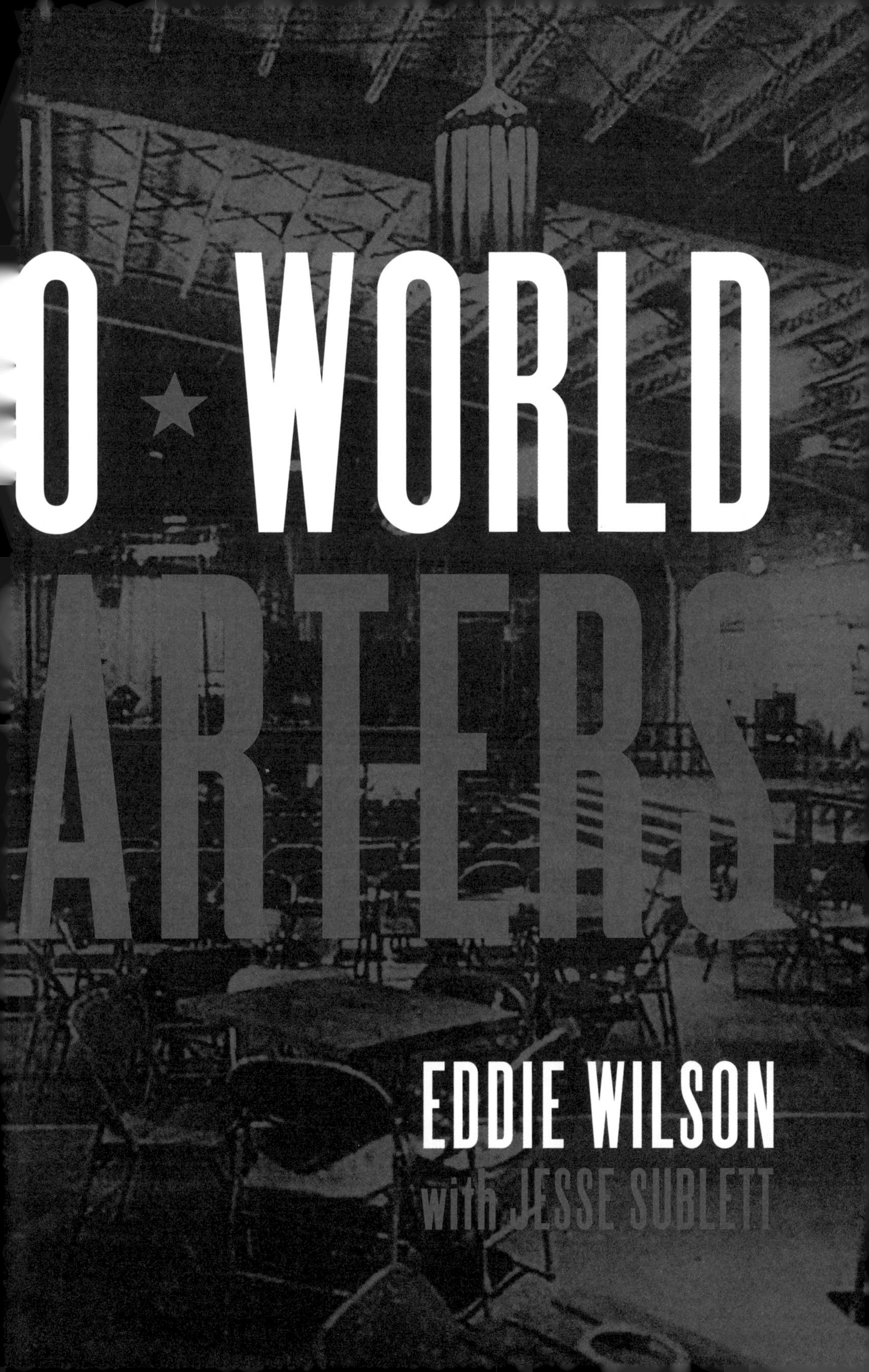

O ★ WORLD

ARTERS

EDDIE WILSON

with JESSE SUBLETT

Published by
TSSI Publishing
6416 North Lamar Blvd
Austin, Texas 78752
Telephone: 512-574-2544
Fax: 512-451-3256
geninfo@threadgills.com
www.threadgills.com

Distributed by
University of Texas Press
P.O. Box 7819
Austin, TX 78713-7819
Telephone: 800-252-3206
Fax: 512-232-7178
info@utpress.utexas.edu
www.utexaspress.com

ISBN 978-1-4773-1382-4 (cloth : alk. paper)
ISBN 978-1-4773-1415-9 (library e-book)
ISBN 978-1-4773-1416-6 (non-library e-book)

DEVELOPMENT, DESIGN, AND PRODUCTION
Lindsay Starr Communication & Book Design

COPYEDITING AND INDEX
Abby Webber

PROOFREADING
Lynne Chapman

PRINTER AND BINDER
Four Colour Print Group

Printed on acid-free paper

Facing: Burton Wilson and Sandra Wilson,
October 18, 2000. Family snapshot.

FOR BURTON & SANDRA

"IT REMINDS ME OF WHAT THE BEAVER TOLD THE RABBIT AS THEY STOOD AT THE BASE OF HOOVER DAM: 'NO, I DIDN'T BUILD IT MYSELF, BUT IT'S BASED ON AN IDEA OF MINE.'"
CHARLES TOWNES

"IT IS THE JOB OF ARTISTS TO PUT FEAR IN THE HEARTS OF ADULTS."
JIM FRANKLIN

"FAILURE IS THE ARCHITECT OF SUCCESS."
M. K. HAGE JR.

CONTENTS

FOREWORD ix

PREFACE xi

ACKNOWLEDGMENTS xv

Introduction 1

Earning My Hippie Card 11

Now Dig This 31

Cosmic Justice 47

Head Honcho 75

The Armadillo Art Squad 91

A King, a Domino, a Captain, and a Leo 103

Digging for Progress 117

Living the Dream 129

A Cultural Refinery 135

Things Were Looking Up 145

The Great Redneck-Hippie Merger 159

A Breed Apart 185

Being Thankful for What We've Got 191

Not Your Daddy's Beer Joint 199

The First Willie Nelson Picnic 215

Armadillo TV, or What Might Have Been 227

Then the Rains Came 233

Home with the Armadillo 237

Long Live Longnecks 247

Pot, Big Red, Acid, Coke, and Pumpkins 257

Feeding the Legend 267

Crosstown Competition 275

Traveling Armadillo Blues 299

Dear Lone Star 303

The First and Final Annual AWHQ Newsletter 311

Rough Waters 317

One Last Swing for the Fences 333

Eddie Has Left the Building 351

The Raw Deal and a White Rabbit 355

The Armadillo Emerges 369

Last Call 383

Full Circle 395

APPENDIX: A SELECTION OF GIG POSTERS FROM AWHQ 413

A NOTE ON SOURCES 475

NOTES 477

INDEX 487

FOREWORD

Like all the greatest stories told about the '60s, Eddie Wilson's starts in the '70s. It stars a batch of redneck hippies, plus a slew of politicians, an occasional jock, and many others, often involved in nefarious activities, sometimes in alleyways, more often in the statehouse. Eddie and his crew set out to change the world, and at the very least, they turned Austin into what it is today, God help us all. Eddie's story is by turns hilarious, informative, and the living spirit of its age, illuminating a previously under-detected transition point between the psychedelic peace-and-love crowd and a world where Shiner Bock—warm Shiner Bock—is the ideal social lubricant. Technically, it's the story of the joint where Bruce Springsteen found an audience about as far from New Jersey as you can get, and where Don Meredith discovered his true home field. But Eddie Wilson serves up even better than that. Eddie piles the most unlikely anecdotes on top of one another, creating a land of enchantment and an order of chemically altered consciousness that rescues an era I'd thought not so much lost as forgotten. Not only am I thrilled I've read this story and wish I was in it, I wish I'd written it.

Dave Marsh
April 2016

Ann Richards, AWHQ reunion, 1994.
Photograph by Burton Wilson.

PREFACE

I SHARE MY BIG DREAM WITH THE RICHARDS FAMILY

Ann Richards, governor of Texas from 1991 to 1995, made the following remarks when she delivered the keynote address at the South by Southwest festival in 1993.

I'm delighted to welcome you to Texas in Austin, Live Music Capital of the World. You know, the natives believe that we are the center of the musical universe, and this week, that is literally the truth. We are proud to have all of you and glad that you can experience firsthand what Texans take for granted, and that is that the amount and the quantity and quality of live music that you hear in Austin, Texas, on nearly any night is the best that the country has to offer. Texas music has become much more than what you hear in a bar with the chicken wire stretched between the band and the patrons.

Over twenty years ago, a friend of mine named Eddie Wilson called me and my husband and said that he wanted us to go see a building because he was about to make a dream come true. And so we went with him out to South Austin to this great, big, old, barny place, and it had all the windows broken out of it and it looked like it was about to be demolished in the interest of the health and safety of Austin, Texas. You must understand that these were in the days, as Ray Wylie Hubbard said the other night, before Willie Nelson brought the rednecks and the cowboys together.

So my husband and I walked in with Eddie to this big, old barn, and it was dirty, and Eddie said, "We're going to make a music center of the universe right here." And as usual, we thought something was wrong with Eddie, that for one reason or another, his vision had become blurred, but of course that was the beginning of the Armadillo World Headquarters, which indeed was one of the most exciting, and remained one of the most exciting, places in the United States for the years that it was in operation. I saw a little of everything at the Armadillo, and it was one of the great experiences of my life.

I met Ann and Dave Richards in the 1960s when I was a college student in Denton. David, an attorney, was involved in politics, and Ann was known for, among other things, Democratic fundraisers in which she and other women performed their scathing "Political Paranoia" parodies of Texas politicians.

The Richardses divorced in 1976. Ann died in 2006. Dave is still a good friend. The following was originally published in his memoir *Once Upon a Time in Texas: A Liberal in the Lone Star State*:[1]

Eddie, who is a true genius and especially adroit at spewing and spinning ideas, came and grabbed us one day to show us his dream project. He had located an abandoned National Guard armory just across the Colorado River in South Austin. He was going to turn it into a music hall and cap-ture the emerging Austin music scene. The place was vast, full of junk, and looked impossible to resurrect. We underestimated Eddie's determination and energy. Shortly, the Armadillo World Headquarters burst on the scene and became the embodiment of Austin funk of the 1970s. With Jim Franklin as resident artist and sometime master of ceremonies, the 'Dillo radiated a deranged quality that defied normalcy and attracted all sorts of people.

The astonishing thing was the wide acceptance of the Armadillo mes-sage. Here was a rock-and-roll joint peopled by stoned freaks and hippies that managed to achieve mainstream acceptance. The city of Austin ended up naming its shuttle bus service "the 'Dillo." The Lone Star beer company began a major promotion featuring Jim Franklin's armadillo art. Arma-dillo was the kind of place that would have been regularly raided by the cops in an earlier era, and yet it became a chamber of commerce icon, one of the things you brag about in promotional materials.

*All kinds of music came through the place. I saw such diverse perform-
ers as Bette Midler, Bill Malone, Ray Charles, and Commander Cody.
The rise of redneck rock and the outlaw image was intimately associated
with the Armadillo. Its opening somewhat coincided with Willie Nelson's
return to Texas and the emergence of an anti-Nashville movement led by
Nelson, Waylon Jennings, and Jerry Jeff Walker, among others. Although
the state abhorred the lifestyles presented by the Armadillo and these
musicians, the "don't give a shit" attitude they personified hit a responsive
chord in the Texas psyche. Everyone seemed to share the sentiment from
"London Homesick Blues" of wanting to "come home to the Armadillo."
So a strange little snuffling nocturnal creature came to replace the longhorn as the state's favorite beast.*

The Richardses had four children, Cecile, Daniel, Clark, and Ellen.
Cecile is well-known today as an articulate figure in progressive politics
and the longtime president of Planned Parenthood. She remembers that
visit to the "old, barny place," too.

*When we moved to Austin, I remember Eddie Wilson taking us all to this
abandoned armory over there off Barton Springs. It was completely empty,
and Eddie explained that he had this idea that he was going to make it into
this important music venue, and it sounded completely cracked at the time,
but of course then it became the Armadillo. And it became such a center
of not only great music and people who probably never would have performed in Austin, but it was a cultural cornerstone. It was amazing. And I
think that was a time when progressive politics really took hold in Texas.*

*Other people, like Esther's Follies and the people involved in that, were
part of that community, too. And then, of course, after the Armadillo kind
of folded, Eddie opened the Raw Deal and then Threadgill's. Those were
important cultural places for a group of freethinkers, if you will, and political liberals, and it led to a lot of people running for office and getting elected.*

*The Armadillo is really where we as kids grew up, because, to my par-
ents, the Armadillo was the place, and it was better than a babysitter. It
was a huge part of our upbringing, and an entire decade, if not more, of my
parents' lives.*[2]

THREADGILL'S

"EAT YOUR   VEGETABLES"

BEULAH WILSON

HOME COOKING

EDDIE WILSON, PROPRIETOR

EST. AUSTIN, TEXAS

ACKNOWLEDGMENTS

I am deeply indebted to the many people who have contributed to my wonderful life and to this modest rendering of it. If I paid just the interest on that debt this page would be far longer than the book. That is reason enough to use the cover of the Threadgill's menu here with Kenneth's name and Mother's picture, and a very sincere thank you to all the rest.

Eddie Wilson

ARMADILLO ★ WORLD
HEADQUARTERS

Jim's genius was at work when he did his "Heads and Necks" handbill. In addition to predicting what was to come of the local social scene he managed to advertise more than one location and multiple residencies in one effort. Ironically, both venues on the handbill burned down within quick succession. The next night I got the key to the future AWHQ. Jim was understandably paranoid. Poster for the Hub City Movers residency at the Cactus Club and Bonnie's. Artwork by Jim Franklin.

INTRODUCTION

★

If not for the coincidence of a swollen bladder and a flimsy lock on a derelict building, there might never have been a place called Armadillo World
Headquarters. What followed is such a strange and unlikely story that,
forty-five years later, I sometimes wonder if it really happened at all.

But it did happen, starting on a night in July 1970 after I had consumed several warm beers watching a band called the Hub City Movers
at a South Austin bar called the Cactus Club. I needed to take a leak, but
a long line of guys waiting to use an overflowing urinal stirred a primal
instinct to venture outdoors.

Joining me on this quest were band members Jimmie Dale Gilmore
and . We crossed the parking lot and found a wall that suited our purpose.
Normally, I might have told them how much I'd enjoyed their set, but as
I stood there relieving myself in the dim light, I was having a fantastic
vision, one that compared with the best chemically enhanced hallucina-
tions I've ever experienced—and I've had some doozies, skull epics that
would compete with the best of Steven Spielberg and Cecil B. DeMille.

My epiphany was prompted by the sight of a cinderblock wall, maybe
two hundred feet long and more than twenty feet tall. High up were rows

of metal-framed windows, some of them broken. There had to be a huge room on the other side.

If I said a word to Jimmie Dale or John, I don't remember it. After zipping up, I left them and walked around the building in the dark until I found a loading dock door on the west side. It was even darker there, because of a giant oak tree looming overhead, but I was still able to jimmy the lock and slip inside. The only light came through the overhead windows, but what I could see was enough to make my heartbeat shift into jackrabbit gear. The blend of fear and excitement was just as strong as when, four years earlier, after being tricked into joining the marine corps, I had gotten lost and stoned in the wilds of Mexico and gone bull riding.

I went back to get "Big Blue," my '66 Dodge Charger, and drove around to the building. I raised the garage door, pulled in, got out, and held my breath. It was an auditorium, enormous and scary. Scary, because I knew that I was looking at my future.

There were doors in every direction. I walked along a wall, opened a couple, and saw nothing but pitch black. Not until I opened a door along the giant south wall did I find enough light to see even further into the future. The floor rose abruptly about three feet. It was a ready-made stage.

I stumbled into another room and flicked my cigarette lighter. Before me was a Texas-sized restroom with enough urinals to empty the bladders of an army—which made sense, because in one of the building's past lives, it had been a National Guard armory. I tested a sink; the water worked. Though I had pissed only a few minutes earlier, I tested one of the urinals, just for luck.

Apparently, the building was available. It was crying out to be used, and I wanted it. Although I didn't have the faintest idea how to go about making it mine, somehow I knew that I would.

It seems incredible now, but with the help of a few friends and like-minded misfits, Armadillo World Headquarters (AWHQ) opened its doors for business just three and a half weeks later. We started out with 16,000 square feet of space and ridiculously cheap rent—$500 a month— free parking in every direction, and a passionate staff willing to work for next to nothing. Those three things were absolutely essential to the success of our strange enterprise.

I take credit for being the "founder," the one who saw the empty, huge, ugly building, immediately "flashed" (as we used to say) on its potential, and started the legwork for making it happen. The small, tight cadre of individuals who ended up being partners in the new enterprise were for the most part people who showed up and pitched in during the hectic couple of weeks before we opened. These were people whose arms didn't have to be twisted before they joined the parade. Mike Tolleson was a good example. He came in when the sawdust was flying and the paint drying. As it turned out, Mike had come down from Dallas with the idea of starting a music and cultural incubator himself. "I saw it and I got it immediately," says Mike. "The thing I was looking for was already coming together, so I talked to Eddie, moved down from Dallas a couple days later, and started doing Armadillo stuff twenty-four hours a day."[1]

Jim Franklin was already at the Dillo making murals and signs and, in general, helping build out the place in his own inimitable image. He was one of the first people I called after that night at the Cactus. Jim recruited Bobby Hedderman, a fellow veteran of the Vulcan Gas Company, Austin's short-lived, premiere psychedelic music emporium.

There were others, particularly Genie Wilson, whom I was married to at the time. Genie had a good job, and we were all essentially unemployed but too busy to get jobs. Without her, we probably would've starved to death. Carlotta Pankratz kept our books. Mike Harr climbed aboard our leaky ark on the bleary-eyed, litter-strewn morning after our first night. Hank Alrich showed up a little later. Just in time to save our asses.

And, not to make this sound like an acknowledgments page, it would be a crime not to mention the bar and kitchen staff, the gang of hippie carpenters, and the army of general volunteers. But as things shook out over the first two years, these were the seven people, along with me, who constituted the core team. We eight were the ones who would become the official shareholders two years later, but from the beginning, Armadillo World Headquarters was a d.b.a. of Armadillo Productions Incorporated. I'll go into more detail later, but trust me, during the first two years, the casual business structure suited everyone just fine, because other than expenses and debts, there really wasn't much for any of us to claim ownership of. We were in it for the music and the lifestyle, not the money. Nowadays, that might sound like a bunch of hippie-dippy hyperbole, but it's the damn truth.

Armadillo World Headquarters opened on August 7, 1970, and closed its doors for good on January 1, 1981. At the midpoint of the decade, we

Jim Franklin and Eddie Wilson onstage at
AWHQ, 1972. Photograph by Van Brooks.

were enjoying creative and financial success. We had gained a world-wide reputation as a great music hall, and bands went out of their way to play the Dillo because of our high standards of production, profession-alism, and hospitality. It was a happening place where audiences knew how to make a band feel welcome. One way to measure the good times at the Armadillo is in gallons of beer: only the Astrodome sold more draft Lone Star Beer than we did. That's right, the famed 44,500-seat domed stadium, often referred to in those days as the "Eighth Wonder of the World," was the only joint in the Lone Star State that moved more kegs of LSB than our 1,500-capacity hippie music emporium.

The next five years were a reminder that what goes up must come down, and one of the casualties of that period was my own position as head cheerleader, ringleader, and buck-stopper. In November 1976, I turned the reins over to Hank Alrich, who had already done more than anyone could humanly expect to help keep the place running.

During its remarkable and unlikely ten-year run, the Armadillo helped nurture and grow an Austin music scene, spreading its gospel around the world. In the thirty-five years since, the reputation of Austin as a music city has experienced exponential growth, and no small part of that is due to the work we did at AWHQ. Today, Austin is renowned for hav-ing an astounding abundance of resident musicians, venues, studios, and other essential organs for a thriving music scene infrastructure, along with music festivals that are the envy of the world. The biggest of them all, South by Southwest, began in 1987, six years after the Armadillo run came to an end.

One of the other big Austin festivals is Austin City Limits (ACL), where you'll find even more Armadillo DNA and connective tissue. The ACL music festival originated as a spinoff of the PBS series of the same name, the longest-running live music program in television history, which is produced by KLRU and first aired as a series in 1976. At the Armadillo, we were heavily involved in video production and had been putting per-formances on cablevision ever since the place opened. In fact, we pro-duced a show called the Armadillo Country Music Review in partnership with KLRU, then KLRN, in July 1973 and were involved in various aspects of developing a music series when the TV station decided to produce its own show. Some of my cohort remained involved for a time, even after that show was produced and picked up in 1975 as a series under the name

AWHQ staff, 1974. Photograph by Coke Dillworth.

Austin City Limits. Even after our involvement in the production ended, the Armadillo got a shout-out every week—"I wanna go home with the Armadillo / Good country music from Amarillo and Abilene"—in the chorus of the theme song, Gary P. Nunn's "London Homesick Blues."

In my opinion, AWHQ was quite simply the best music hall in the country—maybe even the whole world. Thousands of musicians played there: Willie Nelson, Frank Zappa, Bruce Springsteen, Taj Mahal, AC/DC, Charlie Daniels, the Ramones, Roy Buchanan, and Bette Midler, to name a random few. The interesting thing is that so many of them kept coming back. They loved the place: the acoustics, the people who worked there, the huge nachos and other scrumptious food we served them, and the way the Armadillo made them feel a part of something bigger.

Another secret to our tenacity might have been our affinity for the lowly nine-banded armadillo. We named the place Armadillo World Headquarters primarily because the anachronistic armored mammal had already been established by Jim Franklin as the icon of Texas hippies and, as such, we identified with the armadillo for spiritual as well as artistic reasons.

Artists at the University of Texas humor magazine the *Ranger* first began incorporating armadillo images in satirical pieces in the early sixties. Frank Erwin—the head of the UT Board of Regents who was held in special disdain by our community for his overarching, fascistic, redneck influence—reacted as if the snide references to the mammal were evidence of some sort of leftist plot or cult, a reaction that naturally inspired even greater demand for armadillo imagery and *Dasypus novemcinctus* itself.

In the late sixties, artists Gilbert Shelton and Jim Franklin pioneered a new visual style and vocabulary for the underground scene. Franklin had taken over from Gilbert at the Vulcan Gas Company. Armadillo images figured prominently in their handbills and other work created to promote the venue. Gilbert departed for San Francisco, and the Vulcan folded in 1970, but Franklin dug in his heels in Austin and brought the emerging visual vocabulary and attitude to the Armadillo on day one.

Music historians have also credited the Armadillo with being the place where two previously clashing groups of people—rednecks and hippies—found themselves under the same roof, enjoying a new blend of country music and rock, along with cold beer and cheap pot. The movement was already under way before Willie Nelson played AWHQ, but once he did, he joined our armored mammalian mascot as another icon of the cultural melting pot.

Jim's first armadillo, the rest is history. Poster for a
concert at Wooldridge Park, September 29, 1968.
Artwork by Jim Franklin.

On the outs with Nashville, Willie had recently moved to Austin and started to grow his hair long. We met, shook hands, and booked a show. Rednecks and hippies met under the arched roof of the Armadillo at his first gig on August 12, 1972, and struck up a lifelong relationship. The convergence was a boost to our business and spawned a many-named movement: cosmic cowboy, progressive country, and redneck rock, among others. That music and the Armadillo were practically joined at the hip, and in a larger sense, so were the music and Austin. The Armadillo nurtured the fan base of other long-haired country rock artists who followed in Willie's wake, a handful of the best-known names being Waylon Jennings, Michael Murphey (later on he started calling himself Michael Martin Murphey, but we all knew him as Michael Murphey during the Dillo days), Billy Joe Shaver, and Steve Fromholz. But less than two years after Willie's debut on our stage, he bought his own concert venue, the Austin Opry House, and became our chief competition.

We were always struggling behind the scenes, sometimes in public, just to keep the place going. The size of the venue, one of its big assets, also made it almost impossible to manage. The place had no air-conditioning, no heat. So we were constantly forced to innovate, adapt, and experiment. No wonder it often resembled a bunch of adolescents' Mad Scientists Club. Some of those experiments, like the beer garden (an attempt to get people to come out during the summer months), were great successes.

Drawing on my background in the beer business, I worked on countless pitches to beer companies for cross-promotions. One of those campaigns was the "Long Live Longnecks" slogan that was vividly brought to life with Jim Franklin's brilliant posters combining images of longnecks and armadillos. Decades later, those posters are collectible works of art. Some of them are worth a lot of money, but more important, collectively, they are significant links to an amazing period in history, links that trigger heavy emotional responses in the people who experienced that period.

During the lifespan of the Armadillo, it helped define the Austin lifestyle, culture, and identity. Word spread that AWHQ was not only a great, unique music hall, but a place where having a few cool ones in the beer garden could be a life-affirming or even life-changing experience. For many visitors, a trip to the Armadillo was first on their list of important things to do.

Seems like a lifetime ago, doesn't it? Well, it *was* a lifetime ago. In 1970, Austin was a city of 252,000 people, known primarily as the home of the state university and the state capital, not as a place where people traveled from far-flung locations to indulge themselves in an orgy of live music, planning spring breaks and vacations around it. Today, Austin is the eleventh most populous city in the United States and the third-fastest-growing large city. For the entire lifespan of the Armadillo, the property was for sale at a price of $1 million to $1.5 million. Today, that's the price of a nice condominium or family residence in the neighborhood.

Never again will local economics allow for such a curious enterprise as ours.

After the Armadillo closed its doors on January 1, 1981, I was sad, I was relieved, and for the longest time, I was haunted. I'm writing the story of the Armadillo as I knew it, which means there may be some mistakes, and there will surely be parts that annoy the hell out of some people. But I don't know any other way to do it.

I am doing this not just for myself, but for all those people who pitched in and hung on during the ten-year tug-of-war to keep the joint alive and kicking, the people who risked all to try to keep the doors open and the music playing. With volunteer help, chewing gum, duct tape, gumption, bits of string, and a heaping helping of want-to, we worked miracles on a daily basis.

When I was growing up, my mother, Beulah, constantly impressed upon me the idea that if I put my mind to something, there was nothing I couldn't do. All that we achieved at the Armadillo makes me cherish her words and her guidance, even though, as a stern Baptist, she did object to certain things that went on under the roof of our music emporium.

EARNING MY HIPPIE CARD

Before the Armadillo, I had zero experience running a music club. I was twenty-six years old, and my post-college experience included serving a stint in the marine corps, teaching school, coaching football, lobbying for the Brewers Association, and spending a couple of extended sojourns in Zihuatanejo, Mexico, looking for Timothy Leary. In the months leading up to July 1970, I had assumed the job of band manager for a country folkie hippie group, Shiva's Headband. Their sound was rooted in folk and country music but featured extended, trancelike jams powered by the bandleader's untamed electric violin. I got the job mostly because I was the only person bandleader Spencer Perskin knew who owned a suit and tie.

Shiva's Headband was the only band in Austin that had a recording contract with a major label. Capitol Records had made a deal with Perskin in which he was advanced funds not only to create a debut album but to seek out and develop other similar bands in the Austin area. Despite sounding like big business, my initial task for the band was a humble yet difficult mission: find a place in town where they could gig for a few hundred dollars a night, ASAP.

Shiva's Headband in the AWHQ office before the remodel,
December 27, 1970. From left to right: Shawn Siegel, Spencer
Perskin, Leo Rudd, Ike Ritter, and Mike Cooper. Photograph
by Burton Wilson.

For the past few years, Shiva's had been the house band at the Vulcan Gas Company. It's hard to imagine now, but this hippie hangout was located downtown at 316 Congress Avenue, just a few blocks from the state capitol. The walls were plastered with Day-Glo art bathed in black lights, and it had an in-house psychedelic light show. After opening in 1967, the Vulcan booked local and regional bands like Shiva's Headband, the Conqueroo, Georgetown Medical Band, and Bubble Puppy; veteran Texas bluesmen like Mance Lipscomb and Lightnin' Hopkins; and touring acts that ordinarily wouldn't have passed through Austin.

The Vulcan hosted shows that were landmarks in Austin music history. Muddy Waters's two-night stand, August 2–3, 1968, was one of them. The opening act was Johnny Winter, the lightning-fast, gravel-voiced albino blues guitarist from Beaumont. Johnny was twenty-four years old and had been touring and recording since he was a teenager. Muddy and his touring band were impressed as hell with him. Although they pulled into Austin feeling jaded and fatigued from traveling, and turned in a less-than-stellar performance the first night, the Chicago bluesmen ratcheted up their show on the second night, and Muddy struck up a lifelong friendship with Johnny.

Backed by his white-hot rhythm section, bassist Tommy Shannon and drummer Uncle John Turner, Johnny Winter recorded the iconic album *Progressive Blues Experiment* at the Vulcan that same year. (One reason the record has such a great "live" sound is that, during the recording, a microphone was hung down into an old cistern behind the building, capturing that great underground reverb sound.) When Johnny signed with Columbia Records in 1969, the six-figure deal was the largest ever offered to a solo artist.

The 13th Floor Elevators is another famous band closely associated with the Vulcan. The first band to use the term "psychedelic" to describe its music, the Elevators exploded onto the Austin music scene in late 1965 with its first single, "You're Gonna Miss Me." The band electrified club audiences with its soaring blend of garage rock, surf rock, and blues, a mix that became truly mind-bending with the addition of electric jug player Tommy Hall and singer Roky Erickson. Roky, an eighteen-year-old dropout from Travis High, sang with the swagger of Mick Jagger and the raw sex howls of James Brown and Wilson Pickett. The Elevators not only coined the term "psychedelic" for the genre, they went out

Poster for a 13th Floor Elevators, The Swiss Movement,
The South Canadian Overflow, and Shiva's Headband
show at the Vulcan Gas Company. December 8–10, 1967.
Artwork by Gilbert Shelton.

Johnny Winter Band at the Vulcan Gas Company, August 2, 1968.
Left to right: Tommy Shannon, John Turner, and Johnny Winter.
Photograph by Burton Wilson.

Otis Spann on piano, Muddy Waters and Luther Johnson on guitar, and S. P. Leary on drums. The Vulcan Gas Company, August 2, 1968. Photograph by Burton Wilson.

Jimmy Reed at the Vulcan Gas Company, March 17, 1969.
Photograph by Burton Wilson.

Mance Lipscomb and James Cotton at the Vulcan Gas Company,
October 8, 1969. Photograph by Burton Wilson.

James Cotton onstage at the Vulcan Gas Company,
October 8, 1969. Photograph by Burton Wilson.

The Fugs onstage at the Vulcan Gas Company. From left to right:
Ken Weaver, Bill Wolf, Ed Sanders, Ken Pine, Bob Mason, and
Tuli Kupferberg. Photograph by Burton Wilson.

Typical crowd at the Vulcan Gas Company.
Photograph by Burton Wilson.

The Vulcan Gas Company concessions area.
Photograph by Burton Wilson.

Big Mama Thornton backstage at the Vulcan Gas Company,
March 21, 1969. Photograph by Burton Wilson.

Sleepy John Estes onstage at the Vulcan Gas Company,
April 19, 1968. Photograph by Burton Wilson.

to San Francisco and blew the minds of the top bands in the Bay Area. Those bands—Jefferson Airplane, the Grateful Dead, and Moby Grape, to name a few—were so impressed with the Elevators' psychedelic sound that they immediately began the process of psychedelicizing their own repertoires.

The career arc of the 13th Floor Elevators could hardly have been more like a meteor, burning brightly through the sky and crashing to earth in a zillion brilliant colors. The ingestion of a large volume of drugs, including LSD, mescaline, and speed, often on a daily basis, helped inspire and fuel the Elevators' psychedelic sound, but it proved to be an unsustainable lifestyle. Roky Erickson's drug use apparently exacerbated existing mental health problems that would not be correctly diagnosed for several decades. And in the Elevators' case, they didn't need drugs to be paranoid: each member of the band had been under police surveillance since shortly after they played their first gig. Two of the primary Austin Police Department officers who carried out the surveillance and busts, Harvey Gann and Burt Gerding, repeatedly admitted in recent years that it was their intention to destroy drug bands and radical groups in Austin in the sixties. "They were threatening my culture," said Gerding, "and I liked my culture."[1] Roky was busted for a second time in 1969 for possession of a single joint. In an ill-advised ploy to avoid a long prison term, he pled insanity. He was incarcerated at Rusk State Hospital and, for the next three years, was subjected to electroconvulsive therapy and Thorazine treatments. Instead of lending his genius to the rock 'n' roll scene, he was playing in the Rusk State Hospital band, whose members included rapists and murders.

The Vulcan Gas Company had also been the roost for Austin's underground poster artists, thanks mostly to Gilbert Shelton, best known for creating the Fabulous Furry Freak Brothers and Wonder Wart-Hog. Gilbert designed oversized posters for the Vulcan until he moved to San Francisco. His successor, Jim Franklin, not only carried on the tradition of featuring armadillos in his work, but brought it to a new level. In Franklin's hands, the humble, hard-shelled mammal was a portal to other dimensions, as well as a mirror reflection of our own identities.

It's hard to explain the expectations we were dealing with when word got out that a new hippie music joint was about to open. There were many people in the community who missed the Vulcan Gas Company. The very

Gilbert Shelton, 1970. Photograph by Burton Wilson.

The Fabulous Furry Freak Brothers mural at AWHQ, artwork by
Gilbert Shelton, 1971. Photograph by Burton Wilson.

Jim Franklin and Houston White standing in front of the Vulcan Gas Company, 1969. Photograph by Burton Wilson.

The Vulcan Gas Company, 1967. Photograph by Belmer Wright.

existence of the place had given them hope. It was part of their identity. Sadly, the Vulcan was a money pit for Don Hyde, and he'd only kept it running for as long as he had because he believed in the music and arts scene that it served.

The Vulcan Gas Company might have been a dump, but it's a very important part of Austin music history. Don Hyde lived the story, so he was gracious enough to lend a few words giving an inside point of view:

> *The club always lost money. The Monday after the second weekend we were open, I was informed that the* Austin American-Statesman *would no longer run advertising for the Vulcan Gas Company, nor would any reviews be printed.*
>
> *Before long we realized that the 13th Floor Elevators would not be our house band. In fact, they were on a tragic downhill slide. It was a major blow to us, as no other local band could draw more than one hundred people.*
>
> *We had to take chances, so we started booking big-name bands. I booked Canned Heat, the Steve Miller Band, Moby Grape, and the Fugs. Working with Al Smith, I was able to book the Chicago blues greats: John Lee Hooker, Muddy Waters, Jimmy Reed, Big Joe Williams, and Big Mama Thornton. Houston White, a Delta blues aficionado, booked Sleepy John Estes, Fred McDowell, and Lightnin' Hopkins. Johnny Winter came and honed his act for a year, then signed a massive deal with Columbia.*
>
> *We had some great shows, some of which made history, like the Velvet Underground. Some of them made money, others did not. Most of the time we lost money, and I was the person who threw money at the club to keep it afloat.*
>
> *There were four partners when the Vulcan opened in 1967: Gary Maxwell, Houston White, Sandy Lockett, and myself. Gary and Houston had already produced some San Francisco–type shows in Austin and Houston, operating under the name Electric Grandmother. For Austin shows they were renting the Doris Miller Auditorium, but the place was impractical for a lot of reasons, one being that the acoustics were horrible.*
>
> *My search for a venue led me to the funky Victorian storefront at 316 Congress Avenue. I made a handshake deal with the owner, Joe*

Don Hyde and Al Smith. Photograph by Burton Wilson.

Darcy, an elderly Lebanese merchant I'd known since childhood. Gilbert Shelton created our logo and served as art director, with help from Tony Bell. Around February 1968, Gary and Gilbert left for San Francisco, and Jim Franklin moved in upstairs and took over.

In the spring of 1969, an officer from the APD vice squad came in to talk with me. I'd known Jerry Spain since I was a kid. I'd even mowed his yard and babysat for him. He told me that there was tremendous pressure on APD to shut the Vulcan down. They were aware that my name was on all the permits, that I was putting up the money to keep the place going. "If you don't stop," he said, "half a pound of pot will be planted in your office and you'll do fifteen to twenty-five in Huntsville."

I thanked him for the tip and gave him assurances, then sold my house and left town.

The truth was that, from 1967 to 1969, certain people I knew from California, particularly Terry the Tramp, Owsley Stanley, Melissa, and Mountain Girl, had a tremendous influence on Austin music. The fees for all those Chicago blues legends and cult favorites, like the Fugs and the Velvet Underground, not to mention our utility bills and other mundane expenses, were supported by sales of LSD. If people in Austin had not enjoyed getting high and expanding their consciousness, the Vulcan wouldn't have lasted more than a couple of weeks.

Somehow, the Vulcan limped along until the spring of 1970. A few months after it closed, Armadillo World Headquarters opened. Things changed. There were a couple of longhairs on the city council. The people at the Armadillo were able to bridge the gap between the old Austin longhairs and the redneck peckerwoods. Austin was on its way to becoming the Live Music Capital of the World.

The brave souls who took over the helm at the Vulcan after Don Hyde's departure attempted to establish a music-and-arts joint that wasn't reliant on beer sales for financial stability, and they failed. That didn't stop me from wanting to give it another shot.

Spencer Perskin wanted me to consider taking over the Vulcan. I'd been there once before, not to see a band but to warn Houston White about the determination of local law enforcement to shut them down. It was an awkward experience. Back then I was working for the Brewers

Association and had come straight from a meeting of the Disciplinary Control Board. That's where I heard military police officials talk about working with the Austin Police Department to raid that hippie joint and put them out of business.

So, immediately after leaving the meeting, I drove over there. Visiting the place during daylight hours was not for the faint-hearted. Once upon a time, the storefront windows had displayed samples of footwear that was sold within. The same windows now showed off Jim Franklin's shock art: toilets with manikin body parts protruding from bowls and tanks, another manikin dressed in military garb lying there as if mortally wounded.

Stepping around a pile of trash at the entrance, I saw a wine bottle with a hypodermic syringe inside. There was a group of eight or so guys. Long-haired, wearing scruffy T-shirts and jeans, they began backing away as I entered. My suit and tie spelled C-O-P, I reckoned.

I asked for Houston White. No response.

"I'm just trying to get word to him that there's a bust coming down," I said. Still nothing. It was wasted breath.

Two of the suspicious, mutely hostile hippies in the group turned out to be Don Hyde and Bobby Hedderman, who later became close friends of mine.

The Austin underground scene could be a tough nut to crack. The terrible thing was that Austin hippies were hoping that another place just like the Vulcan would arise to take its place. In view of my experiences there, this was going to be a difficult task.

My writer friend Edwin "Bud" Shrake, who had made himself so indispensable to his bosses at *Sports Illustrated* that they let him live in Austin, gave me a check for $1,000 to try and save the Vulcan. So I went back there again to give it another look. On this trip, I learned that the toilets in the front window had been removed from the restrooms, which were nonfunctioning. As the son of a plumber, I knew then that saving the Vulcan was beyond our grasp. It was a dump beyond redemption.

For the time being, Austin hippie bands like Shiva's were making do with another dive, just south of the Colorado River/Town Lake divide, called the Cactus Club. On that fateful night in July 1970, I went there with Spencer Perskin to see some friends play in a band called the Hub

City Movers. Spencer brought along his violin so he could jam with them, and he brought me to show his hippie friends that I was cool, that he trusted me. Which was nice, since not even the other members of Shiva's trusted me.

The Cactus was one of three bars at the corner of Barton Springs Road and Riverside Drive, a short block off Congress Avenue, the city's main street. The other two bars were La Fuentes and the Squirrel's Inn. All three were classic Texas beer joint shacks.

As a potential alternative to the Vulcan, the Cactus had little to recommend itself. Instead of an elevated stage, the bandstand was the lowest part of the room. The ceiling was low, the tables wobbly. Dinette chairs squawked against the concrete floor when moved, there was no ventilation, and the beer was warm.

But next to the Cactus was a building complex that featured a two-story structure with a Quonset-style arched roof and a skating rink called the Skating Palace. Shuttered, dusty, and dormant, these big, empty spaces sat there, so obvious that they were invisible. Bringing the story back to plumbing again, I might never have noticed them myself if the Cactus had had better restrooms.

The Wilson family, 1960. Left to right: Eddie holding Frank, Beulah, and Woody. Family snapshot.

NOW DIG THIS

★

As the nation's young men marched off to fight in World War II, more than a few of them married on the run and got their brides in a family way. My father was one of those soldiers. A thin, pipe-smoking army staff sergeant with a couple years of college, he was on his way to Signal Corps school when he passed through Lumberton, Mississippi, in early 1943 and met a sweet young thing named Beulah Risher. They were married three weeks later.

I came bawling into the world on November 15, 1943, bearing a name bigger than I was: Edwin Franklin Osborne Junior. Beulah told me that my father was a writer who'd received small checks for magazine stories. He was athletic, too. She had pictures of him running the hurdles in high school and college, but the pictures that mean the most to me are those of him holding me in front of Granny Risher's big porch. I was just a little squirt, and my father was heading toward the end of his life. He was killed on the Pacific island of New Guinea on August 7, 1944.

Beulah found herself thrust into the void where war widows dwelled, alone with the love letters her Edwin had written her. She kept them in an old Dover iron box that she passed along to me. The only one I've read is one he sent to his mother, telling her, "The girl I'm going to meet is as pure as driven snow." When the Armadillo had been up and running for three or four years, my mother reminded me that the date we celebrated the joint's birthday was the anniversary of my father's death. I still keep the War Department telegram that told us the news. It sits folded and brittle, yellow with age, in the same case with his purple heart. I don't open the case often, but each time I do, the telegram threatens to turn to dust.

The shock of my father's disappearance from our lives was something that didn't leave us easily, but it didn't define our existence. I was surrounded by the love of Beulah's eight brothers and sisters. Uncle Oscar, my mother's kid brother by a year, became my surrogate father and best pal. Beulah kept herself busy working alongside her sister Frances at Camp Shelby in Hattiesburg. The three of us shared an apartment, and later my Aunt Ione also moved in. It was strictly a Risher family affair until a plumber named Woody Wilson came looking for romance.

He was nine years older than Beulah and making good money installing plumbing in a new subdivision near Mississippi Southern University. After learning his trade in the Civilian Conservation Corps, he had joined the navy and served in the construction battalions, or Seabees, where he became a journeyman in the plumbing trade.

When Woody shipped out for the Pacific campaign, he left a pregnant wife behind. He returned home on emergency leave, but too late; both wife and baby had died during childbirth. When a high school classmate of Beulah's introduced her to Woody at Main Street Baptist Church, they were both painfully eligible.

In the final days of her life, Mother would sometimes get wistful after chemotherapy treatment and divulge things that I'd never dreamt of asking her about. Once, when I mentioned the "pure as driven snow" letter, she said that the day before she married my father, he held her by a handful of hair and got one kiss. Woody, being more passive, took a full year to court her and had to wait until after they were married for Beulah's first kiss.

The newlyweds lived next door to the plumbing shop where quiet, patient Woody worked until 1948. That year, Woody and his friend Vernon Weddle uprooted their families and moved to Texas. The year before, a ship's cargo of ammonium nitrate had exploded at the port of Texas City. It was the worst industrial disaster in US history, killing 581 people and destroying nearly one thousand buildings. Now there was a major rebuilding project under way. Woody and Vernon found jobs, and then they found land where they intended to build homes.

Everything looked fine and dandy, a blue-collar version of the American dream, but Texas City, home to a complex of petroleum and chemical facilities, struck Woody and Beulah as a less than ideal place to live and raise their young son.

Woody went to Austin to look around. While he was there, he took the test for his plumber's license and passed it. Lloyd Meyers, a local plumbing contractor, said to him, "I can keep you working overtime for the next two years." With that, Woody packed up Beulah, Granny Risher, and me and brought us to the town that would define all of our lives, mine most of all.

We put down roots on what was then the north side of town in a neighborhood called Hyde Park, which had begun its life as Austin's first subdivision. Our house on Avenue B did double duty as the home of Beulah Wilson's Day Nursery School.

Looking back, I realize that Beulah worshipped me, and I took ready advantage of that. I knew that she would overlook much of my mischief, and Woody was so busy working that he didn't notice. Only Granny Risher seemed to sense that whatever I was up to wasn't necessarily good. Any sign that I might be having a good time was grounds for an order to practice the piano.

The piano, a Mason & Hamlin baby grand, was two or three decades old when Beulah bought it, but it was still a beautiful instrument, as were Beulah's ambitions that her son would someday become a world-class pianist. Sadly, I gave her a poor return on her investment, unless you count the piano's later life as the house piano at the Armadillo, where it was lovingly played by everyone from Fats Domino to Leon Russell.

The house had a spare room next to the garage that became my bedroom. I had an army cot out there, a clock radio, and access to Woody's truck and the family car, a late-model Cadillac. Late at night, beginning at age twelve or thirteen, I'd go riding around town in one of the vehicles. I'd slip it out of gear and push it out of the garage and down the dirt alley before starting the engine. Never got caught, by my parents or the law.

In those days, racial segregation in the public schools I attended was a fact of life, even as the constitutionality of it was being challenged and refuted. After Allen Junior High burned down in 1954, the Mexican

The Mason and Hamlin baby grand piano.
Photographer unknown.

students who attended there were shipped to University Junior High. The daily schedule was altered so that the school's white kids, yours truly included, could begin classes an hour early, with the school day ending after lunchtime. As we marched out under watchful eyes, the Hispanic kids from Allen marched in.

The inequity of all this wouldn't occur to me until later. At the time, my intellect was more attuned to the opportunities for peddling contraband to the former Allen students. The hottest items I sold were cigarette lighters with naked women on them. Loaded dice and marked cards with dirty pictures were also fast movers. Switchblade knives were a cheap thrill.

The school coaches lurked around every corner, keeping watch on us, so transactions had to be made on the fly. *You like it? How much? Yes/No.* That was all I had time for.

I did it for the thrill of the deal and because I admired the merchandise—not for profit, because there was none. And I did it because it made me feel useful.

Every Saturday I took the bus downtown to prowl Woolworth's, White's Pharmacy, the basement of Scarbrough's department store, and my most important stop, Liberal Outlet, a storefront on Sixth Street that was a paradise for young scalawags, stocked to the rafters with switchblades, throwing knives, brass knuckles, and other illicit items I trafficked in.

Two beautiful clerks worked there. Chip was a tall blonde, Dale was a short brunette, and I was in love with both of these sexy, sweet, glamorous, attentive girls. If I expressed an interest in an item in the display case, they would unlock the case and let me examine it. Then they'd consult the boss about a discount.

Chip and Dale were local celebrities on a television show called *Now Dig This*. It was a teen music show broadcast on KTBC-TV, then the only station in town. Chip and Dale would lip-sync to a selection of the latest hit songs. A panel of teenagers would debate the merits of each song. The final verdict was announced with a bell ring for a hit song. A gong was thumped for the misses.

The show aired on Saturdays at the same time I rode the bus downtown to buy magazines, books, and contraband. Consequently, I'd never seen the show, but I never told Chip and Dale.

One Saturday, as soon as I walked in, both girls approached me. Chip touched my Sal Mineo spit curl and twirled it around her finger. Dale told me I was cute. I tried to stay cool, but it was all I could do not to pee my pants.

As it turned out, they were rounding up panelists for *Now Dig This* two Saturdays from then and wanted my assistance. I told them I never missed the show. They asked whom I would suggest inviting besides myself. I seized the opportunity to make up my own dream team, naming the five cutest girls I could think of. The girls giggled and said they appreciated my effort but I would have to share the spotlight with at least one guy. Thinking quickly, I volunteered a football player named Sidney. He was so big and dumb I felt certain that he'd be no competition for me with the girls.

Chip and Dale wrote everything down, thanked me, and said they looked forward to my television debut. As I left the store, I began to ponder the difficulties of getting laid without a car.

Saturday came and went and I still didn't cancel my weekly downtown prowl in order to watch the show. Logic suggested that I should do some research, but I didn't care. I didn't realize until later that I'd already developed the habit of doing things that I'd never done and knew nothing about, getting a thrill out of improvising.

Television really wasn't a big part of my life, and to some extent I blame Granny Risher for that. The day our big Capehart console was delivered to the house, my parents were away and Granny was in charge. The deliveryman set the console on the nursery floor and plugged it in. I saw the same Indian head test pattern I'd seen in the window at Sears, and then I saw Abbott and Costello doing their "Who's on First?" routine. I laughed so hard I hurt my chubby stomach, and I would've laughed more if Granny hadn't growled, "Turn that thing off! Go practice your piano!" and yanked the plug from the wall.

Granny could tell that uncontrolled laughter in a nine-year-old boy was surely the fault of the devil, and the best way to exorcise the devil was to practice selections from *The Broadman Hymnal* until any hint of mischief had been wrung from the fingers by numbness and fatigue. Any piano-playing aspirations I had nurtured up to that point died around that time.

In my room was a red GE-model radio that I'd bought with earnings from working at a fireworks stand. I'd tune it to KVET 1300 AM to hear Dr. Hepcat, the cool-talking black disc jockey, preacher, and recording artist who authored the definitive book of hip lingo, *The Jives of Dr. Hepcat*. My other favorite station, KTAE 1260 AM, broadcasting from the town of Taylor in the farm country northeast of Austin, was home to another black deejay, Tony Von ("The only color TV on the radio!"). Dr. Hepcat and Tony Von filled my ears and head with tunes by Little Willie John, Etta James, Bobby "Blue" Bland, and other performers I held in great regard.

The first record I bought was "High Noon" by Tex Ritter. By the time I got home, the record had been fried by the sun, and it was warped like a potato chip. I disdain physics to this day. Damn, I wanted to hear that big voice booming low, "Do not forsake me, oh my darlin' / On this our wedding day."

Ritter's low voice stirred my first feelings of manliness and sparked my incurable romantic streak. I was a twelve-year-old boy who couldn't wait to start kissing girls. Popular music was the soundtrack for such activities, and to Granny Risher's chagrin, my relationship with church music went out the window.

When my big day on TV with Chip and Dale arrived, I was nervous to the tenth power. I went scuttling to the men's room at KTBC and quickly ran into the show's host, Cactus Pryor. Cactus had been a local star and a fixture at the station for years, but the first time I'd seen him he was as bald as a cue ball. Now he was running a wet comb through the glossy strands of a toupee. He glanced at me and said, "Nice ducktail, kid. Let's go play *Now Dig This*."

As the show got under way, I got the impression that Cactus assumed he was some kind of guiding light for musical tastes in young people. I didn't know what other kids listened to—I didn't talk radio or music at school, just contraband and girls—but I was damn sure I knew the difference between good music and bad, and I intended to prove it to Cactus Pryor.

When the *Now Dig This* panel was asked to judge "Blueberry Hill," not the original by Fats Domino but the white-bread cover version by Pat Boone, I was appalled. I couldn't even appreciate the effort Chip and Dale put into their lip-syncing act.

When I got a chance to speak, I said, "Why weren't they singing to Fats?"

Cactus was ready with a smug retort, saying that these girls probably wouldn't be very convincing imitating Fats Domino.

White stations had been playing Pat Boone's cover for weeks, but I didn't care. I voted that his version would be a *miss*. Everybody else voted *hit*.

The rest of the show was a blur. Afterward, the girls went downtown with Sidney to see a movie at the Paramount. I left alone and ventured down past the taverns and barbecue joints on East Sixth Street to see a low-budget Lash LaRue flick at the Ritz. I never went back to Liberal Outlet.

In 1959, when I was fifteen, Beulah decided that I should have a car of my own so I wouldn't get killed driving with other reckless teens. I can still see Woody standing silent and knowing as she said it. Woody played along, too, when we went to pick out a '57 Ford coupe that turned out to be the fastest car in town. When I picked up an FM tuner and had it installed, it was also the coolest one.

The scene of my junior-high-dance period was Hancock Recreation Center, the clubhouse of the golf course in Hyde Park. It had been the first Austin Country Club, built around the turn of the century when Hyde Park was on the edge of town. By the fifties, the place looked worn around the edges. Events there were corralled and chaperoned, but there were still opportunities for mischief and juvenile hijinks.

My path to higher education took more turns than Marco Polo. I started at Wharton County Junior College near Houston and then headed to North Texas State Teachers College in Denton. I took courses in literature and philosophy, with little regard for what I might apply them to later on. Mostly, it was a tactic for avoiding science, math, and language courses as long as possible.

I read Jack Kerouac and became infected with a desire to be on the road. The desire simmered even as I traveled back to Austin and managed to pick up a degree in English from UT. I confronted my fear of being drafted by joining the marine reserves. I figured that if I had to serve in the military, I wanted to pick the branch, and I liked the idea of the physical regime that went along with being a jarhead, the first to strike, and all that.

The Beat wanderlust struck hardest during my short stint with the marines, and I went AWOL, ending up in Zihuatanejo, Mexico, on the Pacific coast about 150 miles northwest of Acapulco. I stayed in Z for the first six months of 1965. There were times when I felt like I could stay forever.

It was there that I learned that a "faggot" is a bundle of sticks, like the ones you see stacked on a burro. I learned to smoke pot, and unfortunately, took up cigarettes again, an old habit. I read Hemingway, Faulkner, Steinbeck, and Melville on the beach. I handled counterfeit money, but I was far too scared to pass it on my travels up the coast to Acapulco.

I watched a bunch of would-be grave robbers get conned by an old woman who dealt in forged pre-Columbian artifacts. I saw the bust of a grand car theft operation. I was hoping to catch up with Timothy Leary and his entourage, who had taken up in Z after being run out of Harvard. I had lots of questions to ask him about his experiments in mind expansion. It turned out that I had just missed him, and I was forced to experiment on my own.

I married a woman named Genie Lyon whom I had met the previous year at North Texas State. Genie was a beautiful brunette with full lips, and she had been the chief attraction in my Shakespeare class.

Genie, being whip smart and much more focused than I was, graduated with a major in English and a minor in Spanish. She worked for General Telephone in Denton while I finished another year of school. We visited Austin that summer and discovered there were precious few jobs unless you had connections or a special talent. It's hard to imagine today, but in the sixties and seventies, the only big employers in Austin were the state and the university.

Just after Labor Day, a friend named George Brown called me. George had graduated and got a job teaching school in Van Vleck, a small town near the Texas coast south of Houston. George said that the school district there was so desperate for a Spanish teacher—meaning Genie—that they would hire me, too. The catch, he said, was that I would have to teach and coach at Herman High, an all-black school.

I liked that idea. When the school superintendent, Wayne Cornelius, came to Austin the following Sunday to interview us, I had my fingers crossed for luck. Cornelius was an old-fashioned Southern racist who made a huge effort to cover it up while pressing all the right buttons to make sure we were both on the same white-supremacist page. He carefully explained that I'd only have to work at the "nigra" school for one year, because after that, federal-court-ordered integration would be sweeping across the Lone Star State. Because the district had built a new $500,000 football stadium at Van Vleck High, Cornelius assumed that

Genie Wilson, 1970. Photograph by Burton Wilson.

the colored boys would come across the road and gratefully sign up just for the privilege of playing there.

I got the job. We worked through the fall and the spring. In the second semester, our track team won district and finished second in the state. Later, Cornelius and a couple of the white coaches gathered all the black athletes in our gymnasium to deliver an impassioned speech about how they should sign freedom-of-choice forms. This would enable the students to attend the white school and represent it for the greater glory of all, and all that crap. About the fifteenth time he said "nigra," one of my favorite students, an outgoing, type A class clown, put his head down between his legs and boomed, "That's negro, N-E-E-E-G-R-O-O-O."

Cornelius's face turned crimson red. He'd been busted. Not a single black athlete came forward to sign his damned forms.

Around that same time, a pickup truck from the white school came over and unloaded all kinds of equipment at Herman. There were overhead projectors, movie projectors, visual aids, and various other items. It was a surprise, because in our segregated district, black students were always given the whites' hand-me-downs. Shortly after the brand-new equipment began arriving, an inspector was making the rounds, inquiring as to how federal public school funds were being spent. By the time the inspector got to my classroom, the tables across the back wall had been stacked with things that I'd never seen before. Cornelius stood nearby, glaring at me.

"Have you been using this equipment to your advantage in your school teaching?" the inspector said.

"No, sir," I said, stealing a glance at Cornelius before continuing. "I haven't really had a chance to use it yet. But I'm planning to use it quite a lot between now and the end of the year."

To no one's surprise, our contracts were not renewed after that.

My next stop was the Texas Employment Commission in Austin. While I was filling out paperwork, a counselor asked if I'd consider traveling. I said yes. After teaching school for a couple of semesters, nothing sounded better. The counselor asked, did I have any compunction about doing public relations for beer? Surely he was dreaming, I thought.

The Brewers Association was looking for a retired teacher to be its mouthpiece. Although "retired" and "fired" were not necessarily synonymous, I said I was just the man the brewers were looking for.

Before the job interview, I ran into an old high school chum named Bobby Jackson. When I told him about this dream job, he told me it was my lucky day. The guy doing the hiring at the Brewers Association was a friend of his father's. "Don't wait for them to call," Bobby said. "Just drop in and tell Homer Leonard that my dad said to say hi. Don't let that job slip away waiting on a phone call."

So, by golly, I did just what the man told me to.

I walked stiffly into the dark-paneled office of the Texas Brewers' Institute dressed in the forty-five-dollar brown suit I'd just bought at Scarbrough's and told the secretary I was looking for a job. She looked a bit puzzled but sent me to an office where a tiny old man was scrunched down in a big chair. This seemed to be my day for getting puzzled looks. Where had I heard of this job opening, he wanted to know. Instead of relying on Bobby Jackson's family name, I told the little old man that the employment office had sent me.

"Well, son," he said, "you go tell the sumbitch who told you that, that Homer Leonard is alive and well, his job well filled, and he can kiss my ass."

It turned out that the little, shrunken, pissed-off man, Homer Leonard, was the former Speaker of the Texas House of Representatives and now a very powerful lobbyist. Not only that, but he'd just returned from a two-month hospital stay during which he almost died. Apparently, I was the only person in Austin who didn't know that.

My counselor at the employment commission thought it was pretty funny, too. My biggest blunder of all was that I hadn't even gone to the right place. The job opening was at the Texas division of the US Brewers' Association, not the Texas Brewers' Institute.

When I finally found the right place, I got the job. My boss was Charles B. Alexander, "Alex," a man with a gruff pit bull exterior but a puppy dog personality. When he interviewed me, he asked why I wasn't teaching anymore. I told him about my disagreements with Wayne Cornelius on the subject of equality and civil rights.

Alex had worked on civil rights issues in the military. He treated me like kin from that day forward.

I was twenty-three years old, less than half the age of anyone else on the staff, most of whom were retired from the military, law enforcement, and teaching—dedicated beer drinkers one and all. My job was to drive through East Texas and visit schools to talk about the evils of underage drinking. A second task was to take note of beer joints. Entering them, I would shake hands and introduce myself, do some backslapping and joke telling, pass out business cards, and buy rounds for the house. Life was good.

I remember stopping at a domino parlor in Sweet Home, a small community in the middle of nowhere, where all these old guys were slapping down tiles on the table and drinking Shiner, the local brew. I sidled up to the barmaid and said I'd like to buy a round for everyone.

"You want one, too?" she asked.

"Sure," I said.

"You want it cold?"

"Sure."

She reached into the icebox and opened a cold bottle for me, then pulled a warm case from under the bar and started opening bottles for the old guys. This was an old-school beer-drinking bunch who preferred their German soda pop at room temperature.

That same weekend I met a Falstaff Beer distributor named John Monfrey. He was an old Mafia type with a glass eye and a *Twilight Zone* stare. Monfrey controlled the beer business in San Antonio, the best beer-drinking city in Texas. Despite the fact that Pearl and Lone Star were both brewed there, he sold more Falstaff than the local brands combined.

When a waitress asked what we wanted to drink, Monfrey looked my way. He wanted me to order first. You could have heard a pin drop as heads turned and everybody waited to see what the young pup was drinking.

"I'd like a warm Shiner, if you please, ma'am," I said, having learned from my stop in Sweet Home.

Monfrey broke into a big grin. He said, "Alex hired him a good German boy."

I'd landed in high clover. An expense account for buying beer was a hell of a perk, but the longer I was on the road, the faster my sleek light-heavyweight body became encased in fat. I was up to 235 pounds.

I had other options. I could've gone back to UT to finish the four hours standing between me and a degree in English. Law school was another option.

Then Spencer Perskin came along and offered another alternative. At the time, I still had short hair and looked more or less like other straight

Spencer Perskin, 1965. Photographer unknown.
Photo courtesy of the Austin History Center.

people you'd see walking down the street heading to their nine-to-five jobs. On the inside, however, I viewed the world through the prism of Vietnam, race riots, the Kennedy assassinations, and other events in the decade that often has the adjective "tumultuous" attached to it. My swerve toward hippie culture was already under way. Spencer, a well-known Austin hippie with a lion's mane of curly hair, said that he trusted me. Me, an ex-marine, boxer, and weightlifter, a guy who took meetings with squares from the legislature.

Spencer gave me some LSD one day. Everything in every direction turned all squiggly, and I went on a crazy ride for a few hours. Despite the patterns and pulsating colors making crazy sounds, there was also a sense of dawning clarity. Once my vision came back into focus, I felt a growing sense of purpose. I could see my future, and it wasn't me wearing a suit. My future was called Armadillo World Headquarters.

Intersection of South First Street and Barton Springs
Road, c. 1940. Photographer unknown.

COSMIC JUSTICE

★

For hippies fed up with the straight world, Armadillo World Headquarters became a refuge, a kind of Noah's ark for the hippie world. Its shape even resembled an upside-down ark. It was easy to see that there were cosmic reasons for it all.

It wasn't always easy to interpret the workings of the cosmos in Texas, but the environment here at least made for a healthy respect for nature. You only had to live through a few cycles of drought and flood, or one average summer, to become educated. Along with the natural beauty of the hills and limestone outcroppings that underpin the Austin area, the Colorado River has always been one of Austin's most valuable natural resources. Over the years, however, the river has seemed somewhat ambivalent about the relationship. Prior to the mid–twentieth century, extended seasons of drought periodically reduced the river's flow to a trickle. Dry periods were followed by torrential rains and murderous floods that swept away homes, businesses, crops, livestock, and bridges. During Austin's first century, the Congress Avenue Bridge was destroyed and rebuilt several times. Dams were erected with great hope and ceremony, only to be swatted away by the petulant river.

Efforts to harness and corral the Colorado River upstream from Austin finally progressed with assistance from FDR's New Deal, leading to the creation of the Lower Colorado River Authority (LCRA) in 1935. By 1951, a series of dams for flood control and power generation had been completed, creating the present-day chain of Highland Lakes in the hills west of Austin. Then, in 1960, the city of Austin completed a dam at Longhorn Crossing in East Austin, which created what was originally given the not-so-creative name of Town Lake. The area around it was gradually enhanced with greenbelts and hike-and-bike trails, thanks in large part to the leadership of Lady Bird Johnson. After her death in 2007, Town Lake was renamed Lady Bird Lake, and it remains one of the proudest symbols of the Austin groove today.

But until the river was tamed by the LCRA, no development of consequence existed on the south bank of the Colorado. Even then, for several generations, South Austin remained more rural and funky. It was the capital's ugly stepsibling, the place where Austin let its shirttails hang out. South of the river, Congress Avenue was lined with bars, feedstores, tourist courts, roadhouses, dance halls, used-car lots, wrecking yards, landfills, whorehouses, tent revivals, and carnivals. It was the domain of people who needed cheap rent and of enterprises that needed to be a respectable distance from courthouses, churches, and schools.

During the 1940s, the future site of the Armadillo fit this profile as well as any other block on the south shore. For years, the property at the corner of Barton Springs Road and Riverside Drive was mostly occupied by a small carnival that featured pony rides, a Ferris wheel, and a tiny wooden roller coaster.

In 1949, M. K. Hage, an enterprising Lebanese immigrant, bought the land and built the Skating Palace, with street-front offices and a warehouse following in the second phase of construction. Hage collaborated closely with the architects and even worked alongside the construction crews. The warehouse was a concrete-and-brick structure that was 150 feet long and 95 feet wide, topped by an arched, lamella-style roof.

"My father had been working as a stonemason since he was ten, carrying rock, trimming rock, helping in construction," said M. K. Hage Jr. "He had very strong hands. He liked to build things. He loved the idea of having a big space without columns."

Because structural steel was still scarce after World War II, wooden beams were used to support the sixty-foot-wide roof of the Skating Palace. According to Q. S. "Pee Wee" Franks, who worked on the project, it was the largest wooden-support roof in the state at the time.[1] The warehouse was built with an outer shell of steel beams and reinforced concrete pillars. The absence of interior columns created a wide-open space inside the building as well. It's as if Hage had a dream that envisioned some grand, unarticulated purpose for a future tenant.

During the Cold War era, the spaciousness of the warehouse also had practical implications. With its Quonset hut resemblance, the warehouse was suitable for use as an armory, complete with an underground firing range that would become our beer vault. And soon after completion, the federal government leased space in it for the National Guard. The Bureau of Internal Revenue also leased space.[2]

The building complex was never a big financial success, and in April 1953, disaster struck. Just as Hage was leaving on a European vacation, a fire broke out on the property. Everything was destroyed. Hage had no insurance coverage.

In a testament to first-generation immigrant determination, Hage decided to rebuild on the property and essentially had new versions of the original structures erected on the site, with a few improvements.

A local promoter named Owen Davis stepped forward, staging prize-fights and wrestling matches in the warehouse under its new name, Sport-center. Occasionally, the parade of twentieth-century gladiators was interrupted by a music show. Surely the most historic of these was the appearance of Horace Logan and his *Louisiana Hayride* in August 1955.

Louisiana Hayride was a traveling show broadcast every Saturday night on KWKH radio in Shreveport, Louisiana. Riding on fifty thousand watts of clear-channel power, the show could be heard throughout the South. The star of the 1955 season's *Hayride* was a handsome, young truck driver from Tupelo, Mississippi, named Elvis Presley. Elvis had a few hits under his belt by this time, but in the entertainment hype of 1955, he was billed as the "Folk Music Fireball."[3]

From the scant press I've seen about the show, the billing hardly mattered; Elvis could've been called Mr. X and he still would've set the room ablaze, with women old and young throwing their undies at him. A sellout

Program from Elvis Presley's performance at the Sportcenter, August 25, 1955.

crowd filled the Sportcenter at fifty cents a head, with an ad campaign promising "4 solid hours" of entertainment. Elvis was promoting his first hits for Sun Records, the pioneering Memphis label that introduced the world to Johnny Cash, Jerry Lee Lewis, Roy Orbison, Carl Perkins, Rufus Thomas, and Howlin' Wolf. The show's "Special Autograph Program," which sold for fifteen cents at the show, noted that Elvis was breaking new ground with the singles "Blue Moon of Kentucky" and "That's All Right," describing the former as an "unusual pairing of an R&B number with a Country standard." Elvis was introduced to the public as a "big, blond guy who likes nothing better than to spend an afternoon practicing football with some of the youngsters in his neighborhood."[4]

The idea of Elvis with blond hair still spins my hat around, even if that was his natural hair color. (Sammy Allred was there and asked the young rock 'n' roller what the real color of his hair was. Elvis answered, "Purple.") The big surprise for me was that Elvis played our building, fifteen years before we came along and renamed it Armadillo World Headquarters. Elvis played Austin several other times in the fifties before he joined the army in 1958 at the peak of his fame. I'd known that he played Dessau Hall and the Skyline Club in 1955 and the City Coliseum in 1956, but somehow the Sportcenter show had slipped through the cracks of the Elvis-in-Texas legend.

Looking back now, it makes perfect sense to me that Elvis rocked the house that M. K. Hage dreamed into existence—twice—before the Hippie World came along and made it our hippie boot camp, trade school, music hall, art pad, and home. It's cosmic, man.

★ ★ ★

Fifteen years after Elvis and the *Louisiana Hayride* left town with the crowd howling for more, M. K. Hage Jr. still owned the building built by his father, who had died in 1966. Well-known in Austin, M. K. Hage Jr. had grown up swimming in Barton Springs and making deliveries for his father's store. As a philanthropist, he devoted a lot of his time to public school education. He served twelve years on the Austin school board and helped establish Austin Community College, but he opposed desegregation and caused an angry outcry when he said the ACC board should be composed of "a black, a woman, a Mexican American, and someone who knows what he's doing." He bought a sizable tract of land midtown, between Thirty-Fourth and Thirty-Eighth Streets, as the first step in developing a new, state-of-the-art medical complex. After several of the primary facilities had been completed, Hage talked the people at Seton Hospital into moving there.[5]

Hage was an odd duck. At our first meeting, after a few minutes of small talk, he confided that he'd had a mistress for years. Although the thought hadn't previously crossed my mind, I had the feeling he wanted to reassure me of his heterosexuality. (Or was I the one he was concerned about?) He also mentioned negative comments he'd seen in the *Statesman* regarding hippies and the Vulcan Gas Company. He was concerned that our place might attract the same bad vibes.

He was talking about comments by Wray Weddell, a dedicated hippie hater who wrote a city column on a typewriter that he apparently dipped in caustic acid every week. I told Hage that we were going to run a tight ship, that we wouldn't sell beer, and that I'd had experience enforcing the peace in my time as a marine, boxer, football coach, and lobbyist for the Brewers Association.

And although I tried not to sound desperate, I let him know that I really needed and wanted a chance to rent the old, weird, ugly, vacant building. A few minutes later, I agreed to pay $500 a month for the privilege. Over the next ten years, there were incremental increases in rent as new spaces within the office building became available to us and we expanded our operation; but even when the monthly rate was triple the original amount, it was still a bargain, the main drawback being the short-term lease.

There was one stipulation added to the deal: Mr. Hage wanted his son, M. K. Hage III, to work with us. I told Mr. Hage that would be fine; we needed all the help we could get. Mr. Hage gave me the key and then, taking note of my physique, complimented my biceps.

Heading out the next morning, I decided my first stop would be the Cactus Club. I wanted George Davis to know that I would be a good neighbor, that I wasn't going to sell beer. I also hoped to pick up some advice from him. But when I got there, there was nothing left but a pile of ashes. The Cactus had burned down the night before.

★ ★ ★

Jim Franklin said we should call the joint the Armadillo. Various riffs on that idea were tossed around until we came up with the grandiose name "Armadillo National Headquarters," which made ironic reference to the building's former incarnation as a National Guard armory. Bud Shrake chimed in with some good advice. The word "national" had negative connotations during that era of Vietnam, Nixon, and Kent State. Young men still faced being drafted into military service to fight in a stupid war in Southeast Asia. The draft lottery had just gone into effect. Every US male aged nineteen to twenty-five was assigned a number according to his birth date, and all 365 numbers were drawn randomly out of a shoe box to determine the order in which the men would be called up to serve in the military.[6]

Shrake said it would be better to call the place the Armadillo *World* Headquarters. It was a winning suggestion.

The armadillo was already the cultural icon of hippiedom, as well as a prominent symbol in underground art. The armadillo itself was a perfect metaphor for Texas hippies. Both were at-risk species in the Lone Star State in the sixties and seventies; both had endured ill treatment, disrespect, and violent harassment, and yet both had survived.

With their hard, bony shells, armadillos seemed to inspire grim visions among know-nothing squares and rednecks, despite the fact that the only thing the animals truly desired was to root around in the soil for their dinner, and to avoid being flattened by highballing semis and pickup trucks with a gun rack in the back window and a sticker on the back that said, "America: Love It or Leave It."

Leading up to the opening of the Armadillo, people kept making comparisons to our forerunner, the Vulcan, as if the Armadillo was simply going to be a larger version of that place. But they were way off-base. From the very beginning, our goals were far grander than that.

We were determined that the Armadillo would be more than just a rock club or an auditorium for musical performances. In fact, I tried to discourage use of the words "club," "nightclub," and "auditorium." I wanted to have all kinds of music, not just rock.

And that was just the preamble; we wanted Armadillo World Headquarters to be a community of the arts. All the additional space and extra rooms cried out to be used for art galleries, head shops, an art supply store, arts workshops, a nursery for the children of the staff, and many other possibilities, while the stage itself suggested the staging of plays and screening of underground films. Most of those ideas for using the building were realized before long.

Fortunately, a handful of local heroes were willing to provide the cash infusions we desperately needed. Spencer Perskin contributed $3,000 of his band's $10,000 advance from Capitol Records. Bud Shrake pitched in $1,000.

The check from Bud Shrake was drawn on an account for Mad Dog Inc., a company that existed primarily in the minds of the Austin writers and free spirits who partied under that moniker, sometimes donning strange costumes, superhero capes, and other theatrical garb to enhance their swashbuckling adventures. Shrake, the head Mad Dog, was often accompanied by Gary Cartwright, also a journalist. Both later became well known as book writers. Other members of the Mad Dog crew were the writers Jan Reid and Blackie Sherrod, the Austin attorney David Richards, and David's wife Ann Richards, the future governor of Texas. I had been a student at North Texas State University in Denton when I was introduced to Ann and David Richards by Stan Alexander, my English professor at the time. Alexander was a great country singer, mentor, and longtime devotee of Kenneth Threadgill's Wednesday music nights.

Bud Shrake, who figures in many of my favorite Mad Dog memories, passed away in 2009. He always seemed to have a good time. As Cartwright put it, Bud was "a giant of a man with a poet's soul and a lumberjack's appetite."[7] In the years ahead, he would help us again and again, with wisdom and money, seeking nothing in return. His company was always an additional reward.

★ ★ ★

Jim Franklin was our de facto poster artist, master of ceremonies, underground figurehead, and, as one wise reporter put it, "resident genius."[8] And Jim brought us Bobby Hedderman. Lanky and stoic, Bobby grew up in Oak Cliff and for a while had wanted to become a famous rock 'n' roll singer. After moving to Austin, he skirted fame as the booking agent at the Vulcan.

It was a boiling-hot August afternoon when Franklin was near the university in the "Frog," his 1934 Ford, and spotted the tall, lanky longhair

Bobby Hederman, 1970. Photograph by Burton Wilson.

walking down the Drag. Partly out of compassion, partly out of good business sense, Franklin offered him a ride. Franklin told him that he ought to come meet Shiva's new manager.

After Franklin described me as a "guy from the Brewers Association . . . razor haircut and sharkskin suit," Bobby said he'd met me before, mentioning the day I had unexpectedly popped in to the Vulcan to warn them about an impending heat wave.

Yes, Bobby had assumed I was some kind of a cop that day. But later on, I had invited him and some of the other Vulcan paranoiacs over to my house for dinner with Genie and me.[9]

So Jim and Bobby pulled in at the Armadillo parking lot, a wasteland of rocks and giant potholes. Driving around back, they saw the magnificent oak tree, along with the open garage door on the enormous building, and heard the sounds of music and construction.

At first, Bobby wasn't all that impressed. "I just stood there," he said later, "wondering how I was going to get back across town."[10]

First impressions of the interior took longer to sink in. "It looked like a real stage," he said. "It was made of concrete, brick-faced, but a real stage." He looked up at the high ceiling. He counted the doors around the interior and came up with fourteen. He tried to estimate how many people could fit inside. The official capacity of the original layout, according to the Austin Fire Department, was 750.

Bobby couldn't help but wonder about the "older fellow in overalls and plumber's cap, fiddling with something in his paw-like hands." The older man glanced at Bobby "the way someone looks at a stray dog" and resumed his work. No mistaking that description for anyone besides Woody Wilson, my stepfather.

Bobby thought he recognized somebody near the stage, but the last time he'd seen the "big bear of a guy," his wavy, black hair had been razor cut and he'd been in a suit. "Now his hair was just starting to get long, and instead of a suit, he was wearing cowboy boots, jeans, and a snap-button denim shirt with the sleeves rolled up high over his thick biceps."[11]

That's when I introduced myself again and mentioned that we needed a booking agent. Bobby seemed open to the idea, so I suggested we smoke a joint and talk about it.

"I remember a couple of weeks later we were all driving somewhere in Eddie's Dodge Charger," said Bobby, "and Eddie's throwing out a new idea or scheme every thirty seconds, like usual, and he says, 'You know, I think we've got a gold mine going here.' And I remember thinking that was the first time I'd ever been associated with anything like that."[12]

Around this same time, Mike Tolleson showed up. He was with a friend named David Davis, a UT student who was writing a story about the Armadillo for the *Daily Texan*. Mike was a young lawyer from Dallas who'd been involved in the music business for several years and was actively scouting locations in San Antonio and Austin to develop a music and arts venue for live performances, music and videotape production, and other cultural ventures. Under that calm exterior, he was ambitious, inspired, and excited.

Mike recently shared his own first impressions of the work in progress. As he recalls it, we were about a week away from opening. According to my recollections, by that time, we had pretty much exhausted the $4,000 of funding that had been pooled from various sources.

"There were guys running around the place, painting, building things, doing the murals, and all that stuff," Mike said. "Eddie gave me a tour of the building, walked me around, and talked about what they were going to do. There was a lot of talk about Shiva's record coming out, doing the publicity, going on tour, in addition to getting this place ready to open."[13]

Mike was impressed. We were doing pretty much the same thing he'd been dreaming about. He was blown away. But he didn't think we knew much at all about the music business. He said, "I'm available to get involved with you."

I said, "Great, we need you, but I can't pay you." He was fine with that. All he wanted was a place to stay. I told him he could move into my house. Bobby and his girlfriend had just taken one bedroom, and Mike took the other.

He went back to Dallas, picked up his stuff, and moved in a couple of days later. From there, as he put it, "Eddie and I started doing Armadillo business twenty-four hours a day."

★ ★ ★

While the Armadillo was being made semi-presentable, I had a chance to work with somebody who'd been a hero to me since I was an adolescent: Kenneth Threadgill, Austin's grand old man of country music. Shiva's Headband had been booked to headline a party honoring him, called the

My Thomas Jefferson, the first person to ask if he could join the
effort: Mike Tolleson. Photograph by Burton Wilson.

KT Jamboree. The event was to be at the Party Barn in Oak Hill, on the southwest outskirts of Austin.

In the fall of 1933, just before the Volstead Act was repealed and Prohibition officially ended, Kenneth Threadgill was a twenty-two-year-old country music lover, a bootlegger, and the operator of a Gulf filling station on North Lamar, then known as the Dallas Highway. Kenneth had been selling booze illegally out of the gas station for years, but immediately after Travis County voted to go "wet," he stood in line all night long, waiting to obtain the first beer license in Austin. Travis County Beer License No. 01, dated December 7, 1933, was held by Kenneth Threadgill for the next forty years.

Every Wednesday night, Threadgill's gas station was a hopping place, and not just for gas and beer sales. The place was renowned among musicians and night owls as an after-hours joint where working musicians hung out, jammed, and gambled. One of the performers at the late-night sessions was Kenneth himself, who idolized Jimmie Rodgers and tried gamely to yodel just like him. The fact is, Kenneth wasn't a great singer or yodeler, but his love of the music was infectious, and over the years, his love and dedication to it planted some of the seeds for what would become the Austin music scene.

Being an adventurous adolescent, I would walk over to Threadgill's from our house and talk to Kenneth. I liked the old man. When I was a sophomore at McCallum High, I went there a few times, trying to catch a date with Dotty, his daughter. Dotty was a senior and she already had a steady boyfriend, but I've always been persistent.

In the sixties, curfew laws and annexation put a damper on the vice action at Threadgill's. A new crowd was going there, not for illegal hooch and gambling, but for something else that seemed rare and vintage. Kenneth Threadgill was singing his Jimmie Rodgers songs and presiding over weekly hootenannies. Friends, fans, and professionals passed the microphone around, sharing songs. The weekly gathering of folk and traditional music enthusiasts had originated on campus, where it also entailed bonding over progressive politics and pot.

When I was a freshman at UT in 1961, my English professor, Stan Alexander, invited me to come down to Threadgill's on a Wednesday night to hear him and some friends of his sing country music. I started going there again to listen and soak up as much as I could. Kenneth sounded like a

From 1933 through the sixties Threadgill's had a very limited menu. A gallon of pickled eggs sits on top of a butcher case containing rat cheese, bologna, and wine. Photographer unknown.

Kenneth Threadgill and band onstage at Bevo's Tap Room,
April 27, 1972. Photograph by Burton Wilson.

piece of history, his yodeling a bright novelty, a lightning-bolt link to the yodeling brakeman Jimmie Rodgers. But Stan Alexander turned out to be a fine country singer, the best of them all.

One of the folkies who came to take a turn at the microphone was a homely, wild-haired UT co-ed named Janis Joplin. She came out of Port Arthur with charisma to match her big voice, and after she won the hearts of the Threadgill's crowd, she hitchhiked from Austin to San Francisco in the trademark fashion of Texas hippies. Next thing any of us knew, she was the lead singer of one of the biggest psychedelic bands in the Bay Area, Big Brother and the Holding Company.

Now Janis was back in Austin, with the wreckage of Big Brother behind her and a grand plan to start a new band. As we were getting ready for the KT Jamboree, rumors circulated that Janis was going to make a special appearance. The general assumption was that she would sit in with Shiva's Headband. We'd been expecting about three hundred people to show up, but the rumors threatened to blow that number up.

I still didn't know whether to believe we'd get that kind of crowd, but then five thousand people showed up, looking for Janis.

We scrambled like hell to adjust to the new reality; obviously, we were now doing an outdoors show. We moved the PA and band equipment out of the Party Barn, hurriedly setting up a makeshift stage made of planks, plywood, and cinder blocks. The thing was about as sturdy as a wooden trampoline. Microphone stands and speakers swayed with every step. Stomp your foot while singing and the microphone would punch you in the mouth.

Thank God Janis appeared. She made a flamboyant, swaying entrance, and around her neck was a feather boa and leis fresh from Hawaii. Rude, arrogant, and loaded, she brushed off most everyone but her friends Julie Paul and Chuck Joyce, who played in the Velvet Cowpasture. After huddling with them a few minutes, she went onstage accompanied by Julie, Chuck, and Kenneth Threadgill. She tested her microphone, then took off one of her leis and, sweetly draping it around Kenneth's neck, said to the crowd, "I always promised Kenneth a good lei."

When the laughter stopped, Janis turned serious about the music she was going to perform, saying, "You keep an ear open for a guy named Kristofferson. He writes songs like this." And then she proceeded to sing the Kris Kristofferson songs "Me and Bobby McGee" and "Sunday

Kenneth Threadgill and Janis Joplin at the Newport Folk
Festival, July 1968. Photograph by David Gahr.

Morning Coming Down." She was knocking them out, breaking hearts with her soulful, blues-drenched voice, but the spell was broken, temporarily at least, when a girl in the back of the crowd was bitten by a rattlesnake and needed immediate medical attention. All in all, it was a night to remember. While it's true that Janis was loaded and kind of obnoxious, it was pretty special that she had canceled a $15,000 gig to play for Kenneth's birthday.[14]

★ ★ ★

The last couple of days before the Dillo's opening night, hammers were still pounding as Spencer Perskin and I huddled with attorney Dave Richards to formalize our business as Armadillo Productions Incorporated. Shiva's Headband would headline the first show, naturally, and Hub City Movers would also be on the bill. A third opening act, Whistler, broke up at the last minute, so Jim Franklin threw together a reunion of his Vulcan-period band, Ramon, Ramon and the Four Daddyos. Unfortunately, the Daddyos were not on the poster, since Jim had already drawn it and had it printed.

A story in the *Rag*, the influential underground newspaper published in Austin, boosted our spirits. The reporter raved that our opening, just a week hence, would be "the most exciting development in Community Arts to happen in Texas." After dropping in to visit the venue, the "Roving Rag Reporter" "rapped for a couple hours, and got nothing but good vibes the whole time, and came away infected with enthusiasm. . . . A community is All the People, and all the people can be beautiful if they have a chance to turn on."[15]

Even for 1970, the tie-dyed lingo was a little over the top, but all I could think was, *Right on, brother!* By showtime, I was pretty high on the place myself. Gazing around at the carpet sample squares that passed for seating and the telephone wire spools that passed for tables, I felt like a young commander on the eve of a great campaign.

The Armadillo World Headquarters officially opened its doors on the evening of August 7, 1970. It was hotter than nine kinds of hell, as any August night in Texas tends to be. Before the music began, I mounted the stage and took a good look around. There was much to be proud of, not least the fact that in Austin, there was a sizable enough community of hippies to merit a room this huge and a project this ambitious.

One of the great logos of any era. How many other creatures
on the planet can say they haven't evolved in the last 60 million
years? Armadillo World Headquarters grand opening poster,
August 7–8, 1970. Artwork by Jim Franklin.

No longer a lobbyist, and no longer jollying up legislators and spreading goodwill and cheer through beer, I was now an aspiring long-haired hippie in pursuit of a higher consciousness. Or something like that.

I wanted to make damned sure that no one confused the Armadillo with another music venue called the Chequered Flag. It was a little folkie joint on Lavaca Street, barely a block from the state capitol. The place had opened in 1967, around the same time as the Vulcan Gas Company. The guiding light at the Chequered Flag was Rod Kennedy, a square, uptight Republican back in the day when Republicans were the oddball minority in Texas. Kennedy had cornered the road show market in Austin, and his tastes in music favored the safe, white-bread, nonthreatening purveyors of the folk genre. The décor and logos of the place were meant to make customers think of folk music and car racing at the same time. Get it? I never did, either. Especially since Kennedy insisted that patrons remain silent during performances, paying worshipful attention, as if they were in church or at a funeral. It was time to do something completely different. The size of the Armadillo alone demanded it, but the negative example of the Chequered Flag did its part as well.

Kennedy's status was in danger the moment I shed my fancy duds and started growing my hair out, and I wanted him to know it. The Armadillo was going to be a very different place. Silence wasn't part of our vocabulary. Rowdiness would be our trademark.

On opening night I stepped up to the microphone and said, "My name is not Rod Kennedy, and this is not the Chequered Flag. Welcome to the Armadillo World Headquarters."

The bill on our first night made a powerful statement, I thought, about what the Armadillo was all about, and by extension, the Austin music scene and hippie community at that time. There was nothing generic or stereotypical about it. I certainly wasn't a stereotypical hippie. Neither were the musicians.

None of the bands really fit the psychedelic label. Loosely speaking, Ramon, Ramon and the Four Daddyos was an offbeat, artsy, fifties rock 'n' roll band. Shiva's Headband had their roots in folk and country music, refracted through a hallucinogenic lens and Spencer's hyperactive electric fiddle. The Hub City Movers were into folk and jug band music, although at least one of their songs had originated during an acid trip.

Artist Gilbert Shelton had written "When I Set My Chickens Free" after granting freedom to his chickens while under the influence of LSD.

When I think back on it, the musicians in the Hub City Movers all looked as if they had stepped out of one of Shelton's underground comics. The two guys on guitar, who looked like demons from another dimension, were Ike Ritter, famously frazzled, and , his eccentric West Texas counterpart. Ed Vizard, on sax, looked like an elf who'd stepped out of a cow patty mushroom field. Jimmie Dale Gilmore, the thin-as-a-whisper singer-songwriter from Lubbock, warbled High Plains melodies in a spacey, ghostlike voice that seemed to emanate from a scratchy old 78 rpm record.

The night was full of strange surprises. Many people who walked up to the ticket booth came to a dead stop after they learned the price of admission. "Three dollars?" they whined. "Music's supposed to be free."

An amazing number of them had stories about why they shouldn't have to pay. Some had contributed volunteer labor, and that was one thing, but others claimed exception simply because they used to work at the Vulcan, or because they "just needed to come in for a minute to take a piss." Then there would be some character who swore that he'd bought a ticket but lost it. Next up was the dude who just wanted to come in and look around for a minute or so. Would that be cool? No, man, it would not.

A pack of youngsters denied entrance loitered in the parking lot, drinking beer and smoking pot, laughing, grumbling. If you went out there, they would make a circle around you and chant about how music should be free. We were ripping them off, man.

Another bunch of them gathered behind the chain-link fence out back. At some point I heard them yelling and cheering. I looked up and saw a girl in the process of climbing the fence. I got there just as she made it over the top. I grabbed her ass with both hands, crouched, and pushed up as if throwing a medicine ball. She flew up and over the top of the fence like a badminton bird. Obviously, I'd lost my temper. Only as she went airborne did I think of the razor wire and the potential bloodshed that might occur and regretted the hell out of what I'd just done. Fortunately, she landed safely in the arms of her comrades. They booed and called me a pig.

There was some kind of trouble brewing everywhere. People were popping out of the overhead windows. The hot water heater died, meaning no hot water for the ice cream shop or the restrooms. Wet paint reached out hungrily for bare skin and clothing. The nursery overflowed with crying, unattended babies. Marijuana smoke billowed in all the wrong places. One guy became so unruly that it took several of us sitting on him to immobilize him. He still managed to poke my eye with a cigarette. He ended the night strapped to a table in the infirmary at UT.

Finally it was time for Jim Franklin, master of ceremonies, to introduce Shiva's Headband. Jim worked himself into the kind of fevered, operatic pitch that only he could muster. The band followed this dramatic setup by taking a few minutes to tune their instruments and adjust their amplifiers. Spencer Perskin addressed the audience, saying, "I didn't think anybody could find this place."

Maybe it was the wrong thing to say, because the band never found their groove. I'd never seen them play so badly. Bobby Hedderman and others agreed. Early in the set, people started talking, then talking louder and completely ignoring the band. By the end of the show, half of the audience was gone.

When the music stopped and the lights came on, I got my first look at rock 'n' roll afterbirth. Cigarette butts dotted the floor between the beer cans and bottles, visual evidence that both nearby convenience stores had sold out of beer. Leave it to hippies to stimulate the neighborhood economy. The shin-splintering telephone wire spools had been spun around the room. It reeked of good times and smelly people.

In contrast to all the goofballs outside who thought that music should be free, the three bands were all jammed into the office, clamoring for cash. "How many tickets did we sell?" demanded the nine-fingered bass player for Ramon, Ramon and the Four Daddyos. "How many were sold in advance? How many at the door? How many people does this place hold?"

I had no answers. My poor performance was noted by all. Not being trusted takes some getting used to.

When everyone was gone, I sat down on the stage, so exhausted that I dozed off for awhile, then awoke with a start. On my way home I spotted a young couple trying to hitchhike. Their car had broken down. Turned out they'd been at the Armadillo. When I asked what they thought of the place, the guy said, "Well, that woman with Shiva's sure can't sing."

★ ★ ★

The aftermath of an AWHQ show.
Photograph by Jim Richardson.

The next morning I met my first long-term volunteer. Waiting at the door was a skinny kid with long red hair who introduced himself as Mike Harr. He said he figured somebody would have to clean up. In return for his labor, he asked for living space in one of the small rooms at the back of the building. He said he'd been living with a bunch of fellow Cajuns in a crash pad on West Sixth and had had enough. Mike got the job: official sanitation engineer of the Armadillo World Headquarters, a.k.a. the Righteous Scrub Company. Every week for the first three years, I wrote a check to the Righteous Scrub Company, treating myself to the illusion that I was being conscientious about our business.

Mike began push-brooming the trash into piles while I retreated to the office. A few minutes later I heard a knock at the door. I recognized my visitor as a teaching assistant at UT, but didn't let on, as if the old fedora pulled down over Dealer McDope's eyes was an adequate disguise.

McDope held a large bundle wrapped in red wax paper. "You're doing the work of the Lord," he said. "Use this as you see fit." He handed me the package, turned, and left.

Under the red paper was thin, white tissue paper with purple mimeographed text. Each line of text ended with a blank space filled in by pen. It said: "Location *Guerrero*; Altitude *229 kilometers*; Cuantos *2.2 pounds/1 kilogram*; *!El Armadillo Vive!*"

In the weeks that followed, I paid each member of the crew with two hits of Clearlight acid, a bag of pot, and thirty dollars. Mike Harr split his money with his buddy Tracy Frederick, who became his partner in the Righteous Scrub Company. Nobody worked harder than Righteous Scrub. The debris in the Dillo often threatened to overwhelm them, but Mike and Tracy patiently educated us in the use of trash containers. Attention to cleanliness, if practiced by up to 1,500 people, could make a difference in the workload of two skinny guys at the long end of a push broom after a long night of boogie.

The second night, a wide-eyed kid from the crew informed me that a gang of bikers outside wanted a word with the boss. The bikers were bunched around the entrance like a band of Comanche warriors, restless and spoiling for trouble. Their leader, a would-be diplomat with grease under his fingernails, volunteered that they would be only too happy to keep trouble from happening; free admission was all they asked in return.

Calling the cops, I realized, was not the thing to do. I got the leader to promise to hang on peacefully for a minute and said that I'd be right back with a special gift for him.

I returned with one dose of Clearlight acid. Because the hit itself was hard to see in even the best of light—it was transparent as well as thin and small, about an eighth of an inch square—I'd wrapped it in a sheet of notebook paper, folded repeatedly until it was a package about a quarter of an inch square.

The acid had been an Armadillo housewarming gift from Don Hyde of the Vulcan. The container was a small clear-plastic cube holding one hundred hits. Even with that amount, I had to hold the container up to a light in order to see them.

In hushed, reverent tones, I told the biker about the new acid I'd just imported from California. The others crowded around, straining to hear, grumbling in complaint. The leader shushed them. He feigned familiarity with the subject, though his expression called him a liar, an acid newbie.

He wanted it badly. I warned him that it was extremely powerful, that I only had four hits, and that there were no more to be had in Austin. I was giving him two hits, I told him, as I handed him the package containing one hit, and keeping the other two for myself and my old lady. Acknowledging my generosity with a nod, he accepted my gift and stuck it in his jacket.

"Be careful," I said again. As he fastened his jacket, the girlfriend on the back of his bike cooed and reached for his pocket. He jabbed her with his elbow and growled, "I ain't said you get one, bitch."

He cranked his bike. The others grumbled, "What about us?" But he roared off and they followed, bouncing through the potholes of the parking lot. I was sweating and shaking, but by the time I got back inside, I felt good about everything. Entering my office, I found a gang of hippies milling around. I went off like a Roman candle. "Get your asses into the hall! This is a business office! The show's out there, not in here!"

The last to leave was Gary Scanlon, another Vulcan expatriate. From his no-ass backside to his pencil-thin mustache, he had the wry, sinister demeanor of a sleazy dealer. On his way out, he sneered at me: "Nobody has ever made a business out of one of these places. Lots better men than you have tried."

An empty AWHQ. Scarlet scraps of curtain transformed
the warehouse lights. Photograph by Jim Richardson.

When he was gone I punched a hole in the door. The hole would be my daily reminder of the challenge I'd undertaken, but also a message to the staff that I had a temper.

Sunday, I came in early to think about things and get started on the week. I loved the place when it was empty. When the *Rag* ran a review of our opening, the critic praised the Armadillo's "good vibes" and claimed he'd had "about the groovingest night I've spent since the Gas Company."

Eddie Wilson in front of Jim Franklin's giant mural
of the Conqueroo and Johnny Winter at AWHQ,
April 13, 1972. Photograph by Burton Wilson.

HEAD HONCHO

★

"Head honcho," "trail boss," "owner," and "cheerleader" were just some of the more positive-sounding titles attached to me during my tenure at AWHQ. One article called me "Armadillo's well-known bouncer," which I also took as a compliment. Ever since I'd sniffed out the place and put wheels under the parade, I had been in charge. Right or wrong, I called it my place. Someone had to be in charge, whether it was by acclamation, default, or benevolent dictatorship, and I guess it was me by a combination of all three.

The business operation evolved in a strange way, in part because the Armadillo's original purpose had been to answer the question, where can Shiva's Headband play on the weekends and make money? In addition, the old armory appeared to offer much, much more. So, even before opening, we had developed plans for other uses, some of which were operational by the time we opened. How many music joints, for example, have a nursery where the children of their staff can be taken care of during their shifts? How many nightclubs have their own resident artists, art gallery, and advertising agency? We were proud that we were able to have all those things, but the sheer size of the place seemed to demand more ideas and schemes than we could successfully execute.

We avoided more formalized official partnership arrangements by operating the place as a d.b.a. of Armadillo Productions, which was the company that Spencer Perskin had formed when he signed with Capitol Records. Armadillo Productions was the company Capitol advanced funds to for the Shiva's Headband album and the development of other musical acts. Spencer was supposed to find these bands and record demos that would then be sent to Capitol, who had right of first refusal on them.

Not long after the Armadillo opened, however, Spencer started getting distracted, which didn't make our jobs any easier. Mike Tolleson recently described it this way:

> *Eddie and Bobby and I and a couple of other staff people would show up every day. We were trying to find gigs for Shiva's, working on the publicity for the album, trying to book shows for the Armadillo, and other things that would help keep the doors open. Spencer would drop by in the afternoon, smoke a joint, talk about stuff, and go home. He wasn't involved in running things. His family got bigger and bigger. After Capitol Records turned down a second album, the band wasn't gigging very often, and only one time that I remember did they have a big gig out of state, at Winterland in San Francisco, opening for Steppenwolf.*[1]

The original plan for live music at AWHQ sounds pretty modest now. Shiva's Headband was to play on weekends, with local bands taking turns as opening acts, but only a trickle of people turned out to pay the $1.50 cover charge. From opening night on August 7 to the end of 1970, AWHQ grossed approximately $25,000. A few years later, we would typically gross that much in one week. It was clear we needed bands that could draw more people.

We weren't the only hippie outfit running into brick walls. The *Rag* was in dire straits, but they were always struggling. As editor Thorne Dreyer put it, no underground paper worth its salt was ever founded with the expectation of making money anyway, and if they weren't always on the verge of being shut down by the powers that be (in their case, the UT regents), they weren't doing their job. Around the same time, one of our mutual pet concerns, the People's Free Community Clinic, was in danger of becoming defunct. Another shared interest, a food co-op, had already closed down.[2]

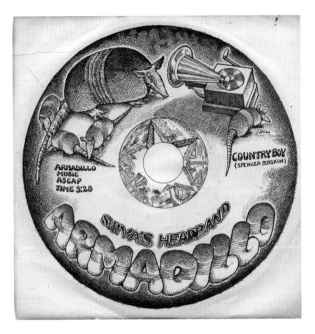

Jim Franklin designed the armadillo-studded label for Shiva's Headband's first 45 RPM single released on their own Armadillo Music recod label.

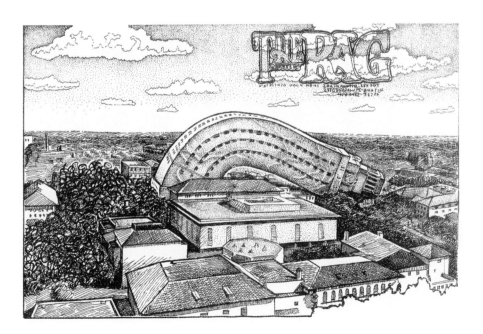

Cover of *The Rag*, 1970. Artwork by Jim Franklin.

It could drive you crazy. On one hand, we were racking our brains to figure out ways to make money so we could make all of our wild-eyed schemes work out. On the other, we were constantly reminded by our idealistic but unrealistic contemporaries that making money wasn't cool, man. We were both inspired and haunted by the ideals of the sixties.

And the new decade always had another downer in store. There was simmering outrage over the fatal shooting of four unarmed war protestors at Kent State University in May, just three months before we opened. On September 18 we learned that Jimi Hendrix had died from complications of drug and alcohol use. On October 4, Janis Joplin was found in a Los Angeles motel room, dead of a heroin overdose. Both musicians were twenty-seven years old, and both had set the world on fire with their talent, Jimi with his electric guitar and wild theatrics, Janis with her voice and raw, soulful persona.

I still think of Janis as the greatest white female blues singer ever. She was the classic outcast who never fit in, a product of a dreary childhood in Port Arthur, taunted and tormented in high school and then subjected to even worse treatment at the University of Texas in Austin. But once she started singing at the Chuck Wagon on campus—where the folkies and lefties tended to gather for meetings, socializing, and folksinging—and at Threadgill's on Wednesday nights, her sense of identity grew stronger, along with her supernatural gifts for communicating emotion and pain using the R&B forms that had worked so well for her role models, Bessie Smith and Big Mama Thornton.

A number of people in our circle of musicians and friends had remained close to Janis after she found stardom. We felt like she was one of us, but then again, she made people feel that way who'd only heard her voice and perhaps seen her image on a record sleeve. She had powerful gifts.

Only years later did I learn that Janis had donated funds for a tombstone on the grave of Bessie Smith, the great black diva of the 1920s and 1930s who had been Janis's model, not only for her singing style but for her bold, trailblazing ways. For various reasons, Smith's grave in Sharon Hill, Pennsylvania, had gone unmarked all those years. The stone was put in place on August 7, 1970, the day that AWHQ first opened for business.

When I heard that Janis had died in the manner in which she did, I was more numb than shocked. According to the stories going around our community, Johnny Winter was also chasing the dragon (I don't think any of us

Burton Wilson never used a flash. This photo of Janis Joplin
was taken at the Matrix, a dark bar north of San Francisco,
August 18, 1970.

Mance Lipscomb onstage at AWHQ, October 9, 1970.
Photograph by Burton Wilson.

dreamed that he would live another forty-four years). Fortunately, the Armadillo crew wasn't strung out. Maybe it was a good thing that we couldn't afford heroin. Unfortunately, I understand that it's much cheaper these days.

In the midst of our young heroes dying off, I guess it was appropriate that a great musician in his mid-seventies not only lifted our spirits but had a small but loyal base of fans willing to pay a cover charge. Born in the Brazos River bottoms around Navasota, Texas, in 1895, Mance Lipscomb was the son of an ex-slave father and a mother who was half Choctaw Indian. His birth name was Beau De Glen Lipscomb; was short for Emancipation.

Mance was a tenant farmer who played on weekends even after he was "discovered" in 1960 and began recording for Mack McCormick and Chris Strachwitz's Arhoolie label. Lean as a POW, he had elegantly long fingers shaped by a lifetime of hard work and "dead thumb" fingerpicking. He didn't play what people often think of as Delta blues; he was what he preferred to call a "songster," somebody who could play from a vast repertoire of popular and traditional music that had been handed down and passed around since the Civil War era and earlier. A soulful, natural-born performer, he had a voice that was mellow, almost childlike. He'd played for Frank Sinatra on Sinatra's private yacht, but he wasn't about the money.

Mance was already familiar to Austinites from the folk-revival movement and playing at the Vulcan. On his first gig at the Dillo, he drew many more people than Shiva's Headband. We brought him back as often as he could make it. For every hour he was on our stage, he must've played another three or four in the living rooms of hippies who would take him home after the show.

One of our biggest bookings in 1970 came out of nowhere. A record promoter named Bill Ham, a native of Waxahachie, Texas, came to us pitching a new blues rock band from Houston. He wanted two weekend nights and a $750 guarantee. We'd never heard of them. The guitar player was Billy Gibbons, whose last band was the Moving Sidewalks, a Houston band inspired by the 13th Floor Elevators. Even their name was a tribute, as both elevators and moving sidewalks were conveyances for taking you somewhere. Moving Sidewalks had a couple of hot regional singles, and they had toured with Jimi Hendrix.

The new band's name, ZZ Top, included the names of the two most popular brands of rolling papers, Zig-Zag and Top. The band had formed in 1969, then went through several shuffles of personnel. They'd released a single on their own Scat Records label and now had a deal with London Records, with an album due in 1971. Ham said he was confident that they could fill the hall. In fact, he said, he was willing to rent the place for a flat fee rather than have us take on any of the risk.

The road crew brought in by Ham to handle the sound and lights gave my people an education in setting up for a show. I learned a few things, too. Bill Ham had made it seem as though he was doing us a favor by renting the hall and taking the gate, but the show turned out to be a big success. By avoiding risk, we missed out on making a sizable profit.

The following year, after we had enlarged the hall, I was still mad at Bill Ham. The next time, as Bobby Hedderman recalls, "we charged Ham $300 for the rental, but we paid for security, which brought it down to about $200."[3]

We made a little more money than the first time, but Ham made a whole lot more. He ran over me like a train over a frog.

I remember that he ran the box office by himself. "Just Bill Ham and his gun," adds Bobby. At one point one of our guys, John Harms, opened the door, stuck his head inside, and found himself with a gun in his face. He told Ham he just wanted to help. Ham said, "I don't need any help. Get out and shut the door."

About two years later, ZZ Top sold out the eighty-thousand-seat Memorial Stadium at UT. From then on, calling them a "little ol' band from Texas" had to be done with a wink.

There was an important lesson in all this: to stay in business, you have to make a profit. But I knew I didn't want to make a career out of fighting a daily war with "all-bidness" types like Bill Ham. I was happier doing things as part of the community, organizing benefits, workshops, and events that fell under the none-of-the-above category. Those things were all basic to our original mission for the Armadillo.

Lightnin' Hopkins, the swaggeringest of all Texas blues cats, graced our stage the weekend immediately after ZZ Top's first show at the Armadillo. The volume was much lower and the stage production couldn't have been more different, but just as his name suggested, Lightnin' was a force of nature. He came with his own generating station.

ZZ Top on the original AWHQ stage at the south end of the hall, November 7, 1970. Dusty Hill on bass, Frank Beard on drums, and Billy Gibbons on guitar. This is the same stage Elvis Presley played on in 1955. Photograph by Burton Wilson.

Lightnin' Hopkins with Rex Bell on bass and Uncle
John Turner on drums. AWHQ, November 13, 1970.
Photograph by Burton Wilson.

During those shaky five months after we opened, there were a couple of other local blues rock bands who rocked the joint on weekends, Krackerjack and Storm. Krackerjack had a deep pedigree in the Dallas-Austin axis. They had a gifted and flamboyant singer in Bruce Bowland of Oak Cliff, the unbeatable rhythm section of Tommy Shannon and Uncle John Turner—formerly two-thirds of the Johnny Winter Trio—Mike Kindred on keyboards, and a revolving cast of superb guitar players that included Robin Sylar, Jesse Taylor, John Staehely, Gary Myrick, and Stevie Ray Vaughan.

Stevie's older brother, Jimmie Vaughan, had moved to Austin from Dallas the summer we opened the Armadillo. Jimmie, whose earlier band, the Chessmen, had opened for Jimi Hendrix in Dallas, formed a new blues band called Storm. With their guitar firepower at least doubled by the presence of Denny Freeman, Storm began playing AWHQ in October 1970.

Krackerjack, Storm, and many other local blues bands often filled local clubs three and four nights a week, but unfortunately, they just couldn't pull the numbers that we needed to justify headline billing at the Armadillo. Some of the local blues musicians resented the fact that we didn't book them more often. Somehow, they just couldn't understand how the numbers added up in the "Trying Not to Go Out of Business Blues" at the Dillo.

In many ways we lived a charmed life. God had made almost all of us young and good-looking, Satan had put an apple in each of our pockets, and romance was in the air, languidly mixing with all the pot smoke. As in the case of booking decisions made while stoned, drug-influenced decisions about sexual intercourse could also have a downside, but fortunately, it was after the advent of birth control but before the outbreak of HIV.

In a time of no money, physical affection was a trusted form of currency. Sex was frequent, privacy and discretion not so much. Sometimes, it seemed as though the most challenging thing about relationships was not to indulge in casual sex with friends and coworkers.

Instead of couples counseling, there was the threat of grudge fucking. Sexual affairs in the office were so commonplace that it began to interfere with other office activities, such as business, and caused bad feelings between various groups and departments. Sometimes, it seemed that our counterculture arts laboratory had rejected everything about the straight world except for sexual hedonism in the office.

Storm onstage at AWHQ, February 28, 1971. From left to right: Lewis Cowdrey on harp, Otis Lewis on drums, Jimmie Vaughan on guitar, Doyle Bramhall on vocals, and Danny Galindo on bass. Photograph by Burton Wilson.

Poster for a Storm, Rockinghorse, and Greezy Wheels show at AWHQ, June 11–12, 1970. Artwork by Jim Franklin.

To paraphrase the old saying, sex at the Armadillo was like pizza: when it was good, it was really good, and when it was bad, it was still pretty good. Unfortunately, as good as it sometimes was, it was too good to last.

★ ★ ★

Brainstorming about what acts we wanted to book in the future was fun as well as scary. As I recall, we were always high during these sessions. Everyone talked up the dream acts they wanted us to book, and sometimes the grandiose ideas worked out. Sometimes they evaporated like smoke or turned into train wrecks.

The most significant of the first wave of touring acts we booked was the Incredible String Band. ISB, as the psychedelic folk band from Scotland was generally referred to by their fans, was one of the first bands to incorporate a lot of theatricality and multimedia into their shows. They had formed in 1968 and released a bunch of albums in a short time, including their most recent, *The Hangman's Beautiful Daughter*, which had a thirteen-minute track called "A Very Cellular Song" that was not about cell phones but about love, life, and amoebas.

ISB played two nights at the Dillo in November 1970. They were exactly the kind of band that you'd want to see on LSD, and that was what I proceeded to do, but unfortunately that's about all I can remember about their show. I do remember one thing from after one of the shows. We went to some sort of outdoor campout where there were strange doings in the dark. Distracted by the light show in my head, I kept losing the money bag, over and over.

★ ★ ★

Doug Kershaw, the fiddle-playing Louisiana Man, was our last booking of the year, playing from December 30 through January 1. Jim Franklin painted a mural of the self-described "Ragin' Cajun" by the main entrance. We rounded up a local backing band and booked Tiger Balm, a jug band/country swing/bluegrass amalgam from San Antonio, to open each show. We actually sold a few advance tickets.

It's hard to believe now, but only rarely did a band who wanted to play at the Armadillo provide us with a demo recording. Tiger Balm may have been the first. One explanation for this rare professionalism was that Hank Alrich played in the band.

Doug Kershaw backstage at AWHQ, January 2, 1971.
Photograph by Burton Wilson.

Jim Franklin's mural depicting the "Ragin' Cajun," Doug
Kershaw, at AWHQ. Photograph by Burton Wilson.

Fresh off an army hitch as an X-ray technician, Hank gradually became a fixture at the Armadillo. First he was driving up from San Antonio for the folk music, then playing gigs. The next part is a little fuzzy, but basically, Hank started crashing there and helping out. He was always around to jam with somebody or push a mop, whatever was needed. Pretty soon he was working on recording gear in the space behind the stage, a facility that eventually became his studio, Onion Audio.

During Doug Kershaw's three-night stand, Hank was one of the bright spots in a sour and disappointing experience. Although Kershaw was on the tiny side, we came to think of him as a giant pain in the ass. At showtime on the first night, Bobby Hedderman walked into the office to find the diminutive Cajun sprawled on a table, babbling incoherently, clutching a plastic cup filled with firewater against his shiny shirt. The composer of "Diggy Diggy Lo" was having a hard time guiding his cigarette to his lips.

The musicians in the backing band we'd put together knew the arrangements of his songs, but derangement was the order of the night once the rude, drunken, pill-popping egomaniac took the stage. Barely five notes into his signature show opener, "Louisiana Man," Kershaw stopped and made the band start over. Throughout the set he would jerk his fiddle bow in the direction of drummer Jerry Barnett, trying to intimidate him into keeping the mystery beat hidden in Kershaw's scrambled brain. It looked like he was more intent on humiliating the band than winning over the audience.

Somehow, the show went on, everyone survived the three nights, and the audiences were more or less entertained, but it was easily the worst show of the year, and one of the worst in the history of the Dillo. I hate to say that's the way we ended the year, but that's the way we ended the year.

Deep in the Heart of Texas mural at AWHQ. Painting by
Jim Franklin. Photograph by Burton Wilson, 1972.

THE ARMADILLO ART SQUAD

★

The poster artists who ended up being part of what we called the Armadillo Art Squad did a lot more than advertise shows; they helped to define Armadillo World Headquarters for the local community and spread the word around the world. The Armadillo's unique, eye-popping gig flyers were often the first thing that clued people in to our very existence. The whole place was infused with art, inside and out. The old armory quivered with the energy of the artistic power bubbling within.[1]

If any single image sang the loudest about the heart and soul of the place, it was *Deep in the Heart of Texas*, Jim Franklin's giant portrait of the great Texas blues guitarist Freddie King, showing King wringing every ounce of sorrow and joy from his electric guitar as a nine-banded armadillo burst from the left side of his chest. If you ever set foot inside the Armadillo, that painting was likely the first thing you saw, and I'm confident it made an impression. It's unforgettable, really, and for many of us, it's a symbol of the magic of that place that will always burn brightly in our memories.

Jim Franklin was actually living in the building, off and on, until 1975. Our goal was to make the Armadillo a community of the arts, and it wasn't long before we had attracted a colorful band of like-minded artists

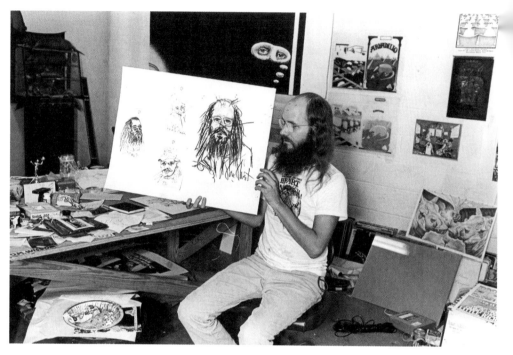

Jim Franklin in his AWHQ studio, May 13, 1971.
Photograph by Burton Wilson.

from all around the state. Each one had an individual style, and each one attracted a particular fan base. Collectively and individually, the Armadillo Art Squad created art so fine and enduring that it still makes my calcified old heart go thumpity-thump-thump.

Spencer had introduced me to Jim. It was the summer of 1970, and Jim had just returned from the Charles Manson trial, where he had done courtroom sketches. Besides being the ruler of the Austin underground, Jim had been everywhere and seen everything.

We got along right away, even though he proved to be better informed about every subject, had an opinion about everything, and had very little patience for those who disagreed with him. One time, I thought I'd unearthed an obscure bit of knowledge that would earn me at least an eyebrow lift of surprise, so I gave it a shot. During a conversation with Jim as he worked on a painting, I offhandedly mentioned that Robert Rauschenberg was from Port Arthur. I figured that, at the very least, Jim would be impressed that I even knew who Rauschenberg was.

Without even looking up from his work, Jim said, "Yeah, when he asked me where in Texas I was from and learned it was Galveston, he told me his mother had once been a contestant in the Miss Splash Day contest. I didn't believe him, but I've never checked it out."

So much for trying to one-up Jim Franklin.

The first wave of artists to follow Jim Franklin arrived as part of a package deal in the summer of 1972, when a visionary hustler named Michael Osborne came to me with the idea of creating an alternative advertising agency. Because the Armadillo was one of the primary, maybe one of the only, places that would be in the market for its services, he came to me seeking a working relationship.

I asked Mike just one question: "Do you have an *e* on the end of Osborne?" He said he did, and I told him the gig was his. The hippie advertising company was called Directions Agency, and one of the best things that came out of it was that we began a long and fruitful relationship with a team of incredibly gifted and committed artists. We needed them, too, because by the time Osborne came around, Jim Franklin was either with Freddie King's European tour, serving as the emcee and house artist, or commuting between Austin and Tulsa, where he had been engaged to paint Leon Russell's swimming pool. As a result, our house artist was out of the house a good deal of the time.

Our procession of Osborne-approved artists began with Micael Priest, a wild child from suburban Fort Worth with an incredible eye for loopy caricature. He not only stepped into Franklin's shoes as our star and emcee, but became a leader who often negotiated on behalf of the artists as a group. Micael went on to do the logo for Moon-Hill Management, the Austin agency that handled Michael Murphey, B. W. Stevenson, Steve Fromholz, and Rusty Wier. They were folkies in cowboy hats, for the most part, but they had a good buzz going in the early seventies.

Ken Featherston was a buff, gregarious surfer from Corpus Christi with a thick mane of dark hair. His posters were elaborate, Maxfield Parrish–inspired fantasies, so we called on him when we needed an image that could visually impart the same vibe as a good acid trip.

Kerry Fitzgerald, better known as Kerry Awn, had solid credentials, having been the original illustrator for the *Rag*. Later, he and some other former *Rag* people moved to Houston and founded *Space City!*, a new alternative mag. Kerry decided to move back to Austin, where he got the gig as house artist for Soap Creek Saloon. Never lacking for energy or creativity, he also produced his characteristically styled cartoonish renderings for Armadillo events.

Bill Narum was raised in a family of painters in Austin but was living in Houston, working with ZZ Top, when he came to Austin with the band in November 1970. One look at what we were doing convinced him that the Dillo was the place to pursue his interest in merging music and video. Bill moved his Space City Video operation to a commune in Taylor, a small town about an hour northeast of Austin that was an agricultural hub for the area. Space City Video morphed into Taylorvision, a cable TV system with a local programming channel.

Any of the 420 cable subscribers in Taylor who were still awake after midnight could watch a recording of the previous night's concert at the Armadillo. Taylorvision wasn't just about music, either. Some programming featured local fare such as council meetings and parades. Bill and his friends also got serious about raising tomatoes and chickens at the commune, so sometimes members of the community would be urged to call in and contribute their tips on gardening and animal husbandry.

Although Bill was a master of understatement, he also contributed some of the biggest ideas in concert production of the era. He not only designed logos for ZZ Top but was the band's stage production manager,

Kerry Awn in Jim Franklin's original studio at AWHQ, 1971.
This space was subsequently turned into a kitchen and Jim's
studio was moved upstairs. Photograph by Burton Wilson.

the guy who wrangled a Longhorn steer and a turkey buzzard for their historic Worldwide Texas Tour of stadiums and arenas in 1976–1977.

Danny Garrett was a Vietnam veteran from Baytown who wandered in on his own. Danny painted with a vengeance. In addition to the posters he did for us, he went on to become chief poster artist for Antone's. He created the "I Want You" image of Willie Nelson as Uncle Sam. Educated in history and theology, in college and in the war zone, he did engraving and filigree with shrapnel in his eyes and lust in his heart.

Guy Juke, alternately known as De White or Blackie White, was a trained artist and gifted musician from the West Texas town of San Angelo. He's certainly not the only artist from the West Texas region skilled at showing us the surreal side of real life, but there's never been anyone quite like him, either. In particular, Juke's cubist-styled works, such as the cover for Joe Ely's *Live Shots* album, are instantly recognizable and unforgettable. One of the Armadillo's most influential artists, Juke split his time between graphics work and performing with Lubbock singer-songwriter Butch Hancock and other bands.

Sam Yeates came out of North Texas, another guitar slinger and professionally trained artist. The most accomplished painter of the Art Squad, Yeates created the "Sorry, Pardner" sign that hung over the kitchen door at the Dillo. He was at his best when he had to hustle a budget to make four-color reproductions of his paintings. The pinup girls he drew for magazines were, pardon the expression, his cash cows.

Henry Gonzalez was our triple threat: bouncer, stagehand, and artist. The son of a sign painter in Corpus Christi, Henry had arrived in Austin in 1966 with Cesar Chavez, the Chicano labor organizer, on a campaign for minimum wage for migrant farmworkers. Henry knew he'd found paradise the moment he saw Barton Springs Pool. Ken Featherston sealed the deal by introducing him to Jim Franklin and Micael Priest. A fifteen-dollars-a-night gig as a bouncer gave him a foothold at the Armadillo, which he augmented with odd jobs, including sign painting and poster commissions. In a way, it was a shame Henry ever had to bruise his knuckles keeping the peace, but it was one of his gifts.

When it came to their work, every one of these guys was pure of heart and soul. It was always art for art's sake, not money, which was fortunate for us because we paid them less than a pittance for their artwork. With AWHQ as their home base and part of their identity, they traded ideas

Micael Priest working on the Armadillo Country Review
mural at AWHQ. Photograph by Linn Scherwitz.

Burton Wilson's photographs often served as source material for the art
squad's posters. Above: Mance Lipscomb, Bill Neely, and Taj Mahal backstage
at AWHQ, October 22, 1971. Facing: Poster for a Mance Lipscomb benefit
concert starring Taj Mahal, May 24, 1973. Artwork by Micael Priest.

GET YOUR TICKETS AT OAT WILLIES, INNER SANCTUM & ARMADILLO BEER GARDEN.

and techniques, taught each other, and worked together and alone. They created images for T-shirts, signage, murals, bumper stickers, tickets, and album covers. They worked with struggling and emerging bands, helping them establish a visual style that let them stand out from the pack.

It bears repeating that the Armadillo Art Squad didn't just promote the Armadillo but helped establish the visual vocabulary of the era in Austin. Jim Franklin's beer logos, Mike Priest's design for KOKE-FM, Ken Featherston's Oat Willie's signage, Kerry Awn's street murals, and many other iconic works helped spread the news about the Austin scene to the rest of the world.

Our artists shared resources, talent, and work spaces with a collective mindset not unlike that of a band, and at times the same sorts of rivalries would flare up, but there was a lot more cooperation and nurturing among them than cutthroat competition.

Since the mid-1960s, there had been an Austin-to–San Francisco axis in the music and art scene. Critics can debate the merits of San Francisco art versus Austin art, but the way I see it, the big spark for San Francisco psychedelic artists was LSD and other hallucinogens. In Austin, inspiration was fueled primarily by a combination of beer, summer heat, world-class swimming holes, and mind-expanding drugs in roughly equal parts. Granted, a professional critic would stress other aspects of the respective cities' artistic output, including techniques, disciplines, and artistic influences. But then I'd have to remind said critic that starting in the mid-sixties, some of the best, most influential creators of music poster art in San Francisco were from Austin. In particular, Gilbert Shelton and Jack Jackson moved to California after honing their craft and establishing much of their visual vocabulary here in Austin. If you don't trust my artistic opinions, then do the math. During the late-sixties heyday, the combined output of the Fillmore, Avalon, Family Dog, and other concert promoters equaled a grand total of about 475 posters. In Austin in the 1970s, artists working for the Armadillo *alone* turned out 500 posters.

Our artists showed up each day with their latest work, talking excitedly about the performers they were immortalizing. When I saw the bags under their eyes, I couldn't help but think of fighters who'd spent the night in the boxing ring. I constantly worried about them. How many fights did they have left in them? Their efforts seemed unsustainable. I was embarrassed that we couldn't pay them more, but they never bitched about it.

Fans eagerly plucked their posters from bulletin boards and telephone poles, thereby canceling the advertising potential of the artwork. Years later, Sam Whitten, a professor of library science at UT, buttonholed me at a party and told me that he had an "ethical" Armadillo poster collection. He explained that he'd always waited until after a show to harvest a poster. It's fortunate that he was able to assemble such a magnificent collection.

When times were good, the overabundance of music, art, and community spirit all seemed like some kind of ongoing miracle. When times were bad and it felt like the Armadillo was cursed with horrible luck and an unhappy staff ready to mutiny against their clueless leader, well, the art was still pretty damn great.

My favorite photograph of Freddie King, taken by Burton Wilson.
That smile could disappear in the tiniest portion of a second.
Backstage at the AWHQ, October 3, 1970.

A KING, A DOMINO, A CAPTAIN, AND A LEO

★

Following in the staggering footsteps of the Ragin' Cajun, Freddie King kicked off 1971 at the Armadillo. The towering blues guitarist, a.k.a. the "Texas Cannonball," had been popular since the early 1960s, when records like "Hide Away" packed the floor at sock hops and even made it onto the Top 40 charts. In his first weekend at the Armadillo, back in October, Freddie had done very, very well, and his fee was only $300.

On this night, however, the temperature was below freezing outside, and it was almost as cold inside the hall. Aside from body heat, three small space heaters were the only sources of warmth. The dampness in the concrete floor seeped up through my cowboy boots. So we were a little nervous, especially since, as showtime drew near, Freddie was nowhere to be seen.

Storm had the opening slot and were also contracted to be Freddie's backup band. As their last song came to an end, I saw Bobby Hedderman frantically waving at me from the backstage door. When I stepped outside, Freddie King, wearing a floor-length fur coat, was standing next to a shiny black Cadillac, his enormous outline making the lead sled look small. The trunk was open, a guitar case inside. Freddie had a huge smile on his face as he draped a big, muscular arm around Bobby.

Crowd watching Freddie King perform onstage at AWHQ, 1970.
The photograph shows the original stage as pictured from the
upstairs rooms. Photograph by Burton Wilson.

"What you worried about?" Freddie said. "I don't go on for five minutes."

Freddie grabbed his guitar and amp and nodded at Bobby to walk him onstage. He took off his coat, laid it across a chair, nodded hello at the band, plugged in his guitar, turned to the microphone, and got down to business.

His first number was "Hide Away," and suddenly, the chill started leaving my bones. Nobody could get down to business with a thunder and fire like Freddie King.

It's hard to imagine anyone playing that ugly frozen room without complaint, but Freddie gave us the full treatment. He was the gold standard for Texas roadhouse blues. Over the next few years, he developed a huge following at the Armadillo, and he saw every improvement we made—in part because the business he brought to us made them feasible. Freddie liked to call the Armadillo the "House That Freddie Built."

At the end of January 1970, six months into the Armadillo's existence, I was still staring at a succession of dark, empty nights when a smooth talker named C. C. Courtney breezed into my office, offering to help us break new cultural ground. In an earlier life, Courtney had been a Top 40 disc jockey in New Orleans, where he was known as the "Duke of the Dial in Dixie." Now he was trying to interest me in a quirky country-western musical about the village idiot of Ruston, Louisiana, titled *Earl of Ruston*. Perhaps he had heard that I had the same title in Austin.

The musical had been written by C. C. Courtney, his cousin Ragan Courtney, and Peter Link. Link and C. C. Courtney had previously collaborated on *Salvation*, which had been a hit on Broadway.[1] The band that would play in *Earl of Ruston*, Goat Leg, had some of the best female singers I've ever heard.

The show was a success. The acting and singing had our audiences laughing, clapping, stomping, and shouting. Critics liked it, too. The *Daily Texan* gave it a favorable review, although the Armadillo was described as "bleak." A writer in the *Texas Observer* more charitably described the place as an "arts laboratory." So what if we were unconventional? At least we had a stage and were willing to take chances. Whatever the Armadillo was, we launched *Earl of Ruston*, which eventually made it all the way to Broadway, but the sophisticated New York theater audiences failed to get it. It opened on May 5, 1971, at the Billy Rose Theatre and closed on May 8.

Jim Franklin showing his genius on behalf of the Earl and his
Louisiana Tribe. *Earl of Ruston* handbill. Artwork by Jim Franklin.

Although we were beginning to deliver on our promise of offering artistic productions that went above and beyond expectations, the *Rag* continued to warn readers that we were about to go under. We couldn't issue any denials, because we were always about to go under.

Captain Beefheart was the kind of artist that inspired intense passion from a small cult following. The small crowd that showed up to see him at the Dillo couldn't have been more excited. Being in awe of the Captain's immense, rare, mysterious talents, I was as excited as anyone there, but if the record company hadn't been underwriting the tour, it's hard to imagine how we could've booked the show. Fortunately, they were. The show was a double bill with the Captain's sometime guitarist, the brilliant Ry Cooder.

The Captain's given name was Don Van Vliet. The opportunity to meet him and spend time with him was a rare privilege. He was far out, in the best sense, wearing a wackadoodle expression, artistically sculpted facial hair, and a top hat. A lot of his music was rooted in Delta and Chicago blues, filtered through jerky beats, dissonance, and overall weirdness. His voice was a Howlin' Wolf howl, rasping but authentic. To some people, it was off-putting, noisy, or weird for weird's sake, but his fans got it. It seemed as though the Captain was speaking directly to them, whatever it was he was singing about.

Seeing Captain Beefheart and Ry Cooder on the same stage made for a truly eclectic and satisfying evening. Cooder's playing channeled everyone from Johnny Cash and Blind Alfred Reed to Hawaiian slack-key guitarists. It was hard, maybe impossible, to imagine such a night happening anywhere else in Texas, maybe even in the whole world.

The Captain was also a painter, and to no one's surprise, he found a kindred spirit and admirer in Jim Franklin. On the night of the show, Franklin did a drawing of the Captain while the Captain simultaneously did one of Franklin.

"He was a great intellectual," Franklin said years later. "The day before the Beefheart show, I went by the hotel to meet Captain Beefheart. Accompanying me was Mincemeat Mercer, who played with Ramon, Ramon and the Four Daddyos. The three of us ended up going to the gift shop, where we bought toy fishing poles with plastic hooks. Beefheart was an animal lover and didn't want to hurt any fish. From there we strolled down to Town Lake and went fake fishing with our fake hooks. We didn't even catch a cold."[2]

Poster for Captain Beefheart and the Magic Band and Ry Cooder show at AWHQ, February 20 and 21, 1972. Jim Franklin's illustration is the visualization of an epigram by Don Van Vliet (a.k.a. Captain Beefheart) that was included in a promotional piece from his record company: "A whirling dervish, honey of two white pigs bore snoots 'n touched tusks on either husk of the sun 'n moon / an apple dropped thru membrane arches broke embryonic picked out seed cores."

Many great performers graced the Armadillo's stage, but during those early days, no one quite compared with Mr. Antoine "Fats" Domino Jr. One of the most singular pioneers of rock 'n' roll, Fats Domino, from the Ninth Ward of New Orleans, had achieved fame with such hits as "Blueberry Hill," "Walking to New Orleans," and "My Girl Josephine."

The privilege of seeing Fats Domino play was thrill enough, but there was more. The grand piano the great man played was the same Mason & Hamlin my mother, Beulah, had bought for me when I was twelve, the same instrument Granny Risher had tortured daily with selections from *The Broadman Hymnal*. Beulah, who still called me Edwin, was as proper as a church supper and had preferred not to think about what her adolescent boy was up to while the piano gathered dust at her nursery school. Never did she dream that the piano would end up in a joint like the Armadillo.

The crowd was small that night, but despite the fact that it was forty-two degrees outside and we had no heaters in the hall, they worked up quite a fever. They were going nuts from Fats's first chords until his last chorus. Fats said thanks by belly-bumping Beulah's baby grand all the way across our great wide stage. I never told Beulah or Granny Risher, but I think it was love.

Fats brought his own security team: two large, well-dressed black men who stationed themselves next to the backstage door to guard Fats and his abundant jewelry. Undoubtedly, they had been through this drill in a thousand different joints. Armadillo regulars, pickers without portfolios, and kids were all turned away with a raised eyebrow. The security team's scowls alone had the power to transform men into mice. Certain men in business suits, acknowledged with no outward sign, came and went. Females were carefully scrutinized and some were allowed entry.

We all stood back and observed as one of the behemoth bodyguards stepped into the dressing room to help Fats change into his stage clothes. With his short, round frame, Fats stuck his arms straight out and his man went to work, slipping the famed ivory pounder out of his black velvet jacket and into fresh trousers, gleaming patent leather pumps, and a black Mexican wedding shirt. Reminding me of a diva backstage at the opera, Fats nodded at his assistants, signaling that the star was ready to meet his public.

A busty woman in a tight sweater stepped forward. "My name's Choo-Choo," she said. "Would you please give me your autograph?"

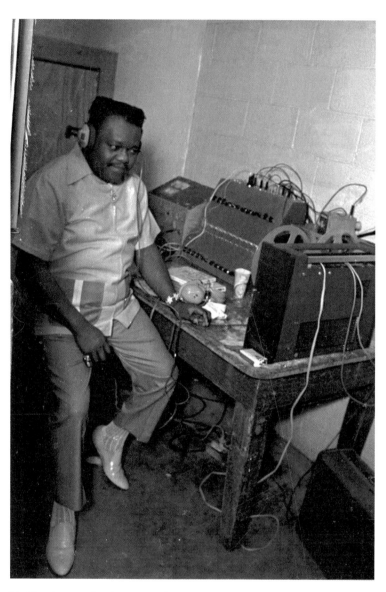

Mr. Domino was the ultimate gentleman.
Photograph by Burton Wilson.

Fats Domino onstage at AWHQ, February 28, 1971.
Photograph by Burton Wilson.

Choo-Choo tugged on the neck of her sweater on the left side, expos-
ing one of her gigantic breasts.

"Why, of course, my dear," said Fats.

Choo-Choo's girlfriend offered a ballpoint pen. As he cupped the
mammary Choo-Choo offered, its heft overflowing his grasp, he shook
his head. "I need the felt-tip pen."

A felt-tip pen instantly appeared. Putting tip to teat, the rock 'n' roll
star carefully inscribed it with "F-A-T-S" in big block letters. After he
was done, he released his grip on the breast, but the pen remained poised
to write. At first surprised, then pleased, Choo-Choo yanked down her
sweater further to expose the other breast, where Fats proceeded to print
"D-O-M-I-N-O." As he finished the last O, she started to step back and
let others take their turn with the star, but Fats stopped her with a look.

"We've got to use good grammar, now," he said. With one last, deft
motion, he added a comma.

Her breasts now said: "Domino, Fats."

Beulah could never have imagined it, Granny Risher would never have
approved of it, and I'll never forget it.

Leo Kottke was the first act I picked up at the airport. I had no idea
what to expect. Some people said he had extra fingers, and after listening
closely to the amazing polyphonic fingerpicking on his records, it didn't
seem like such an outrageous idea. There were rumors that the guy was
ancient. There wasn't a photo of him on his first album, *12-String Blues*,
or on the second one, *6- and 12-String Guitar*. Even if he called out to say
hello to me as he got off the plane, how would I know it was him? The new
LP had no vocals on it. In the liner notes he explained that it was because
his singing voice sounded "like geese farts in the wind on a muggy day."

The second album had also blown our minds because the cover featured a pretty fair drawing of a full-grown armadillo. When it came to
armadillo drawings, we were pretty hard to please, but in this case, it
looked as if illustrator Annie C. Elliott had channeled Jim Franklin. Even
to this day, people call it *The Armadillo Album*. Kottke didn't know it, but
he was already one of us.

The fact that he walked off the plane carrying two guitar cases gave
him away. Tall and clean-cut in a button-down Oxford shirt, Leo Kottke
looked more like an Ivy League rowing team captain than a rock 'n' roller.
But before we could shake hands, he whispered hoarsely, "I don't think I
can play tonight."

What a stunning talent was Leo Kottke and what good, easy
manners he had. Jim Franklin's accessorized toilets didn't faze
him, and he told the same knock-knock joke three or four years
in a row, August 4, 1971. Photograph by Burton Wilson.

Poster for Leo Kottke and Greezy Wheels show at AWHQ.
July 23 and 24, 1971. Artwork by Jim Franklin.

"Why?" I asked.

He was clearly in pain. "I cut my finger," he said. "Maybe to the bone."

The cut could not be seen because he was carrying the two guitars, so I took his word for it until we got in the car. He explained that he had restrung his twelve-string on the plane and after returning it to the case, he noticed the end of a small E string sticking out. Instead of opening the case and pushing the string out of the way, he had taken hold of it with his left hand, resulting in a deep cut on the little finger at the first bend.

Once we were in motion, he took out his twelve-string guitar and ripped off a few runs at incredible speed. When he needed to reach a note with the injured finger, he screamed but didn't slow down. He kept playing. A minute later he screamed again. After the third scream, he stopped playing and said, "Well, I guess it's nothing I can't work around."

Kottke seemed to fall instantly into the Armadillo groove. Not surprisingly, since they shared an off-center sensibility and view of the world, he bonded with Jim Franklin. Before the show, Franklin created an elaborate stage set with panels of painted bluebonnets, or "blue vomits," as he liked to call the state flower of Texas, and used the panels to create an illusion-like entrance for Kottke. This was one of the occasions when Jim really put a lot of "ceremony" into his job as master of ceremonies. At the end of a particularly convoluted and dramatic introduction, delivered in Franklin's inimitable Vincent Price–on-LSD voice, one of the panels moved aside to reveal Kottke sitting there, guitar in hand, ready to play.

"Just call me Tammy Wynette," the musician retorted. And on the second night, that's exactly what Franklin called him.

Kottke began his set by telling a knock-knock joke. He loved the joke so much, he continued using it every time he played the Armadillo for several years running. Decades later it would become the title of an Academy Award–winning film.

Knock, knock.
Who's there?
Argo.
Argo who?
Argo fuck yourself.

Eddie in AWHQ parking lot stading between "Big Blue,"
his 1966 Dodge Charger and Genie's Dodge Dart, 1972.
Photograph by Burton Wilson.

DIGGING FOR PROGRESS

My friend Ann Richards, the future governor of Texas, once called the Armadillo a "barny old place," and as gifted as she was with colorful, barbed expressions, we were probably lucky she left it at that. Outside, the caliche parking lot was a moonscape, with potholes big enough to swallow an entire Volkswagen, and it created clouds of dust that came inside and coated everything, except when it rained, and that meant mud-caked cowboy boots, sandals, and bare feet. Beautiful Texas!

When I originally secured the lease with M. K. Hage Jr., I promised not to sell beer. It had seemed like the right thing to do at the time. Beer created drunks, drunks caused fights, and fights created trouble that brought the cops. Our people were already paranoid about the police. In 1970 hippies were routinely harassed, singled out, and arrested just for their appearance or for having a peace sign sticker on the back of a car or a VW bus.

On the other hand, my experience with the Brewers Association, not to mention high school and college, told me that beer also brought people together. As a come-on to get people to a show, beer had no peer. And we desperately needed to get more people coming to the great shows we were putting on.

Beer was also a response to the climate. A person doesn't have to live in Texas for long before learning that beer makes the summer heat more tolerable. Our building had no air-conditioning. Real air-conditioning was financially impossible at the time, but getting a beer license was doable, and that was one of the most important early improvements we made to the Armadillo after our first year in business.

It was obvious, as well, that we needed some structural improvements that would make the joint more inviting to people. The only seating we had was the floor, where dirty carpet remnants were laid out, checkerboard style, in what was euphemistically called "festival-style seating."

Our initial goal was to double the Armadillo's income by increasing our capacity from 750 to 1,500. We built a grand stage at the opposite end of the hall, moved the entrance/exit, installed a box office, and hung curtains that would serve double duty as dividers for smaller shows. We also installed a glorified bar and hangout by the kitchen where food and beer would be served. The Cabaret, as we called it, was elevated and had room for tables and seating where people could sit and watch the show from what was now the back of the hall.

The success of the renovation project depended heavily on channeling the approach used in Mark Twain's classic, *Tom Sawyer*, when Tom entices his friends to take over his job of whitewashing a fence without pay.

We had a good-sized crew of helpers. Everyone with nothing better to do wanted badly to be in our gang and hang out. And they had no choice but to work if they wanted to hang. The harder we worked, the harder they worked. They showed up every morning, sometimes bleary-eyed, always scruffy. Most were looking for companionship, not employment. Sometimes the ranks would swell with friends of friends, cousins, newcomers to town, or folks just passing through and in need of gas money.

We began the interior makeover by tearing out fourteen rooms that surrounded the large room. I did not ask the landlord for permission, I just ripped up his building. Tearing out the walls was relatively easy.

We kept the crew going with giant, greasy Schlotzsky's sandwiches, buying them at the original storefront next door to the Continental Club on South Congress Avenue, where the now countrywide sandwich franchise started out just a few months after the Armadillo opened.

When we lacked cash for sandwiches, we served them rice and beans in a tub. Cheap refreshments, in the form of Mexican pot and ninety-nine-cent six-packs of Texas beer, also kept us going. I didn't allow pot to

A typical AWHQ crowd, 1974. This photo shows the new bar in the background, and carpet scraps still on the the floor before the risers were installed. Photograph by Burton Wilson.

Galen Barber consulting with his man on the mop, Bill Pankratz. Photograph by Burton Wilson.

An empty AWHQ. Photograph by Jim Richardson.

View of AWHQ bar after renovation. This was the original location of the stage, which was moved to the north end of the hall. Photograph by Jim Richardson.

slow us down, however, having recently learned the difference between volunteers who were stoned and those who were high. The ones who got high were the guys who found the experience exhilarating enough to show up the following day, ready to go; the ones who got stoned were missing in action.

My coaching experience, not to mention marine corps boot camp training, served me in good stead. My locker-room pep talks at the start of the day leaned toward theatrical and military imagery. "We have to keep the theater open," I said to whomever was around and needed motivation.

At other times, I'd say, "The show must go on. Our job is bigger than the unpleasant thought of having to spend time in a foxhole with someone you don't particularly like." Sometimes I threw in references to Noah's Ark and the Alamo. With so many people working so hard for little or no money, someone had to keep the pressure on.

Through a combination of hard work, worthwhile goals, comedy, pot, and my corny motivational speeches, we developed a sense of camaraderie and community. Plus we got an impossible job done.

The temperature must have been 120 degrees in the offices when we started the tear-out. The work was hard, hot, and dirty, but the nastier it got, the harder we laughed. The scene reminded me of my stepfather's photographs from World War II, when they were building runways in the jungles of the Pacific islands. South Austin in 1971 was a long way from there, but sometimes it felt almost like war.

The renovations took just over two weeks. During that time, we radically changed the innards of the hall by moving the stage and installing the Cabaret and new bar. Beer sales were initiated with a little two-keg beer box. Our gross potential was also enhanced by expanding the capacity from 750 to about 1,500. We also upgraded the stage lights and PA. The previous sound system had been owned by Bloodrock, the Fort Worth hard rock band whose single about a gruesome plane crash, "D.O.A.," had somehow reached number 36 on the *Billboard* Top 100 earlier in the year. We bought the new PA from Showco Productions, a concert production company in Dallas run by Jack Calmes, who became my good friend.

Jack was an important figure in the music business in Texas. He and another Dallas promoter, Angus Wynne III, then a visionary nineteen-year-old, were responsible for booking Bob Dylan in Austin at the Municipal Auditorium on September 24, 1965. It was Dylan's first Austin appearance and also his first gig with his new electric band, featuring members of the Hawks, later known as the Band. Two months earlier, at the Newport Folk Festival, Dylan had performed an electric set (backed by several members of the Electric Flag) that did not sit particularly well with many in the audience, who viewed the electrification of Dylan's rootsy material as a trashy sell-out. Austinites, however, were enthusiastic about the Dylan show. Few complaints were heard, and in fact, Dylan's first show in Austin is remembered today as a transformative event. For decades after, many musicians talked about it in reverent tones, like teenagers going over an old comic book that tells the origin story of their favorite superhero.

Jack Calmes liked us and looked out for us, which was a good thing since his partners didn't like us at all. We bitched about the sound system from the git-go, and their attitude was, if you don't like it, buy another one. Jack was always sending us spare banana plugs and other parts to make it work better.

Jack was also Freddie King's manager. Unlike Mance Lipscomb, Lightnin' Hopkins, Jimmy Reed, Bo Diddley, and other great blues musicians, Freddie had radio hits in the early 1970s, and he worked all the time. Jack Calmes was responsible for much of that. He also had a great story to explain how he got the job.

Previously, Freddie had been signed to a booking agent named Sam Copeland, a guy who had a reputation for being difficult and threatening. Freddie was certainly no wallflower, however, and on more than one occasion, the bluesman found it necessary to collect his money from Sam Copeland at gunpoint.

Jack wanted to work with Freddie, and he knew he could do better. Jack planned to inquire about getting Freddie released from his contract with Sam, so he asked Freddie how much time was left on the contract.

"I don't know," Freddie told him, "but we can just have him killed."

"No, no, let's don't do that," Jack said. "I've got $1,500 in the bank. I'll offer that to Sam."

Jack met with Sam and brought the $1,500 to purchase Freddie's contract. To sweeten the deal, Jack gave the agent some advice. "I promise you, if you don't take the money, Freddie's going to spend the money to get somebody from Chicago to kill you," he said. "I'm trying to keep him from doing that."

Freddie King and Leon Russell discussing the set list before
the grand reopening show, 1971. The beer garden was full
and beginning to rumble. Photograph by Van Brooks.

Sam signed the release. Freddie and Jack became business partners.

By the fall of 1971, things seemed to be coming together. For the grand reopening, we had Freddie King, who was red-hot at the time and newly signed to Shelter Records. Even better, Freddie would be recording a live album at the Armadillo, with Leon Russell producing and doing some of the songwriting.

Shelter had been founded by Leon Russell and Denny Cordell in 1969. Leon was on fire in the early seventies, one of the biggest names in rock 'n' roll. He had great momentum from the *Mad Dogs & Englishmen* tour, where he basically stole the show from Joe Cocker, and his self-titled solo album would continue to generate hits for other artists for years to come. He had recently worked with Bob Dylan, Delaney and Bonnie, and George Harrison, among others.

When the Shelter Records gang arrived and walked through the doors, the first thing that caught their eye, of course, was Jim Franklin's masterpiece, his portrait of Freddie King with an armadillo exploding out of his chest.

"It's a monster," said Leon. In practically no time, Leon had hired Jim to paint the swimming pool at his house in Tulsa, and Jim would also end up painting Leon's studio. For the next year, Jim commuted between Austin and Tulsa, lending his many talents to Leon, Shelter, and Freddie.

At showtime on the first night of Freddie's two-night stand, Jack Calmes, Angus Wynne, and Leon Russell collected and led a huge entourage that proceeded to do a snake dance across the Dillo stage. They were hollering, dancing, and beating drumsticks, beer bottles, and cowbells. The joint rumbled with joy.

Two weeks later, we got all pumped up for the sellout show by Ravi Shankar, the Indian sitar superstar so admired by the Beatles. At Ravi's request, it was a no-smoking show, which was a definite first. We posted people at the door to explain the smoking ban and to hand out incense, despite the fact that when burned, incense creates you-know-what. By showtime, my hippie idealist bubble had burst several times. When I was on chauffeur detail, Alla Rakha, Ravi's tabla player, had asked me to pull over at a liquor store for a pint of bourbon and at KFC for some fried chicken. I had hired a macrobiotic kitchen for the night, whose cooks prepared what they hoped would be a respectful and acceptable local interpretation of Indian fare. When Ravi's band members asked if we could fetch some white bread to go with the meal, it was a sad sight to behold.

Poster for Ravi Shankar show at AWHQ,
May 1, 1971. Artwork by Jim Franklin.

John Sebastian with wife,
Catherine, backstage
at AWHQ, October 29,
1971. Photograph by
Burton Wilson.

Vassar Clements and Earl Scruggs backstage at AWHQ,
November 5, 1971. Photograph by Burton Wilson.

After the momentum of our grand reopening, I learned all about speed bumps. One month after the grand reopening, we lost more money on John Sebastian than we had ever dreamed of losing. It had seemed like a sure thing. Before going solo in 1968 and playing Woodstock the following year, Sebastian had written and sung all the hits for the electric folk band the Lovin' Spoonful. They were songs that just about everybody liked: "Summer in the City," "Do You Believe in Magic?," and "Did You Ever Have to Make Up Your Mind?," to name a few. There was even a hit song by the Mamas and the Papas, "Creeque Alley," that mentioned their friends from the Lovin' Spoonful. Jerry Garcia said that it was after seeing Lovin' Spoonful that the Grateful Dead decided to go electric.

Sebastian's fee seemed quite reasonable. Surely he would sell a thousand tickets, we reasoned. Only three hundred people showed up, and it felt like less. We lost a lot of money.

The next week, banjo picker Earl Scruggs, a folk and bluegrass favorite, put us another $2,500 in the red. We hired the Geezinslaws, a local hillbilly duo, to open the show, making out a check for $150 to the duo's Sammy Allred, who also happened to be Austin's favorite country music deejay. The following Monday morning, Sammy went on the air and blasted the hippies at the Armadillo who had paid his band with a hot check.

It was the only time in the Armadillo's history that we bounced a check to a performer.

Bud Shrake pulled our asses out of the bacon grease that time. We were at the Cabaret bar when he pulled out his personal checkbook and wrote out a check for $3,500.

When winter arrived, our struggles with nature began anew. With only those three little space heaters, it was so frigid in the hall that we retreated to the Cabaret end of the building, using a curtain to cordon off the space. We had some good shows, but they were financially disastrous. In 1971 we grossed about $45,000 and lost about $13,000. We found that by enlarging the building, we had increased not only the gross potential but also our loss potential.

Armadillo Daily Bread Bakery cartoon, 1971.
Artwork by Jim Franklin.

LIVING THE DREAM

★

Not long after we opened the joint in 1970, a couple of playboy drug smugglers came up with a bright idea to build a concession area around an ice cream parlor. Sure, why not? Someone else asked if hippie bakers could bake bread. The concession area would be open at night, and the bakery would operate during the day. I kept nodding my head, sure, let's go for it.

The playboys turned greedy. They wanted a cut off of all concessions, not just the ice cream. Not a chance, I told them. So they told me they didn't like the bakery using their space. It seemed their ice cream kept disappearing, and unknown parties kept spilling honey and cooking oil on the concrete floor without cleaning it up.

Tensions rose after the drug dealer/ice cream investors saw their ice cream business was running a distant second to the bakery, which was run by women who flaunted unrestrained breasts and left their underarm and leg hair to grow unmolested by razors. With their bare-bones, back-to-nature style, the earth mothers had a way of seeming confrontational to such guys, even when the women were just minding their own business.

Every morning, wealthy West Austin socialites cautiously navigated their Cadillacs and Mercedes into our dirt parking lot. They tiptoed inside the big, ugly building and looked around warily as their eyes and noses adjusted. Then they strode purposefully to the bakery and purchased warm loaves of fresh whole-wheat bread. In the backwater that was Austin in the early 1970s, no one else had anything like the Armadillo's Daily Bread Bakery.

The bakery hosted free community dinners every Sunday. The serving line was an exercise in what I called "point and grunt, scoop and plop." From old, dented pots, servers shoveled gobs of sticky, gray gruel onto plates. Rice, oats, molasses, and certain unknowns were combined to create some of the worst shit I have ever tried to eat.

These banquets entailed no real overhead, but we managed to lose money anyway. The donations can was almost always empty. Hippies kept coming, and a large proportion of them brought their dogs. One day, after picking up my plate of glop, I took my place on the floor at a splintery spool table with my friends and unwittingly sat on top of a fresh, wet pile of dog turds. That was it, I'd had more than enough. I put up a large sign on the doors that said "NO DOGS!"

And we called it civilization.

The playboy drug dealers were gone soon enough, but the earth mothers of the bakery became an Armadillo fixture. As with most communities, the people who really want to be there are the ones who hang on through thick and thin.

★ ★ ★

If you come across a classic photograph of a night at the Armadillo, there's a good chance it's the work of a man who was nearly fifty years old when I met him. That may not sound old to our generation now, but back then it was twice the age of most of the staff.

Burton had a very formal way of speaking. The first time we met, he made a proposal. "My name is Burton Wilson. I'm a freelance photographer," he said. "I take a lot of photographs of musicians, and if you will be so kind as to allow me access to Armadillo World Headquarters, I will make available to you copies of any pictures I shoot to use as you please."

What a fine deal it turned out to be. Burton had already documented many of the acts that played the Vulcan; now he wanted to document the

Self-portrait by Burton Wilson.

Armadillo's acts. Besides being incredibly talented and skilled in the photographic arts, Burton was always cool, calm, and collected.

"Burton, you've got a great name," I said. "Just tell anybody who asks that you own the place. You'll never need a backstage pass."

★ ★ ★

As chaotic as the Armadillo was, my home life was maybe more so. The house was on a double lot across from a small city park in Tarrytown, then Austin's snootiest neighborhood, except for maybe Pemberton Heights. Genie and I kept the lawn green and trimmed. We tended our garden. We probably had the nicest-looking hippie crash pad for miles around.

Bobby Hedderman and his girlfriend had moved in soon after he came to look at the Armadillo with Jim Franklin. Mike Tolleson moved into the guest room soon after. Shiva's Headband practiced in a converted shop in the backyard. Spencer Perskin and his brood stayed on the back porch, but not permanently. Later, Spencer's brother Pete and his wife moved in. When Pete started taking banjo lessons, it was a bad time for everyone. It was lucky we didn't kill each other, and it was really, really lucky for Pete.

★ ★ ★

If not for the Armadillo's volunteer staff, we wouldn't have survived more than a few months. Volunteers were people who showed up and stuck around long enough to figure out where they fit in: kitchen, security, production, maintenance, or somewhere else. Some of them had been unable to make it in the outside world, but at the Armadillo, they helped breathe life into our strange enterprise.

Lloyd Goering was the perfect department head for maintenance, electronics, and sound. A master electrician and mechanic, radio expert, pilot, and outdoorsman, Lloyd was no hippie; in fact, he was antislacker and, like many people of genius I've known, kind of a grouch. But if someone made a good suggestion, he could admit it was good and analyze its cost-efficiency in a heartbeat. He was as valuable to the Armadillo as the ground it stood on.

A parade of talented gearheads worked alongside Lloyd Goering. Jerry Barnett, who at various times had played drums for Hub City Movers and Shiva's Headband, conducted strange experiments in the pit that became the game room. Jerry later earned a degree in electronics engineering.

AWHQ stage and maintainance crew.
Photographs by Burton Wilson.

Charlie Sauer, another alumnus of the Hub City Movers, used my old Wollensak reel-to-reel tape recorder to record Janis Joplin on her final pass through Austin. Charlie later became a star in the technology world, highly regarded as a systems architect specializing in networking, system modeling, multimedia, and Internet software development; before he had his own company, Technologists.com, he was vice president of software and technology at Dell.[1] Another volunteer, Tim Elliott, took care of our mechanical and electrical problems and tried valiantly to keep the place patched together.

Probably our brightest volunteer was M. K. Hage III, our landlord's eighteen-year-old son. His birth name was Mitry Kalil Hage III, but I called him "Three." He was smart, articulate, and enthusiastic about what we were doing. The senior Hage had been concerned about Three's apparent lack of focus and ambition, and to see his son excited about working with us, as unconventional as our enterprise may have seemed, gave the father hope.

We all had our problems, but not too many of us had to deal with being the son of a rich and influential man—one who had built a huge medical complex. While other teenagers scoured the streets for drugs, Three had ready access to the keys of the locked offices that held the pharmaceutical treasures of Austin's midtown medical complex.

Yet I never saw Three loaded. Sometimes he would wait until everyone was gone to knock gently on my office door. He'd apologize for bothering me, but I was always tickled to see him. Most of the time, he just wanted to hang out or hear me talk. He shared the excitement of my expectations and my agony over things I couldn't control. He knew he was too young to sway his family's interest in the prime real estate we occupied, but he was acutely aware that his time was coming. His interest in our enterprise was my secret weapon. My wildest schemes and dreams were like bedtime stories to him. He hoped to wake up someday with an important role in making them all work out.

A CULTURAL REFINERY

★

Exactly why armadillos are taking hold as a youth symbol is a matter for speculation. Armadillos are paranoid little beasts who prefer to mind their own business. They love to sleep all day, then roam and eat all night. They are gentle, keep their noses in the grass, and share their homes with others. Perhaps most significant, they are weird-looking, unfairly maligned and often picked on, and have developed a hard shell and a distinctive aroma. They do far more good than harm.

BUD SHRAKE

That Bud Shrake would write about us was no surprise, but for it to appear in the pages of *Sports Illustrated* was a real kick.[1] Armadillos had taken over precious magazine pages that were normally occupied by fire-breathing linebackers and bust-your-nose boxers. Such validation! What was next?

One night at the Armadillo, Shrake brought along two Dallas Cowboys stars: Don Meredith and Pete Gent. They were hardly the typical gridiron bubbas. Don had already been transformed from star quarterback to TV star on *Monday Night Football*. Pete would go on to write *North Dallas Forty*, which is as good a football novel as there's ever been.

Now they were sitting on my rump-sprung sofa in the office, drinking adult beverages from paper cups and laughing at all the right places as I told the story of the Armadillo's origins.

Freddie King was rocking the joint. During a break, Bobby Hedderman walked into the office and whispered that ten men of a certain description were in the house; from their butch-waxed buzz cuts, Ban-Lon shirts, and bad sport coats, it was obvious they were agents of the Texas Alcoholic Beverage Commission. Before Bobby could finish his sentence, two of the TABC agents waltzed through the door.

I tried to take charge, but the lead dog ignored me and went straight to Shrake, as if he was a chew toy. The agent sniffed at the cup the sportswriter was holding and scowled.

"This is alcohol," he said.

Shrake gave him a so-what stare.

All I could think of was that the Armadillo was doomed. Booze on the premises was all the TABC needed to turn out the lights on this hippie menace.

Then Meredith rose from the couch and approached the agents. It was an amazing thing to behold, seeing these hard-asses transformed into fawning hero worshippers. Most any old Dallas Cowboy might have done the trick, but this was Don Meredith, Dandy Don, the Danderoo. He introduced himself, shook their hands, and generally made the tension evaporate.

Meredith signed autographs. Not for the agents, of course, but for their sons, daughters, and distant relatives. *Whatever you say, fellas.* He put his arm around one of the agents, as if he were a long-lost pal, and walked him out the door and into the parking lot. The other agents followed like puppies.

Bobby quickly ducked into Jim Franklin's living quarters/studio, fetched a trophy, and brought it back. It was one of the gaudiest high school basketball trophies I'd ever seen, originally awarded to the Texas School for the Deaf and for some cosmic reason abandoned at the Armadillo and never thrown out, possibly because it appealed to our sense of the ridiculous.

After Freddie King finished another set, I walked onstage. Informing the audience that the Armadillo had a new hero, I summoned Don Meredith to join me.

Dandy Don walked out, and under lights so dim no one would have noticed if Howard Cosell had been at his side, he accepted the trophy with the deadpan aplomb that instantly made him the perpetual toast of the Dillo. "You may not know it," he said, "but this is what I really always wanted."

The crowd went wild. He was one of the most recognized faces in the nation, and he was hanging out in our joint. No one outside the backstage inner circle had a clue that he'd just stepped in to save our collective asses. One thing was certain, though: the Texas Alcoholic Beverage Commission had a new, if somewhat ambiguous, respect for the Armadillo hippies.

★ ★ ★

Through the auspices of the university's Student Cultural Entertainment Committee, we booked the legendary San Francisco–based rock promoter Bill Graham for February 2, 1972. A refugee of the Holocaust raised by a foster family in New York City, Graham had moved to the Bay Area in the early sixties and entered the rock concert business after managing the San Francisco Mime Troupe with Chet Helms, founder of the Family Dog. The concerts that Graham and Helms staged at the Fillmore West and Winterland Arena launched the careers of the Grateful Dead, Jefferson Airplane, Big Brother and the Holding Company featuring Janis Joplin, and numerous other Bay Area bands. Helms and Graham shared credit for putting the San Francisco scene on the map, but Bill Graham was the name everyone remembered, whether the encounter was in the flesh or from watching behind-the-scenes concert footage. Graham was always the guy yelling, barking orders, and basically chewing the scenery.

By the time of the Graham date, we were all a bit nervous about meeting the man. We were anxious to see what we could learn from him, not only because of his experience in concert promotion, but because we were huge Dead Heads and fans of the other major San Francisco bands. Plus, with our mutual connections with people such as Janis and Chet, we almost felt as though we already knew the great man.

We were also wary because of his reputation for being confrontational. Gruff and aggressive by nature, Graham responded best when provoked. He thrived on conflict and crisis.

Bill Graham on AWHQ stage, February 5, 1972.
Photograph by Burton Wilson.

So Graham came to the Armadillo, shared his ego, told some stories with us, and stomped on a lot of toes. Sensing that Graham was a time bomb waiting to go off, a local theatrical character named Doug Dyer tried heckling him, but Graham quickly cut him to ribbons. It was over so quickly it was anticlimactic.

Not surprisingly, Graham and I didn't hit it off. When the gig was over, I drove the great man to the airport in Genie's Dodge Dart. The car had last been used for a vet appointment for our puppy, who was so upset about the trip that he pooped all over the backseat and floorboard. I'd been far too busy preparing for the gig to clean it up, and the famous concert promoter gagged and complained all the way to the airport.

By the time we got to the terminal, Graham was shouting at me that the Armadillo would never survive in the business world because we were a bunch of hippies. "Guess what, Bill," I said. "I'm the hippie who talked the University of Texas into shelling out the $5,000 for you to fly down here so you could lecture me about my lack of capitalist ambition." About that time, I noticed that John Henry Faulk, the native Austin writer, liberal commentator, and literary lion, was standing in line behind Graham.

Faulk gave me a wink and said, "You got him back pretty good, son." Faulk had stood up to senator Joseph McCarthy during the wave of anti-commie hysteria in the 1950s. A compliment from him might not have been the equal of an endorsement from Warren Buffet or Ed Sullivan, but I sure was proud to get it.

A few feet closer to the terminal entrance, I encountered Bud Shrake and his friend, the actor Dennis Hopper. Hopper, who had achieved great status as a counterculture hero through the 1969 film *Easy Rider*, appeared to be using Bud for a crutch. He leaned against Shrake at such a sharp angle, I wondered if he was asleep. When Bud greeted me, Hopper brightened considerably and sort of straightened up. He beckoned me toward him with a tiny hand movement. As I came closer, the smell of ether almost choked me.

"You're doing the work of the Lord," Hopper mumbled. I'd heard that line before, from my friendly dealer friend, McDope, but it still sounded good.

A couple of years later I ran into Bill Graham again. This time, the scene was backstage at a theater on Broadway in New York, where the

Tony Award–winning actress Elizabeth Ashley was starring as Maggie in a revival of Tennessee Williams's *Cat on a Hot Tin Roof.*

The vice president of Warner Bros. Records had introduced me to Elizabeth the previous day. I wasn't intimately familiar with her track record as a star of film and Broadway, or the fact that she was born in Florida and raised in Baton Rouge, but her Southern roots were obviously genuine, not rehearsed, and I guess I felt I had at least as much business visiting Elizabeth's dressing room as Bill Graham did. Maybe even more. As I glanced around, I happily noticed that she had plastered her dressing room wall, mirror, and door with the "Long Live Longnecks" stickers and posters I had given her.

When the king of rock promoters saw me, he seemed to shrink back against the wall, his eyeballs rolling upward, as if he might be having a stroke or something.

After I left, she and Graham talked about me a little. "Bill said you were really into hunting dogs," she said later.

It was nice to know I had made an impression on him.

★ ★ ★

The Austin establishment was still having trouble accepting us. In March, the *Austin American-Statesman* editor Sam Wood bemoaned Austin's emerging reputation around the United States as the "Hippie City." Wood railed that hippies were streaming into town and that flower vendors on street corners were in fact "dope pushers, dope addicts, [and] petty criminals." As for those Austinites who had previously complained about the newspaper's scorn for "young people . . . engaged in free enterprise," the editorialist had a stern retort: "Flower salesmen on busy street corners step out to pass a flower to a motorist while brakes screech, automobiles line up and traffic snarls. For anyone else in Austin this type of free enterprise would be a trip to the hoosegow." Worse, it seemed, it was only March, and with Austin's abundance of summer sunshine and warm weather, even greater numbers of the flower-pushing horde were expected to converge upon the capital city.[2]

No doubt the right-wingers in Austin were concerned that the Armadillo was a magnet for radicals. We prided ourselves on being the chamber of commerce for the counterculture. The Underground Press Syndicate came to Austin for its four-day conference in the spring of 1971.

And where was the gathering of alternative newspapers from around the country supposed to meet, the Holiday Inn?

There was a lot of hostility out there, but the more our enemies tried to mobilize the public against us, the stronger we became. In addition to providing for the conferencing needs of the underground press, we welcomed groups from the straight world as well. We hosted ballet, the symphony, and the National Lawyers Guild, who held their four-day convention at the AWHQ in February 1973.

The Greenbriar School and the People's Free Clinic were two places that were always in need, and it made no sense to let the Armadillo sit empty if we could help them out and make a few hundred people happy. Even though my association with Shiva's Headband was starting to wind down, the band was always eager to play a fundraiser at the Dillo, and so was John Clay, one of Austin's most popular folksingers.

During the first two years of the Armadillo's existence, we hosted benefits for the Oleo Strut coffeehouse near Fort Hood, the Food Co-op, the striking UT shuttle bus drivers, and many others I've forgotten. Although we made no money from these benefits, we profited by integrating ourselves into the fabric of the community. We thrived on the hugs, handshakes, and good vibes sent our way.

We also worked hard to embrace the fine arts, presenting a wide variety of entertainment. In late 1972, the San Francisco Mime Troupe did a four-night stand at the Armadillo. The Abelard String Quartet had a no-cover, weekly residency gig in the beer garden. We staged a hot rod show, and, just to show the Austin Chamber of Commerce that we weren't anti-capitalist, we founded the Austin Freak Merchants Guild.

We looked for every kind of entertainment that might put a few people in the big building. Stanley Hall, formerly with the Austin Civic Ballet, set up his own Austin Ballet Theatre at the Armadillo. Starting in the fall of 1972, Austin Ballet Theatre held a performance every second Sunday of the month. It was a win-win situation, as Sunday had always been a hard day to book, and Hall's bunch not only paid for using the space, they spent money on food and drink. Their audience wasn't messy, so the next day cleanup was minimal.

The ballet mothers and our kitchen staff didn't always get along. One Sunday, a mischievous dishwasher donated a big bag of weed to the bakers for a batch of brownies. The moms grazed on the brownies during the rehearsal break. Several were heard to say, "These brownies are delicious!" Has a well-executed *brisé* or *petite battement* ever caused straight-laced west-side mothers to break out in such unseemly giggling and hooting? Not that I know of.

Later on, we hosted the Guatemalan Ballet, which was literally a blast. The Guatemalan dancers had a bigger fetish for fireworks than a drunk redneck at the lake on the Fourth of July.

Not all of our cultural experiments are remembered with fondness. *The Armadillo World Series* was a theatrical show directed by Doug Dyer, whose sensibilities and mine were like two cheese graters being rubbed together. In the late sixties, Doug had directed a production at UT called *Now the Revolution* that was busted for nudity. I had a feeling he was determined to bring the vice squad down on the Armadillo next. Bobby Hedderman and I kept thinking that any minute everybody onstage was going to end up naked, and we would end up being the guys they took off to jail. It brought out the redneck in us.

We never wanted to see Dyer or have anything to do with him ever again. Doug is gone now, but Esther's Follies, the comedy club and satirical comedy show he founded with Shannon Sedwick and Michael Shelton on Sixth Street in 1977, is still going strong.

When we first opened the joint, we hoped that someday we'd be able to book the heroes of the day, like Timothy Leary. He finally made a trip to Austin to do a gig in 1979.

Yoga wasn't nearly as mainstream in the 1970s as it became later, but we gave it our best shot. Our People's Yoga program was probably doomed from the start by the fact that it was never quiet enough in our cavernous venue for people to reach the proper meditative state. Despite all the tofu and macrobiotic food our kitchen served to the masses, the Armadillo was better suited for skateboards, volleyball, and half-court basketball—activities that helped keep you warm in the winter and made you sweat enough to cool down in the summer.

Another entrepreneurial idea we came up with was a telephone message service for music listings. At the time, there wasn't a reliable source to find out who was playing where on a given night other than radio and newspaper listings. Despite the cool poster and logo, designed by Micael Priest, the public never dialed in. Another pipe dream evaporated.

Another service we created was the Entertainers Information Guild, a nonprofit clearinghouse for musicians in the days before cell phones, faxes, and e-mail. Through this service, working musicians and their families could remain in contact with each other no matter where their gigs and private lives took them. The head of the guild was Prissy Mays, whose husband, Mike Mays, was the only banker in town who had the courage (and backing) to give us loans. It had seemed like a good idea, but the funding ran out and it went the way of so many other projects dreamed up in the Armadillo's back room. As Captain Beefheart would have said, "They were gone like a turkey in a storm."

Bobby Hederman and Bob Northcott begin work on
the beer garden construction with the help of Doug
Scales's wrecker, 1972. Photograph by Burton Wilson.

THINGS WERE LOOKING UP

★

The summer of 1972 began another major chapter in our struggles to deal with Texas weather and saw one of the most dramatic episodes in the Armadillo's history. Tearing out the inside offices to enlarge the hall the previous summer had created a mountain of rubble. We had no money to have it hauled away, so we started piling it up on the south side of the property. Eventually, we borrowed a pickup truck and started taking loads of the Sheetrock and insulation away every night, dumping them at a nearby apartment construction project. After a week of dumping, a twenty-four-hour guard appeared at the construction site. We had already gotten rid of most of the debris that wouldn't burn, so we pushed all the combustibles into a big pile and set it ablaze. Watching the bonfire was immensely satisfying. After sending out for beer and pizza to feed everyone, I settled back to watch and supervise.

As the plume of smoke rose and coiled itself above the hills of South Austin, three fire trucks came screaming up, carrying grim-faced fire-fighters. They weren't there for the beer and pizza. The fire department had received over one hundred calls. It took only about two minutes to extinguish our fire, and a good deal longer to placate the representatives from the fire department. They did not regard us as hardworking, industrious volunteers, but as dirty, hairy, half-naked hippies with a pyromaniacal streak.

Their commander became more reasonable as I explained the situation. At one point he said it looked as though we had enough scrap sheet metal to build an incinerator. If we had an incinerator, we could burn all the trash we wanted.

The fire trucks had not been gone long before we had a homemade incinerator constructed and a blaze going again. The smoke soon turned dark, heavy, and voluminous. We later learned that the fire had ignited the asphalt parking lot, creating a column of black smoke that made it look like all of South Austin was burning down.

The fire trucks came roaring back, sirens screaming. Grim-faced responders squelched the fire, flattened our incinerator, and flooded the entire area. We were warned not to start any more fires whatsoever, not even to light a cigarette.

When we got around to clearing off the burned debris, we found ourselves looking at a large crater in the pavement. It occurred to me that if we could make a bigger hole in this same spot, we could create something.

Like a beer garden.

When I was a kid, Granny Risher used to get very nervous whenever I had nothing to do with my time. The idea of a child with free time seemed to strike terror in her heart.

"Go dig a hole, Edwin," she'd say, serious as a heart attack. "Really, if you don't have anything to do, then go dig a hole."

"What do I do when I finish digging it?" I would ask, even though I already knew her answer.

"Then you fill it up, Mr. Smarty Pants."

The Armadillo beer garden and beautification campaign was one of our finest hours. The hardest part was completing the excavation of the parking lot. Our volunteers worked from dawn to dusk with picks and shovels, digging out telephone poles that had been laid into the asphalt. One day Doug Scales, the big redneck guy who owned the body shop next to us, ambled across the parking lot and took me aside. I was cautious; Doug's antagonism toward hippies and rock 'n' rollers was well-known.

"Listen, I've been watching y'all," he said. "There's a much easier way to do this job. I'll bring one of my wreckers over here, put a chain around them poles, and pluck them out like asparagus."

The beer garden almost completed. Woody Wilson's plumbing truck to the rescue. Photograph by Burton Wilson.

The offer, which we gratefully accepted, lessened our workload considerably. Doug Scales and the Armadillo folks never looked at each other the same way again.

Next, we scrounged old bathtubs from junk heaps around town and arranged them along the chain-link fence, then planted them with bamboo we liberated from places where it grew wild around town. We also liberated landscaping plants from residential properties that were being demolished to complete the MoPac Expressway. The plants would create a free privacy fence that would shield us from the view of the Social Security office next door, and vice versa.

Beulah joked that the Armadillo renovation proved I had the Great Depression in my genes. Her encouragement got Woody Wilson on board, and he ended up doing the plumbing in the new outdoor restrooms, the kitchen, and the bar.

We still needed a big chunk of money to complete the beer garden, and we were thousands of dollars in debt. Hank Alrich was mopping the floor one day and asked me what was wrong.

"We're not gonna make it," I said. I told him I thought that the whole enterprise was doomed to fail.

Hank had reasons to be discouraged himself. He was living in a school bus in the parking lot. He'd taken over the job of guitar player in Shiva's Headband only to realize that the band wasn't going anywhere. It was ironic, since the band was the original reason for the Armadillo coming into being. After a couple of rehearsals, Hank realized the band had no work ethic. They seemed to have no real desire or energy to make things happen.

After Shiva's Headband's first album was released, Capitol Records elected not to pick up the band's option. While we were running the Armadillo, we worked on raising the money to put out their second album. Spencer Perskin was staying home and making more babies instead of promoting his band. He had three or four kids and what was a kind of 1960s underground comedy version of a tribe of barefooted hippies.

It was ridiculous, now that I think about it.

On the day that Hank stopped mopping to have this conversation with me, the unfinished beer garden was full of customers. The new stage was gig tested and ready. We were booking shows and coming up with new schemes for the future. But the fact that we were still losing money weighed on me like a lead cowboy hat.

"How much would it take?" Hank said.

"At least $50,000," I said.

Hank leaned the mop against the stage and pulled a checkbook out of his hip pocket. He wrote a check for $25,000 and handed it to me. "I'll give you another one next week," he said. "Hang tough. You're doing a great job." With a twinkle in his eye, he went back to mopping.

In addition to funding the completion of the beer garden and some other improvements, Hank's hip-pocket loan resulted in a new owner-ship structure for AWHQ. Up until the spring of 1972, Spencer Perskin still owned Armadillo Productions Inc., of which the Armadillo was a d.b.a., but he had no real involvement in the day-to-day business of the place. As Mike Tolleson put it, "Spencer used to come down to the office every afternoon and smoke a couple of joints with us, and that was pretty much the entire extent of his involvement in the day-to-day running of the Armadillo."

Harking back to the original purpose of the Armadillo, Mike remem-bered, "Bobby, Eddie, myself, and a couple of other staff people were meeting every day, trying to find Shiva's Headband gigs, book shows at the Armadillo, and basically make ends meet. So no one knew what was going to happen, because we were just focused on day-to-day survival. We never stopped to talk about how to divide things up."[1]

In mid-1972, we gave Spencer some cash to repay his investment and buy out his share of the corporation. From then on, Armadillo World Headquarters continued to be a d.b.a. of Armadillo Productions Inc., but I split the ownership of the company equally among eight sharehold-ers. It wasn't too difficult to look around and decide which people would become shareholders; they were in positions of responsibility and man-agement, people who had been there since day one or not long afterward.

The eight shareholders were Jim Franklin, Bobby Hedderman, Mike Tolleson, Hank Alrich, Carlotta Pankratz, Genie Wilson, Mike Harr, and me. The group became known as the "founders" and "owners."

★ ★ ★

Everybody remembers 1972 as the year Willie Nelson first played the Armadillo, bringing out not only our usual crowd but also old died-in-the-wool C&W fans, including rednecks, who tended to be allergic to hippies and their environment. But a lot of good things were already under way before Willie's first show at the joint on August 12. It was the second full year of our existence, and the press was taking notice of the various miraculous happenings at our grand cultural experiment.

As noted in the *Daily Texan* during the week of our second anniversary, the Armadillo was already "a country-western center" where local favorites Greezy Wheels, Freda and the Firedogs, and Balcones Fault played "a mixture of country-western and boogie which can be found nowhere else."[2] The Armadillo offered "a new sound, style and place with no parallel elsewhere in the country."

Although the writer called me "Ed Wilson," he accurately quoted me saying that the operating strategy of the Dillo was to be a music hall that developed and evolved along with the artists who worked there, rather than the other way around. We had succeeded so far, despite the challenges. "The economics of the thing were totally impractical," I said. "Everything about the place was totally impractical. To replace a light bulb we needed a 30-foot ladder, not to speak of a bulb big enough to fit."

My definition of success was carefully worded: "After close to two-and-a-half years of six to eight people working here 18 hours a day for almost nothing, there are 40 people down here working at a salary."

Jim Franklin was rightfully recognized by the *Daily Texan* as our "resident genius." The reporter wrote that "his work covers the walls of the hall and outdoor garden, and his studio behind the stage is something to behold, filled with large murals, armadillo shells, manikins and interesting pieces of trash."[3]

Another *Daily Texan* article focused on the great range and depth of the city's music scene. Willie wasn't mentioned. This article also singled out Greezy Wheels, Balcones Fault, and Freda and the Firedogs as the most popular of the country rock hybrids, or "proponents of what has [come] to be known as 'the Armadillo sound.'" The article noted that the best place to see such hybrids was in "their natural habitat—the Armadillo World Headquarters."[4] The *Daily Texan* writers also pointed to our friends Mance Lipscomb, Kenneth Threadgill, and Freddie King as important artists not only to the Armadillo but to the richness of Texas's music heritage.

Another favorite group of regulars at the Dillo was the Texas Flatlanders, a trio of Lubbockite singer-songwriters: my old friend Jimmie Dale Gilmore, who was still playing with the Hub City Movers at the time, plus Butch Hancock and Joe Ely. The band later dropped "Texas" from its

The Flatlanders onstage at AWHQ, October 6, 1972. From left
to right: Steve Wesson on autoharp, Tony Pearson on mandolin,
Butch Hancock on guitar/voals, Joe Ely on guitar, and John X.
Reed on bass. Photograph by Burton Wilson.

name. Alvin Crow and the Pleasant Valley Boys was another of our favorite hip country bands, which gave the Armadillo the right to call itself the world's biggest full-service honky-tonk. The group also played traditional honky-tonks, beer joints, and dance halls.

In the months before Willie came around, we had shows by some of our favorite touring acts: John Prine, Shawn Phillips, John McLaughlin, and Dan Hicks and His Hot Licks. It was a good year for female-oriented rock bands, as we had Fanny, one of the very first all-female rock groups, plus Joy of Cooking, another band fronted by women. During 1976, our sixth year, the old armory rocked to the Runaways, the most famous all-female band until the Go-Go's.[5]

Our 1972 fundraiser for the striking city bus drivers turned into a showcase for Freda and the Firedogs. The Firedogs were young Austin musicians who embraced hardcore country music roots and mixed them with counterculture values. During their Sunday night residency shows at the Split Rail, they could instantly transform a mellow crowd into a rapturous throng of hooting, hollering shitkickers. Women, in particular, hollered their support for Freda, the stage name of Louisiana-born pianist Marcia Ball, especially during the band's rendition of the Tammy Wynette classic "Stand By Your Man," which the Firedogs performed as "Stand By Your Male Chauvinist Pig."

One important champion of the Firedogs was Townsend Miller, whose country music column was featured every Saturday in the *Austin American-Statesman*.[6] Another champion, James White, owner of the Broken Spoke on South Lamar, wasn't so sure about the Firedogs at first. Hippies in a hardcore honky-tonk dance hall seemed to make about as much sense as fire twirlers in a hayloft. When the Broken Spoke hosted a benefit show for a young politician named Lloyd Doggett, then running for the state senate, a packed dance floor and impressive beer sales made White into a Firedogs fan. With the support of other important local venues, like Soap Creek Saloon and the Split Rail, the band was getting enough work to make a living. With the help of a major-label record deal, they might have had a great career ahead of them.

It almost happened. One night when the Firedogs were playing at the Split Rail, in walked Jerry Wexler and Doug Sahm with Malcolm John Rebennack, the great New Orleans musician most of us know as Dr. John the Night Tripper. Wexler was working on a comeback album with Sahm

Marcia Ball and her new Freda and the Firedogs band met Burton
Wilson in the AWHQ beer garden for a photo shoot, July 30, 1972.
The firedog that showed up, sat down, and then wandered off was not
brought by the band or Burton. From left to right: David Cook, Steve
McDaniels, Marcia Ball, Bobby Earl Smith, and John X. Reed.

Dr. John at AWHQ, April 15, 1974.
Photograph by Burton Wilson.

and also helming Willie Nelson's first post-Nashville recordings. Wexler's hit-making talents had worked for Ray Charles, Aretha Franklin, Wilson Pickett, LaVern Baker, Solomon Burke, Dusty Springfield, and the Drifters, to name only a few. Doug Sahm was the one who had hipped him to Freda and the Firedogs.

By the end of the night, the band had impressed everyone so much that Doug might've been expecting a finder's fee. Wexler offered them a deal with Atlantic. The band cut a demo but then wasted so much time trying to decide whether to sign the contract that the contract did what contracts always do in situations like that: it went away.

Of all the local bands we liked in the early days, Greezy Wheels was always the most dependable draw at the Dillo. They took old country standards and reshaped them through semipsychedelic jams. A freewheeling character from New York named Cleve Hattersley had formed the band after being busted at Austin's Mueller Airport with a suitcase full of pot. The bust by notorious APD vice chief captain Harvey Gann ended in conviction. Cleve was sure he was going to prison, so he decided to go down singing. That sort of cachet gave Greezy Wheels a big boost in the local underground.

Greezy Wheels had an edgy, vaguely alien quality. Cleve, the original front man, had the ability to bellow, cajole, and tease his way into people's hearts. He reminded me of Captain Beefheart gone country. He was a strange cheese, sharp and slightly foreign. In 1971 the band consisted of Cleve, bassist Mike Pugh, and guitarist Pat Pankratz, but Cleve's sister Lissa later joined on mandolin, and Tony Laier took over on drums.

Then one night at a joint on the Drag, Cleve was transfixed by a quiet, mysterious fiddler from New Mexico who was playing with Kenneth Threadgill. She went by the name Sweet Mary Egan. Cleve recruited Sweet Mary for the band, and she quickly established herself with her spot-on fiddling and her short dresses.

Greezy Wheels' cosmic country jams grew more powerfully hypnotic and hip, with Cleve's handpicked pickers adding more depth, variety, and professionalism. In a terrible case of irony, once Cleve and his gravelly vocal chords were shipped off to Huntsville, the Wheels rolled on, sounding better and better.

Lissa Hattersley stepped up into a prominent role alongside Pat Pankratz, a fine singer, tall and lanky, with hair down to his back. Pat also

Greezy Wheels backstage at AWHQ, March 15, 1974. From left to right: Pat Pankratz, Cleve Hattersley, Mike Pugh, Tony Laier, Sweet Mary Egan, Tony Airoldi, and Lissa Hattersley. Photograph by Burton Wilson.

Sweet Mary Egan. Photograph by Burton Wilson.

brought his parents, Lucky and Chickie Pankratz, into the fold, and they eventually became the godparents of Greezy Wheels' fan base. The Wheels' fan base and support group grew out of a small community of South Austin hippies and became the largest group of followers of any local band.

Lucky Pankratz was a housepainter possessed of more brains than required for his job. He had a dancer's physique, a head of wavy silver hair, and a ready smile that promised mischief. He'd grown up building postwar Austin as it spread to the north, at a time when painters and paperhangers used to stop at Threadgill's for breakfast, which was generally a thirty-cent can of Campbell's Soup and two Texas beers for a quarter.

Chickie was Lucky's mirror image. She had a perfect coif of curly hair and glowed with the light of affection for her mate. Lucky and Chickie Pankratz were two of South Austin's greatest natural resources, welcoming anyone and everyone with an open attitude and offering unconditional love to all under their tent.

Even those of us with perfect parents like Beulah had to wonder why our parents couldn't be more like Lucky and Chickie, tolerant of our weird friends and their dangerous assortment of party favors. Lucky had at one time been busted for smuggling pot from South Texas to Austin, charged with income tax evasion, and stripped of most of his worldly possessions. But he never stopped smiling, and he rarely spoke of his troubles. While he and Chickie raised their own two boys, Lucky kept putting up Sheetrock, painting houses, and mentoring a legion of young people.

Poster for the Flying Burrito Brothers and Greezy Wheels show at AWHQ,
February 28–March 2, 1975. Artwork by Jim Franklin and Micael Priest.

Poster for Earl Scruggs Revue and Rat Creek at AWHQ,
November 5 and 6, 1971. Artwork by Jim Harter.

THE GREAT REDNECK-
HIPPIE MERGER

★

Of all the legacies attached to the Armadillo, none compares to its storied role in the rehabilitation of country music. The change, which had
begun in the late sixties, was very much like an intervention by friends
and family who were determined to save country music from its pious
and self-righteous self.

A steady stream of local and touring acts flying the country rock flag
had been welcomed and nurtured at the Armadillo from the beginning.
The Flying Burrito Brothers, one of the early marquee names of the genre,
came through for a two-night stand in the summer of 1971. Over the next
couple of years, we brought in Gram Parsons, Guy Clark, Goose Creek
Symphony, Brewer and Shipley, the Nitty Gritty Dirt Band, Earl Scruggs,
and others. Call some of them rockers or folkies who'd added an extra
little twang to their rock 'n' roll. Call others hillbilly and country singers who'd let their hair grow long around the same time that their guitar
players were swapping fingerpicking for playing power chords through a
Twin Reverb or a Marshall stack.

Willie Nelson had obviously taken note of these things, and he started
paying even more attention to them as his dissatisfaction with the Nashville scene grew into a powerful sense of alienation. I don't know exactly

when he first thought about playing the Armadillo, but I can tell you exactly when and where my side of the saga began.

I was out in San Francisco crashing at the abode of my friend Joe Brown. A member of the expat-Texan community, Joe had written some copy for Gilbert Shelton's Fabulous Furry Freak Brothers underground comics, a thing that really enhanced his counterculture credibility. As for me, I was trying to make contact with the Grateful Dead and working on moving a few pounds of Mexican weed in order to pay the rent on the Armadillo.

The live album Willie Nelson recorded at Panther Hall in Fort Worth in 1965 was constantly on the turntable at Joe's place. Most people call it *Live at Panther Hall*, even though the record says *Live Country Music Concert*. Panther Hall was a thirty-thousand-square-foot former bowling alley shaped like a flying saucer. Willie was still a Nashville cat at the time and had a regular spot on a weekly TV show broadcast from Panther Hall called *Cowtown Jamboree*. *Panther A-Go-Go*, which catered to rock 'n' rollers, was also broadcast from there. Shiva's Headband had played there.

On the record cover, Willie looks like a Nashville slickster, with Brylcreem-shiny hair, a clean-shaven face, white shirt, dress jacket, skinny tie, and Fender electric guitar. A closer study reveals details that tell a different story. In place of a studio band, Willie was backed by his regular touring sidemen, Wade Ray and Johnny Bush. These road veterans gave the music an immediacy and bite not heard in the usual Nashville schlock of the day. Willie even covered the Beatles' "Yesterday," nailing the wistfully melodic tune with precision and soul.

My friend Joe kept the album on replay because he was trying to get over a bad case of homesickness, but the record worked an even more powerful spell on me. I'd heard that Willie had left the Grand Ole Opry and was moving from Nashville to Austin. I was determined to find him when I got back to town. I wanted to introduce him to my hippies.

Strange how things can work out. A week after I got back to Austin, I was at the Dillo drinking a beer when I turned around and saw the country singer from Abbott, Texas, standing there with his sparkling brown eyes and impish grin.

"I've been looking for you," I said.

"You just found me," he said.

"I want you to play here," I said.

"I want to play here," he said.

Willie Nelson backstage at AWHQ, November 4, 1972.
Photograph by Burton Wilson.

We shook hands and sealed the deal on a 50/50 split of the door. The date was set for August 12, 1972.

Willie was thirty-nine and I was twenty-nine. Next to him, I felt like a green, wannabe rodeo cowboy trying to stay on the bull until the buzzer went off.

People around us recognized him. Some approached in awe. I noticed that he suffered fools gladly, and as long as someone was talking to him, he never broke eye contact. I had noticed the same thing in two other people: Ann Richards, when speaking with children, and Muhammad Ali, when talking to girls.

Willie was accompanied that day by Paul English, his longtime drummer, sidekick, best friend, music publishing partner, business manager, and chief protector. Paul had a big, bright, shiny smile of pearly teeth, exquisitely sculpted sideburns and goatee, and tattoos that looked like the work of a lowrider pinstriping master. He reminded me of a cross between Satan and Zorro.

In the past, struggling to survive before he made it, Willie had sold Bibles and vacuum cleaners door to door. He had a calm, nonthreatening, almost tender countenance. Paul had run collections for gangsters and pimped, among other things. Both men exuded a sense of Zen calmness, not unlike that of a gunfighter, a meditation guru, or a super-slick gambler.

Poster artist Micael Priest, newly arrived at AWHQ, came to my office to discuss his first project, which was to be a poster advertising Willie Nelson's first appearance at the Armadillo.

"Do you have any ideas about the kind of poster you want?" he asked.

Funny, Jim Franklin had never asked my opinion before he made a poster. I told Micael I wanted an image of an old cowboy crying in a mug of beer, with a jukebox in the background playing Willie's song "Hello Walls" and a little picture of Willie on the wall. The next day, Micael brought back that very image.

Three weeks before Willie's debut, I was performing my emcee duties during a rock 'n' roll show, and when I mentioned that Willie Nelson would be performing at the Armadillo, only a handful of people clapped. I repeated the announcement, a little louder this time, for those who might be hard of hearing; there was very little change in the reaction in the room. So the next time I repeated the information, I added, "Willie is

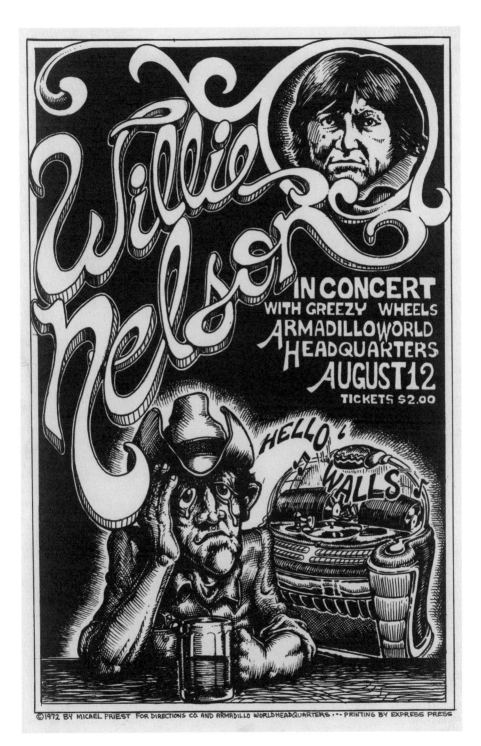

Poster for Willie Nelson and Greezy Wheels show at
AWHQ, August 12, 1972. Artwork by Micael Priest.

only the Bob Dylan of country music, you hippie assholes." Maybe some of my sense of indignation sunk in, because over the next couple of weeks, a buzz began building.

On the night of the show, some four hundred people paid two dollars at the door. Probably about half of them were there to see the opening act, Greezy Wheels, but another one hundred or so were newcomers to the Dillo. They were Willie's longtime, hardcore fans and friends. Considering it was August, the turnout was impressive.

I was curious about how our regulars would take to this outsider. I felt that if our long-haired regulars would just listen, they'd recognize the artistry of this great songwriter and performer. Greezy Wheels seemed to be nervous themselves; they rushed through their set as if being chased by the cops. Considering their history, it could've been more than just nerves.

Willie's hair was still cut and styled in the Nashville way, and his face was clean-shaven; by the end of the year, he would be long-haired and bearded. Backstage before the show, he was open and talkative with our house attorney, Mike Tolleson, and he let Burton Wilson take all the photos the photographer wanted.

Cool as Frank Sinatra under a Vegas spotlight and calm as a preacher at a nighttime prayer service, Willie led his band up onto our big stage. There were just two of them, Paul English on drums and Bee Spears on bass. Willie was still pinching pennies then, playing rhythm and lead guitar. Paul English looked splendid, dressed in all black except for the red satin underlining of the black satin cape draping his shoulders. Bee Spears wore a headband and moccasins, a look that fit right in with our crowd.

The room quickly warmed to Willie, cheering and clapping as the opening bars announced timeless classics such as "Crazy," "Hello Walls," and "Funny How Time Slips Away." Many of the songs had been made famous by others; for some in the audience, it was the first time they had heard the original versions. The arrangements were short and tight, with few guitar solos; only rarely did the band pause between songs. The latter was a trick picked up from Willie's biggest influence, Bob Wills, the icon of western swing.

Bob Dylan, the Shakespeare of my generation, never wrote anything near as honky-tonk cool as "Hello Walls." Not even "Like a Rolling Stone" was as deep as "Crazy," which had been such a giant hit for Patsy Cline. Not to pick on Dylan, but he was an aloof Yankee loner. By contrast, Willie was accessible, warm, and friendly. He was a Texan, and an Indian to boot. Watching him perform up close, I was more impressed than ever.

Willie's piercing gaze seemed to be just as effective from the stage as it was when you were standing next to him. He never blinked, never looked away. He was charming, as always, to the older female fans who were new to the Armadillo, and he won over the hippie chicks, too.

The roar from the small gathering grew louder and louder. The feeling of mutual recognition was a two-way affair. The set went long, and it kept on going—the "stay all night, stay a little longer" approach we later came to expect. At one point in the set, Paul got tangled up in his cape, falling backward from his stool, but hardly anyone noticed.

Finally the show came to an end. The music stopped, the house lights came on, and the audience slowly filed out into the parking lot. Even as they were getting into their cars, you could still hear them saying Willie's name.

In the next weekend's *Austin American-Statesman*, Joe Gracey, who at this date was still wearing his rock critic hat and writing a weekly Rock Beat column, not only gave the show a giant nod of critical approval but saw it as a cultural shift in the making. Willie's Armadillo audience had consisted of "a sizeable and sociable crowd made up of the most amazing assortment of country music fans I have ever seen," Gracey wrote. "Ponytails and bouffants. Pantsuits and moccasins. Gentle amazement and, best of all, mutual understanding. It was a joyous homecoming for Willie Nelson; he played way past normal into the Texas summer night. Everybody there Saturday night agreed that it was fine, and nodded yes, we ought to do this a whole lot more, and agreed that Willie looks younger and younger every year. And he does."[1]

Townsend Miller, whose weekly Country Music column ran alongside Gracey's, also praised the show. "Willie Nelson's experimental 'let's get country music fans to mix' at Eddie Wilson's AWHQ last Saturday was beautiful," he wrote. "He alternated sets with the popular local Greezy Wheels group, and everyone had a ball."[2]

Almost everyone had a ball at the picking session that followed the show at the Crest Hotel just across the river, especially country music–loving UT football coach Darrell K Royal. Then in the middle of a two-decade career as the winningest coach in UT history, Royal dearly loved orchestrating picking sessions in motel rooms, living rooms, or wher- ever. He ran them with a coach's sense of order: no matter who they were, guests were expected to listen with both ears. At one point Gary Cart- wright was singled out by the coach. "Jap, you can stay if you shut up and listen," snapped Royal. "Otherwise, butt out."

Cartwright, who happened to be a cohost of the jam session, shut up and hunkered down like a flattopped freshman Shorthorn.

Our gang of hippies and Willie's gang of hardcore country fans had communed together over the same music in the same room, finding com- mon bonds at the Armadillo World Headquarters. The world's biggest full-service honky-tonk suddenly had a much larger community of music fans.

A great deal has already been written about what happened the first time Willie and his band graced the Dillo stage, the convergence that took place, and the history that followed. All I know is that a bunch of people were drawn together by cold beer, cheap pot, and fine music. Willie him- self has said that he just saw some people headed somewhere and he man- aged to get in front of them.

Willie told writer Ed Ward in 1980 that, although he wasn't the first country act to perform at the Armadillo, he was the first well-known one to do so. "I knew what kind of audience it was, and I wanted to do it," he added. "It's not like I was a genius or anything." Willie didn't suggest that we were geniuses for booking him, either. What he said was: "I think the success of Armadillo had a lot to do with my becoming successful."[3]

★ ★ ★

The hippie/country confabulation stimulated our imaginations, con- fidence, and ambition sufficiently that we hastily organized a nine-city tour of the state featuring Willie Nelson and Michael Murphey, which we called the Armadillo Country Music Review. The last word should've been spelled "revue" and sometimes was, but more often it was spelled "review," perhaps because we expected so many rave ones in the media.

Willie Nelson shared the headline spot with Michael Murphey, a flaxen-haired folkie in a cowboy hat. Murphey had achieved critical and commercial success with his first album, *Geronimo's Cadillac*, and was quite popular with the fraternity and sorority students at UT. Early the

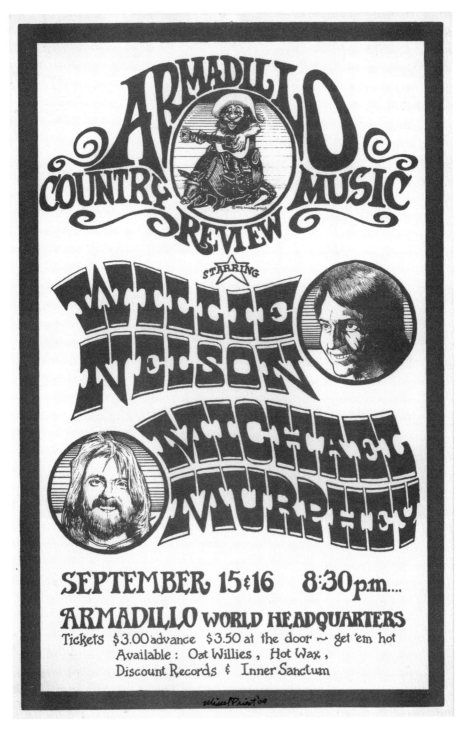

Poster for the Armadillo Country Music Review featuring Willie
Nelson and Michael Murphey at AWHQ, September 15 and 16, 1972.
Artwork by Micael Priest.

next year, the song "Cosmic Cowboy, Pt. 1" on his second album would become a top-selling, sing-along hit, as inescapable as an annoying chewing gum jingle or the buzzing mosquitoes that ruined your last picnic.

The rollicking success of the trial show of the Review at the Armadillo gave us confidence that it could work anywhere in the state. Our egos and expectations soared as our supporters in the music press said we were onto something big, unique, and world shaking. After Austin, the stops included San Antonio, Abilene, Lubbock, Arlington, and Wichita Falls. Hank Alrich bankrolled the tour. (The fact that Hank and I often thought alike was a hallmark of our friendship, but unfortunately, the convergence wasn't always to his advantage.)

Taking the Armadillo on the road was an eye-opening, character-building experience. How quickly we learned that Austin is very different from the rest of Texas. In Austin, Nelson and Murphey were a can't-miss combo, but not so in the rest of the state. Not yet, anyway. Ticket sales were abysmal. It was the Texas tour from hell.

We were all hurting. Phone service at the Armadillo was cut off. Offices upstairs were moved to a clustered suite of rooms up front by the stairs. If we needed to call someone, there was a pay telephone downstairs. We fielded incoming calls by running a wire from downstairs to the upstairs office, where it was connected to a pink princess telephone someone had donated. Doing business that way was awkward, but there wasn't a whole lot of business going on.

The $2,000 I was able to pay Willie after the tour wasn't even enough to make his payroll, he said. Murphey got the same amount for his own band. Even with their discounted fees, the whole venture lost $12,000. Hank Alrich never got his money back. He had cheerfully fronted us the cash, and when I told him that I'd lost every cent of it, he answered with a philosophical shrug. Naturally, I just assumed that Hank was loaded. Later on, I learned the facts: yes, he did have an inheritance, but thanks to me, it was quickly being exhausted.

Despite the depressingly empty venues at the shows that weren't canceled for absence of interest, Willie remained cool, doing the same great show no matter what. Murphey, on the other hand, became moody and physically weakened, and at the end of our tortuous mini-tour, instead of channeling his angst with his axe at the Armadillo homecoming show with Willie, he called in sick.

Jerry Jeff Walker gamely agreed to stand in for Michael Murphey. At that point, Jerry Jeff had fashioned a career from one great song, "Mr. Bojangles." He had a reputation for gregariousness, which wasn't necessarily a euphemism for being a beer-guzzling fool, but sometimes even the latter was an understatement. At showtime at the Armadillo, the troubadour swaggered to center stage and proved that our misgivings and low expectations were justified. The fact that his backing group, the Lost Gonzo Band (who also supported Michael Murphey), played with fiery intensity and professionalism made the singer's buffoonery all the more bizarre.

Jerry Jeff, who might be the first country rocker known for tossing a TV set into a motel pool, continued his clownish rampage backstage after the show. He took a piss in a beer pitcher and tried passing it around the room. When he failed to get a dial tone from the princess phone, he yanked it from the wall.

Eventually, even the most foul-smelling fart leaves the room, and thus, with a shake of his head, Jerry Jeff stumbled in the direction of the door. After a couple of painful arguments with gravity, he made it outside, careened through the beer garden, and disappeared into the night.

★ ★ ★

Our big media break came that fall in *Rolling Stone*. The title of the article was "Uncle Zeke's Rock Emporium," the byline, Chet Flippo.[4] Chet was one of us. Raised in an evangelical Christian household, he now used his great intellect and writing talents to describe the Austin country music scene. In the days when people got much of their information from print media and radio, our core audience depended on the biweekly editions of *Rolling Stone*. It's hard to believe now, but *Rolling Stone* was for many years a cutting-edge alternative magazine, the periodical bible of the youth movement and our music.

Flippo caught up with me on a good day. The beer garden was open, Willie was about to play, the weather was nice, and all was right with the world. We were cocky, just a little bit high, and damn proud that we had defied the odds and the naysayers. We were young, long-haired, and full of beans.

Flippo quoted me about losing big money on John Sebastian ($5,000), then waxed poetically about the beer garden, the new stage, and other

Jerry Jeff Walker onstage at AWHQ, March 7, 1971.
Photograph by Burton Wilson.

improvements of the past year. There were kind words for our neighbor, body shop owner Doug Scales (described as "a gigantic, granite-jawed retired colonel"), and Scales's begrudging admiration for the hippie work ethic, which had begun after a dramatic dialogue in the parking lot "straight out of *High Noon*."[5]

On the afternoon of the interview, I had pontificated, while smoking Camels and drinking Lone Star, with a hippie country band rehearsing in the beer garden, about who we were, why we were doing what we were doing, and the broader implications for our survival. Flippo was bullish on Austin, and therefore he gave my own bullish comments full rein:

> "Ohhh, yeah," he exhaled Camel smoke. "There's gonna be a scene develop here. Nothing nobody can do to stop it. There's all kindsa musical talent here and more moving in. Willie Nelson just moved from Nashville and lives down the street. Michael Murphey moved here and so did Jerry Jeff Walker. And we've finally got a 16-track studio here. People are moving in, in droves."

Later in the article, I was quoted on my reaction to criticism of our iconoclastic attitude toward booking policies and the music business in general.

> "We've got a very local attitude around Armadillo," Wilson conceded. "I've had folks say they thought we were too eccentric to be in the rock & roll business. Agents from some of the biggest bookin' agencies in the United States have screamed at me over the phone for doin' unpardonable shit, like not bookin' a three-piece band from England that plays so goddamn loud it makes you bleed. We didn't book 'em because we didn't wanna hear 'em. I figure we didn't need any better reason than that. . . . But I'd like to put out the word now that we're alive and well and just salty as shit. And we're gonna have some fine entertainment but we're not gonna have any of that shit crammed down our throats."

Some may have interpreted my remarks as arrogance, but we had just recently emerged from the darkness, and we did feel pretty damn salty. Our philosophies about booking talent and operating a business weren't just metaphors or boasts, but ideals that we discussed and debated daily as we fought not to compromise too greatly with the establishment in order to keep the doors open. Faithful readers of *Rolling Stone* likely understood the philosophical tug-of-war going on behind the scenes and between the lines.

"Uncle Zeke's Rock Emporium" was a fine article, and Chet Flippo's continuing coverage of the early-seventies, down-in-the-trenches music scene in Austin surely helped influence the coming land rush. Perhaps the article's accompanying photo of Jim Franklin, with a serene smile on his face and a live armadillo atop his balding head, offered visual proof that there was indeed something special happening here.

★ ★ ★

Jerry Lee Lewis, alias "the Killer," had been a rebel hero to all of us ever since our teens. One of the most original and dynamic of the rock 'n' roll pioneers, he was famed for his explosive performances on vinyl and in person. He also had a reputation as an unpredictable and volatile person. The public backlash after a 1958 news story revealed he had married his thirteen-year-old first cousin had pretty much killed his career for almost a decade. The Killer came roaring back in 1968 after releasing a string of "pure country" singles. The new sound, which some called "hard country," really wasn't so new after all, especially if you had listened to songs like "Crazy Arms," which had been part of his repertoire from the beginning. The Killer enjoyed a slew of hits that extended well into the late 1970s, his hard country sound rocking right alongside his high-octane, old-school rock 'n' roll.

We booked the Killer for October 14, smack in the middle of that history-making fall of 1972. "It was the first show after we opened the new bar we called the Outpost," remembers Bobby Hedderman. "It was a big deal for us. His fee was a guarantee of $5,000 versus 50 percent of ticket sales. We ended up grossing a little less than $10,000."[6]

The drama began the afternoon before the show. We hadn't heard anything from Jerry Lee. He had a terrible reputation, so we were all pacing the floor, wondering if he was going to show or not. Around five thirty that evening, we started to panic. We actually called the airport and talked to the people in the control tower. It's hard to even remember stories like these from the days before cell phones, but we got a call later from the

Poster for a Jerry Lee Lewis show at AWHQ, 1972.
Artwork by Jim Franklin.

tower. The guy said the band had just left Tennessee, and they hadn't filed a flight plan yet, but the control tower expected to hear from the pilot in a little while. The next call, they said, "We've got him over Bastrop." They had overshot the airport, so they'd be turning around and landing in a minute or so.

Hank Alrich and I jumped into Hank's little '34 Dodge pickup. It was small up front and back, the bed of the truck probably no more than three and a half feet wide. We rushed out to Mueller Airport (this was prior to the airport being moved to Bergstrom Air Force Base), and to save a few minutes' time, Hank pulled off Airport Boulevard and crossed the bar ditch to drive straight onto the tarmac, bypassing the airport entrance. Imagine trying to do something like that now.

The guy in the control tower had told us they didn't have room to park the plane, so they were going to let the pilot pull up in front of the café. And there it was, a big, black plane with gold trim, real fancy looking, a 727 or something like that. They pulled the stairs up to the plane and out came all these polyester cowboys, guys with big bouffant hairdos. The band members were wearing light-blue suits with white piping around the lapels. They were all waiting for the Killer to deplane first. Jerry Lee came storming out, wild-eyed, glaring down at us. He said, "Goddamn it!" and came charging down the steps.

"I brought the wrong goddamn band," he said. "Nobody told me this was a hippie gig. I brought the country band. I didn't bring no rock 'n' roll band."

I assured him it would be OK, that our audience was ready for whatever he had. When he saw Hank's truck, he said, "I wanna ride with y'all."

We could only get the guitars in the back, and there really wasn't room up front for three people, but we crowded in, Jerry Lee sitting between us. He talked a blue streak the whole time. He said, "You boys just think you have long hair. When I was twenty-one years old my hair was twenty-one inches long. I bet neither one of you has hair twenty-one inches long." It was like that the whole way, *blah-blah-blah-blah-blah.*

"He called everybody else 'Killer,' too," Bobby remembered. "Just like Waylon called everybody 'Hoss.' He was really well-mannered. It was the thugs he brought with him that made us nervous."[7]

In the office, we had a Victrola with a collection of old 78 rpm records, and these thugs were pulling them out and trying to sneak out with them.

The scariest thing, though, was what the thugs might do to me. During the show, I stayed close to Jerry Lee the whole time because he was playing Mama's piano, and if he did any of his wild antics, like stomping on it or even setting it on fire, like he had done once when he was forced to open for his arch rival, Chuck Berry, well, I'd have to tackle him and stop it. And I knew those thugs would eat me alive.

But Jerry Lee didn't do any of that—didn't hurt the piano at all, in fact—and he put on a hell of a show. The response was tremendous, too, and everyone could tell that he was really getting off on it.

The day after the Killer, we switched gears with Shawn Phillips. A sensitive singer-songwriter type with a beautiful voice that was operatic in range, Phillips could cast a spell on a room, particularly on the women in that room, and because of his first show at the Dillo in May, we knew that the room would be full, too. His list of credits was so impressive, it almost sounded made up. Like quite a few great musicians, Phillips was born and raised in Fort Worth. By early 1972, he had done session work with Donovan and the Beatles and was a veteran of the folk scenes in Greenwich Village, Los Angeles, and London. He also did some stage acting. He had the longest, straightest hippie hair I'd ever seen.

Over the years, Phillips became tremendously popular with our audience. He was a groupie magnet, too. The first couple of times he played the Armadillo, however, he wasn't a big draw there, or anywhere else. One morning before his second time playing the hall, a distinguished gentleman in a suit showed up and introduced himself as James Phillips, father of Shawn. He asked how I thought the show was going to do. I told him I had to be honest with him, that I didn't have any reason to think it was going to sell at all. Mr. Phillips asked if I had any ideas for a solution.

"Giant ads in the *American-Statesman*," I told him. "But that's very, very expensive, a whole lot more than we can afford."

He asked for directions to the newspaper, wished me a good day, and departed.

Friday morning, the phone started ringing off the wall. Joe Bryson, owner of Inner Sanctum, the coolest record store in Austin, called and said, "Get me more Shawn Phillips tickets down here quick." I grabbed a newspaper and it fell open to the biggest Armadillo ad I'd ever seen, approximately one-third of a page, and it was different from any other Armadillo ad I'd ever seen.

Large print at the top of the ad read: "When he was ten years old and growing up wild in Fort Worth, Shawn Phillips was busted for blowing up mail-boxes with giant firecrackers. He's been making noise ever since, but the arrangements are better now . . ."

The remainder of the ad was fairly straightforward: "In concert this Friday and Saturday, 8 p.m., at the Armadillo World Headquarters, the internationally-known rock singer, guitarist, and composer, Shawn Phillips."[8] The print size was bigger than any other ad on the page, yet there was still so much white space left over, it made all the others look crowded and stingy by comparison. This was my first lesson in New York–style advertising white space.

This savvy move made more sense when I learned that James Atlee Phillips was a successful spy novelist. He had been a pilot and journalist in the years before, during, and after World War II, serving in China, India, and Southeast Asia, so he had a good deal of experience in exotic locales to draw upon for his writing.[9] A little closer to the music world, he wrote the screenplay for the 1958 Robert Mitchum bootlegging movie *Thunder Road*.[10] James's brother David worked for the CIA and is a subject of interest in JFK assassination conspiracy circles.

In his later years, Shawn Phillips moved to Port Elizabeth, South Africa. When not performing and touring, he kicks back by working as an emergency medical technician, firefighter, and sea-rescue specialist. Apparently, the adventure bug runs strong in the Phillips family.

The Moods of Country Music, Austin's most popular boot-scooting country-western dance band, had the first weekend of November, but then the bill got a big boost with the addition of Boz Scaggs. Scaggs had played with his old private school friend from Plano, Texas, Steve Miller, but was now a solo act, crooning bluesy love songs like a new Bing Crosby. His second solo album, featuring the Muscle Shoals Rhythm Section and Duane Allman, got great reviews, though it wasn't a big seller. Despite the unusual combination, everyone was happy with the bill; the Moods would play the opening set for the same $300 fee, but they would be playing to a much bigger crowd. The only problem was, it was too late to do a new poster. What we had was the Moods' generic show poster, which showed the band in their matching outfits, hay bales in the background, and a blank space below to fill in the name of the venue and the date. Using a big felt pen, I added the pertinent information: "And, featuring BOZ SCAGGS and his red hot San Francisco band!"

Boz Scaggs backstage at AWHQ, November 3, 1972.
Photograph by Burton Wilson.

Boz's younger brother, who worked for the band, wasn't happy with the customized poster. He told me that Boz would have a shit fit over it.

So we did what we could to get the word out about the star attraction and ended up having a good crowd after all. Boz played the Dillo again later on, though after the Texas Opry House opened, he jumped at the chance to play there for bigger guarantees, air-conditioning, and other deluxe comforts befitting his status as a big-selling blues crooner—but that's a story for later on.

Booking Waylon Jennings at the Armadillo may have seemed like a no-brainer, but the scenario was quite different in the fall of 1972. Before booking Waylon, I went to see him on a Friday night at the Big G Club. Located just outside of Round Rock, a half hour's drive north on the interstate, Big G was a hardcore, no-nonsense honky-tonk dance hall.

By this time, I'd become quite comfortable working with Willie Nelson. I got along well with the Moods of Country Music, and I had survived Jerry Lee Lewis and his entourage of Memphis thugs. Why not screw up my courage and step into a real shitkicker dance hall? My beard was trimmed, my hair was big and fluffy, and I was in good physical shape because LSD and pot, rather than beer, were my recreational drugs of choice. The moment I stepped inside the Big G Club, however, I felt intimidated.

A woman grabbed the neck of my cowboy shirt and stapled a theater ticket to the collar—a technique that would never work on hippies wearing T-shirts. No one picked a fight with me, but trouble erupted anyway. The band had just started a song when a big drunk hollered something nasty at the band. Waylon halted the music with a hand gesture, and the room fell into a hush.

"Hoss," he said into the microphone, "I think there's something you ought to know." Waylon addressed everyone as "Hoss," but with his voice booming over the PA, the effect was chilling.

"Yeah, what's that?" asked the heckler. The people near him moved away. "Tell me something smart."

Waylon unshouldered his guitar, signaling that he was ready to rumble, then said, "I've lost my last dozen fistfights, buddy, so it stands to reason that I'm due to win one."

The crowd roared with laughter just as a fireplug of a man, Big G himself, grabbed the drunk in a hammerlock and hustled him from the

Waylon Jennings backstage at AWHQ, January 25, 1974.
Photograph by Burton Wilson.

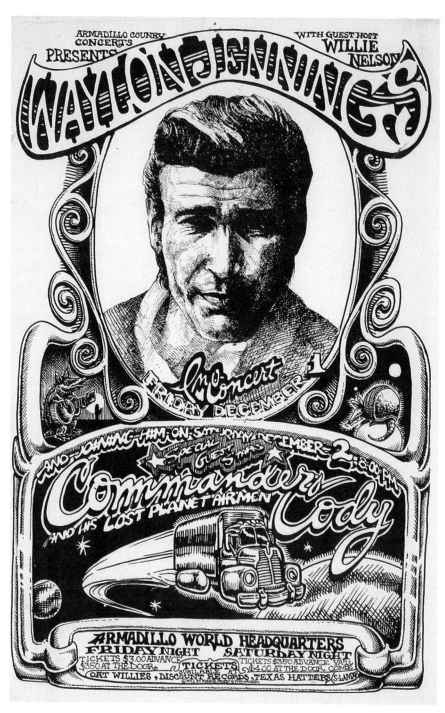

Poster for a Waylon Jennings and Commander Cody and His Lost Planet
Airmen show at AWHQ, December 1, 1972. Artwork by Micael Priest.

building. Waylon grinned his handsome grin, ran his fingers through his ample cowlick, ducked back under his guitar strap, and ripped into the next song with his band.

After a few more songs, I returned to the safety of the Armadillo. Did I really want such people mixing with our hippies?

Waylon required a bit of arm-twisting, as well. He wanted $5,000 for Friday and Saturday, December 1–2. We offered him $2,500 versus 50 percent, with advance tickets at $2.50, and $3.00 at the door. If things went gangbusters, we'd sell four thousand admissions and Waylon would take home between $5,000 and $6,000. I got a friend to intervene and let him know what a great thing we had going, that Willie had already tapped into it, and that he'd be missing out if he didn't give it a shot.

Despite misgivings on both sides, the gig was finalized.

At showtime on Friday, I saw that Waylon looked about as nervous as I had felt at the Big G. Willie was there to lend support, acting as the emcee and host of the show and waiting with Waylon backstage before his set. Waylon's anxiety was not exactly soothed by the sight of so many long-haired, bearded men and hippie chicks. I suppose he was maybe halfway jesting when he turned to Willie and said, "What have you gotten me into, Hoss?"

Willie gave him a reassuring grin and said, "Just trust me."

Willie's endorsement of Waylon was probably equally important to the Dillo crowd. Willie was better known, but Waylon was a rocker at heart. Back in 1958, he was in the studio with Buddy Holly, producing Holly's first single, when Holly hired him as the Crickets' new bass player, a position he held until Holly's tragic death in 1959. Watch some video clips of Waylon and his band from the late sixties or real early seventies—he's got one of the best slicked-back ducktails I've ever seen, and the guitars are cranking through Fender Bassman combos. You just know that everything not screwed down was being rattled by Waylon's heavy groove.

But we were still relieved and thrilled when, following Willie's introduction, Waylon and his band, the Waylors, took the stage and rocked the Armadillo like they owned the place. They rocked harder than Willie and his family band ever did. Both nights were sold out.

The opening acts that weekend were in their own way equally historic. Friday night, Billy Joe Shaver played the first slot. Billy Joe was a gnarly

Billy Joe Shaver onstage at AWHQ, 1972.
Photograph by Van Brooks.

piece of work with the wrinkled face of a shar-pei dog. A great songwriter who could punctuate his lines with a fine hillbilly howl whenever appropriate, he was also an impressive guitar strummer despite having lost several fingers on his right hand in an accident in a lumber mill. I hadn't known him for more than twenty-four hours when I realized he had more soul than the next fifty or so songwriters put together.

Any random slice of Billy Joe's life had material for a dozen classic honky-tonk songs: his father deserting the family before Billy Joe was born; the heroine overdose death of Eddy Shaver, his son and guitarist; his many divorces and remarriages to the love of his life, Brenda; and the night he felt compelled to shoot a man in a bar in Lorena, Texas, to name a few. The important thing was that all the hard luck, irony, and pain came out in his music and words, and despite all the songs about failure and loss, Billy Joe came off as one tough SOB. Bob Dylan recognized it and even mentioned him in a song. In "I Feel a Change Comin' On," Dylan sings, "I'm listening to Billy Joe Shaver, and I'm reading James Joyce." And, like Willie Nelson, Billy Joe Shaver was a songwriter most people first came to know through other singers' versions of his songs. As with other artists, I was proud that the Armadillo was one of the places that helped introduce him to a brand new audience.[11]

Saturday night, Commander Cody and His Lost Planet Airmen opened the show, and again we fretted over the billing, wondering if the combination would go over. For their part, the Northern California band was happy just to make their Armadillo debut. Sharing the stage with the outlaw in black was icing on the cake.

Commander Cody was the stage name of George Frayne IV, a graphic artist who founded his band in Ann Arbor, Michigan, in 1967. Four years later the band moved to San Francisco and released its first record, *Lost in the Ozone*. Its influences ran to western swing—hillbillies playing jazz—and obscure country songs from the 1940s and 1950s. As a gang of technically superb and insanely inspired hippie rockers, the band had no equal.

We liked a lot of the other rock bands who were jangling their cosmic spurs at the time—bands like the New Riders of the Purple Sage, the Byrds, and the Flying Burrito Brothers—but they weren't in the same class as Commander Cody and His Lost Planet Airmen. We seemed to be cut from the same cloth; their songs hit us where we lived. "Down to

Seeds and Stems Again Blues," an original weepy ballad about being out of pot, set to a traditional, tear-in-your-beer country melody, was our cross-cultural anthem. And these guys were authentic weed heads, our kind of guys. "Hot Rod Lincoln" was a cover of a 1955 country boogie song about a drag race and became a Top 40 pop hit. How could we not love this band?

Saturday night, Commander Cody and His Lost Planet Airmen went on first and blew the roof off. Waylon came on and won the crowd over, then Cody came back for all the people hanging around for "Hot Rod Lincoln" and "Down to Seeds and Stems Again Blues." If we hadn't asked them to do that second set, they would've paid us for the privilege. Although the gig was a triumph for Waylon, for us, Cody and company was the bigger deal. It was the beginning of a love affair, the tightest relationship our place ever had with a touring act.

By the end of 1972, the Armadillo's place in honky-tonk history was as secure as a boot in a bucket of concrete. We were getting lots of media attention for being ground zero for the "progressive country" movement. It was great to be recognized, but sometimes it got annoying. For one thing, we never intended to cater to a single music genre. We were still booking lots of blues, jazz, folk, and rock of various stripes, from retro fifties stuff to heavy metal, not to mention the weekly ballet and other cultural happenings. For another, I hated the term "progressive country." Calling it "progressive" sounded as if you were trying to con people who didn't like regular country music. We were trying to encourage rednecks to mix with hippies, and for rednecks throughout the South, marketing something as "progressive" is a good way to start a fight with somebody. It's been that way since before the Civil War, and it's still true today.

Whatever it was called—and it was called a lot of different things, including cosmic cowboy, country rock, and progressive country—the country/rock merger continued gathering steam, and the Armadillo's failure to fail continued on through the new year.

A BREED APART

As at any bar, club, honky-tonk, theater, or other venue where the music gets loud and the booze flows freely, especially in Texas, there were nights at the Armadillo when the natives got restless. When the good vibes turned gnarly, it was the bouncers who squared off against the sons of bitches who had eaten nails for breakfast.

My chief deputy, Dub Rose, rode herd on a posse of cowboys who had taken LSD before riding bulls and army veterans who had faced the Viet Cong in the jungles of Southeast Asia. These guys had faced phalanxes of nightstick-swinging riot police on campuses and city streets, and none of them were impressed with bullies who emerged from a drunken mob in a music hall, their bravery artificially enhanced by the combination of alcohol, other substances, and a depleted brain cell inventory.

Dub really cared about his job, however, and despite the formidable capabilities of his crew, he worried to the point of almost breaking out in hives at the approach of every big-league show. Before every show, he carefully followed an established routine: double-check each door to make sure the inside security crew is in place; go to the office, get the change drawer and the money bag, then escort our beautiful head ticket taker, Linda Wuenche, and her assistant to the box office; then, with the yammering crowd eager to get in, slip into the beer garden to check in with the outdoor crew; and, if the outdoor crew is ready, duck back inside and wait for the precise moment to open the doors.

Dub reminded me of a sharp private eye. If he saw someone for a split second, he could describe that person to a T. He could spot trouble before it happened.

Austin has a legacy of bare-knuckle badasses in its population. Call them the spiritual descendants of Big Gil Stromquist, a former boxer who ran a hardcore country honky-tonk out on South Congress. They included full-time hoodlums like Timmy Overton, tough guys who seemed to thrive on physical combat the way your average musician loves jamming. These characters were as native to the Austin area as live oaks, cedar fever, and armadillos. They were bent-nose, scarred-knuckle toughs who just loved to fight—not necessarily because they had something against the other guy, but because of a primal need to measure their own physical aggression against that of another combatant. The ancient impulse to pummel someone may sound like something out of the Stone Age, but in the 1970s, it was still pretty common in Austin, Texas. In places where strong beverages were sold, such confrontations were frequent and took little time to ignite.

One badass I had to deal with on a regular basis was Bill Campbell, a white blues guitarist from East Austin best described as large, scary, and usually drunk. Bill was a veteran guitarist in the 1960s East Austin blues scene going back to the days of Charlie's Playhouse, Ernie's Chicken Shack, Sam's Showcase, and the IL Club. Just about every well-known blues guitarist who came out of Austin since then, from Stevie Ray Vaughan and Eric Johnson to Gary Clark Jr., followed in Bill Campbell's footsteps in one way or the other. Too bad that music wasn't Bill's only influence or impact on the community.

Then there was Paco, a handsome troublemaker who sold Cuban sandwiches on the Drag. He thought he had first call on any available woman at the Armadillo, and he had promised to kick my ass. We'll never know how that fight might've turned out, because before Paco could give me a chance to save my own hide, he got killed by someone else he'd pissed off.

Another big, handsome local tough—who will remain nameless— was one of those beer drinkers who could be quite charming when sober but, when drunk, turned obnoxious and threatening. I was pretty sure he could take me, and for two years I steered clear of him to avoid the knuckle fest that was sure to happen.

Finally, one night at closing time, he refused to leave. Drunk and swaying on his feet, he threw down the ancient gauntlet, saying, "Are you big enough to make me leave, you son of a bitch?"

Losing my cool, I pushed him lightly with my left, just touching his chest for the setup, but before I could throw a haymaker right that I hoped to God would take his head off, he fell to the ground, sobbing and howling. "Please don't hit me," he begged. "Please, please don't . . ."

If only all of our beefs ended that way. My sermon to the bouncers was simple: hug, don't hit, and holler really loud for backup. On most occasions, we could quickly outnumber the troublemakers, so I really stressed the need to hold on and wait before things got out of hand. I knew the incidents were going to increase as soon as we opened the Cabaret and started selling beer. We briefly floated the idea of restricting drinking to the Cabaret but concluded that it would be totally impractical. Therefore, we had beer everywhere, and everywhere beer goes, trouble often follows.

Hard drugs inevitably appeared on the scene, making the bouncers' job even more difficult. Speed made troublemakers more difficult to reason with and harder to disable or hurt. The combination of alcohol and speed took the worst of both highs and quadrupled it. Downer freaks, on the other hand, were mostly obnoxious but harmless. No matter how badly they wanted to hit you, they mostly hurt themselves.

One night somebody kept fucking with Jose Cerna, our bouncer of bouncers. Jose chased the guy outside, where another asshole was waiting to stab Jose with a sharpened tire tool, which the asshole did and escaped. Jose was stitched up, and he recovered. On another night, we told a pack of Bandidos that wearing their colors in the club would cause trouble, so they retaliated by carving up a couple of our bouncers. Thank God for the ambulance and emergency room crew, or our guys would've bled to death. It must have taken a thousand stitches to put them back together. When the doctor doing the suturing on one of our boys thought he was almost done, he asked the patient to sit up, only to discover that the cuts went all the way around his body.

When Bill Brown, one of my brighter friends, told me he was leaving his job on the Texas Legislative Council, I talked him into coming to work for me as a bouncer. I asked him to give us some ideas on humane techniques for keeping the peace. His only suggestion was not letting the bouncers drink. I knew that wasn't going to work. It's hard to explain, but drinking within reason was too deeply ingrained in the culture. General attitudes about drinking were quite different back then as well. In Texas, it was still legal to drink and drive as long as you weren't legally drunk. I was good at it, I believed, and I practiced a lot to stay in shape.

One night Bill Brown told a Himalayan-sized drunk that he was going to have to leave, which made the drunk want to whip Bill's ass.

"OK," Bill said, "let's step outside and get it on."

As the man-mountain stepped out the nearest exit, Bill pulled the door shut and bolted it, then ran to the main entrance, where he figured the guy would soon appear, boiling mad. Bill alerted Jose Cerna, who was already stationed there. Jose waited, and when the big angry dude came storming through, Jose dropped him like a bad habit.

Jose Cerna had been working for us only a short while when Bobby Hedderman saw him turn a burly, rowdy cowboy into a blubbering baby without doing much more than touching him. Jose was short and extremely stout—not the kind of build you'd associate with speed, but Jose was a sixth-degree black belt. He was modest to the point of being close-mouthed about his skills in self-defense, but after seeing him in action, some of the other bouncers asked if he would teach them some tricks.

"There are no tricks," he told them. It was a discipline, he explained, that required an attitude built around Zen philosophy and meditation.

One quiet afternoon, I was cleaning up in the kitchen when Jose wandered in and asked if he could help. I'd just finished filling the big sink with hot water. I reached in to retrieve a knife and yelled with pain after scalding my hand. Jose calmly reached into the water up to his elbow and pulled out the knife.

How the hell did he do that?

"Most pain is just in the mind," he explained. "I've learned to shut it down for little things."

I looked at my own arm, red and puffed up, the nerve endings still sending angry messages to my brain that were anything but Zen. Jose's arm wasn't even red.

The security guys eventually talked Jose into instructing them in karate and meditation. Despite being hippies at heart, they undertook the most rigorous regime of strength and endurance I'd seen since marine boot camp. They were good students. Although none of them seemed comfortable discussing it, Jose's spiritual guidance and physical discipline actually seemed to influence their general demeanor. They gained a new level of confidence, especially when dealing with loudmouth drunks.

One day Bobby Hedderman was talking with Wichita, a tall West Texas cowboy with a black hat the size of an umbrella. Bobby appeared uncomfortable, while Wichita was energized and passionate.

Later, when Bobby was alone, I said, "What in hell were you and Wichita talking about?"

"Oh, he was just explaining to me how he was learning to acquire a transcendental state," Bobby said.

Craig Hattersley was technically part of our security force, but he was another one who didn't seem the type. Rail-thin, laid-back, and sunny, Craig kept an eye out for trouble in the parking lot while sitting cross-legged and barefoot in a chair, banjo on his knee. People tended to ignore him as they walked across the parking lot, but he played exceptionally well. On a night when Frank Zappa and Jean-Luc Ponty were inside, playing "Orange Blossom Special" accompanied by Sweet Mary Egan, Craig matched their whipped-up frenzy note for note. At a salary of ten dollars a night, Craig was a bargain.

★ ★ ★

One night, I was drinking a beer in the beer garden with Robert Gower, our stage manager. We were sitting with a couple of the other guys at a table in front of the bar. The place was about a third full. The band was setting up onstage. A couple of girls had joined us. Someone on the staff introduced their parents, who were visiting from out of town. Meeting parents always made me self-conscious about the place; I didn't want anyone's mom and dad to think we were a bunch of dirty, immoral hippies. I remember feeling relieved that the joint looked pretty good that night and most of the waitresses were wearing shoes.

Gower, by the way, was a big guy who wore a gorilla suit better than anybody I ever saw. The costume really seemed to bring out his inner gorilla. Bobby Hedderman knows how it all began.

"Robert and I grew up together in Dallas," said Bobby. "We used to watch the Ernie Kovacs show all the time, and one of our favorite skits was the Nairobi Trio, three guys in gorilla suits wearing top hats or bowlers—some kind of hat—doing these musical numbers. It was really funny. So that's where it came from."[1]

"I'd put on the suit for Halloween and hang out in the audience before the show," said Robert. "I played a foam-rubber guitar onstage with Jo Jo Gunne, went to Dallas with Balcones Fault for a debutante-ball after-party, and did all kinds of special events."[2]

On that peaceful day when Robert Gower and I were enjoying a couple of beers, a strange sight suddenly appeared just inside the entrance gate. Bearded and curly-haired, a man was standing there, slowly scanning the terrain of the beer garden. After a minute or so, he stretched his arms wide and, in a booming voice that reminded me of Charlton Heston as Moses in *The Ten Commandments*, said, "I AM THAT I AM."

Unlike Charlton Heston as Moses, however, this guy was completely naked. His hair was red and so was his beard and the hair on his chest and shoulders. In the late-evening light he seemed to be glowing orange.

Fortunately, the parents had already left.

"Shit, we gotta get this guy outta here," I said to Gower.

He nodded reluctantly, and together we strode purposefully toward the entrance. As we got closer, we realized that the naked guy was tall enough to remind us of a giraffe, and almost as thick as Gower.

Just as the naked guy announced "I AM THAT I AM" once more with feeling, Gower grabbed one arm and I grabbed the other. We walked him out to the parking lot, and he offered little resistance other than repeating that he was who he was. We tried to get an actual name out of him, but before we got anywhere, some people showed up who claimed to be his friends and said they'd take care of him.

Gower and I went back to our beers, our existential identities intact. We were who we were.

The weird, the strange, and the deranged were as common to the Armadillo as our kitchen's greasy nachos, but unlike our nachos, such people could potentially be dangerous. It was one of the things that kept life at the Armadillo interesting.

BEING THANKFUL FOR WHAT WE'VE GOT

★

Leon Russell and Willie Nelson were introduced to each other by Jim Franklin the day before Willie's first show at the Armadillo in August 1972. Franklin had been in Tulsa painting at Leon Russell's house, and Jim and Leon traveled to Austin together for the occasion. Anxious to check in at the Dillo, Jim met Willie during sound check. Willie had heard that Jim was working for Leon and said he'd really like to meet Leon.

Jim gave him Leon's phone number in Tulsa. If Willie had been in a bigger hurry to meet him, though, he could've popped into Jim's studio that night, where Leon was enjoying his celebrity status with some of his female fans.

"I wanted Leon to experience what was going on all over the country where his audience was," Jim said. "Six girls were there who were willing to take care of his every need. He spent that one night sleeping on a mattress on the floor with all of them."[1]

The next day, Jim took Leon to meet Willie Nelson at his apartment on Riverside Drive. "Doug Sahm, Leon, and I spent the rest of the afternoon there, sitting around, playing songs," Jim said. "That night, Leon stayed at Willie's apartment."[2]

Leon Russell onstage at AWHQ, November 23, 1972.
Photograph by Burton Wilson.

A lifelong friendship was forged that weekend. Leon Russell was one of the biggest rock names in the world, and Willie Nelson, who had run out his string in Nashville, was in the process of reinventing himself in Austin. Willie wanted Leon's star power and mojo. Leon wanted to rub up against Willie's authenticity and country credentials.

Leon Russell became a frequent sight in Austin after that. He was in town on Wednesday, November 22, 1972, the night the Grateful Dead played Palmer Auditorium. I was at the show, too, not only as a fan but because the Armadillo kitchen was catering the gig.

The Grateful Dead was the one band that the staff most fervently wanted to play the Armadillo. We loved the Grateful Dead. When we imagined ourselves as a band, we were the Dead. By coincidence, Jerry Garcia and I were both bushy haired and dark bearded, and I was even mistaken for him once at a joint-rolling contest in Victoria, Texas. Our fantasy Dead show at the Dillo never came to pass, but appropriately enough, on Thanksgiving Day, we got the next best thing.

I knew Sam Cutler, Chesley Millikin, and Frances Carr—who handled tours for the Dead and Ramblin' Jack Elliott, among others—having met them at the Fly By Night travel agency, located next door to the Dead's office in San Francisco. The agency's name and motto, "Home Today, Gone Tomorrow," were right in line with the kinds of ideas offered by my own Five Dollar Name company.

When Sam Cutler called to ask if we could cater the show, I immediately said, "Hell, yes!" The Grateful Dead was the band who set the standard by which all other rock 'n' roll organizations were measured. They were the epitome of the San Francisco psychedelic drug band. Their superfans traveled long distances to catch every show, following them to undiscovered corners of outer and inner space during the Dead's extended jams. Confounding the expectations of outsiders, the band's support system was one of the most professional outfits of its kind in the world. The Dead employed a top-shelf road crew, quality support staff, and an ingenious custom-designed sound and light system.

The Palmer was just on the other side of South First Street from the Dillo, so the band came over to the joint for dinner before their show. It was kind of like having the Pope drop in on your church. We fed the Dead the most elaborate spread the kitchen had ever whipped up. Doug Sahm was there, holding court and bogarting joints. All the diners had been warned to wear their heaviest coats, as we still had no heat.

Thanksgiving Day meal at AWHQ, November 23, 1972. Left to right: Phil Lesh, Eddie Wilson, and Genie Wilson with backs to camera, Jerry Garcia, Doug Sahm with breath held, and Bob Weir. Photograph by Burton Wilson.

Thanksgiving Day jam session at AWHQ, 1972. Left to right: Leon Russell on piano, Sweet Mary Egan on fiddle, Phil Lesh, Jerry Barnett on drums, Jerry Garcia on pedal steel, and Doug Sahm. Photograph by Burton Wilson.

After the dishes had been taken away, Jerry Garcia, also known as Captain Trips, leaned back, gazed around the building, and uttered the magic words: "I want to play here."

I tried to be cool, but I was so excited I could hardly speak. "When?"

"We don't have a gig tomorrow," he said.

"When?" I repeated, as if it was the only word I could remember how to say.

Garcia hesitated. Details such as time were probably trivial to him.

"I really need to know," I said.

He looked at Doug and said, "How about three o'clock?"

Exhaling smoke from a joint that had been passed to him quite some time ago, Doug said, "Cool."

Later that night at the auditorium, Garcia was walking offstage after the show when he came face to face with Leon Russell. As they shook hands, Garcia said, "We're playing the Armadillo tomorrow afternoon."

"I'll see you there," said Leon.

The next morning was Thanksgiving Day. I did a phone interview with "Good Karma" KRMH-FM. I didn't mention any band names, but I did say that there was a really big jam going down at the Armadillo that afternoon.

There was a lot to do. Jim Finney was enjoying Thanksgiving dinner at the home of Lucky and Chickie Pankratz when I found him.

"Where are your drums?" I said. "How long will it take for you to get them here?"

"What's the big rush?" he said.

"It's a secret," I said. Then I told him that the Dead were going to jam at the Dillo and they needed a drummer.

Finney said he was in. As soon as he hung up, he excitedly shared the news with his dinner companion, Leon Russell.

My brother Frank was at my parents' house. He and the neighborhood strongman, Mike Inmon, loaded Beulah's piano on Woody's plumbing truck and brought it to the Armadillo so Leon would have something to play on.

The Thanksgiving Day jam at the Armadillo felt like a dream come true, an acid trip, and just a bunch of musicians meeting up to trade songs and licks. For many of us, it truly was a combination of all three. Jerry Garcia played pedal steel and Phil Lesh played bass. Leon Russell played

Thanksgiving Day jam session at AWHQ, 1972. Leon Russell,
Jim Finney, unknown, and Jerry Garcia lighting a cigarette.
Photograph by Burton Wilson.

piano. Doug Sahm played guitar, sang, and pretty much wrangled the session, throwing out songs, calling the keys, and basically being Sir Doug. Other local players included Benny Thurman (who'd played with the 13th Floor Elevators but was managing a Piccadilly Cafeteria at the time), Sweet Mary Egan of Greezy Wheels, Jim Finney, and Jerry Barnett.

It was a loose jam for sure, with many high spots threaded together by inspired vamping and noodling. A lot of good weed was passed around. Years later, after Jim Finney heard a tape recording of the jam, he found it really difficult to listen to. Maybe the technical quality was bad, but I remember the rapt faces of the people in the audience. Maybe the sounds and feelings just didn't make the transfer to audiotape.

Word of the big Turkey Day jam spread like wildfire. With the Dillo, Dead, and Leon all being uttered in the same breath, our credentials turned platinum. People were finding out that what we had going on in Texas wasn't like anything else.

Backstage at AWHQ, February 21, 1973. From left to right: Gram Parsons, John Guerin, Emmylou Harris, Gretchen, Kyle Tullis, unknown stage hand, and Jock Bartley. Photograph by Burton Wilson.

NOT YOUR DADDY'S BEER JOINT

Gram Parsons, a revered figure ever since his work with the Byrds and the Flying Burrito Brothers, came to town in February of 1973. The show drew large numbers of fans out of the woodwork, many of whom happened to be attractive young females. People seemed to see whatever they wanted to see in Gram: to some, he was a cowboy maharajah; to others, a bad boy; and to still others, a stoic romantic poet. From what I saw, his jowls were going soft from bad food, bad liquor, and hard drugs. But there was a spiritual vibe there, or maybe that was from the reflected glow in the eyes of his singing partner, Emmylou Harris. She might well have been an underage preacher's daughter who'd run off with the bad boy and gone pagan, and was now wildly intoxicated by a renegade spirit.

"We completely blew off the top of the AWHQ in Austin," Emmylou said years later. "In fact, we had to go back and redo a song for the final encore because we had been called back so many times that we didn't have anything left. So we started to do the show over again."[1]

While they were in Austin, we learned that Gram's band needed a place where Gram could teach his new guitarist some country licks. We moved the band into the pit under the Cabaret, which was about to be converted to a game room, so they could rehearse. Now all they needed was some weed. Lucky Pankratz came to the rescue, bringing what Gram Parsons said was the biggest bag of weed he'd ever seen. "Texas ounces would be close to a half pound anywhere else," he said.

Together, Emmylou Harris and Gram Parsons were mesmerizing. More than a few fans followed them to Houston for their next performance. The girls who followed Gram, the so-called Grievous Angels, did a lot to establish him as a cult figure, but a lot of the real heat coming off the stage was stoked by his main squeeze, Emmylou.

Man Mountain and the Green Slime Boys had done a great job as opening act at the Dillo, and our pals at the Houston venue, Liberty Hall, also booked the band for the Houston show. Ron Rose, Man Mountain himself, called it the highlight of his career. Gram Parsons's song "Sin City" was one of the band's most popular songs, a real crowd-pleaser. As the opening act, however, the band felt that playing the song before their hero's set was a no-no. As it worked out, Gram left the song off his set in Austin and again in Houston. During sound check before the show at Liberty Hall, Ron finally found the courage to ask Gram if he minded.

"Up until the moment I mentioned 'Sin City,' Gram had been real standoffish," Ron said years later. "As soon as I told him our dilemma, he changed. He turned into a puppy."

That night, Man Mountain and the Green Slime Boys "played [their] asses off" and were called back for an encore. "When we went back out to do 'Sin City,'" said Ron, "Gram and Emmylou came out with us. Gram waved out at the audience, and here came Neil Young and Linda Ronstadt to join the chorus. Best backup singers I ever had."

Gram Parsons was dead six months after he played our place, overdosed on heroin. When Emmylou Harris returned a few months later to publicize her solo album, she seemed to be a changed woman. She wore high-buttoned collars and floor-length dresses. She seemed something like a widowed prairie schoolmarm, shrouded in mourning, uptight and defensive.

It was a sad thing to witness. So much country music has been inspired by alcohol-influenced infidelity and misery wallowing, but heroin seemed a lot more evil and insidious.

★ ★ ★

I was never much for hanging with the musicians who came through, with some notable exceptions, such as Freddie King, Loudon Wainwright III, and members of the Grateful Dead, Commander Cody, and Asleep at the Wheel. Some of my close encounters with other bands made me realize they weren't like you and me. Fortunately, encounters like those stood me in good stead when the bookings for the spring of 1973 rolled around. Every night, we seemed to be in the presence of completely different, vivid personalities. Just looking at the calendar for the middle of the month of March, I have to scratch my head in wonder. I took great pride in the fact that the Dillo had become so much more than a big hippie music hall. But how did we deal with the weekly parade of royally quirky personalities?

3/8/73 Thu, French Italian Theatrical Troupe
3/10/73 Sat, Frank Zappa, Jean-Luc Ponty, Blind George McClain
3/11/73 Sun, Austin Ballet Theatre
3/15–3/17/73 Thu–Sat, Freddie King, Al "TNT" Braggs
3/18/73 Sun, Staff Party in Luckenbach, Kinky's first gig
3/22–3/23/73 Thu–Fri, Kinky Friedman and the Texas Jewboys, Texas Instruments
3/24/73 Sat, Bette Midler, Barry Manilow

In the space of fourteen days, we welcomed Zappa, Kinky, and Midler. What a combination. Then there were the regulars: the theater and dance people, the bluesmen like Freddie King—who was like family by then— the folkies, the country rockers, the jazz fusion guys like John McLaughlin, and the legends of traditional jazz, such as one of my all-time favorites, Mose Allison. Most all of them were super talented and interesting in some special way or other, and some of them we'll never be able to forget, no matter how hard we might try.

Frank Zappa intimidated me before we ever shook hands. Zappa and his band, the Mothers of Invention, were the most expensive act we'd ever booked, but their edgy, experimental brand of rock music appealed to our customer base to the point that the Dillo brain trust agreed the hefty performance fee was worth the expense.

Zappa's contract stipulated that an Armadillo loading crew had to be on hand to unload the band's eighteen-wheeler truck and have their equipment set up by noon. Four hours were blocked out for rehearsal, and a one-hour sound check was scheduled after dinner, before the doors opened at seven for the first of two shows that night.

We were already well aware that there was no slop factor in the timetable. Zappa's reputation for exactitude was informed by stories of tantrums, rages, fits of stubbornness, and last-minute cancellations if his demands weren't met.

It was the first time we'd ever attempted two shows in one night. That alone scared me stiff. The idea of ending one show, emptying the hall, cleaning it up, and refilling it with 1,500 more hippies, many of whom had bought tickets to both shows, all in less than an hour, seemed a bit far-fetched. I had a hard time picturing anything but resistance from 3,000 ticket holders who'd paid a premium price to see Frank Zappa. Dillo-philes were used to endless encores by bands who fed on rowdy applause and thunderous roars of appreciation from their rabid fans in our house.

The contract stipulated that the opening act be a solo performer and that the opening act's equipment must be set up and removed without moving any of the Mothers' equipment. I booked Blind George McClain to fill the bill and to prove to Zappa that he wasn't the only weirdo in the business.

The truck with the Mothers' equipment didn't arrive before noon as scheduled. It didn't arrive by one o'clock, either. It pulled up to the building shortly after five, by which time the bandleader was thoroughly steamed. I walked up behind him onstage as our guys were hauling the stuff off the truck and thought I saw smoke coming from his ears. It turned out to be smoke from a Winston, one of hundreds I saw Zappa suck down before the night was over.

By the time everything was in place, a huge gaggle of ticket holders had gathered in the beer garden. At seventeen minutes before showtime, some of the first-come-first-serve regulars began pounding the giant wooden doors, which created a booming jungle-drum effect. My nuts began to ache and shrivel. I was visualizing a standoff between Zappa and a riot of angry ticket holders.

Zappa's eyes were coal-black, angry slits when he turned to a very nervous band, strapped on his guitar, raised its neck like a conductor's wand, and brought it crashing down in a thunderous roar of rock 'n' roll. The crowd outside fell silent. A four-hour rehearsal and a one-hour

Frank Zappa onstage at AWHQ, March 10, 1973.
Photograph by Burton Wilson.

Frank Zappa and Blind George McClain backstage at AWHQ,
March 10, 1927. Photograph by Burton Wilson.

sound check were squeezed into those seventeen minutes. I didn't know they would end at showtime until Marty Perellis, Zappa's road manager, looked at his watch, pointed to Frank, and moved his finger across his Adam's apple, indicating that time was up. The band nervously filed off-stage followed by a thoroughly pissed Zappa, who snorted, "Some fucking sound check!" The doors flew open and a hoard of happy hippies surged in.

I chose this moment to approach the Mother Superior. "Frank, I doubt if you usually have much interest in your opening act, but I thought you might want to meet Blind George McClain."

Distracted but polite, Zappa said, "What's he do?"

"He plays the piano and sings," I said. "He's kind of a cross between George Jones and Ray Charles. He's blind, crippled, and mostly deaf."

Zappa squinted at me. "I'd like to meet him right now."

I led Zappa backstage and upstairs toward the office. I said to make sure to speak up because Blind George really was hard of hearing. We walked into the office where Blind George was sitting on the sofa, crumpled down into the cushions, waiting to be led to the piano onstage. Blind George had a skinny, twisted physique, and dark-black circles framed his sightless eyes. I leaned down and spoke loudly, "George, I'd like you to meet Frank Zappa."

Blind George tilted his head back at me, and a glowing smile appeared on his face. He held out his bony hand, and Frank took it gently.

"Hi, George, I'm Frank Zappa," said Zappa, his voice a low whisper.

George shouted, "What?"

Startled, Frank leaned down lower and spoke in a much louder voice, "Did you hear our sound check, George?"

"Yeah!" George yelled back. "You were way too fucking loud!"

During the day on Saturday, I drove Zappa out to a mesquite and cedar forest west of Austin, where a small group of philosophers, architects, teachers, and designers lived in yurts, round Mongolian huts with sloping roofs. There were four single-room yurts occupied by single individuals or couples surrounding a larger yurt that functioned as a communal kitchen, den, and living room. Another yurt, designated as the John Yurt, had a restroom and showers.

The yurt folks were a cordial bunch, so I talked Zappa into checking it out. He listened with rapt attention to the tales of the yurt dwellers, fixing his eyes on them as they proselytized and asking them questions. They regaled him with tales of catatonic and schizophrenic patients making dramatic behavioral improvements after living in yurts for three weeks. Frank was captivated.

As we drove back to the Armadillo, swerving our way in and out of a gravel ditch, Zappa suddenly snapped his fingers and snorted, "Shit!"

"What's the matter?" I asked.

"It won't work." His face had fallen. He had a glum and disappointed look.

"What won't work?" I asked, still in the dark.

His brow furrowed, and the corners of his mouth turned down.

"If something is going to save the world, that something has to pass several tests. One of those tests is it's got to work in New York City."

I realized right then and there that yurts would not save the world.

Zappa didn't do illicit drugs. He chain-smoked Winston cigarettes and drank coffee by the gallon, but he was more vocally antidrug than any musician I'd ever met, even though his Dada-absurdist music was the soundtrack for millions of LSD trips.

Jan Beeman learned that the way to Zappa's heart was through his stomach. The Armadillo kitchen even got special thanks on Zappa's *Bongo Fury* album, most of which was recorded at the Dillo with Captain Beefheart in 1975. That was after Jan learned that the mere scent of weed was sufficient to piss him off. After the band had been served, Zappa appeared in the kitchen and summoned her backstage. He was waiting for her in the greenroom with his coffee machine and his cigarettes. "You smell like marijuana," he said. "The next time I come back here, don't let me smell any marijuana around you."

"You've been smoking and drinking coffee ever since you got here," Jan said. "What do you have against marijuana?"

"I'm allergic to it," he said.

Zappa returned to the Armadillo the next year. At one point during the show, he made a request to the audience. Pointing to the open doors of the emergency exit at stage right, he said, "Please blow your smoke that way."

Not long afterward, the show was stopped because of a bomb threat. The hall was cleared, with everyone directed to leave through the aforementioned exit. Had the caller been an irate pot smoker? We never found out. After the place was searched, people were allowed to reenter, and Zappa resumed the show on the exact note where the band had left off.

Zappa was constantly on the watch for scofflaws on his crew. If anyone was caught with contraband, they were fired immediately and had to pay their own way home. Apparently, his policy dated back to an experience with a former Armadillo employee named Leon Rodriguez. On a tour with Zappa in England, Rodriguez and another crew member were partying in their hotel room with two girls when the London bobbies busted them. Zappa picked up their legal tab—bailing them out of jail, paying their lawyers, sending them back to England for their court dates, and then paying for their return to the United States. Understandably, he never wanted to have to do that again.

Zappa was extremely business oriented, especially for a musician, always aware that he was running an organization as well as leading a band. He hired several of our crew to go on the road with him, and that raised his already significant profile around the Armadillo. Since his crew included some of our people, we went out of our way to accommodate the crew whenever they wanted to discreetly get high. We let them use the Chicanoline, the break room for security where roadies and staff could drink and smoke weed out of public view. Zappa knew all about the Chicanoline and told his crew to stay the hell out of there if they wanted to keep their jobs.

★ ★ ★

Kinky Friedman called me late one night and asked if we could meet for coffee. We'd never met before. After we decided on a place, he said, "I hear you look like Jerry Garcia."

"That should make me easy to spot," I said.

"I'm easy, too," he said. "Look for somebody who looks like a swarthy Arab skyjacker."

Mike Tolleson had already cautioned me to be patient with the singer-songwriter, who preferred to be called "the Kinkster" and who routinely referred to himself in the third person, as crowned heads of state traditionally do.

We met, and within a short time I decided that I was impressed with Kinky's intelligence, cunning, and guile, all of which he bragged about possessing. I agreed to join his conspiracy, and we drew up plans to

Poster for a Kinky Friedman and the Texas Jewboys show
at AWHQ, March 22–23, 1973. Artwork by Cliff Carter.

promote the debut of Kinky Friedman and the Texas Jewboys at an Armadillo staff party, which would be held at an old dance hall in a rural community west of Austin called Luckenbach. The population there was in the single digits.

At the time, only a handful of people outside the Texas Hill Country could've found Luckenbach on a map. It was completely off the cultural radar. Not until the following summer did bands start playing there regularly. Then, in 1977, Waylon Jennings's recording of a song by Bobby Emmons and Chips Moman called "Luckenbach, Texas (Back to the Basics of Love)" touched the little German settlement with the gilded brush of fame.[2]

Our promotion of the Kinkster's debut on FM rock stations in Austin and San Antonio attracted an audience that was just about as hip, tolerant, and open-minded as Kinky could have hoped for. But the night got off to an unsettling start. Just as the targeted demographic began to arrive, all the benches around the dance floor started filling up with big, husky German farmers—women with white- or blue-tinted perms and men with silver pomaded hair and complexions that had turned beet red after decades of hard work under the unforgiving Hill Country sun. This was their community hall, after all, and we were interlopers from Austin. If you're familiar with the history of German settlements in Texas, you'll know that the Germans immigrated here beginning in the 1840s, and that many of them were progressive thinkers, abolitionists, and seekers of a utopian ideal. That was then, however, and this was now. The descendants of the original immigrants were not known for having a tolerant attitude toward long-haired dope smokers seeking their own utopian experiences.

Kinky and the Texas Jewboys looked frightened. I was frightened.

"Wilson, I can't go out there," Kinky said. "Those Germans will tear me apart."

"Kinky, you've got no choice," I said. "You don't stand a chance against me and this hammer."

Kinky bravely took the stage and sailed into "Get Your Biscuits in the Oven (and Your Buns in the Bed)." He followed with one classic after another—"The Ballad of Charles Whitman," "Ride 'Em Jewboy," and so on.

Caught off guard by the laughter from the city kids as well as by the edgy style of the country music, the Germans seemed oblivious to the lyrics. Somewhere in there was the key to Kinky's survival.

On the following Thursday and Friday, Kinky Friedman and the Texas Jewboys played at the Armadillo. Initially, critic Joe Gracey wasn't impressed. He didn't like the band and commented that there was a certain "overblownness" to Kinky's act. The world would soon realize that for the Kinkster, "overblownness" was just a starting place.

★ ★ ★

What a season. After Zappa, then three nights of Kinky, we had the Divine Miss M on Saturday. Bette Midler, the showstopping song belter newly signed to Atlantic Records, was on her first national tour, and the Armadillo was her only Texas date. There were far glitzier places to play in the state, but here she was at our hippie palace.

The show attracted a large contingent of black cross-dressers. Splendidly attired in flowing gowns and high heels, they all appeared to be over six feet tall. It was quite the sight. Despite the fact that Midler had jump-started her career performing at the Continental Baths, a gay bathhouse in New York City, the sight of our Lone Star queens of color seemed to freak her out. They crowded close to the edge of the stage, trying to touch her dress.

I admit that Bobby Hedderman, Hank Alrich, and the rest of us were a little freaked out, too. We hadn't known that there were enough drag queens in Austin to fill a VW Bus, much less the Armadillo.

Bette Midler was one of the sharpest entertainers I ever met. A minute before she walked onstage, she grabbed me by the collar, pulled me down into her intense gaze, and said, "OK, stud, you've got sixty seconds to tell me everything about this little town."

"Pardon me, ma'am," I said, "this is the capital of Texas. Our university has a three-hundred-foot-tall phallic symbol that glows on the tip when there's a victory by the mighty 'Horns."

"Far out," she said, whistling through her oversized, toothy grin. Charging onto the stage, she ripped into a routine that sounded like it had been put together by a team of top-shelf comedy writers. Her backing band was led by pianist Barry Manilow, of whom you may have heard.

Poster for a Bette Midler show at AWHQ,
March 24, 1973. Artwork by AMSEL.

Bette Midler onstage at AWHQ, March 24, 1973.
Photograph by Burton Wilson.

The Divine Miss M left the sellout crowd panting for more. In her wake, we wondered about all those cross-dressers. What other communities existed out there that we didn't know about? Every night at the Dillo could turn out to be an education.

In mid-May we saw even more glitter and makeup on men, with big teased hair, flashy earrings, platform shoes, and other feminine flourishes on both sexes. The occasion was a show by Slade, a glam band from the UK who had a string of hit singles to their credit, songs with catchy hard-rock hooks and slangy titles: "Cum On Feel the Noize," "Skweeze Me, Pleeze Me". . . you get the picture. Slade owed a lot to the David Bowie–New York Dolls glam scene. Years later, bands ranging from the Ramones to Nirvana would claim to have been influenced by the band.

Under the makeup and bangles, the guys in Slade looked like British street toughs. The singer, Noddy Holder, had puffy muttonchops and a pug face. He wore plaid suspenders and a top hat with mirrors all over it. Illuminated by spotlights as he sang and danced, the hat doubled as a disco ball.

Slade was the loudest band ever to play the Armadillo. Even Jesse Sublett, whose band the Skunks was reputed to be the loudest rock band in Austin in the late seventies, said that the band was "painfully, excruciatingly loud."

The backstage-door security man, Steve Russell, a huge Native American who went on to be a lawyer, writer, and judge, made his only ever request/demand that night. Steve asked to be moved to parking lot duty during the show. Guns and knives in the dark, he said, were far less risky to his health.

Cars inch along Highway 290 headed toward Willie Nelson's first Fourth of July in Dripping Springs, Texas, 1973. Photograph by Burton Wilson.

THE FIRST WILLIE NELSON PICNIC

★

The town of Victoria, Texas, wasn't exactly a hotbed of alternative thought, but the civic leaders there were eager to promote their town. Their annual Armadillo Confab was just another gimmick, but we were always looking for gimmicks that could ensure our survival. When the pay phone rang and a fellow named Fred Armstrong said he had heard that we were the center of the armadillo universe in Texas and would we be interested in being involved, I rallied the troops, and we took the Armadillo Country Music Review back on the road.

The dates were Friday to Sunday, June 15–17, 1973. The caravan of Armadillo stars who played on a flatbed-trailer stage with our Armadillo Country Music Review backdrop were Willie Nelson, Greezy Wheels, Man Mountain and the Green Slime Boys, Diamond Rio, and D. K. Little. Diamond Rio was the band that resulted when Hank Alrich joined Shiva's Headband and Spencer Perskin stayed home. They were good. D. K. Little hailed from Lubbock. He was a good-looking, charismatic, tough-emoting front man in the classic rock 'n' roll mode. His band had Bill Campbell on guitar and Tiny McFarland, the gentle giant, on drums.

Overall, the show was a good experience, although the local organizers had included several events that tended to make us squirm when we thought about them years later. The Miss Vacant Parking Lot and "cigarette" rolling contests were good tongue-in-cheek fun, but the armadillo races and barbecued-armadillo recipe competition were things we'd rather not have been associated with.

The history-making event of the summer was the first Willie Nelson Fourth of July Picnic. We coproduced the show with Willie practically on the fly, hustling everything together at the last minute and making things up as we went. The fact that it came off at all was something of a miracle.

Woody Roberts remembers the details well, partly because he's a really smart guy and also because it was his first experience working with the Armadillo. Woody was a veteran radio station manager and promotions guy from San Antonio who had been coming to shows at the Armadillo for a while. Before coming to work with us full time, Woody was vice president and general manager at KTSA in San Antonio, which was then a powerhouse of Central and South Texas. I'd met Woody before and so had Mike Tolleson, but we'd never worked together on anything.

The job started when Willie walked into the office at the Armadillo and said he wanted to do a festival at the Hurlbut Ranch outside of Dripping Springs on July 4.

Mike Tolleson remembers that day. "Willie had cooked this thing up," said Mike. "He had some backing from his friend, the Houston lawyer Joe Jamail. Joe's office had put together a corporation for Willie called Nelson Prospecting Corporation Inc. Willie, Larry Trader, and Billy Cooper were the directors. Willie was waving it around, saying, 'Look at this, I'm a corporation.' He started talking about the concert, saying he wanted to call it the Willie Nelson Fourth of July Picnic, and he wanted us to help produce it."[1]

By this time we'd done a number of things with Willie, and this idea had a lot of potential, but the show was only three, maybe three and a half, weeks away. No tickets had been sold. No promotions had been done. The thing had "disaster" written all over it.

It was going to be held at the Hurlbut Ranch just outside the town of Dripping Springs, twenty-six miles west of Austin. The year before, some promoters had staged a country music festival on the same site called the Dripping Springs Reunion. They'd had Willie Nelson, Waylon Jennings, Kris Kristofferson, Ernest Tubb, and Tex Ritter. Very few people had showed up.

Poster for Willie Nelson's Fourth of July Picnic, 1973.
Artwork by Jim Franklin.

I called a powwow at my house and asked Woody Roberts to come. I told him we needed help.

"I'd never even heard of Dripping Springs," said Woody. "I remember driving up to Austin to Eddie's house. Everybody was sitting on the floor around a coffee table, passing joints, talking."[2]

Willie Nelson was there with Larry Trader, his promoter friend and all-purpose outlaw. For the Armadillo, we had Mike Tolleson, Bobby Hedderman, Woody Roberts, and me. Beers and joints were passed around. There was a coke mirror, but nobody partook. The tone of the meeting was pretty serious.

We had a poster for the show. The slate of performers included Willie Nelson, Waylon Jennings, Kenneth Threadgill, Kris Kristofferson, Rita Coolidge, Billy Joe Shaver, Jerry Jeff Walker, Freda and the Firedogs, and a few others.

At some point someone mentioned Leon Russell, which got Woody's attention. Leon was committed to play, but we weren't allowed to advertise him. Woody said, "Shit, that's the only thing that sounds interesting about this festival. It's a country show, except for Doug Sahm and maybe Michael Murphey, but nobody on this bill can fill an arena."

After some more discussion, I suggested that we turn all the radio promotion over to Woody. Larry Trader seconded the motion. We took a vote and Woody got the job. A couple of Willie's friends weren't happy about it.

"I took control of the radio promotion budget," said Woody. "All the money they were going to spend in Houston, Dallas, and San Antonio got redirected. My plan was to pull all the money away from these country stations they'd bought from and put it all on Top 40 and FM rock stations."

Discussion followed, some of it heated, but in the end, we gave Woody the ball and he ran with it. Woody cleverly spread the word about Leon Russell's participation in the picnic by telling lots of important people that it was top secret. Woody tells it better than anyone, because his fertile mind sprouted this mushroom field of great ideas.

We produced a commercial where it sounded like we were having a picnic, having a big time, and sent it out all over the place. Then we called all the radio stations. We'd tell the program directors and music directors, "You're invited to this thing, and we can't say it on the commercial and you can't say it on the air, but Leon Russell is going to be there," and they perked up. . . . Then we'd say, "Here's the other thing, they're saying that Bob Dylan's going to show up with Doug Sahm, but we have no way to say if that's true, so don't even mention that."

So right away, the word is out. Leon Russell is going to be there, and there's a rumor that Bob Dylan might show up. And that was the campaign. It was an incredible mess, but when it was all over, it had been a big success.

Woody's savvy radio promotion made a critical difference. He had realized that Leon Russell was the key to selling the event. Willie was still largely unknown to rock audiences, even in Austin, but Leon had heavy airplay on FM rock radio stations around the country.

Two days before the picnic, a potential disaster happened at the concert site. The roof somehow fell off the stage. Without it, there would be no shade for the performers during the day and no lights after dark. The contractors assured me that there was no time to build a new roof. It was a big problem.

An idea came to me: perhaps Lloyd Fortenberry of Uranus Urethanes could make us a roof out of urethane foam. We had just used Lloyd's new spray product to insulate our underground beer keg room. Jim Franklin had fallen in love with urethane as a sculpting material and used it to create a giant cowboy hat, a guacamole headdress the size of a Volkswagen Beetle, and a giant smoking jacket.

After considering my idea, Lloyd agreed and rounded up all the materials and equipment. We laid down a canvas tarp large enough to cover the stage and stretched light-gauge chicken wire on top of it. Lloyd then sprayed four inches of foam over the whole thing. Within minutes, the huge, orange mass had hardened and was ready to be hoisted into place. It looked like a horizontal sail. We held our breath, attached the supports, and grinned nervously as dozens of hippies cheered.

Lloyd only charged us the cost of the urethane. I felt like the cocreator of a masterpiece. It was the same feeling I'd had when Micael Priest took my directions and created the first Willie Nelson poster.

In the days leading up to the picnic, Willie's friend Geno McCoslin was a major pain in the ass. Geno ran a string of topless bars and nightclubs in Dallas and seemed to love the life and image that went with it. He was notorious for carrying guns and whipping them out on the slightest

Willie Nelson's Fourth of July Picnic, 1973.
Photographs by Burton Wilson.

whim, putting out the vibe of a real badass. We feuded and cussed over every little detail. In a not-so-subtle way, I let it be known that I was looking forward to getting within arm's reach of him.

On the day before the picnic, everybody on the Armadillo staff showed up wearing "Go Ask Eddie Wilson" T-shirts. Geno had made them up and passed them out. He even showed up wearing one himself. I told him to round up every one of the shirts my staff was wearing and bring them to me. I'd give them away to the people who really needed a shirt, and he did as I asked.

On the day of the show, which the Texas Legislature had declared "Willie Nelson Day," a whole bunch of people came. How many? More than enough to call it a success, and way more than our stretched-beyond-the-seams infrastructure at the site could handle. We were overrun. Estimates ranged from twenty-five thousand to three or four times that many. According to one rumor, someone had gotten a flat tire on the road out to the site, and once he pulled over, every car behind him started pulling over, starting a bottleneck that stretched for miles, all the way out to the highway.

The areas we had designated for parking were pretty much ignored. A barbed-wire fence around the perimeter was knocked down early in the day. Sweaty, dust-covered people lugging heavy beer coolers trudged through the mesquite brush shoulder to shoulder, a mob of happy picnickers "as thick as the Chinese Army at the Chosin Reservoir," as my Uncle Clarence liked to say.

The dirt road to the site was fenced in on either side. The concertgoers were supposed to converge on an opening where we had set up a Winnebago with a table in front. People were supposed to stop at the table and pay the admission. There were some serious flaws in this plan, as Mike Tolleson noticed when he went out to inspect the logjam.

"The plan was for the people at the table to collect the admission, then pass it to the Winnebago," Mike explained later. "Carlotta Pankratz was inside. She'd count the money for the Armadillo, then hand it over to Larry Trader, who was counting for Willie. Larry then sacked it up and took it away.

"Clearly, we were understaffed. I spent most of the day out at the last intersection, where the cars were in gridlock and the sheriff was towing vehicles and threatening to shut us down. Herds of people just swarmed in. They just walked past our two little ticket takers standing in the middle of the road."[3]

Some stopped to pay admission, others moved forward in a human wave, shrugging with annoyance at being asked to pay. Why should they pay if nobody else was paying? That wasn't the only surprise, as Mike explains. "The money that Larry Trader collected was never seen again by any of us," Mike said. "We never got an accounting as to the total. The only totals we knew about were from the ticket outlets we collected from."

Then there was the heat. This was July in Texas, so that was expected, but still, it was a thing of awesome proportions. The audience area was like an experiment in ultraviolet torture. Backstage was miserable, too. The only shade was inside Willie's bus. When combined with artificial stimulants, the heat contributed to several ugly meltdowns. Bobby Hedderman was working the stage when Joe Jamail confronted him, saying, "Do you know who I am?" and spit in his face. Bobby, who had extensive training in karate and other martial arts, really wanted to avoid hurting him. Bobby left the stage in frustration, screamed like a banshee, and hurled himself face-first into a chain-link fence. After untangling himself, he went back to work.

The Mad Dogs' favorite doctor had agreed to run the medical tent, but on the day of the picnic, he found other things to do. Tom Daniel filled in at the last minute. Tom Daniel was a young physician from La Marque, Texas, who'd gone to school with Jim Franklin and Kay Bailey Hutchison, who was then a member of the Texas Legislature. Dr. Daniel ended up being the sole professional physician on-site, tending heatstroke victims, drug overdoses, and one gunshot wound. Apparently, when a young redneck hippie sat down on a rock, the pistol in his back pocket accidentally discharged, causing a painful wound in a most tender area of the body.

From beginning to end, the event was a "heathen stomp," a phrase I borrowed from the writer Billy Porterfield, who knew what to call it when he was in the middle of one. Most of my time and attention were consumed with just trying to keep everything running—a task made more complicated by the chemicals swirling around my brain, although that was standard operating procedure for the time and place. Paul English might have been pacing himself, as he and his fiancée, Diane Huddleston, planned to get hitched at sunset, with the reception following

John Prine onstage during Willie Nelson's Fourth of July Picnic,
1973. Photograph by Burton Wilson.

at the Armadillo beer garden after the show. In case any of us had such a great time we suffered amnesia afterward, there was a very cool wedding announcement poster created by Micael Priest with the names of the members of the party and caricatures of them below.

There was something bittersweet about watching the sun come up on July 5, casting its glow on a field littered with debris. I was sitting onstage next to John Prine, both of us wearing tired "illegal smiles," as he so famously termed an expression of stoned contentment. My feet were so swollen that there was only one solution. With Prine lending a helping hand, we cut off my cowboy boots. When a person does a grand favor like that, you never forget it.

My memories of the show are highlighted by certain images. Willie was in fine form. He wore a white "Shotgun Willie" T-shirt and ruled the stage, generously trading off the spotlight with Kris Kristofferson, Waylon Jennings, Leon Russell, and a heavy-duty mix of rock and country up-and-comers. For the most part, the music transcended the bullshit.

Mike Tolleson was proud of our achievements. "We managed to produce the first Willie Nelson picnic and come out of that thing alive, with very few people burned or hurt or not paid," he said. "We didn't get ripped off, nor did we rip anyone off. Everybody came out feeling pretty good about that."

Among those who thought they got burned were members of Waylon Jennings's band. The Waylors were still wailing thirty years later about Willie being the only one who got paid, which wasn't true. In late 1974, when *The Improbable Rise of Redneck Rock* was published, I was surprised to see author Jan Reid quote Willie Nelson saying that I was the only one who made any money on the picnic. It was a ridiculous thing to say. I figured I could say my feelings were hurt or that I was pissed off, or just say what the heck, let them print the legend, and laugh about it.

We weren't laughing much at the Armadillo the day after the picnic. I remember that every time I looked out at the parking lot, another lead sled rocked into view, with characters from Willie's entourage spilling out, swaggering into the beer garden like hermit crabs emerging from the surf. Loud arguments erupted over money like busted radiators exploding on a July afternoon. Every one of these characters seemed to have a pistol or two tucked into his jeans or bulging under his cowboy shirt. These were guys with rough and ragged résumés. They were hard cases, hustlers, and losers from the mean streets, creeping out of the woodwork from the gutbuckets and honky-tonks that some of them were raised in, a world where guns were a fact of life.

For some people, guns were even a necessity. You could understand why guys like Freddie King and other blues musicians who played the roadhouse circuit would as soon go out with no pants on as leave their cannon at home. Promoters and managers like Bill Ham, ZZ Top's manager, were in the same class, keeping Smith and Wesson as their bodyguards, the bulge or flash of steel always present as a reminder.

That was the world they came from, and I understood that, but the Armadillo was different. Guns in the Dillo made some of the peace-loving hippies on our staff nervous and upset. The tension in the beer garden would escalate when black and whites rolled into the parking lot: someone had called the cops and reported guns on the premises.

The response from Willie's people was less than classy. Instead of apologizing, Billy Cooper was livid. Billy was Willie's official driver and a favored member of his entourage. Our hippies had betrayed him, he said. The acid-head bull riders on our security staff grumbled about fetching their own heat. Bobby Hedderman got so mad, I thought he was going to fire everybody and shut down the garden.

Bobby swore that unless the guns were kept out of the Armadillo, he would never have anything to do with Willie again. I agreed with Bobby's attitude about all the guns invading our place like some kind of cancer, but his response still startled me. I'd never seen him so mad before.

Willie Nelson onstage during the Armadillo Country Music Review
in Victoria, Texas, June 17, 1973. Photograph by Burton Wilson.

ARMADILLO TV, OR WHAT MIGHT HAVE BEEN

★

> Armadillo moves from one extravaganza to another. Sunday night they are taping a television concert to be simulcast over KLRN-TV, KEXL (San Antonio), and Krum-ha [KRMH] in Austin. The performers for the session include Mike Murphey, Willie Nelson, Billie Joe Shaver, Diamond Rio, Greezy Wheels, and D. K. Little.[1]

Despite the friction between Willie's camp and the Armadillo gang, we continued working together for a while, including one last big gig for the Armadillo Country Music Review. The show was on July 8, 1973, just four days after the picnic in Dripping Springs, and as Joe Gracey wrote in the *Statesman*, it was taped for broadcast on KLRN (the Austin/San Antonio PBS affiliate, now known as KLRU in Austin) and other PBS affiliates in the state. Willie got top billing, followed by Michael Murphey, Billy Joe Shaver, Greezy Wheels, D. K. Little, and Diamond Rio.[2]

We envisioned the TV show as a chance to prove that an exciting music performance program could be produced in a real music venue here in Austin. We'd been spitballing and pitching a live music television series for some time. From the very beginning of the Armadillo, Mike Tolleson and Bill Narum had been working to get Austin musicians and their music on televisions in homes everywhere.

Woody Roberts helped us get the show simulcast on FM radio, which was really important, since the sound on regular television was pretty awful in those days. Although the first show was billed as the Armadillo Country Music Review (ACMR), we thought of the words "Armadillo Country" as representing a place bubbling over with great music of all kinds, not just country. When we proposed the show as a series, we called it *Live from Armadillo World Headquarters*, although *Armadillo Music Television* might have been even catchier. If the thing had gone on to become an annual music festival, there were many great possibilities for a name: AWHQ Fest, Dillo Fest, Dillopalooza, Armadillostock, etc.

Leading up to the ACMR broadcast, we'd been doing live radio broadcasts on KOKE-FM. Bill Narum and the Taylorvision commune were cablecasting videos of shows at the Armadillo within a few hours of the performances. In *The Improbable Rise of Redneck Rock*, Jan Reid made several mentions of our video obsession ("The Armadillos were always taping everything").[3] We'd been taping our shows on half-inch black-and-white video, but the ACMR show would be the first color, broadcast-quality taping, and the radio/TV simulcast on Austin and San Antonio FM stations would be the first of its kind.

Naturally, Mike Tolleson assumed responsibility for coordinating the shoot. Rounding up the equipment to produce a high-quality, multiple-camera shoot was a tall order. At the time, KLRN had a very modest studio facility, but they did have a mobile video van. Tolleson called his friend Bill Arhos, a producer at KLRN, and talked him into taping the show at the Armadillo. KLRN also took on the task of editing the concert down to two one-hour shows, to be broadcast on successive weekends. Bruce Scafe received credit as director; Mike Tolleson, Bill Arhos, and Charles Vaughan were credited as producers.[4]

The first segment of the Armadillo Country Music Review was to air on Friday night, July 20, 1973, but the schedule was shifted around at the last minute due to breaking news from Washington. The Watergate hearings were in session, and the committee investigating the White House had been informed just days earlier that President Nixon had secretly recorded conversations with his henchmen in the Watergate affair. Townsend Miller expressed his frustration in his column the next day.

I tuned in to KLRN-TV Friday night to hear the videotape of the Armadillo show, as originally scheduled. All I got was the significant but ridiculous Watergate hearings. Sunday night I tuned in to KLRN-TV to hear Doc Watson and the Dillards. I heard the Armadillo show! Then they tell me Part II was slated for 10:30 p.m. Sunday, July 29. I wondered when Doc Watson and the Dillards would appear. I thought I'd watch when the Watergate hearings were scheduled. Who knew?[5]

The ratings were not encouraging, but that didn't mean the Austin music series was a dead idea. Leon Russell didn't think so. Our friends at Lone Star entertained the idea of sponsoring such a series, with Leon and Sheltervision handling the production.

Bill Arhos still thought it was a good idea, too, and so did some of his associates. Later, in 1974, Arhos applied to PBS for a funding grant to produce a music concert series and was awarded $13,000 for development. His timing was good. A massive building boom was underway at UT, and one of the projects completed in 1974 was a new, state-of-the-art KLRN studio on campus, designated Studio 6A.

Mike Tolleson was enlisted as a consultant. "Bill Arhos called me to say they wanted to produce a pilot for a music series in their new studio and wanted my suggestions for talent," said Mike. "So I told him that Willie was the obvious choice for a headline act, and with his agreement, I called Willie and booked him. B. W. Stevenson was also booked for the pilot. And Bill also wanted help rounding up other musicians for future episodes, and with that in mind, we began to make a list."

The pilot was shot at KLRN's Studio 6A on October 14, 1974. B. W. Stevenson's set suffered technical glitches, and his part of the program had to be scrapped. Willie's performance, however, was sufficiently impressive.

During a PBS pledge drive in early 1975, a sufficient number of PBS stations pledged a portion of their budgets for the purpose of extending the series, which was to be called *Austin City Limits* (*ACL*).

After more than forty years on the air, *ACL* has piled up so many accolades it almost seems to wear a Kevlar vest against criticism, yet, as Mike Tolleson puts it, "[Their] version of an Austin-based music show became as good as can be done in a studio environment, but it was not the down-home rock 'n' roll lifestyle variety show we wanted to present from the Armadillo."

On the show's website you can read the official history of the series, with heavy emphasis on awards from the National Endowment for the Arts, Rock and Roll Hall of Fame, and so on, with a dramatic conjunction linking its years of success with an ostensibly unscripted and unlikely beginning:

But no one knew it would be any of those things back in 1974. That was the year KLRU program director Bill Arhos, producer Paul Bosner and director Bruce Scafe hatched the idea in response to PBS's call for original programming from its member stations.[6]

The three of them were not exactly big names in the world of live music television, but to be fair, that world did not yet exist. Bosner, who was living in Dallas, said he was a dedicated fan of the so-called cosmic cowboy scene in Austin, and Scafe had directed a music program in Illinois.[7] Next, according to the official ACL history:

> After [Bosner] turned Arhos on to Jan Reid's book *The Improbable Rise of Redneck Rock*, the trio came up with the idea of a TV program to showcase Austin's diverse mix of country, blues, folk and psychedelia. Thus *Austin City Limits* (title courtesy of Bosner, who saw the sign every week when he commuted from Dallas to Austin) was born.[8]

Bill Arhos told this version of events many times over the years. He told it to Jan Reid, and it's repeated in the text and on the dust jacket of a revised edition of *Redneck Rock* published in 2006. But the story makes no sense, because *Redneck Rock* wasn't published until 1974, the year *after* Tolleson enlisted Arhos in the shooting, editing, and broadcasting of the Armadillo Country Music Review, all of which happened between July 8 and 29, 1973. You can find Bill Arhos's chronologically impossible assertion almost everywhere: music books, dissertations, Wikipedia, and every place where amateur historians have tried to describe the Austin music scene of the 1970s.[9]

Arhos died in 2015 at the age of eighty, and I never got around to having a discussion with him on this particular topic.[10] It would sure be nice to see Armadillo given proper credit for putting Austin music on television, but I'm not saying we were ripped off. We had a lot of other irons in the fire at the time. Plus, as Mike Tolleson points out, "KLRN had the money and gear and we did not."

Early on, we had at least a hand in the production of *Austin City Limits*. Arhos had tapped Mike Tolleson to book the talent for the first season. "We were consultants," said Mike, "but we wanted a role as coproducer." Music video had long been one of Mike's passions and areas of

legal expertise. He laid out the need for clearing rights to the musical performances for commercial use following the PBS run. But unfortunately,
his advice fell on deaf ears.

"This was all new to them," said Mike. "Arhos and his people were
just focused on getting shows on the air, making their budgets, things like
that." There were other things that Mike Tolleson and the *ACL* people
didn't see eye to eye on, including his role as consultant. Eventually, the
two entities parted ways, and Mike's job was taken over by Joe Gracey.

Even though music from "Armadillo Country" went on without us
under a different name and with different people in charge, for many years
Austin City Limits continued to draw from the Armadillo talent pool. And
during its third season, the show famously began using Gary P. Nunn's
"London Homesick Blues" for its end credits. So we got a shout-out ("I
wanna go home with the Armadillo / Good country music from Amarillo
and Abilene") every week for the next several decades.

★ ★ ★

Let's return to July 8, 1973, the night we taped the Armadillo Country
Music Review. I was rightfully proud when I went onstage to introduce
Willie, but I also felt compelled to make a sideways reference to what we
all knew, that buzzards were circling over the Nixon White House:

> There's a story going around the United States of America, going
> around about the same time that the government's crumbling, and
> the economics are falling apart and the prices are going up, and the
> story . . . is that there's something weird going on in Austin, Texas.
> And what seems to be weird is that the cowboys and the hippies
> are getting along better, probably, than anywhere in the world. And
> maybe it's because the cowboys took a look at the hippies a couple of
> days ago and said, "They look more like my grandfather than I do."[11]

Another historic thing happened that night after the taping. Mike Tolleson and Carlotta Pankratz brought Willie back to the office to discuss
booking another date at the Armadillo. Bobby Hedderman, who was
still simmering from the last dustup, saw visions of Willie's friends spit-
ting on the floor; of gun-toting slimeballs pulling their redneck, used-car-
salesman, mafia-intimidation tactics on our security team; and of every

good-old-boy friend of Willie's slipping in and out of the box office as Willie was being adored by his new, young fans.

"Willie, I'd love to have you do a show," Bobby said, "but you have to control your friends. I can't have them pushing around the staff and packing heat in the building."

Willie glanced over at Mike and Carlotta, a little grin on his face. In his Blackland drawl, he said, "They don't all carry guns."

Mike and Carlotta went pale. Willie's eyes reminded Bobby of an eagle's—dark, piercing, and yet unknowable.

"We can both make some money here," Bobby said, "but we don't run the Armadillo like a saloon."

"Bob," said Mike, attempting to intervene, "Willie comes from a different—"

"I'm not having my staff endangered by those guys," said Bobby. He was fuming. "Willie, we want you to play here, but you've got to control them."

Willie retained his trademark cool, his voice soft, his eyes sparkling. "I can't be responsible for what somebody else does."

Temporarily shelving the disagreement, Bobby asked Willie if he wanted to schedule another date.

"Call my manager on Monday," Willie said.

Neil Reshen was Willie's manager, and Monday morning, Bobby called Reshen's office in New York. He had hardly begun talking when Reshen interrupted.

"Willie said, 'Fuck you,'" said Reshen. "If his friends aren't good enough for you, then neither is he."

"Yeah," Bobby said, "he's probably right."

Bobby hung up the phone, and that was that. Less than a year after his first show at the Armadillo, the love between Shotgun Willie and the Armadillo had grown cold.

THEN THE RAINS CAME

★

After we sweated through August, and usually September and part of October, a flood was just about the last thing we worried about at the Armadillo. But then came October 9, 1973. I woke up that morning to the sound of my bedroom door banging open. While reaching for my glasses, I blindly stepped out of bed and into ankle-deep water.

A guy who worked for the Grateful Dead's record label was still asleep in the guest room. He was in town to promote the Dead's new album, which in a bizarre coincidence was titled *Wake of the Flood*.

The bathroom window looked out on the backyard and carport area, where flood debris was stacked up against the gate. The water level was up to the windows of my Dodge Charger. I climbed out on the window ledge, inching along until I reached the gate. As soon as I released the latch, a log the size of a canoe rushed past. Opening the gate lowered the water level in the carport considerably, but on the front side of the house, the water was up to the windowsills and still rising.

Inside, the water was a couple of inches deep, but you could see around the front-door frame that the outside water was really desirous of coming inside. The stereo was high and dry, so I put the Dead's new record on the turntable and cranked the volume, in the hopes it would send a gentle message to my guest as he awakened.

The phone rang. It was Galen Barber, the Armadillo's sanitation engineer. "Boss," he said, "you've got to see this to believe it."

"Oh, I believe it, Galen," I said. "I'll be right down."

The night before, Robert Gower and his brother-in-law had worked late putting the finishing touches on our new basement game room. It was a fully equipped arcade, with coin-operated pinball, shuffleboard, foosball, car-race games, and a new, state-of-the-art Pong machine.

During the night, one of the Colorado River's South Austin tributaries, Bouldin Creek, had turned into a river feeding into Town Lake. When Robert Gower and Bobby Hedderman drove down South First the next morning, they encountered the overflow. They made it all the way to the last block before Barton Springs Road, where they had to pull the car over and wade the rest of the way. The water was waist-high and moving swiftly as they crossed the bridge. Bobby was so worried about the game room, he didn't mention his fear that some of the things going bump against his body might be water moccasins, rats, or other nasty creatures.

They entered the building through the side garage door. There they saw Galen Barber, soaking wet, standing in six inches of water next to the stairwell. The roaring sound they heard was floodwater draining down the stairs, a cascade of doom.

"It's been going like this for a while," Galen said.

Robert desperately wanted to save whatever could be saved. He hesitated for a moment, then bravely climbed down. Down in the game room, the water came up to his knees. Each footstep stirred up about an inch and a half of silt on the floor.

By the time I got there, we were all starting to feel sorry for ourselves. Once a game room, now an underwater cave. I wanted to say something that sounded managerial, but nothing came to mind. Doug Sahm, who usually drew a good crowd, was scheduled to play that night, and we needed the money. Somebody had to call the radio stations to tell them the show was off.

"I think we're fucked," said Bobby Hedderman.

"You know what?" said Robert Gower. "I doubt that anything's ruined."

"Hold on," I said. I took a deep breath to stall for time. "Let me think a minute."

A volunteer appeared. Willis Alan Ramsey, a popular but absurdly low-key Austin singer-songwriter, held two tools, neither of them a guitar.

"Where do we start?" he said, a shovel in one hand, a rake in the other. Other willing helpers soon followed.

"Eddie, do you think it's possible to save this thing?" said Bobby.

"Hell yeah," I said. "Let's drag these carpets out of here." More people showed up. Nobody liked what they saw, but they all pitched in.

That night, eight hundred people showed up for the show. Sir Doug Sahm, the most cosmic of the cosmic cowboys, his shoulder-length hair topped off with a cowboy hat and wearing blue jeans and pointy-toe boots, knew just what to sing for them. For starters, there was the 1965 hit by Sir Douglas Quintet, "The Rains Came." *Rain, rain, rain . . .*

With Augie Meyers's Vox Continental organ percolating skating-rink riffs, the crowd made their own kind of thunder, cheering so loudly they almost drowned out the vocals. But that was OK, because we knew the song so well.

Hippie karma shown in beer pricing. After raising the prices across the board, we went back and lowered Shiner to 30 cents so it would be the cheapest. Photograph by Burton Wilson.

HOME WITH THE ARMADILLO

Neither flood nor folly could put a damper on our dreams and schemes, but Texas weather continued to throw interesting wrinkles into the fabric of Armadillo history. The staff was now on salary. Our beautiful new beer garden, which set the stage for a new era of pleasant experiences, did a booming business in the summer months. Encouraged, we put big, high-speed electric fans inside the hall, but the only difference they made in the environment was an increase in background noise. That winter we had to close the beer garden again, but we had some heating inside the hall, which raised our hopes that we were about to become a year-round venue. We used a smaller portable stage in the center of the hall, erecting curtains to create a smaller space. We grossed $555,000 in 1973 and reduced our loss to $10,000. Having our own upgraded sound system (previously, we had been renting a sound system for larger acts) improved our ability to produce high-quality local shows. And for the first time, we began to effectively market free shows, dollar shows, and weeknight shows. All in all, we had a much more consistent, six-night-a-week operation.

We never stopped looking for new things to do with the old armory building and new ways to market the scene we had going. Jim Finney brought in some recording equipment, and with the beneficent intervention of Hank Alrich, a recording studio called Onion Audio was born. Finney was a South Austin native who spent his teens playing in rock bands and hanging out at the Vulcan. He had an added impetus to hang out at the Armadillo after his girlfriend, a former topless dancer in Dallas, got a job there as a waitress. Finney kept an eye on his sweetheart, and in the bargain, his passion for audio sweetened the Armadillo's in-house radio productions. Before Finney got involved, the commercials we were producing for radio stations were substandard at best.

Finney produced the first radio spots on his four-track recorder. But when I saw him loading more gear into the room behind the stage, I looked at the wall and said, "Why don't we just poke a hole in there? We could run the audio snake [the conduit for all the stage microphones] through there. Then you could actually record gigs."

Finney's friend John Causey agreed to loan us a bunch of gear that wasn't being used by his live sound company, Xeno Sound. Some of it was past its prime or antiquated, but with everything cobbled together, we had the beginnings of a real recording studio. There were little Shure mic mixers that lacked tone controls, pads, and graphic equalizers, but they worked. Finney picked up all the extra expenses. A band who played the Dillo could have a live recording of their set for $150, tape included. The arrangement worked for almost three years, ending when we had to give some of the equipment back.

As with a lot of people who worked at the Armadillo, Jim Finney's real passion was being on the other side of that wall between the studio and the stage. Finney played with several bands, including Homegrown and Caught in the Act. "There was always the possibility of getting a gig down here," Finney said. "Where else are they hiring real long-haired, goofy-looking people?"

Finney was a family man who came to work after dropping his kids off at school. I was in the habit of getting up early every morning for my workout, so we'd both show up around eight in the morning, drink coffee, burn a morning joint, talk music, and plan the day.

Most of the spots Finney recorded in-house aired on Austin's 95.5 KOKE-FM, where a new format called progressive country shared broadcast time with Austin's only Spanish-language programming. KOKE-FM billed itself as Super Roper Radio, its playlist bearing a powerful resemblance to the music that was being performed on the Armadillo stage. On KOKE-FM you could hear Willie Nelson, Jerry Jeff Walker, Michael

Murphey, B. W. Stevenson, Willis Alan Ramsey, Townes Van Zandt, Sir Doug Sahm, the New Riders of the Purple Sage, the Grateful Dead, Commander Cody and His Lost Planet Airmen, and Asleep at the Wheel. In the same way that the Armadillo wasn't your run-of-the-mill, pinkie-ring-wearing concert promoter, KOKE-FM broke every rule in the commercial radio programmer's playbook, and it sounded great because of it.

If only via osmosis, the Armadillo had clearly been instrumental in creating the progressive country format, and had practically midwifed the birth of KOKE-FM as well. It seemed like an opportune moment to meet with Ken Moyer, the station manager, to discuss a business relationship between Armadillo Productions and KOKE-FM.

The team I rounded up for the meeting included Michael Osborne (from the old Directions advertising agency), Micael Priest, and two very talented disc jockeys, Joe Gracey and Fermin "Speedy" Perez. Gracey was multitalented, a savvy music critic, a songwriter, and a singer with a fine voice. Speedy hailed from Lubbock, where his family was prominent in the radio business.

Our pitch to Ken Moyer was to turn the programming over to us. In my mind, it was a perfectly logical suggestion, since KOKE-FM's playlist seemed to be taken almost directly from the Armadillo's calendar of live shows. At one point after we'd articulated our pitch, Moyer excused himself to go to the bathroom.

Speedy whispered to me, "This ain't gonna work. He looks at us like we're trash."

Sure enough, Moyer didn't buy our pitch. In place of our team, he hired a heavyset, humorless broadcaster from the Rio Grande Valley named Rusty Bell. On the plus side, Speedy Perez and Joe Gracey remained on the KOKE-FM deejay roster, and they knew what they were doing. Bell did his best to execute the plan we had articulated to his boss, and *Billboard*, which apparently also liked our style, gave him the Trendsetter of the Year award.

★ ★ ★

Nashville singer-songwriter Tom T. Hall was one of those country entertainers who came off like an old lounge act. He was a jaded singer with a cigarette and microphone in the same hand, a knight in polyester armor and a helmet of razor-cut, Brylcreemed hair. I didn't know if our people would love him or hate him.

Chip Taylor opened the show. Chip was as good a singer-songwriter as they come, and he was so well received, it looked even grimmer for the headliner. The response to Chip was testimony to the clout of KOKE-FM. It looked like half the people there knew the lyrics to the songs. Granted, some of them had been monster hits. He was the original composer of "Wild Thing," the gnarly three-chord garage rock classic that was a hit for the Troggs and many other bands, including Jimi Hendrix, who ran it through his phase-shifted, upside-down Stratocaster and looped it around the rings of Saturn on the way back to the garage. At the other end of the spectrum was "Angel of the Morning," a countrified, anthem-like pop ballad covered by Jackie DeShannon.

Chip Taylor ended his set by thanking everyone on the staff whose name he could remember. He brought out his two preteen children to sing with him on the last songs. One reason for his affection for Austin was that it was the only town where he had measurable record sales. Shortly after the Armadillo experience, he quit the music business for twenty-five years and became a professional gambler in Atlantic City. He finally left there after being banned for card counting.

Tom T. Hall's touring band was super tight, super professional, and super Nashville. The band played an intro number, teasing the crowd before the star made his entrance, finally climaxing with the come-on, "Welcome the greatest storyteller in America!"

Hall oozed loungey charm as he schmoozed with the audience, singing "Old Dogs, Children, and Watermelon Wine," "I Like Beer," and a long string of chart-topping jukebox favorites. To my relief, the crowd ate it up. Things got almost as rowdy as at a real honky-tonk on payday.

After the last song, the crowd called him back for an encore, then another, and another. Microphone in one hand, cigarette in the other, he sang four encores, and if I remember correctly, did the same corny song all four times. The Nashville cat's polyester suit hung heavy with sweat, but his smile was bright and genuine. It was pretty clear that he and the members of his Nashville band were stunned by the reception. As he paused before the final encore of the night, he said, "I don't know what you guys are smoking, but I want some."

The room practically thundered in response. Austin, he said, was surely destined to become one of the three great music cities in America. He didn't name the other two. He knelt at the edge of the stage and shook hands with every hand that came within reach. Finally, as the showman made a final bow and headed offstage, I noticed his right hand cupped around something. As he turned for a final wave, he raised the joint someone had slipped him in a respectful salute.

With shows like this one, there were always doubts. Would the hippies cross over and come see a Nashville act? Would the rednecks cross over and come to a hippie joint? Although Hall's fee was fairly steep for us, we gambled that we would get some of both crowds. We booked him for four nights, hoping that the word would get out and buzz would build. In the end, the crossover happened, but not in sufficient numbers. We took a bath on Tom T. Hall.

Commander Cody and His Lost Planet Airmen returned to Austin in November to record a live album at the Armadillo, in the knowledge that it was really the best place in the world for them to do it. None of their studio albums had come close to capturing the energy of the band that we had seen and felt at our music hall. Every show of theirs at the Armadillo was a beer-soaked, pot-stoked, wild party, from the first chord to the last.

The resulting album, *Live from Deep in the Heart of Texas*, featured cover artwork by Jim Franklin. In addition to capturing the full intensity of the band, the recording also caught the hollering, stomping audience response for which the Dillo was famous. The crowd sounds were so good, in fact, that samples of it were later overdubbed on live albums by other bands.

When Bill Monroe, the Father of Bluegrass, stepped out of his bus and looked out over our moon-crater parking lot, you could see the skepticism on his face. His brow was furrowed like a freshly plowed cornfield. Grumpy and stern, he reminded me of an old preacher or a school superintendent, the kind of person who lacks a slick politician's ability to pretend, even briefly, that everything's fine. Having been absent from Austin for several years, he seemed taken aback at the notion that things might have changed since his last visit.

As the show got under way, however, you could see his stony veneer crumbling before the crowd's vocal embrace of his purer-than-pure bluegrass. They loved him and he loved them back.

"You make sure the man that runs this place has us back," he told the audience. After the last song, Monroe kept going. He talked for a good while, confiding that he hadn't been in Austin since Hank Williams died. Finally, he wished us all a Merry Christmas. "And each and every one of you," he said, "drive carefully on your way home."

Bill Monroe and band onstage at AWHQ, November 22, 1974.
Photograph by Burton Wilson.

During the fall of 1973, in one of the best executive decisions possible, I hired Ramsey Wiggins as our new publicist. Ramsey had deep Austin roots. His brother Lanny had been the driving force behind the Waller Creek Boys, the group Janis Joplin had joined after a Threadgill's hootenanny back in the mid-1960s. Ramsey had also worked on the staff of the *Ranger*, the storied satire magazine at UT, and at Rip Off Press in San Francisco.[1] With his history, it was naturally assumed that, in addition to publicist, he would also take on the responsibility of house intellectual, which he did without complaint.

The November 1973 issue of *Texas Monthly* carried a five-thousand-word article about Austin's new country music scene titled "The Coming of Redneck Hip," cowritten by Jan Reid and Don Roth.[2] It was nice to have a feature article saying that "Armadillo offers some of the best live music in the country," although many other aspects of our emporium were noted with something between severe understatement and faint, grudging praise. The lack of air conditioning was prominently mentioned. Our Art Squad's murals and giant canvases, including works that were destined to fetch huge prices by collectors, were dismissed as "artwork of modest inspiration." The big, greasy nachos and other output of the Armadillo kitchen, whose praises were being sung by performers around the world, were said to be "pretty fair." The acoustics, they said, were "surprisingly good."

The big theme of the story was the boom in progressive country. I give the writers credit for acknowledging the role of Kenneth Threadgill in being the granddaddy and figurehead of the country music community. Another thing they did a good job of conveying was the electricity in the air during an exciting show at the Dillo, when the place was a stew of hippies, rednecks, and other folks "bellowing, stomping" to show their appreciation for good music and a good time. That was the kind of love that put the double *o*'s in the Austin music boom.

"Word has spread among performers that Armadillo's audiences are perhaps the most spontaneous and appreciative in the country," the article said. "As a result the national reputation-makers have been very kind to Eddie Wilson and his Armadillo, and he is now booking acts that he once could barely afford to phone."

The writers described the night in April 1973 when Willie Nelson played with opening acts Greezy Wheels and Man Mountain and the

Green Slime Boys. The crowd, they wrote, was "a visually bizarre mix of beehive hairdos, naked midriffs, and bare hippie feet. . . . But Nelson's music relieved any cultural strain that developed beneath him."

Although the article devoted some space to the other musicians involved in the progressive country scene, Willie was the centerpiece of it. The writers praised him as "the grinning, gentle rebel who made the music industry come to him on his own terms yet somehow remained the almost universally admired nice guy and artist." Others featured included Waylon Jennings, B. W. Stevenson, Jerry Jeff Walker, and Michael Murphey.

"The Coming of Redneck Hip" concluded with a detailed account of Willie's first picnic, sparing no mention of the brawls, security lapses, power failure, and other screwups, but it then pivoted from the topic of recent failures to future potential. The writers were guardedly optimistic that the Austin music boom was just getting started.

"The day after the Dripping Springs fiasco," they wrote, "Eddie Wilson slammed his fist against a wall in anguish and humiliation, but he was already formulating thoughts on how to do it next time."[3] They were right about that, except next time it would be without Willie Nelson.

By the time "The Coming of Redneck Hip" came out in November 1973, a lot of other writers had already covered the coming together of rednecks and hippies in some detail. Not that it was all old news, but a lot of the same material had been in Chet Flippo's *Rolling Stone* feature, "Uncle Zeke's Rock Emporium," published over a year earlier, in October 1972.[4] The emergence of the cosmic cowboy/progressive country genre and resulting cultural phenomena had also been covered in weekly updates by Townsend Miller and Joe Gracey in the *Statesman* and in various features in the *Daily Texan*. At the end of 1972, many journalists were trying to come to grips with what they saw as a phenomenon developing at the Armadillo. In a two-part story in the *Daily Texan* published in December 1972, A. B. Gunter stated:

It is really a good thing when music can bring together two social factions like flower children and cowboys (to be euphemistic) and not result in any confrontations. Surely this is an example of what God had in mind when He created musicians.[5]

Elsewhere, Gunter said that the "best example" of the melting pot of musical styles in Austin was what was taking place at Armadillo World Headquarters:

> Nowhere else will you see longhairs rubbing shoulders with cowboys without any feeling of threat or unpleasantness; nowhere else is there spiritual room for both of these factions.
>
> The credit for this can go to Eddie Wilson, Armadillo's owner. He is trying to achieve something different for Austin, and he is doing it. His two outstanding qualities as a club owner are his desire to have people enjoy themselves and his love of music.[6]

"The Coming of Redneck Hip" helped create more buzz for the Armadillo and the country rock scene in Austin. Sensing a bonanza, Jan Reid liked the subject matter so well that he threw his energies into producing a full-length book titled *The Improbable Rise of Redneck Rock*, which was rushed into print by Heidelberg Publishing in 1974.[7]

All the attention was great for business, and we appreciated the affirmations, but as time went on, it had a weird effect on what the academics refer to as "public memory." Long story short, the Austin music scene, and the scene at the Armadillo in particular, became so closely identified with progressive country and the cosmic cowboy thing that it sucked all the air out of the attention that should have been given to about a dozen other genres of music, all of which we supported and identified with.

Jason Mellard, a scholar of music and history, analyzed the types of bands who played at the Armadillo between 1970 and 1980, crunched the numbers, and came to some interesting conclusions in an article published in the *Journal of Texas Music History* in 2010. He even illustrated some of his points on a bar graph.[8]

From 1972–1974, Willie played at the Armadillo a total of seven times, Waylon played five, and neither of them ever played there again. Other country-influenced acts continued to perform at the Dillo, but they were in the minority. Even in 1973, the year we did Willie's first Fourth of July Picnic, the offerings were diverse. We had everyone from Shawn Phillips to Slade, and in between we had Frank Zappa, Martin Mull, Bette Midler, Leo Kottke, John McLaughlin and the Mahavishnu Orchestra, and Sonny

Terry and Brownie McGhee. Besides continuing to have country and country rock, we also had ballet every month.

Next time you hear Gary P. Nunn sing, "I wanna go home with the Armadillo / Good country music from Amarillo and Abilene," remember that a lot of music besides country rocked and rolled the Armadillo World Headquarters.[9]

LONG LIVE LONGNECKS

★

From the first twinkle of a dream of the Armadillo World Headquarters, an in-house marketing agency had been an arrow we wanted in our quiver, just as surely as we wanted a nursery for the employees' kids, an art gallery, and a jewelry store. And of all the things I tried to do to bring more revenue into the Dillo, our agency was the most successful. The advertising campaigns we did for Lone Star Beer made it possible for some of us to earn a living wage for the first time, and more important, it was creatively rewarding. What a great ride it was.

The new agency began with a simple idea. The Armadillo already had a grip on the young, beer-drinking, music-loving market. We sold more draft Lone Star Beer than any other place except for the Astrodome in Houston, which could accommodate fifty thousand more customers than the Dillo. Adding a sense of urgency was the fact that Coors, after a long delay, was finally coming to Texas. Coors had a sheen of hipness at the time, since it was unpasteurized and had been difficult to get. But we were confident that we could deliver our market to Lone Star.

Looking around at the staff I worked with, it wasn't difficult to round up the team that would make our agency a hit. I'd already been a PR flack for the Brewers Association, and I've always been an idea generator. Mike

Tolleson was one of the sharpest entertainment lawyers in Austin, and he always had his finger on the pulse of the moment. Woody Roberts, radio promotion genius, had saved Willie's first picnic. Randy McCall, Tolleson's pal from Southern Methodist University, was a CPA whose former clients included AT&T and the government of Panama, but he'd moved to Austin because he wanted to play bass more often.

The name of the agency was TYNA/TACI, provided gratis by my Five Dollar Name company. Pronounced "Teena Tacky," the acronym stood for "Thought You'd Never Ask / The Austin Consultants Inc." The short form was "Austin Consultants."

It was the spring of 1974 when we drafted a set of proposals for marketing work we could do for Lone Star Beer. Barry Sullivan, the marketing director for Lone Star, set up a meeting and we drove to San Antonio feeling pretty excited about it. Besides being our first big campaign, this was going to be the spark that lit the fuse on a cultural moment. But what I didn't know until very recently, when four of us got together at Threadgill's to look at some pertinent files and video from that time, was that the meeting with Lone Star might have been staged much sooner, and with only one of the TYNA/TACI team present: Woody Roberts.[1]

Our writer/musician friend Jesse Sublett was with us at the table at Threadgill's, asking questions about how the relationship with Lone Star began. Mike Tolleson and I were trying to narrow down the date that we started communicating with Barry Sullivan. Jesse grew impatient and said, "So, nobody remembers how the first meeting came about?"

Finally, Woody Roberts spoke up.

"Well, I do," he said.

"Oh, you do?" Jesse said.

"Of course," Woody said, speaking between bites of cucumber-and-tomato salad. "There are different sides to the story, the Armadillo side, and my side, and so on."

What Woody meant was that he knew that Barry Sullivan was already acquainted with me as well as with Mike Tolleson, Bobby Hedderman, Jim Franklin, and others at the Dillo. We also knew Sullivan's district sales manager, Jerry Retzloff. But I never knew until this lunch meeting years later that Barry Sullivan had tried to steal Woody out from under us. Woody told it like this:

Barry Sullivan and Jerry Retzloff had been coming up here from San Antonio because they wanted to find out why Armadillo was selling more Lone Star draft beer than any other place in Texas. One night—I think Commander Cody was playing—I was introduced to them by Eddie. And after we talked a while—maybe it was that night or the next time I saw him—Barry said, "I know what you did for Willie's first picnic, and I want to hire you to be the advertising director for Lone Star Beer." And I said to him, "I've got a commitment to Armadillo. We have a radio show, a TV show, and a record company through here, and that's my direction. That's what I'm doing."

Barry said, "I'll give you $60,000 a year." I said, "Give the money to the Armadillo, let them pay me something." Ever since the incredible success of Willie's first picnic, Eddie had been asking me to come join the Armadillo staff. I knew they didn't make much money, and I didn't know what I could contribute to earn my keep up there. Armadillo was almost three years old at that point. But Barry said, "I don't think we can do that."[2]

Barry Sullivan's hesitation was primarily due to the Texas Alcoholic Beverage Commission's "three-tier" law, which forbade beer companies from making cash contributions to retailers such as the Armadillo. Fortunately, being familiar with the ins and outs of the TABC, I knew there was a way around this problem: forming a marketing agency as an entity separate from the Armadillo. Armadillo World Headquarters was our client. We rented our own, separate office space in the building.

"I didn't want to appear to be pushing," said Woody, "because the Armadillo had a great thing going, and I thought this was my chance to be involved and pull my own weight. Eddie, being the spiritual leader and trail boss at the Dillo, came back with the idea of us being a corporation, and he named it Thought You'd Never Ask / The Austin Consultants Inc., which was a great name. Was it legal? I don't know, but nobody ever asked."[3]

Barry Sullivan got a kick out of it. With a wink and a handshake, he agreed that Lone Star was free to do business with the Austin Consultants. Just as important, Mike Tolleson and I were thrilled to work with Woody Roberts, a person we both recognized as a true genius, and I don't mind admitting that Woody's appraisal of our abilities and achievements gave our own confidence a boost. Woody remembered us as the "two main brains" at the Dillo:

Anything they wanted to do at the Armadillo would be accepted there. By the time I got to the Armadillo, I'd quit my vice president/general manager job at KTSA-FM in San Antonio, but I'd been working with talent since I was eighteen. Sometimes it was a great talent, sometimes they were temperamental and stuff, but I recognized in a second that Eddie was a star. So when we started the agency, we ended up with Eddie—he's got brilliant ideas, he's a genius, and he's obviously a great person to talk to people and bring them in. Then there was Mike, the lawyer, and Randy [McCall], the CPA, which was a good idea, and me as the media guy. It was an ideal mix.[4]

For our first big sales meeting, Mike, Randy, Woody, and I piled into a VW Bug and drove to San Antonio to meet with Barry Sullivan. Sullivan's own track record was pretty impressive. While he was still a big-league hockey player in Canada, Sullivan had started working at Falstaff Brewing Corporation during the off-season. At Falstaff in the 1950s, he worked with Hank Thompson, one of the first country singers to have a corporate sponsorship. Hank Thompson was one hell of a cool guitar player and honky-tonk singer. During his long-term relationship with Falstaff, Thompson recorded jingles for the brand, sang the beer's praises on television, toured with his own sound and light system, and flew his own airplane on tour. Thompson's song "A Six Pack to Go," recorded in 1960, had sold more than a million copies.[5]

Barry Sullivan had also helped resurrect Narragansett, a faltering label owned by Falstaff that was brewed in Rhode Island. In 1970, one year after Woodstock, Sullivan came up with a savvy PR campaign featuring a series of mini–Woodstock festivals in every corner of the Narragansett market. Associating the brand with performers like Janis Joplin, Led Zeppelin, and Santana helped turn Narragansett's fortunes around.

Sullivan, who still had the look of a former hockey player or pro fullback, gave us a warm welcome at Lone Star headquarters. He escorted us straight to the brewery's hospitality room, where we began discussing possibilities over pitchers of cold draft beer. At this point in time, Lone Star was a sagging regional brand that was losing sales to the big national labels. They needed us.

We were treated like visiting royalty as Barry Sullivan escorted us around the brewery, introducing us to everyone, including Harry Jersig, president of the company. Jersig was the youngest old man I'd ever met, full of piss and vinegar, defying the aging process by spending as much time as possible fishing, hunting, and drinking.

To our surprise, Jersig wanted us to work on marketing the longneck, the recyclable bottle that had once been the industry standard but had lost favor after the advent of nonreturnable cans and bottles. In the early 1970s, America was still under the spell of the "throwaway" craze: disposable bottles, cans, boxes, and all manner of containers for consumer products were promoted as a modern convenience, as if it were our patriotic duty to waste resources.

Beer in longnecks certainly tasted better than beer in cans. I remembered from my Texas beer history that, in terms of flavor, the next best thing to drinking your beer out of a clean glass the same temperature as the beer is drinking it from a longneck bottle, where the air in the neck of the bottle creates more head. As a beer joint proprietor, however, I hated stocking longneck bottles. Beer in plastic cups was easy to manage. Glass bottles conjured visions of shattered slivers on the floor and weapons that could draw blood when used to conk a bad actor in the head. Even though we got the contract to promote Lone Star Beer in longneck bottles, the Armadillo continued to serve it in pitchers and plastic cups only.

The deal we got was similar to the one that Woody Roberts had already discussed with Sullivan, except that, instead of hiring one advertising chief, Sullivan got a whole agency. We were paid $60,000 a year, or $5,000 a month, plus an override of 17.65 percent on production costs such as renting studio time, hiring musicians and writers, printing marketing materials, and so forth, which allowed us some leeway on costs that earned us some extra money.

We started the campaign by printing up five thousand black T-shirts with a Jim Franklin design of a map of Texas dotted with thousands of tiny armadillos, each bearing a Lone Star Beer logo. We mailed the shirts to hundreds of rock bands. It wasn't our favorite T-shirt design, but it got the word out to the kind of people we wanted to reach, not just in this country but around the world.

The part of the campaign that probably had the biggest reach and longest life, however, was the slogan "Long Live Longnecks," which was coined by Jim Franklin. Under our contract with Lone Star, we hired artists to produce a series of posters for the longneck campaign. Without a doubt, the posters that Franklin produced under this arrangement represent some of the best beer-and-music marketing artwork ever produced.

My favorite Jim Franklin Lone Star poster is probably the one with the Lone Star "prairie schooner." The picture shows a scrubby southwestern landscape with a covered wagon inside a Lone Star longneck bottle, with an armadillo in the lower right corner rearing on its hind legs. Several puns are at work all at once: the schooner was an ocean-going sailing ship used to carry people and cargo across the Atlantic from the 1600s through the 1800s; it was also the nickname of the Conestoga wagons used by millions of Americans in their westward migration in the 1800s; and it was the name of a beer-drinking vessel. The poster depicted a "prairie schooner" in a bottle, as opposed to the usual ship in a bottle. But you didn't even have to realize all those things to dig the poster. It was just visually compelling, funny, and fun to look at.

"The posters were fabulous," said Woody Roberts, "and they're the only thing that remains. But the fact is, those posters only went into certain kinds of nightclubs. They didn't go into kicker bars. But everywhere you went you saw the 'Long Live Longnecks' stickers. They were on pickup trucks, in parking lots, in redneck joints in West Texas, in sophisticated neighborhoods, everywhere."

We had wanted to do bumper stickers, but it was a challenge because we weren't allowed to put the word "beer" on them. I said, "Why don't we do a bumper sticker shaped like a longneck?" Woody wasn't convinced.

Then Jim Franklin brought some of his work over to my house. We were looking at it, and Woody saw Jim's slogan "Long Live Longnecks" under one of his posters and said, "That's it!"

NGNECKS
T.M.

"I went to this guy at a printshop in San Antonio," Woody said, "and told him to make it look like the 'America: Love It or Leave It' bumper sticker, which was real prevalent in Texas at the time."

The Lone Star logo was so small it was hard to see. Sullivan didn't get it at first, but success made a believer out of him.

For the radio commercials, we ventured into new, barely charted terrain, much like those pioneers, but with Woody Roberts as our trailblazing leader. For the first step in our market research, Woody compiled a list of about two hundred potential words and phrases that would elicit positive reactions in radio listeners. The list was delivered to Dr. Tom Turicchi at his psychographic research lab in Richardson, Texas. A market research group was selected using criteria developed by prior research at Lone Star. The typical Lone Star drinker, Barry Sullivan told us, was a thirty-seven-year-old blue-collar male with some high school education. Your basic redneck, in other words. Our goal was to insinuate the Armadillo consumer into that profile.

Dr. Turicchi sent a street team out to Dallas-area malls to recruit twenty-one-year-old college students who liked progressive country music. Each one who agreed to show up at Dr. Turicchi's lab for the marketing test got five bucks. All they had to do to earn another five bucks was listen to some music and react to Woody's list of words and phrases.

The lab was a small auditorium with rows of school desks wired to four-channel galvanometers, or lie detectors. Each subject was hooked up to a galvanometer via metal splints strapped to two fingers on the left hand with Velcro straps. On the desk were four buttons for the subject to push. They were asked to rank words, phrases, and music, registering a positive or negative response by pushing the appropriate button.

After Woody's list of words and phrases was tested on the subjects, Dr. Turicchi analyzed the results on the galvanometer tapes. Some of the results were amusing. Of all the words and phrases, a single one had zero negative responses and a 100 percent favorable response rate: "high."

To a gang of Dead Heads like us, this looked like the best omen since the days when you could buy legal peyote from Sledd's Nursery on Enfield Road for a dime a bud. The kids liked several other words too, especially the sounds of "fine" and "Harry Jersig's Lone Star beer."

Woody trimmed the list to a dozen or so buzzwords, then called Bob Livingston and Gary P. Nunn of Jerry Jeff Walker's Lost Gonzo Band. Woody asked the songwriters if they could write a song about Lone Star Beer that incorporated as many of the favorable phrases as possible. What we got was a song called "The Nights Never Get Lonely." The lyrics made poetry of the test-market-approved words: "Dancing in the moonlight under Lone Star skies / In the Lone Star State with a Lone Star high / And the nights, they never get lonely." And then a low baritone voice intoned, "Harry Jersig's Lone Star Beer. It's really fine."

We booked the Gonzos at Pecan Street Studios and nailed a really good track. We sent the recording to Dr. Turicchi, who played it for a test group. The participants hated the steel guitar on the track, but everything else tested positive. We were up against a deadline with no time to rerecord, so Woody decided to overdub some intellectualization. Chet Flippo got a late-night phone call from us asking if he wanted to do some voice work in the studio.

Chet initially resisted our request. He had the flu, he said, and on top of that, he was worn out from a long trip he'd taken with his wife, Martha Hume. We got the impression that something else was bothering him. Eventually, he came out with it. His parents were Pentecostals, he said, and if he did a beer commercial, his father might disown him.

Assurances were quickly offered. We don't want you to advertise beer, I told him, we want you to tell us about yourself. You're a great music writer, I said. Tell people about the new music in Austin, the stuff some people call cross country, others call progressive country, but whatever you call it, it sounds like this . . .

Chet finally gave in, although it was hard to tell whether it was my gift for persuasion or the fact that he and Martha needed the money. They were about to move to New York, and with Harry Jersig's Lone Star Beer covering the bills, TYNA/TACI paid good money.

Other versions of "The Nights Never Get Lonely" were recorded later, including Freddie King's version, which could've been a big radio hit, but we also loved the versions by the Pointer Sisters and Sunny and the Sunliners. Our campaign was so successful that it's been written about numerous times as an example of cultural branding, but the details often get scrambled in strange ways. An article in *Texas Monthly* in 1982 got a lot of the background right but called the song "Harina Tortilla." *Texas Monthly* ran a story about it again in 2014, this time with a lot of emphasis on Jerry Retzloff and Jim Franklin. Writer John Spong rightfully gives a lot of credit to Retzloff for being a true believer in Lone Star whose eyes were opened by the progressive country music scene he found at Armadillo World Headquarters, and Jim Franklin gets kudos for coming up with "Long Live Longnecks" and making some damn fine art, but TYNA/TACI somehow disappears from the narrative. The effect of this kind of tunnel vision is a little like hiring a big name architect to design a swanky new house; the architect works with all the contractors for building it out, doing the finishing work, and dealing with utilities, furnishing, landscaping, et cetera, and when it's all done, someone gives all the credit to the woman who hung the drapes, the guy who did the mosaic tile in the bathrooms, and the guy who designed the fireplaces.[6]

We also did a series of cowboy commercials that were really a lot of fun. Woody Roberts had done similar commercials before in San Antonio using his friend Gordy Ham as a voice actor. Gordy came up with a character named Ramblin' Rose, and with writer Carolyn Allen they came up with additional characters and storylines that were entertaining, comical, and often laced with drug jokes that usually, but not always, went straight over the heads of the client.

For example, in a commercial during the Christmas season, Santa Claus talked about "snow" giving him a "froze nose." We did get busted on the one that mentioned Alice B. Toklas and magic brownies.

The funny thing is, when we first pitched our services to Lone Star, we didn't know what we were going into. Woody wanted to market something called the "handy keg," a bullet-shaped container in which cold-filtered beer was sold. It turned out to be Harry Jersig's favorite beer. But then Barry Sullivan told us that they wanted us to take on the returnable bottle.

That's what he called it, the "returnable bottle." Not "longneck." Back then you had throwaways and returnables. Nobody wanted returnables. They took up space in the brewery. Rewashing and relabeling them was a process that the industry wanted to abandon. During our discussion with Sullivan, we talked about how returnable bottles were environmentally responsible, but the truth is, the excitement didn't hit us until he mentioned an old brewery term for returnables: "longnecks."

Woody and I looked at each other at the same time, and we knew just what the other was thinking—that we knew where that phallic term came from and that we would have a real good time marketing it.

And we sure did.

Barry Sullivan might not have been the hippest guy around, but he was a genius at marketing. He believed, and rightly so, that the way to sell the cans was through the bottles. That is, if you sold people on the bottles, sales would go up on the cans. He was right. Our "Long Live Longnecks" campaign reversed Lone Star's historic decline in longneck sales to the tune of twenty thousand cases a month over a five-year stretch, and an increase of 1.4 million cases in fourteen months.

The campaign also paid for some of Jim Franklin's best commercial work and, as stated earlier, gave some of us a weekly living wage for a short time. But it also created some bad vibes among some of the staff members who felt that making money off of the Armadillo's hippie vibe was uncool. More about that unpleasantness later.

POT, BIG RED, ACID, COKE, AND PUMPKINS

★

Marijuana was ubiquitous and cheap in the seventies in Austin, and along with cold beer, good music, and the swimming pool at Barton Springs, it was one of the foundations of our lifestyle. In Hippie World, it was hard to think of anyone who didn't smoke pot.

Doug Sahm was probably the king of the Austin potheads. Pot seemed to fuel his loopy persona like batteries fueled the Energizer bunny. No one could keep up with him. Bogart should have been his middle name. God bless him, Doug was the worst person I ever saw at letting go of a communal joint. Behind a bar, in a parking lot, or backstage in a circle of folks taking a break, a joint would leave the lighter's hand to make its way clockwise around a circle of fellow travelers until it reached Doug.

Most likely, Doug would be the one talking, always in a rushed, hoarse whisper, telling a story we all wanted to hear. He'd stop to take in a lungful of smoke, then without letting go of the joint or his breath, he'd start rapping again, voice going deeper and hoarser as a few more sentences were produced, followed by another deep toke and a repeat performance. The story inched forward slowly, haltingly, until finally a new joint would come around the circle from the other direction. Only then would he send the captured doobie back the way it had come, allowing himself to partake of the new one.

John X. Reed and Doug Sahm backstage at AWHQ,
August 4, 1974. Photograph by Burton Wilson.

For years I assumed that Doug was a speed freak. He always seemed to be wired, talking a mile a minute. Then I learned he had a Big Red habit: he drank a dozen bottles a day of the soda pop that tasted like syrup and bubble gum, with the caffeine equivalent of half a dozen cups of coffee per bottle. When Doug kicked Big Red in later years, he didn't slow down a bit, and a new Armadillo adage was born: "Most drugs make you even more like you already are."

Pot was much easier on the body and mind than alcohol or tobacco. Psychedelics were a whole other thing. One day when the schedule was relatively light, I decided that ingesting some mushrooms and peyote would help me reexamine my inner workings. I remember clearly the sense of great understanding that came each time I settled on my pillow, briefly touching down after another curvy race through the mountains and caverns of my mind. Something new and important had just been revealed to me, but I was powerless to explain it, which left me with a feeling of baffled comfort.

Every time I ingested peyote or LSD, I knew it would be a test and my fear of insanity would come into play. Each time, I passed the test and came down feeling more confident, with renewed faith in my potential. Most of all, I came back to Earth feeling humbled. As tolerant of psychedelics as most of us were, the ritual of tripping eventually waned. It was hard work. Drugs wore me out, and I didn't have the leisure of abundant time to come down off a trip.

Psychedelics and marijuana were good drugs, but bad drugs were always lurking in the background. Heroin was no stranger in our world, but most of our crowd knew well enough to keep a distance. We blamed heroin for killing Janis Joplin and for stalling Johnny Winter's career, although moving to New York may have been part of the latter's problem, too.

Pills were confined to certain cliques, including truckers, all-night workers, and country musicians. When people talk about guys like Johnny Cash, Merle Haggard, Roger Miller, and more than a few pedal steel players getting busted repeatedly for speed, they tend to forget how many housewives and other average people in the fifties and sixties were gobbling diet pills, even when they didn't need to lose weight, and also gabbing real fast, because up until the late 1960s most of those "diet pills" were amphetamines. From the time I was with the Brewers Association to the early days of the Armadillo, I was fond of a prescribed diet pill with a muscle relaxer called Eskatrol, which I regarded as the Cadillac of speed. But it was just a minor diversion.

It was ironic that, in our community, the act of getting high in the sixties was almost a political thing, a way of rebelling against the establishment and maintaining our ideals of peace and love; then, during the decade of the Armadillo, a really insidious drug, cocaine, ushered in an age when recreational drug use went mainstream. Cocaine had once been legal. I knew the Coca-Cola story, the Casey Jones story, and how cocaine is for horses, not men. We wouldn't be tricked by the "reefer madness" hysteria this time around. Coke was too much fun. It was supposed to be nonaddictive, too.

I got my first snootful of the white powder backstage at Winterland in San Francisco. Shiva's Headband was opening for Steppenwolf and Buddy Guy. Someone backstage proffered a sparkling little mound of white at the tip of a bowie knife and hollered, "Hard! Hard!" as I attempted to inhale all the powder I could.

In seconds, sweat was dripping off my forehead onto my glasses. I felt lightheaded and dizzy. I made it to the bathroom just in time to throw up in the toilet. Washing my face in the sink, I looked at myself in the mirror and blurted out loud, "Uh oh! This shit's too good." I'd just thrown up and felt like a million. I knew I was in trouble. It was a high unlike any I'd experienced before.

Instead of the quiet introspection brought on by hallucinogenic drugs, or the mellow feeling good marijuana imparts, coke fueled instant confidence and stripped away inhibitions. It cost a bunch—one hundred dollars would keep a party of four high for most of a day; the same amount bought an ounce of premium pot that would keep four people high most of the week—and required repeat applications, like every twenty minutes or so.

The giddiness and euphoria you felt after doing it was followed by a pronounced low. Cocaine filled you with wild and sexy sensations, then drained the lead out of your pencil. It tended to breed assholes and asshole behavior. Social scenes turned ugly. Rooms full of partygoers would roar with loud talk, and a glance would reveal that no one was listening, everyone was talking. Bathrooms filled up with people sharing their stash or hustling a snort while those left behind in the living room waited, either anxious for an invitation or oblivious to why they were being ignored. Decent people turned into slobbering fools. Generous souls turned greedy.

Pretty soon, hearing about another friend or foe biting the cocaine dust became a weekly occurrence. Nobody bitched too much about it, though, other than complaining about its exorbitant price or questioning how much it had been stepped on, diluting its potency. They were too busy snorting it or chasing their high with beer or booze. One of the few positives of coke for our business was that it boosted alcohol consumption like no illegal drug before.

In a strange way, coke consumption improved beer sales, although there were two greater factors. One was the new law lowering the drinking age to eighteen, and the other was Austin's decision to allow drinking whiskey in bars, in addition to beer and wine, and doing it until 2:00 a.m. instead of midnight. The citywide referendum extending the drinking hours had squeaked in by 101 votes. It was like the Earth tilted and the toy box spilled over, spreading goodies to people all over town, our crew included.

Bartenders, waitresses, and doormen could finish working a concert and still have time to head out to Soap Creek Saloon in the cedar breaks west of town, have a fatty and a snootful in the parking lot, down a couple quick shots of tequila inside, and get a nice buzz going before the last set started. It would have been a great party if somebody had just forgotten to bring the cocaine. The shiny cleverness you felt during a cocaine high was inevitably revealed to be a cynical joke by the business decisions you made under the influence.

Even the nice bands did their part to spread the problem. The first time we ever met, Toy Caldwell, leader of the Marshall Tucker Band, walked up to me on the stage while his crew was unloading the truck for sound check the afternoon before a show. He shook my hand and said, "We've sure been looking forward to playing here." He pulled out a long vial containing two and a half grams of cocaine. "Pass this around to those guys unloading that truck, and try to find me an ounce, will you?" he said, walking away. "That's all I got."

I've often said that our Austin scene was predicated on cheap pot and beer. Part of the success of the Armadillo was due to the fact that the cops knew people were smoking inside but we were too big to bust, and we had developed a friendly, cooperative relationship with the Austin Police Department. When cocaine appeared in 1974, things changed, but until then, we had a pretty happy movie.

Even after we got our beer license, relations with Austin law enforcement were reasonably cordial. A big part of the reason, I believe, is that when we called for help, they knew that when they arrived, the trouble-makers would already be hog-tied and ready to escort to the patrol car.

Travis County sheriff Raymond Frank, an Austin original whose successful campaign in 1972 included a "No More Pot Busts" platform, was anything but typical. He dropped by the Dillo frequently. On one occasion, he was being given a grand tour of the joint by a kitchen staffer when he unexpectedly poked his head into the Chicanoline. Not unsurprisingly, he was greeted by the reek of premium skunk weed buds. "You know, there's sprays to cover that smell," he advised his guide. At the end of the walk-around, Frank thanked her for the hospitality and accepted a gift of chocolate-chip cookies.

When Austin police officers like Jerry Spain came around to the Armadillo, most arrived with a tolerant attitude. My office was as big as a handball court and when people knocked, it was a long walk to the door, so I left it unlocked even when we were smoking dope. We usually passed joints around a huge conference table made of recycled lumber.

The door had a peephole, but I had it reversed so that people could look inside and avoid disrupting discreet activity by walking in unannounced. When we were breaking the law, a business card on a thumbtack was used to block the view.

One day, however, after a perfunctory knock at the door, Jerry Spain and a new partner blew right in with grins on their faces. They apparently didn't expect to see anything they weren't supposed to see. They had just interrupted a meeting of my advisors, seated around the table as we hashed out various issues of the day over Texas torpedoes, a pungent cloud hovering overhead.

Spain stopped in his tracks, then began backing out of the room, but I bellowed a hello at him and asked him to come inside. He took a seat next to me, where a seven-inch reel-to-reel tape box held the remainder of the pot we'd been smoking.

He explained that he was looking for a runaway, but it appeared to me that what he really wanted was to impress the new partner with his ability to work with hippies. He was still talking when he picked up the tape box and started absently playing with it. Holding it perpendicular, he started spinning it on the axis of his fingers through the spindle. As it spun around, the pot seeds in the box rattled like marimbas. The sound made the guys on my team quite nervous.

Then, without much preamble, Spain pulled the box open with his thumbs, causing seeds and pot trash to rain out over the table. He closed it again quickly. I happened to be the only one looking. Not even his partner noticed; he was talking to someone at the other end of the table. I looked away, giving Spain a chance to put the box down, sweep the mess off the tabletop, then brush it from his pant legs.

Roy Butler was mayor of Austin when there was a spike in heroin use, particularly around the Drag. Butler said he wanted to bring in federal narcotics agents. I went to his office, along with representatives from the *Rag* and some street vendors. We asked him to assure us that he'd tell the narcs to lay off pot smokers. Butler countered that he couldn't tell the feds which laws to enforce.

We assured the mayor that if he'd just keep the feds out of this, we'd clean up the Drag ourselves, but he said his hands were tied. I got really pissed off. I told the mayor that, according to *Time* magazine, he was the number-one used-car salesman in America, and that proved that he could do anything he damn well pleased.[1] Even decades later, Roy Butler and I still weren't on friendly terms.

In 1971, after we had expanded the concert hall, moved the stage, and obtained our beer license, I sent letters to the Austin Police Department announcing our grand reopening. From my training with the Brewers Association, I believed that law enforcement agencies react to two kinds of stimuli, complaints and requests for advice. If you go to them ahead of time and ask for advice, you put them in the position of being your counselor. This makes it a bit harder for them to come in later and feel good about giving you a lot of shit.

None of that, of course, meant that we were immune to police raids.

We were raided on Halloween night 1972 during the third annual Armadillo Pumpkin Stomp, a pagan rock 'n' roll freak-out that had originated at the Vulcan Gas Company. The Pumpkin Stomp was basically Jim Franklin's party. Every year was a little different, but three constants of every Stomp were a performance by his retro fifties rock 'n' roll band,

Poster for the Fourth Annual Halloween Pumpkin Stomp,
October 31, 1972. Artwork by Jim Franklin.

Ramon, Ramon and the Four Daddyos; an even-more-crazed-than-usual emcee act; and the ritual disembowelment of pumpkins.

The trouble that night started when a new kid working the door smart-mouthed a cop who was only there to investigate a noise complaint. Instead of politely cooperating, the new guy, who was wearing an orange jumpsuit with a silver lamé Speedo on his crotch, asked the police officer if he was in costume and did he have a warrant.

Quicker than you could say "trick or treat," a SWAT unit arrived, wearing the usual paramilitary gear and toting the usual shotguns. The team arrived just in time for the bottle rockets and pumpkin parts flying through the air inside the music hall. For a moment they didn't know how to react. At one point a fifteen-year-old drunk kid got their attention. We'd thrown him out three times, but he kept sneaking back in. When he saw the SWAT team, he smiled and passed out, sliding down the side of the building like melted wax. They busted us for serving a minor.

Another night, a team from the Texas Alcoholic Beverage Commission conducted a sweep and found a bottle of hard whiskey that Danny Cibulka had stashed away in the kitchen, an act that was strictly forbidden. One of the agents, J. T. Seaholm, was a former UT All-American football player who had been drafted by the Chicago Bears in 1954 but had come back to UT to finish his college education and serve in the Texas Rangers. Seaholm was the only guy I've ever known who quit the Rangers, and I know it wasn't because he wasn't tough enough for them. On this occasion, Cibulka was hightailing it from the concert hall with the bottle when Seaholm caught up with him. Seaholm grabbed Danny's ponytail and yanked it hard a couple of times, bouncing Danny's head on the floor like a basketball. Our guys were tough, but TABC guys were tougher.

AWHQ Restaraunt comic, 1975.
Artwork by Micael Priest.

FEEDING THE LEGEND

★

We were pleased as punch that Van Morrison chose the Armadillo to kick off his Caledonia Soul Express tour in January 1974. Van was big box office at the time, and to cover the premium price we paid to get him, we raised the cover to three dollars for his show. All three nights sold out.

Van was supernaturally gifted and more than a little eccentric, but we did our best to keep him comfortable and happy. Genie and I even put him up at our house. During his entire stay in Austin, a young, attractive female companion did all of his talking for him. She was introduced as his "masseuse and interpreter." A typical interaction went like this:

> "Van would like an omelet," said the interpreter.
> "OK, I'll be glad to make Van an omelet," said Genie.
> *Whisper, whisper, whisper.*
> "Van would like me to make his omelet," said the interpreter.
> "Sure thing. No problem."

It was a weird three days and nights.

Looking back on all of this, it almost seems preordained that the former lead singer of the band Them, who popularized the durable-as-a-hammer

Van Morrison and band onstage at AWHQ,
January 10, 1974. Photograph by Burton Wilson.

songs "Gloria" and "Here Comes the Night," would be knighted in 2015 by Queen Elizabeth. His full title became Sir George Ivan Morrison, OBE (Order of the British Empire).[1]

After the last night of Van Morrison's three-night run, we made an inquiry as to how he had enjoyed the backstage hospitality. We were informed that Van enjoyed the spread, but he didn't get the shrimp enchiladas Jerry Garcia had told him about. Jan Beeman promised Van that if he came back, she'd have a big heaping plate ready for him.

Van already had another gig on Sunday, but he was off on Monday. We had nothing on the calendar for Monday. Van was agreeable to another show, so we booked the gig, got the word out, and Monday evening, Sir Van had shrimp enchiladas for dinner.

One year after taking Frank Zappa to see the yurts, I took Van Morrison to see them. Van listened to the spiel about the healing powers and other attributes of yurts, but unlike Zappa, he never asked a question or spoke a word. That wasn't surprising, since he hadn't said a thing during his stay at my house, either.

As we left Yurtsville, I was anxious to know what Van thought about it. "What does Van think about the yurts?" I said.

Whisper, whisper, whisper.

"Van says he really needs his corners."

★ ★ ★

"This is a paradise," Jim Franklin once said. "Look around. Food. Beer. Music. Lots of people . . . and an abundance of armadillo mythology to keep you from feeling isolated."

The beer garden struck many people as a paradise. After a pitcher of Lone Star and a platter of nachos, many folks made up their minds to put down their roots in Austin. Several years went by before I realized how important this combination of things was to the Armadillo's success.

One of the ingredients of the combination was the staff. The Armadillo was the home they'd never had, and they spread the feeling of welcome and belonging to others who came through our doors. Then there was the kitchen staff and the food and hospitality they served, which, unfortunately, took me a long time to fully appreciate. The kitchen put me off for several reasons, maybe because walking through it, you were assaulted with heat and greasy smoke, strange odors, and the peculiar chaos of our food-making operation.

The feedback we got from touring bands made me realize that the Armadillo's kitchen was helping build our reputation in the music world. Our nachos alone—the simple presentation of jalapeno slices on top of a pile of melted yellow cheese on a crisp baked tortilla—were legendary. Armadillo World Headquarters was the first big venue in the country to serve nachos. Popularizing nachos for the masses certainly wasn't our only great achievement, but it's a worthy claim to fame.

Jan Beeman was recruited for the kitchen staff because head cook Betsy Haney was shorthanded. Jan steeled herself before she assumed the job. First of all, the kitchen had a one-stove setup. You could only cook nine nachos at a time. There was no dishwasher on the premises. Then there was the chilling sight of Big Rikke Moursund, also known as the Guacamole Queen. Tall as a lamppost and weighing two hundred pounds, she could often be encountered stirring a pot of beans while clad in only panties and flip-flops.

Big Rikke was the most famous member of the Dillo staff. As part of Jim Franklin's stage show, she would come out onstage wearing a giant guacamole hat made of urethane foam. Loud-talking and larger-than-life, she aspired to be the biggest groupie in the music world. She tried to emulate Barbara Cope, the infamous Dallas groupie they called the Butter Queen because she was known for using Land O'Lakes butter as a sexual lubricant. Barbara Cope's conquests were said to include the Rolling Stones (as immortalized in the song "Rip This Joint"), Joe Cocker, Elton John, and many others.[2]

Instead of butter, Big Rikke used guacamole. The number and fame of her lovers never eclipsed that of the Butter Queen, but she gained immortality through Jim Franklin's artwork. A painting outside the men's restroom depicted a gruff-looking army sergeant with a cartoon speech bubble warning, "If I catch any of you pussies beatin' off in this bathroom, I'm gonna turn you over to the Guacamole Queen!"

Outside the women's room, an image of Big Rikke herself, scowling, said, "If I catch any of you guys in the gals' john, I'm gonna mash you up n' spread you on a salad!"

Big Rikke was just another one of the challenging aspects handled by Jan Beeman, the true queen of the Armadillo kitchen. Jan also had to deal with bar versus kitchen conflicts and ongoing debates among her own staff, which was split between vegetarians and meat eaters. Considering

Ike Ritter and Big Rikke (a.k.a. the Guacamole Queen)
at AWHQ, 1970. Photograph by Burton Wilson.

AWHQ mural and graffiti, 1972.
Photograph by Burton Wilson.

AWHQ kitchen, c. 1974. One glance gives my memory the shakes. Photograph by Burton Wilson.

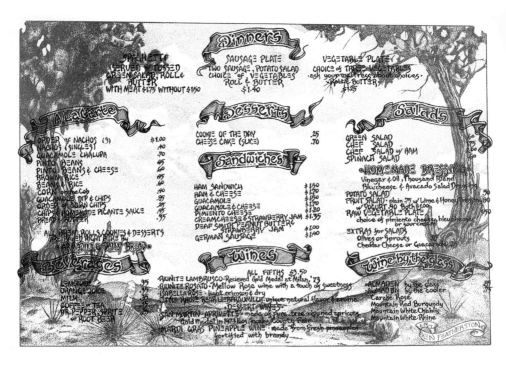

Menu artwork by Ken Featherston, 1974.

the tough job she was given, which included serving as mediator between food factions, I regret not being nicer to Jan, but historically, my attitude toward the kitchen was always negative.

Despite all this, Jan succeeded in making the kitchen the showcase of Armadillo World Headquarters hospitality. What she and her kitchen crew did for musicians on the road created buzz all over the country. Many started clamoring for a chance to come play the Dillo just so they could eat. As soon as a band arrived for load-in, our crew was standing by to do the heavy lifting, while the kitchen did their part by baking choc-olate-chip cookies for the road-weary musicians and their crew. Beer flowed freely. Pot was plentiful, high quality, relatively cheap, and eas-ily accessible. Cocaine could be had for the asking if there was a need. El Rancho and Tamale House No. 1, located just across the river, had all the inexpensive Tex-Mex a stomach could stomach. Barton Springs Pool, where the springwater remained a constant sixty-eight degrees year-round, was a mile down the road. To many road-weary travelers, playing the Armadillo was a died-and-gone-to-heaven deal.

Except for the shrimp enchiladas, there was nothing exotic or cutting-edge about the fare. But we treated the bands and crew like they were spe-cial, something that evidently occurred very seldom in their travels. The kitchen tried to pay attention to what bands liked to eat, and would ask if it was anyone's birthday. If someone was having one, they'd bake a birth-day cake.

If someone moaned, "Oh, man, I've been out on the road for six months, I wish I had a real apple pie," an apple pie would soon appear. Bands who'd played our house before knew the kitchen staff well enough to call ahead and let them know what they'd been eating and what they were craving. Vegetarians knew they could show up and not have to suffer through another plate of quiche, because the kitchen prepared excellent vegetarian dishes that even a carnivore like me could devour.

The guys in the Charlie Daniels Band, who were big old Southern men with big old Southern appetites, were always sent away with boxes of roast beef sandwiches, extra chicken, fruit, and gallons of iced tea, and all that after the preshow spread, which usually featured oven-baked stuffed pork chops—a mushroom-onion-garlic-breadcrumb kind of deal that was the CDB's favorite entree.

Jan's kitchen always made sure to feed and water a band's road crew. Big pitchers of lemonade with fresh strawberries and mint were always waiting, with big pitchers of beer available for the asking. If the roadies were happy, the stars were usually much happier.

Commander Cody left a fat one-hundred-dollar tip for the kitchen after a big weekend, and a personal fifty-dollar tip for Jan Beeman, which allowed the kitchen to pay off the guy who brought shrimp up from the coast with a little left over to invest in some needed utensils.

Word spread. The Grateful Dead told the Beach Boys and Van Morrison about Jan's shrimp enchiladas. Before long, many acts who played at Municipal Auditorium because they were too big for the Armadillo still insisted on catering from our kitchen. The Beach Boys, for example, had cheese sandwiches in their contract rider, making it easy for promoters in the most remote boondocks of the country to accommodate their vegetarian diets. But after the Beach Boys tried the shrimp enchiladas from the Armadillo kitchen, they changed their rider to stipulate that Jan's crew cater any show within one hundred miles of Austin.

CROSSTOWN COMPETITION

Booking Van Morrison helped bring the Armadillo into the mainstream of concert promotion. The boost in our profile coincided with a general growth spurt in the live music and nightclub scene. The state ban on liquor by the drink had been lifted by an amendment to the Texas Constitution in 1970, followed by Travis County approving an option to serve liquor by the drink in local bars. The legal drinking age had been lowered to eighteen, which also had a major effect on the number of people going out at night to see music and do all the other things people like to do in association with booze.

A bumper crop of new live music venues opened, and some of them tried to position themselves as alternatives to the Armadillo. In a capitalist society, competition is supposed to help bring about higher-quality products at lower prices. In some cases, it also brings out the ugly side of some service providers and their former colleagues.

Waylon Jennings pulled off a rowdy two-night stand at the Armadillo at the end of January 1974, with Billy Joe Shaver, who had written the songs for Waylon's breakthrough album, *Honky Tonk Heroes*, opening both nights. Six months later, Waylon canceled a return date in order to play the Texas Opry House, our new competition on the block. He went for a higher guarantee.

Meanwhile, Commander Cody and His Lost Planet Airmen had grown into AWHQ's biggest road act. They came back for two nights in February 1974 to promote the release of the live album they'd recorded at the Armadillo the previous November. John Morthland and Ed Ward, two of the writers flown in by Cody's record label for the show, were duly impressed by the scene and said so frequently in the stories they filed in the music press. (Later, Morthland and Ward gave up writing about Austin long-distance and moved here. Ward took over the rock critic slot at the *Statesman* and Morthland continued as a freelancer.)

Both nights were sold out, which should have been a source of joy, but at the time, I had my hands full trying to build up buzz for Little Feat, who were booked for four nights the following week. Linda Ronstadt was traveling with Lowell George, guitarist and bandleader of Little Feat. It occurred to me that, if we could advertise Linda doing a special guest appearance, it would create a lot of buzz. But I wanted to get their blessing first.

If ever there was a goddess of a musical age, Linda Ronstadt was it for me. So pretty she was hard to look at, so lovely to listen to she could make a he-man cry, she reminded me of a tiny, delicate bird. She was in a class of her own.

Little Feat was playing Liberty Hall in Houston before Austin, so I drove down there and caught the show. Unfortunately, I wasn't able to get an audience with the moonstruck couple. On the drive home I decided to proceed with my plan anyway. Giving added encouragement, Commander Cody agreed to stay in Austin an extra two days and open for Little Feat's first show, without contract or guarantee. We charged three dollars for a triple bill of Cody, Little Feat, and Linda Ronstadt.

Wednesday night, everyone was cool and relaxed before the show except Linda and Lowell, who were holed up backstage, not seeing anyone. Linda was widely known to be shy and delicate to the point of instant hysteria. I just couldn't get an audience with her. She considered me a scummy promoter. I was starting to believe it.

Making matters even more awkward, she had recently shared the stage with Commander Cody and His Lost Planet Airmen in Los Angeles for a television show, yet she didn't recognize a one of them. It was just tunnel vision. She couldn't help it.

Bill Kirchen and Andy Stein of the Lost Planet Airmen came back to the dressing room with their guitars and pretended they were all sitting

Poster for Little Feat show at AWHQ, February 8–9, 1974.
Artwork by Micael Priest.

Linda Ronstadt was an unwilling goddess. Backstage at AWHQ,
February 6, 1974. Photograph by Burton Wilson.

around a campfire or something. They introduced themselves and ended up trading songs, picking, and singing on some old country classics. When it was time for Cody to take the stage, Linda had loosened up some, and it looked like about a 50/50 chance that she might get up and sing.

The opening set by Commander Cody was high energy, though looser and more casual than normal; the boys left their sequins in their suitcases and let their shirttails hang out. After a sizzling set, they came backstage and more or less swarmed Linda and Lowell. The crowd was still applauding and screaming for more, and Bill Kirchen, who is such a likeable guy, just wouldn't take no for an answer.

Linda took herself up the stage stairs, with Lowell holding her hand. Bill Kirchen led the band, which was about half Lost Planet Airmen, half Little Feat. Cody sat it out. I came out and introduced Linda with no fanfare. "Please welcome . . ." The place went nuts.

Bill Kirchen and the guys all knew her music. They made her comfortable and Lowell stayed close, and she mellowed out. Linda's courage grew and they coaxed her into an eleven-song set. It's hard to describe the impact of this improvised set, but there was a feeling of intimacy and hugeness at the same time. It was definitely one of the highlights of the whole Armadillo experience, maybe the biggest one I can recall. And the night was only half over. Little Feat followed with its powerful blend of Southern blues and rock filtered through the Laurel Canyon vibe, and by the end of the evening, the band had secured its place as an Armadillo A-list draw and an Austin favorite. One of Cody's roadies said that night was his biggest payday ever—Linda had insisted that the door be split evenly among everyone, including the crew.

The next night, Linda came to my house with Lowell and chewed me out for what I'd done. She thought it was a terrible breach of ethics. I blamed the media.

Two weeks after Little Feat, Roy Buchanan played. On a stage where guitar heroes were a dime a dozen, Buchanan was a house favorite. In addition to his amazing talent and discipline, he happened to be the only guy to turn down offers to play with Lennon and McCartney, the Rolling Stones, and Bob Dylan. Armadillo audiences appreciated an iconoclast like that.

Touring acts brought in the crowds, but we were continually trying to build audiences for worthy hometown bands. For a one-dollar admission on weeknights, you could see great acts like western swing fiddler

Poster for a Roy Buchanan show at AWHQ, September 18–19, 1974.
Artwork by Ken Featherston.

Roy Buchanan onstage at AWHQ, September 18, 1974.
Photograph by Burton Wilson.

Alvin Crow and his Neon Angels, or our favorite "blue yodeler," Kenneth Threadgill. Alvin had tons more talent than bands like New Riders of the Purple Sage, but he could never build a following in our place. Once he moved over to the Broken Spoke, an authentic honky-tonk that was long-hair-tolerant, Alvin started to develop the following he deserved.

We had some great double bills for only a dollar. We would pair the Conqueroo, one of Austin's original hippie bands, with Leanne and the Bizarros, featuring Sterling Morrison, the former guitarist from the Velvet Underground who had moved to Austin and was teaching at UT. A double bill like that sometimes even earned enough to pay the AWHQ light bill, but not much more than that. We were too big to be a club and too small to compete for the bigger touring acts.

The scene in Austin was growing up and changing fast. There was an influx of talented and pretty people in town, the kind you'd see out and about after dark but not in morning traffic on their way to a nine-to-five job. A good many were thirty-somethings drawn to Austin by its reputation as a place where the living was easy, with perpetual sunshine, a low cost of living, the cheapest pot, and the cheapest beer. They weren't hippies and they weren't straights, but somewhere in between.

An alternative biweekly paper called the *Austin Sun* was taking the underground paper concept of the defunct *Rag* into the semi-mainstream. The content of the paper showed that the Austin scene was becoming more self-aware, and the creators of that content included several fine writers—including Bill Bentley, Michael Ventura, and James "Big Boy" Medlin, who later moved to Los Angeles and played a large part in the music scene, where they were among the founders of the *LA Weekly*.[1]

Clubs sprouted like magic mushrooms in a Bastrop cow pasture after a rain. In four years, the number of local clubs had grown from something like fourteen to fifty. KOKE-FM promoted concerts at the Country Dinner Playhouse, a theatrical venue north of the city, including one with Willie Nelson that Leon Russell tagged along to play, unadvertised. Chequered Flag, Rod Kennedy's intimate listening room, booked a lot of singer-songwriter acts that I longed to get, most notably Bonnie Raitt.

The Bergstrom Air Force Base NCO club booked a *Hee Haw* show, and the Sheriff's Posse Arena tried its hand with a *Grand Ole Opry* show. Alliance Wagon Yard, El Paso Cattle Company, Saddle Club, Feed Lot, Hansel and Gretel, Rusty Nail, Country Dinner Playhouse, Chapparal, Split Rail, Mother Earth, Black Queen, Oasis, Scorpio, Cricket Club,

Skyline, Arkie's Dessau Hall, Abel Moses, Saxon Pub, and many more joints were trying to fill their rooms and pay their bills in the same manner that we were.

One of the newcomers of 1974, the Texas Opry House, decided to go head-to-head with us. So I grabbed the bull by the horns, and in some ways, it was one of the best things that could've happened. For most of 1974, the mere words Texas Opry House would send a chill across the hairs on the back of my neck. The place was built in the midfifties as the convention center for the Terrace Motor Hotel, which had lodging units spread over the hillsides on either side of Academy Drive, just off South Congress. In the years since, the Opry House had aged about as well as a Ford Edsel.

The Opry House's location put it less than a mile from our place. The room was completely devoid of charm and had no soul whatsoever, although it did have basic creature comforts the Armadillo lacked, and the management was willing to outspend us for road acts. The management also had no problem with Willie and his pals hanging out with their friends Smith and Wesson, probably because Willie had agreed to be a silent partner. It became Willie's new Austin home stage.

Before the Texas Opry House opened for business, its people trolled the town for bartenders, waitresses, and bouncers. Wallace Selman, the guy fronting the business, told everyone who would listen, "We're going to put the Armadillo out of business."

The Terrace's convention center had three rooms of different sizes, each with carpeting, wooden dance floors, air-conditioning, and tables. There was a hotel-sized kitchen to serve all three rooms. The parking lot was paved and well-lit, a welcome sight to anyone who'd scraped a muffler or dropped a transmission parking at the Dillo.

Fortunately, Selman's noxious manners stirred public sympathy for our side and infused our staff with a hard-shell toughness that would have made our namesake proud. We burrowed down for the fight. In some ways, it was a relief to have a villain to blame for our troubles. We knew we needed to improve our place, despite the fact that we were on a month-to-month lease and could lose everything we had put into the place if we got the boot from the landlord.

During the same month in which the disgraced president Richard Nixon finally resigned and left the White House, we embarked on building a set of risers intended to improve sight lines in the hall. Dub Rose and his crew of hippie carpenters had their work cut out for them. Fortunately, on a visit to the Armadillo, the architect Cyrus Wagner—whose design work made the San Antonio River Walk what it is today—listened to our ideas and offered some help. He took a pen and some napkins and sketched out a rough blueprint of his idea for elevated seating on either side of the Cabaret. The Rolling Stones also did their bit. The stage for their Dallas show had been disassembled, and when it came up for sale I bought it, saving a lot of money on the lumber for the redesign.

"Hippie carpenters did all the work," Dub Rose said. "A lot of hippies were carpenters at that time, and those were the kind of people we had on the volunteer staff at the Armadillo. Which worked out pretty well for me whenever I needed a work crew."[2]

After the risers were installed, the ceiling of the old armory was sprayed with shredded-paper insulation, which improved the acoustics considerably.

The renovations did little to calm my nerves. I lost sleep. A few long-time employees deserted us for the competition. The Opry House drew crowds with acts who would've otherwise been playing the Armadillo. Waylon Jennings was one of them, Michael Murphey was another. Boz Scaggs went there for the bigger guarantee, and so did the Eagles, the SoCal band of slick country rockers who were about one year away from becoming major-league superstars with their album *One of These Nights*, which yielded three Top 10 singles, and three years away from releasing the song "Hotel California," which many deejays and other canned-music providers simply left on replay for the rest of the decade.

In retrospect, we were doing a pretty good job at what we did best. Over six weeks in the spring of 1974, we had Frank Zappa and the Mothers of Invention, the Austin Ballet Theatre, Freddie King, Kinky Friedman and His Texas Jewboys, John McLaughlin and the Mahavishnu Orchestra, Leo Kottke, the J. Geils Band, and those reliable western swing/rockabilly madmen, Commander Cody and His Lost Planet Airmen.

Cody returned for two more nights, sharing the bill with another western swing band, Asleep at the Wheel. Two guys from Philadelphia, Ray Benson and Lucky Oceans, had formed Asleep at the Wheel in Paw Paw, West Virginia, in 1969. They played some shows opening for Alice Cooper and Hot Tuna in Washington, DC, and in 1970, they relocated to East Oakland, California.[3] I'd met the guys when I was visiting in

Berkeley, hyping up the Armadillo to Joe Kerr, who managed both Asleep at the Wheel and Commander Cody.

"Come to Austin," I told Ray Benson, Asleep at the Wheel's front man. "Y'all can be the house band at the Armadillo." They took me up on the offer and played their first show at the joint in the spring of 1973. The house band promise didn't work out, but we gave them plenty of work. Benson said, "We came to Austin because it's where the music is."

The Wheel was a big ensemble made up of players who lived and breathed western swing. They were brimming with talent, determination, and personality. By now Austin had more than its share of great new-style country bands—Freda and the Firedogs, Man Mountain, and Alvin Crow—along with the hardcore redneck combos, like Jess DeMaine, Johnny Lyon, Janet Lynn and the Country Nu-Notes, and whatever band was currently being led by Bert Rivera, Hank Thompson's former pedal steel player.

When it came to carrying the Bob Wills baton, Asleep at the Wheel gave no quarter. Bandleader Ray Benson was a six-foot-seven-inch-tall, red-haired Jewish boy from Philadelphia. He looked like a baby giraffe with a cowboy hat. If the mellifluous drawl that rolled out of Ray's mouth didn't convince you that the ensemble deserved a place in the pantheon of authentic Texas music, then their hit "Miles and Miles of Texas" would surely do so.

The Wheel's female vocalist, Chris O'Connell, sounded like she'd been raised by Tammy Wynette. Pianist Floyd Domino banged on the ivories, hands crisscrossing, rhythm and counter-rhythm exploding out of the box with the kind of fury that could turn a graveyard into a dancing ballroom. Tony Garnier thumped the upright bass like a beatnik cat. Holding down the pedal steel chair was a fellow who used the name Lucky Oceans but who was known in a previous life as Reuben Gosfield—just as Ray Seifert had become Ray Benson and Jim Haber was now known as Floyd Domino. Leroy Preston, a fresh-faced lad from Vermont with a penchant for writing twisted lyrics (e.g., "Hello, everybody, I'm a dead man") was born with a stage name.

The guys in the Wheel and the Lost Planet Airmen often had their axes handy when they were hanging out, and they were prone to jam at the drop of a hat. The beer garden and the backstage area were never as much fun as when Cody and the Wheel shared the bill at the Dillo. They

From day one, Ray Benson and Floyd Domino knew they were
moving to Austin. Backstage at AWHQ, September 7, 1973.
Photograph by Burton Wilson.

also kept the kitchen busy; each band might have set an all-time record for consuming Armadillo food. In a pound-per-band comparison between those two and the Charlie Daniels Band, you might assume that the latter had the edge, since it took a lot of feed to satisfy a guy like Charlie, who weighed over three hundred pounds. But the two hippie western swing bands were bigger ensembles.

Cody and Ray also burned more energy. They tended to act more like growing boys on vacation at Grandma's house. Instead of napping after gorging, they'd play volleyball against the Dillo crew and then jam some more, teaching each other licks and lyrics they'd recently picked up, laughing like fools.

The Wheel acclimated quickly to Austin. In the beginning, Floyd Domino camped at Bobby Hedderman's house and Ray Benson let his feet dangle off my guest bed until the band scouted more permanent digs. Before a year was up, most of the band members were well established in South Austin.

★ ★ ★

Every time economic pressures started blurring my vision, along came an event that blew away my worries, and such an event sometimes generated the kind of press that you couldn't buy if you wanted to. We hadn't heard all that much about the shy kid from New Jersey, Bruce Springsteen, but Columbia Records was underwriting a national tour and Wild West Productions from Houston had bought the Texas dates, giving us two nights in March at virtually no expense. The record company wanted to make a good impression on Bruce and on his edgy manager, Mike Appel.

We got into gear, working to capitalize on the buzz. Jim Franklin produced his finest, most detailed poster since Leo Kottke's "Vaseline Machine Gun" poster and Frank Zappa's "Do Not Adjust This Nut" poster. Columbia Records passionately believed in Springsteen and spent more money on his tour than we'd ever seen a label spend—so much that we were able to charge one dollar for admission to his first appearance, a Thursday night that was added at the last minute, with Friday and Saturday night dates already scheduled. Alvin Crow was already booked for Thursday, but Springsteen's people were amenable to having Alvin's Pleasant Valley Boys open the show.

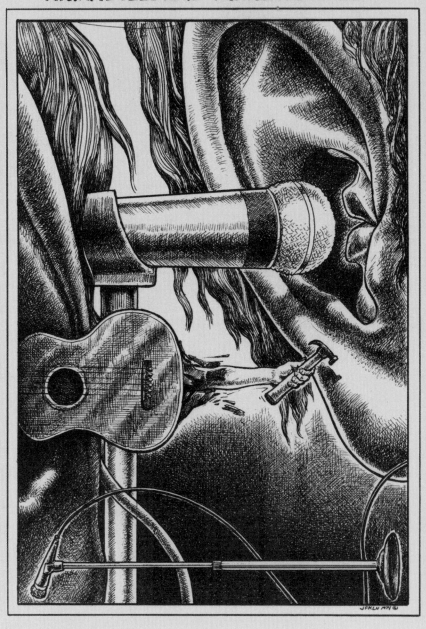

Another one of Jim Franklin's tribute-level posters. He recognized "the Boss" as soon as he heard him. Poster for Bruce Springsteen show at AWHQ, March 15 and 16, 1973.

Bruce Springsteen backstage at AWHQ, March 15, 1974.
Photograph by Burton Wilson.

Apparently, the record company's generosity only went so far. On Thursday Leea Mechling drove down to the bus station to pick up Springsteen and the E Street Band. "They couldn't afford a tour bus," she said. "They were a bunch of gangly kids. I'm not even convinced they had hotel rooms."[4]

The New Jersey musician who was destined to become one of America's best-known faces was just another guy to Leea. He kept hanging around the bar in the Cabaret where she was busy setting up. She figured that he must be a roadie.

"He asked if we were staying for the show," she said. "I told him, 'Probably not, they're just a bunch of Yankees who think they play rock 'n' roll.'"

Alvin Crow and his Pleasant Valley Boys turned in a remarkable opening set, Alvin just blazing on his fiddle and the band swinging with a rock 'n' roll intensity. The crowd was stirred up, and Springsteen apparently took notice. As Alvin worked the crowd into a lather, the New Jersey rocker anxiously paced back and forth. Kenneth Threadgill remarked that Springsteen seemed to be as jittery as a "cocker spaniel trying to pass a peach pit." The New Jersey rockers might have had preshow nerves, but they were hardly intimidated. They delivered the goods in a two-and-a-half-hour marathon performance that came close to levitating the old armory.

Leea Mechling, who ended up staying and working that night, was blown away. When nacho time came around, Springsteen asked her opinion of "this bunch of Yankees." She apologized and told him she thought they were great. Then as Leea and the cleanup crew pulled out their brooms and mops, Springsteen and the guys came out and serenaded them as they worked.

For the next two nights the place was filled to capacity, mostly on word of mouth from the previous night's performance. Springsteen fell in love right back, leaving Austin with a burgeoning fan base.

Springsteen also found a brand-new girlfriend in Austin. Karen Darvin was a leggy, gorgeous redhead who wore the tightest cutoffs we had ever seen on the Drag. She was pictured with Springsteen in *Time* magazine on October 27, 1975, the same week the New Jersey rock 'n' roller was on the cover of both *Time* and *Newsweek* for his new album, *Born to Run*.[5] Karen later left the Boss for Todd Rundgren.

★ ★ ★

Our search for an air-conditioning solution led us to the Houston oil fields, where huge, diesel-powered AC rigs were hauled around on tractor-trailers and hooked up to manholes to provide cooling to miles of underground tunnels for firefighters. We tried the concept at the Armadillo and spread the word about our new system. But as the summer days grew hotter, we realized that while the Dillo may have been "underground" in a cultural sense, it was no tunnel, and the diesel behemoths were no match for a former National Guard armory.

The passing of summer into fall marked renewed efforts to figure out how to make the beer garden habitable in the winter. One of our consultants, Tony Bell, was privileged to be one of the rarest types of celebrities: he was the inspiration for Gilbert Shelton's Wonder Wart-Hog. Tony was also a genius at figuring out solutions to impossible construction problems. After studying the problem, he offered some ideas, but they were all out of our price range.

We worked on a geodesic-dome-type framework we called the Space Knuckle that could support a covering over the beer garden, but the design for a practical cover that could be removed in the summer eluded us. A three-season beer garden is what we ended up with. The giant pecan tree in the parking lot gave us coveted afternoon shade, which made the garden a close-to-ideal place to hang in spring, summer, and fall. Installing a covering on the beer garden would've necessitated cutting down the tree, and no one wanted to do that.

Time magazine capped the frenzy of Austin hype in September with a page featuring pictures of Jerry Jeff Walker and Doug Sahm flanking a wide shot of the interior of the AWHQ along with an article that was short but profuse with praise.[6] "What the Fillmores East and West were to the rock era," the article said, "the Armadillo World Headquarters is to Austin's country-rock set." Doug Sahm was identified as "a 32-year-old fugitive of San Francisco psychedelia," and the joint was described as a "cavernous old armory decorated with surrealistic murals of the burrowing, bony-plated mammal that now ranks second only to the longhorn in Texas esteem."

According to *Time*, the Armadillo crowd was "a curious amalgam of teen-agers, aging hippie women in gingham, braless coeds, and booted goat ropers." What were they all doing at the Dillo? They were "swigging Pearl beer and swinging Stetsons in time to the music."

As an advertisement for the Austin music scene, it was pretty good, including the quote from Doug Sahm about how "leaving Austin now is like climbing off a spaceship from a magic place." Townsend Miller was quoted saying, "Austin music is country picking and basic bluegrass, leavened with rock and lightly glazed with acid."[7]

The brass at Lone Star Beer weren't too happy about the Pearl Beer reference, but that was something we weren't able to control.

★ ★ ★

In November, before we put 1974 to bed, Bruce Springsteen made a triumphant one-night return, but it was just another night in a month that had already seen an abundance of great music. Commander Cody and His Lost Planet Airmen, with Hoyt Axton opening, was one of our favorites. Cody and the band arrived in style, escorted from the airport in a fleet of '59 Cadillacs. Rounding out the month were Dr. Hook and the Medicine Show, Austin Ballet Theatre, British jazz-rock bandleader Brian Auger with his Oblivion Express, the Charlie Daniels Band, the Pointer Sisters, and bluegrass giant Bill Monroe, back for more love from his hippie fans.

We were still losing acts to the Texas Opry House, but we set about trying to "nice" the competition to death. Gracious overtures on our part became easier when word leaked out that they were in trouble. The landlord was suing them for $10,000 in back rent. The IRS was unhappy about their nonpayment of withholding taxes. Making for at least a triple whammy, the TABC pulled their liquor license.

We were only too familiar with the species of vultures that were circling over the Opry House. We had heard the stories of wretched excess, eye-popping scenes involving guns and large amounts of cash, and other sordid tales from friends and ex-employees. Most of us had seen far classier joints than the fifties cheapo modern complex on Academy Drive on similar downward slides. The Opry House's decline was like a fat man tripping on a ski jump and rolling in the snow.

My sympathy glands were not immediately stimulated by the manner in which I heard the news. I learned that Michael Murphey was going to cancel his show at the Armadillo with less than a week's notice to play at the Opry House. Murphey had called his manager Larry Watkins and told him he needed to help out the Opry House by playing a benefit there instead of keeping his date with us. He told Watkins to call us and inform us. Watkins told Murphey to call us himself.

Murphey might have done better to say that he didn't have an album out and knew he wouldn't sell out the Dillo, which would've been terribly embarrassing for him. Instead, he preferred to pretend to be Cosmic Cowboy No. 1, riding to the rescue of the Opry House.

Like a good manager, Larry Watkins called me anyway. He said, "I've got to call you because Michael doesn't have the guts to tell you himself. He's pulling out of the Dillo gig this weekend to play the benefit for the Opry House. He told me to call you, and I told him to call you himself, and by the way, I quit."

During Murphey's sound check at the Opry, I showed up to confront him, and Wallace Selman, too. I even brought my tape recorder to preserve my righteous tirade for posterity. My original plan had been to whip both of them, one at a time, but in the interest of social protocol, I settled for being loud, rude, and bellicose. I trashed everyone in sight, and also Jan Reid, who wasn't there, but whose *Improbable Rise of Redneck Rock* had come out; almost everything about it, including the cover photo of Michael Murphey, had put me in a bad mood. Murphey had assured me that he was going to sue Jan and prevent the book from being published, which I had known was a fantasy.

On the plus side, the book brought a whole lot of attention to a whole lot of good music. But the "redneck rock" aspect of the thing just seemed to trivialize what we had going in Austin. The Armadillo seemed to have been marginalized in favor of focusing on a concept, giving the scene a cute name, and ignoring the bigger picture in favor of name checking every guitar player in town with long hair and a cowboy hat. On top of all that, it was a really fluid, quickly evolving scene, and the book had been rushed to print as a follow-up and expansion of Jan Reid's "The Coming of Redneck Hip" feature in *Texas Monthly* from the fall of the previous year, talking up a scene that already had a good head of steam up by the end of 1972. I'm a big admirer of Jan Reid as a person and as a writer, but at the time, his take on the scene made me think of a loud party for Johnnies-come-lately at the day-old bread counter.

Anyway, I left the Opry House feeling energized and ready to spar with somebody, verbally or otherwise. I was still on the same cranky streak the next day, which was November 15, 1974, my thirty-first birthday and the seventh month since the grand opening of the Texas Opry House. In a spirit of friendship and neighborliness bordering on foster parenthood, the Armadillo hosted the benefit at the Opry House. The big headliner was, no surprise, Michael Murphey. The goal was to float some sort of fantasy that the place might not close after all. That night, as the foster parent emcee, I walked out on their stage and gave a tongue-in-cheek pep talk to the Opry House folks. My remarks were punctuated by flying joints, not periods. In all, I flipped thirty-one joints out to the crowd.

"This show is dedicated to all the bartenders and waitresses in Austin," I said, sending the first reefer somersaulting into the crowd. "When you light up in licensed establishments, you jeopardize their jobs, and you ought not to do it," I said, flipping another doobie, which landed gracefully in a pair of eager hands. "Unfortunately . . ." There went another one. "These fine people here lost their license earlier today . . ." Another launched into the darkness. "So you had to bring your own . . ." Now I was flippantly flipping a big missile with my left. "So nobody's going to lose their job tonight . . ." Another one went sailing up and away. "Though we could get busted . . ." And another. "So be careful . . ."

Finally, with empty pockets and smile on my face, I departed the stage, my exit obscured by a roiling pall of marijuana smoke.

No sane business would have done what we did, lending a helping hand to a despised competitor. But to me, it was perfect PR in the shit-kicker sense of the term, and about as satisfying a birthday as I could've wanted. I couldn't help but get in the middle of it, in the interest of looking good while rubbing their noses in it. We'd lost the Eagles, Waylon Jennings, Boz Scaggs, and a bunch of solid acts to the Opry. Lending a helping hand was also the neighborly thing to do in their time of need.

In the weeks following our make-believe benefit for the Opry House, I started getting along better with Wallace Selman. When I got another request to help out the Opry House, I said yes, a decision I was to regret.

The Opry House had booked Ray Charles with opening act David Allen Coe and paid the fee, but the Opry House was closed, so we took the show. It was perhaps the oddest billing in AWHQ's history: brother Ray sharing the bill with David Allen Coe, a singer-songwriter who desperately wanted to be recognized as a country music outlaw. In one of his more desperate moves, the latter parked his bus on South Congress and left it there for a month in the hopes that Willie would discover him. He fluffed up his bio to turn jail time for petty theft into a murder rap. He staged fights onstage.

David Allen Coe wanted to be a star so badly that he succeeded, although briefly, with his song "You Never Even Call Me by My Name," which is pretty funny as a country music parody.

There was no getting around the fact that the Ray Charles/David Allen Coe double bill was a terrible idea. It made no sense. Ray Charles, who was the greatest in so many different categories, was the opening act for Coe, a minor-league country rocker. The show came to us with no financial risk, and yet the billing was a bitter pill to swallow.

On the night of the show, as Ray Charles began his set, David Allen Coe's liquored-up and downered-out loyalists did their damnedest to shout him down. Coe didn't even have that many fans, but the few who were there acted like a mob, infecting the room like a nasty virus, booing relentlessly. Ray Charles heard them, and probably smelled them, too. I should've tried to quiet them down, but I was so mad I just wanted to go out and slap them all with a shovel. And so the great R&B singer cut his set short and said good night. The assholes booed him for that, too.

★ ★ ★

Soap Creek Saloon, located on the western edge of town down a quarter mile of narrow, teeth-jarring washboard road, was only a third as big as the Armadillo, but it attracted the same core audience. Soap Creek was owned by George Majewski and his wife, Carlyne Majer. Sunday afternoon jam sessions, led by Doug Sahm, filled the place on what was the slowest night of the week for most clubs. George and Carlyne never turned away anyone who had the price of admission. When the space got too tight and people were still coming in the front door, they squeezed folks out of the back door. On a busy night, it was like being inside a sausage grinder. Soap Creek was snagging hip regional acts such as Professor Longhair, Delbert McClinton, and Clifton Chenier. All three would have been solid draws at the Armadillo.

What hurt even more was the fact that many of my favorite people preferred Soap Creek to the Dillo. Hell, they had a point. For one thing, the road to Soap Creek Saloon was so rough, the cops didn't like going out there.

While the Opry House made me fighting mad, Soap Creek made me admire George Majewski, who seemed to be liked by everybody. We

Ray Charles onstage at AWHQ, 1974.
Photograph by Van Brooks.

almost always ended shows at the Armadillo before legal closing time because of noise complaints. The only residence within shouting distance of Soap Creek was the mansion that Doug Sahm rented, and Doug never called the cops. He played Soap Creek like he owned it.

Soap Creek went under when their landlord sold the property. George and his wife set up shop on the far north end of town, taking over the location that had formerly been the honkiest honky-tonk in Austin history, the Skyline Club. Hank Williams and Johnny Horton had both played their last gigs there. By the end of the seventies, George and Carlyne moved again, taking over the old Terrace Motor Hotel lobby on South Congress.

The old Ritz movie theater on East Sixth had a stage and seating, but it wasn't a place we considered competition. Later on, sometime in 1975, Jim Franklin went over there to manage the place and turn it into another showcase of music and art. In his mind, he didn't see it as a permanent move. "I didn't move all my stuff," he said. "I just started staying over at the Ritz."

Jim was more than ready to leave the problems of the Armadillo to me, and I couldn't blame him, since the change gave him a chance to run a place the way he wanted instead of being one of many voices at the Armadillo. His partner was Bill Livingood, owner of Slow Printing, the company that printed Jim's T-shirt designs.

The Ritz was successful enough that it siphoned off some shows that would have been moneymakers for us. J. J. Cale played there. The British band the Pretty Things played there, too.

We still had an abundance of talent with the Armadillo Art Squad, but we really missed Jim's microphone magic. There was never an artist quite like Jim Franklin, and there was never another master of ceremonies like him. We were fortunate that we had Micael Priest, who not only continued to blossom as a visual artist but stepped into the role of emcee and made it his own. Micael had a really great rapport with musicians, too. He seemed to be friends with musicians from every genre and every corner of the Austin music scene. When he introduced a band, his enthusiasm was infectious and genuine, and it made him a great emcee as well as an ambassador to the community. Things like that contributed to the loud, rowdy, passionate audience response for which the Armadillo was famous.

On mornings that I sat at home alone, feeling blue, chain-smoking, and pouring down coffee by the gallon, a deep, syrupy voice threatened my sanity more than anything any rival club owner had ever done before. The voice belonged to the morning jock on KRMH, Austin's so-called underground rock station. One morning he gave a recap of his evening on the town the night before at Castle Creek, another club in Austin. He went on and on about the mixed drinks, the air-conditioning, and the nice digs. Concluding, he wondered why anyone would go to the Armadillo World Headquarters and sit on the concrete floor in a puddle of beer and sweat when such civilized amenities were offered at Castle Creek.

That did it. I charged down to the station, hoping to get my hands on the smooth-talking, blow-dried, polyester piece of shit. Luckily, the building was locked like a tomb. It was a holiday.

TRAVELING ARMADILLO BLUES

★

Sometimes, Jack Calmes at Showco in Dallas would call and invite me to jump on a plane and meet him at a rock 'n' roll event, gratis. Jack seemed to enjoy introducing me to heavyweights in the music industry. One Friday in 1975, Jack invited me to go with him to LA. Showco was providing sound and lights for a string of sold-out Led Zeppelin shows at the Forum. All I had to do was catch a Braniff flight to Dallas to meet up with Jack.

That afternoon, just as I was about to leave the office to catch my flight, a character named Big Ed dropped in to see me. According to reliable sources, Big Ed was the head of a ring of local cocaine dealers. He had that kind of an aura—somewhere between distasteful and downright evil.

Big Ed needed to know the prices for a long list of acts. He was thinking about doing a huge outdoor event but needed to know what kind of fees everyone charged, and he expected me to run the numbers for him. That wasn't a job I wanted, I said, and besides, festival promoters were generally not a class of people with which I cared to be associated. Big Ed obviously didn't like being brushed off so quickly, but I had no time to smooth over his ruffled feathers; I was already running late for my flight.

I wasn't sufficiently sophisticated at the time to intuit Big Ed's overall scheme: his bottom line was promoting rock 'n' roll shows as a means of laundering drug money.

I got away from there, and Jack and I met up in Dallas and hopped on the plane to LA. We checked in at the Continental Hyatt House on the Sunset Strip—the infamous "Riot Hyatt"—and when I walked into my room, the red message light on the phone was already winking at me. Sure enough, it was a message from Big Ed. He wanted to finish our conversation. When? Right now. He was calling from the lobby.

So he came up to my room and continued his pitch. "Just look into the prices," he said, "and just tell me what it's worth for your trouble."

"Oh, hell," I said, "a couple of hundred ought to be enough."

Big Ed flipped open his briefcase. The inside was perfectly packed wall-to-wall with stacks of wrapped one-hundred-dollar bills. I could have as easily asked for $20,000, and it wouldn't have mattered a nickel to him. He pinched two bills from a stack, handed them over, and shut the case.

When Big Ed saw that my jaw had dropped open like a garage door, he reopened the briefcase and fingered the top compartment. Out came a two-gram vial of cocaine. "Have fun tonight," he said, handing it over.

The evening continued in a similar vein of surrealism. I met Peter Grant, Led Zep's whale-sized manager. Grant wore a pair of cute, red tennis shoes that made his feet look tiny. Whenever Grant was involved in a show, promoters dreaded the inevitable cry of outrage from him; he would claim that box office receipts had been stolen, a tactic that enabled him to skim huge amounts of cash. It was said that the money was shipped back to England hidden in sound equipment. Peter Grant was brutish and scary, and he certainly wasn't the kind of person I wanted to hang out with. All of which made him the perfect front man for megarich rock bands.

After the show, I saw a couple of the biggest rock stars in the world enter a room, upon which they closed the door and made loud spanking and squealing sounds. Later, I received a kiss from a towering figure in high heels and a long, white dress, with a white turban on top of long, wavy hair. The kiss had a sandpaper effect, and I noticed an unmistakable five o'clock shadow when the individual said, "You're cute, cowboy," in a heavy British accent. That was my first encounter with Led Zeppelin's lead singer, Robert Plant.

By the end of the evening, I was sure I belonged in Austin, not LA.

Not long after my LA adventure, I flew to New York with a head full of marketing ideas and business pitches. I believed I could sell Armadillo, TYNA/TACI, Lone Star Beer, three bands, and a multitude of concepts all at once. Such was my confidence.

The New York expedition was, in short, one hell of a ride. Among the exciting adventures enjoyed by our sizable Armadillo entourage was our introduction to the actress Elizabeth Ashley, who was then hot as hell on Broadway and starring in the part of Maggie in a revival of Tennessee Williams's *Cat on a Hot Tin Roof*. On or off stage, Elizabeth Ashley was a larger-than-life character, and we got on very well. It was Mary Martin, the vice president of A&R at Warner Bros. Records, who made the introduction. In addition to being a powerful record company executive, Mary Martin (not to be confused with the famous actress from Texas) was legendary for getting the right people together, almost as if she were Fate's right-hand gal. Probably the most fateful meeting she arranged was between Bob Dylan and the Hawks, later known as the Band. When she was managing Leonard Cohen, she was the one who made the call to John Hammond, the producer and talent scout who had sparked the careers of Billie Holliday, Bob Dylan, and many others, and who ended up signing the offbeat, brilliant poet and songwriter. Mary Martin also got Cohen together with Judy Collins, who listened to Cohen's demo of "Suzanne" over the phone and immediately said, "I'm going to do that this week, in the studio." Martin also managed Van Morrison, and from my personal experience with Van, I can only imagine what that must have been like.[1]

It was one hell of a business trip. Memories of some of the details have grown fuzzy in the last forty years, but I do recall Bill Narum and his wife, Paula, drove the truck up, pulling fifty cases of Lone Star in a U-Haul trailer. Gordy Ham, a.k.a. "Ramblin' Rose," rode with them. Fortunately, my old, dusty files coughed up my "New York Activity Report," a detailed and upbeat letter that I wrote upon our return to Austin and sent out to Harry Jersig, Barry Sullivan, Jerry Retzloff, and our other clients at Lone Star Beer—and which is reproduced in the next chapter.

Kenneth Threadgill holding a Lone Star longneck. Bevo's
Tap Room, April 27, 1972. Photograph by Burton Wilson.

DEAR LONE STAR

"The Austin Consultants, Inc.
Thought You'd Never Ask . . ."
525 Barton Springs Rd.
Austin, Texas 78704
Phone 512-477-3623[1]

December 1, 1974

NEW YORK ACTIVITY REPORT

When my Braniff flight landed in New York, a San Antonio–based flight attendant salvaged the only four cans of Lone Star Beer on board, stuck them in her purse, and got me to the Warwick Hotel. She has since agreed to deliver a case per New York flight (two a week) to Chet Flippo and other deserving people.

This flight attendant, Ms. Sarah Putnam, and her San Antonio based crew, are interested in doing all they can to aid our Lone Star campaign and would love to get the "Cook's Tour" of "America's Most Beautiful Brewery" (We started to work on Texas International on the return flight).

As soon as my four cans of Lone Star were gone (about one hour), I ordered a six pack of Schaefer Beer, a local brew, and began the long 24 hour wait for our 50-case truck load to arrive. Sure enough, the can designs are embarrassingly similar (thank God we had ten cases of long-necks). In the new issue of *Rolling Stone,* a regional insert (a new *Rolling Stone* accommodation to get ad bucks) has a full-page ad for Schaefer, billing it as the youth-music beer, and a coupon for a $3.00 poster similar to the one I suggested for Lone Star some months ago. If the poster is as bad as the ad, I'll feel good. I should be receiving one in a week or two.

The first thing we did after checking in was to take the Warwick's paintings off the walls of our suite and replace them with the trappings of TYNA/TACI and Armadillo World Headquarters. A sign on the entrance of the suite announced that "We've brought as much of Texas with us as we could haul up in a truck, and since we're not taking any of it home, please gather up anything you need to take to your home or office…thanks for everything you do to make our stay in New York productive and fun. [Signed] TYNA, The Austin Consultants, Inc."

Since we only had a dozen or so Lone Star T-shirts left in our stash, we took several dozen T-shirts with other [Jim Franklin] Armadillo designs, several collections of AWHQ posters, a bunch of Long Live Longnecks posters, and a couple of dozen prized silver Armadillos for special, deserving folks. These were carried by the box load to every major record company, magazine, and newspaper office, along with a case of Lone Star Beer.

Mary Martin, vice president in charge of A&R at Warner Brothers Records, New York office, brought Elizabeth Ashley (currently starring in *Cat on a Hot Tin Roof* on Broadway) to our suite the night we arrived in New York. Ms. Ashley is currently regarded by most theatre critics as the reigning First Lady of the American Stage. This country boy did not know who she was until after she left in the wee hours of the morning. The next day, a fistful of tickets was delivered to us with the request that we come backstage after the performance. My burned out college memory of American lit did not recall that the play opens with Maggie the Cat screaming about the "no neck monsters" of her in-laws.

After the final curtain, imagine my surprise on finding "Long Live Longnecks" stickers on the dressing room doors and mirrors and my pleasure at discovering that Elizabeth had already sent one to Tennessee Williams.

Copious quantities (for New York, at least) of cold Lone Star turned backstage at the ANTA Theatre[2] into something not unlike the Armadillo, and the cast visited us many times during the remainder of the week.

On my last evening in New York, Ms. Ashley insisted that I don my Levi jacket and help her carry a grocery sack of Lone Star (in 30 degree weather) to Sardi's for her waiter friends. She kept me from feeling the least bit out of place in the presence of more class than I ever knew existed.

We found the Depression already surfacing in New York and a large interest by all media in anti-Depression stories. The *Wall Street Journal* carried a front page story (Nov. 22) on the financial organization of the Grateful Dead. We were contacted by editors and writers who had been told or read of our "successes" and they seemed to all be looking for proof that the arts and entertainment industry will not only survive but flourish to the point of aiding the peace and comfort of the country.

I told several of the wonders of beer and the brewing industry and you can look for story material to come out in several unusual publications before summer that deal with what was my main theme in New York: "Beer and Music, a Comforting Combination for Hard Times."

TYNA/TACI's presentation of "The Nights Never Get Lonely" (by the Gonzos, Freddie King, and Sunny and the Sunliners, plus commercials thus far produced) encountered a dramatic test of comparison and won with flying colors.

Chet Flippo and other music writers had for several weeks been investigating rumors that Randy Newman (considered by many to be one of the very best songwriters in America) had written and produced all the music for a huge new Dr Pepper ad campaign which begins immediately. The cause for the investigation is "R. Newman Management's refusal to admit that Newman has indeed done so."

On Saturday, November 23, several interested record and TV producers and executives and music journalists met with us and played the entire series of Dr Pepper commercials from a very unauthorized copy of Mr. Newman's tape. Pencils and pens flew across note pads, tape recorders whirred, brows knitted up. The tape was played again. We were asked to play "The Nights . . ." People laughed, we drank Lone Star, and both tapes were played again. Dr Pepper was put down. Freddie and Sunny and the Lost Gonzo played all night long and it did not get lonely.

Jack Calmes arrived on Sunday with good news. He has finished financing for the Rainbow Pavilion and contracted with Armadillo Productions to design, install, and oversee beer service. He has also contracted with TYNA/TACI to serve as promotional consultants. The Rainbow Pavilion is 70 acres of sloping, grassy park, in a natural theatre shape, adjacent to Rangers Stadium (in Arlington, Texas) and its parking facilities. It will have a maximum capacity of 100,000 and will include permanent restroom and concession facilities. Mayor Vandergriff of Arlington has already given the project his wholehearted endorsement and construction is expected to begin February 1, with a projected completion date of June 1, 1975. Calmes has tentative [commitments] on 14 major dates at this time.

Freddie King's Monday night performance at the Bottom Line was a remarkable success. Every imaginable music industry heavyweight seemed to be present and the mysterious supply of Lone Star Beer that kept appearing on unsuspecting tables added a great deal of humor and good spirits. According to Allan Pepper, owner, he had never seen a Bottom Line audience, usually a calm and sophisticated bunch, stand in their chairs, screaming for encore after encore.

Robert Stigwood, organizer of RSO Records, Freddie King's new label which is distributed by Atlantic Records, and RSO president Bill Oakes visited the suite after the performance and agreed that, even if they hadn't seen Dr. Turicchi's report, Freddie's recording of "The Nights Never Get Lonely" was a potential smash hit (at our meeting we at last got signed releases for use of our Freddie King tapes. His RSO contract is worth $400,000 and is very tight).

Freddie King, Jack Calmes, and the members of RSO left for London on Friday for the opening of Freddie's European tour. Bill Oakes, president, and Jack will return on Friday, December 7, to finalize plans and procedures for releasing "The Nights Never Get Lonely" early in 1975.

We had delivered to the suite a remarkable complement of audio and video hardware: speakers, amp, turntable, reel to reel and cassette tape players, video monitors, video tape cameras, etc. In effect, we opened our consulting office in New York for one week. Because of a recent and very dramatic rise in the profile of Dr. Turicchi's psychographic research lab in the music industry's upper echelon and because of the national reputation for scientific and promotional skills of two of the Austin consultants (namely, Woody Roberts and Augie Blume), we were doing full-tilt business in less than 24 hours. Record company executives made appointments with us and came to the hotel bearing records and tapes to play for us and ask advice regarding testing, promotion, and marketing.

Offers to buy were made to us on each component of our total product package, but we are insisting on one total purchase to reduce the number of clients we must satisfy to one (or two at the most) and to increase the efficiency of our relationship for non-Texas based projects.

These components are as confidential as our relationship with Dr. Turicchi once was, but for your better understanding of our Lone Star–TACI, Armadillo Productions relationships, I will list briefly what seems to be "in hand."

A. Marketing, promotional, testing control of Freddie King and "The Nights Never Get Lonely" for RSO/Atlantic
B. Armadillo Record Label
C. Sale with the above mentioned control of tapes for Uncle Walt's Band, Joker Moon, and the Doak Snead Band
D. Budgets for additional production, testing, and promotion of other musical groups
E. Sponsorship of a series of high quality TV specials
F. Financing for Armadillo Management, Inc.
G. Budget for production, testing, distribution and promotion for my #1 fantasy, a musical comedy documentary movie of AWHQ with plenty of sex, drugs, violence, and music to ensure sales
H. Production budget for a second screen play which we own
I. A rather large publishing advance for our company Rip Snortin' Tunes
J. National radio syndication
K. Production of Dory Previn's new musical starring Elizabeth Ashley, to open August, 1975, at AWHQ (Broadway meets Hollywood in Texas?)
L. An Armadillo/New York cultural exchange, multi-media art show in New York in the spring of 1975

Specific statements of desire to purchase various parts of this list were made by the decision-making executives for the five major labels in

America. Additional overtures came from one of the country's leading book publishers, a Broadway producer, and one of the largest syndication firms in the world.

The head of one of the major record companies wants to buy Sunny's English version of "The Nights . . ." He thinks it has even more Top 40 potential than Freddie's version. He didn't even know about Key-Lock Records or Sunny's huge sales in 27 states and Europe, and is frustrated to the point of wanting the cut so badly, he's probably going to offer Sunny a foolishly large sum of money.

One lengthy session that cost several thousand dollars involved a seminar with and the hiring of one of American's truly high tech trademark attorneys. With a new degree of Texas enthusiasm and a silver Armadillo on his watch fob, he is registering all of our products and ideas as fast and effectively as he can in every applicable area of trademarks and copyrights. He agrees with us that we have created the foundation of a new, highly profitable industry, which will serve the nation out of Austin, Texas, and understands how we have been scooped by Farah Slacks and *Redneck Rock* and is going to help us keep it from happening again.

NOTE: A lawsuit by Michael Murphey is in the works that will cause *The Improbable Rise of Redneck Rock* to cease being printed and sold pretty soon. He's paying the legal fees but has asked us to sign his petition. It seems they've upset Michael pretty badly and didn't bother to get any releases. I think we'll watch rather than participate. I did get treated pretty well in the book. My feeling right now is that I would like to handle promotion for the book and the press for Michael's suit.

Except for a couple of accounts that Augie picked up for his Northern California test market staff, we declined to take on any more work at this time, explaining that we first must complete the closing of the package that got us to New York.

When we first approached the Marketing Department of Lone Star we announced that our goal was to double Lone Star sales in three years. We were told that such a goal was admirable but absurd.

We would like to reiterate. Now that we have 1) pursued and accumulated information and knowledge of the brewing industry, 2) gauged mass audience response through psychographic testing and demographic research, 3) solidified working relationships with every major publicist in the country, and 4) gotten inexpensive commitments from some of the best known recording artists in America to record "The Nights Never Get Lonely" in 1975, we are now sure that Lone Star Beer sales can be doubled, provided the brewery morale and distribution can get geared for the hard work and jovial efficiency that is going to be required for such a task. We can make a "Lone Star high" one of the most desired conditions in America this coming summer.

Yours very truly,

Edwin O. Wilson
Austin Consultants, Inc.
525½ Barton Springs Rd.
Austin, Texas 78704

Poster for an AWHQ Halloween show, October 31–
November 1, 1974. Artwork by Guy Juke.

THE FIRST AND FINAL ANNUAL AWHQ NEWSLETTER

Well, unfortunately, the nation did not break out into a Lone Star high during the summer of 1974. Jack Calmes's plans for the Rainbow Pavilion, a one-hundred-thousand-seat amphitheater in Arlington scheduled to open in 1975, toppled like a sand castle under a beached whale, crushing both Armadillo Productions' contract to design, install, and oversee beer service for the venue and another lucrative PR gig for TYNA/TACI. It would be pointless to catalog every other item mentioned in my "New York Activity Report" that failed to materialize, least of all the fact that Michael Murphey decided not to waste money trying to halt publication of *The Improbable Rise of Redneck Rock.*

The list of disappointments and follies of 1974 was a long one. At the end of the year, I sat down to compose an annual newsletter to our staff, a first for AWHQ. Besides the usual reasons for such a communiqué, I wanted to address a certain negativity that I'd encountered in the building over the past year. Some of our people were carrying around a grudge as big as a Cadillac. A 1973 Cadillac Eldorado, to be exact.

The story behind the Cadillac started in late 1973, when two West Austin society ladies came into my office. Ada McElhenney and her friend Sally Byram were there on behalf of the Austin Arts Council, they explained. They were on the planning committee for the annual fundraising gala. Ada was married to a prominent Austin physician, Dr. Tom R. McElhenney. Sally was married to John D. Byram, a Donald Trump type in South Austin, except that John D. was better looking than Donald and not quite as rich. Sally was a beauty, pure and simple.

These two West Austin society women turned giggly and girlish once inside Austin's Hippie Carnegie Hall. It was their desire, they said, to hold a huge "Non-Gala" fundraising event at the Armadillo. I was skeptical. They were talking about an event for people like the governor, the mayor, and the powerful, rich people who funded the arts in our fair city. Would those types actually want to attend an event at the Armadillo? Sally and Ada assured me that they would.

On Sunday, January 20, 1974, I arrived early and enjoyed watching the big American sedans of the local elites wallowing into the Dillo's infamous moonscape parking lot. One of the first arrivals was a lady in a big, hairy fur and too much jewelry. As she entered the hall with her entourage, she glanced around the room and said, "What a perfect place to hold a Non-Gala."

Asleep at the Wheel was the no-brainer choice for musical entertainment. Their danceable western swing was irresistible, even to the stuffiest of the stuffies. I retreated to the studio to enjoy some refreshments, listening to the music over the big monitors. During the break, there were speeches, announcements, the usual society business. But then, at some point, I heard them paging "Mr. Eddie Wilson . . ."

My escort walked me onto the stage, where Ada McElhenney was waiting for me at the podium. She took my hand and announced to all, "And now, for his major contribution to the Austin arts in 1974, Eddie Wilson!"

Before I had a chance to speak, a huge gift-wrapped box was wheeled over to us. Ada pulled on the bow, the box fell open, and Sally Byram popped out and jumped into my arms. Sally was 103 pounds of Texas blonde, tanned with a hard body, dressed in a sexy little sundress with spaghetti straps and a short, tight skirt and high heels.

Feeling like King Kong, I stepped up to the microphone and expressed my humble thanks to everyone, especially Sally's husband, John D. Byram, after which I humbly walked offstage with Sally warm and cuddly in my arms.

I took Sally behind the stage and we stepped into Onion Audio. Here was a world that was light-years away from those West Austin Greek Revival mansions and country clubs. She seemed pleased with the hushed room, surrounded by dimly lit recording gear. The aroma of skunk weed hung in the air.

After twenty minutes or so, a security guy came back with a message. John D. Byram was about to have a heart attack . . . something about a missing wife. Sally bid me good-bye and, I'm told, returned to a much more attentive John.

Ada McElhenney and I became fast friends. One day I got a call from her saying that she and her husband were getting a divorce. She wanted me to buy her Cadillac Eldorado. The car was nearly new, and she really wanted me to have it. By then I knew her well enough to understand. She said she wanted to scale back a little and, in the process, get rid of all the vestiges of her ex. But I realized she also liked the idea of me cruising around town, easily recognizable with my wavy, black hippie hair, and knowing that her ex would see me driving the expensive car that he'd paid for. So, for less than I'd have had to pay for a used Checker cab, I got a nearly new Cadillac Eldorado. Some of my colleagues, however, scorned me for not driving my Dodge Charger or a beat-up VW.

There were other thorny issues as well, not the least of which were Hank Alrich's unpaid loan and the fact that we still didn't have a long-term lease on the property. I had issues to figure out, and I've always found that the process of writing often leads the way to possible solutions, or at least tells me what's really going on inside my head.

So I composed a newsletter. Some of the content was predictable, such as the annual accounting of income and expenses, income projections for the future, and a report on the activities of various aspects of Armadillo Productions Inc., including an update on the year's TYNA/TACI activities. No address to the troops would be complete without a discussion of our problem areas and goals for 1975, but I saved that for last, after my writing muscles had time to warm up.

In 1974 we had grossed $900,000 and broken even, our first year without a net loss. We had also found a spray-on insulation for the building interior that improved not only the thermal insulation of the building but also the acoustics, and cut down on noise complaints from the neighbors.

In August we had installed a mobile air-conditioning unit that, while not ideal, added a shred of credibility to the rumor that our music hall had AC.

One goal that almost felt within our grasp was establishing AWHQ as a national showcase in the eyes of the record labels and other moneyed music industry people who were able to provide tour support for artists, which would enable us to lower our ticket prices.

The Armadillo's physical infrastructure needed upgrading. Our business plans needed fine-tuning and capitalization. The building needed a marquee. We wished for a less terrible parking lot. The recording studio needed an upgrade. So did the kitchen.

Some goals were familiar tunes from 1970: organize and finance our record label and a publishing company, continue working on developing TV programs and a national radio show, and bring in legitimate theater.

We had investigated the possibility of getting a loan in order to consolidate our debts, cover the beer garden, and take care of other needed repairs and improvements. About $100,000 should do it. Our study showed us that the investment would likely result in a 10 percent net on our projected gross of $1.2 million in 1975. There was just one little problem. Until we could secure a long-term lease from M. K. Hage Jr., no one would loan us the money.

So far, that had not been possible, but why dwell on the negative? I reminded our staff that we had the most famous music hall in the country and that a lot of people out there looked to AWHQ for good news, not revenue projections. We were doing an awful lot of good work for a lot of people. If we could just keep going forward and with luck find a partner to help us either obtain a long-term lease or allow us to buy the eight-acre intersection, I wrote, we could potentially develop our sliver of land into the equivalent of the big film and television studios in Los Angeles.

Austin is right for this new industry. We didn't see it coming five years ago, [so] we set out to make it happen.... And after a while, people far away from Austin heard it was coming here so they came to see it for themselves. They liked it here and went back home and said, "It's gonna happen in Austin." And some of them packed up and came back to help, or they came back to get a piece. And it had begun to happen.

We didn't guess five years ago that today we'd have a thirty-year-old mayor, another thirty-year-old city councilman, [and a] thirty-year-old state representative, but we do and they are examples of the intangibles that are somehow part of us now and illustrate a change in the times. We would like to see another indication of changing times illustrated by our ability to pull together a fifty-year ground lease on an eight-acre intersection in the downtown part of the fastest growing capital in the United States. We're going to have to be quick and to the point to pull off such a real estate maneuver with no money, but it's our job and I feel that we will find a way.

I credited my tone of optimism to something Jim Franklin had told me in February 1972, when I was severely depressed. What he said turned out to be the most important lesson I've learned about business: "Don't let people know that you're depressed about how bad business is. When they ask, 'How's business?' tell them it's just fine." This approach, he said, would improve things a whole lot faster than pissing and moaning. I've followed that advice ever since.

My end-of-1974 communiqué finished with a reminder that the eight members of the board of directors of Armadillo Productions Inc. were Bobby Hedderman, Jim Franklin, Hank Alrich, Mike Harr, Carlotta Pankratz, Mike Tolleson, Genie Wilson, and me. I gave heartfelt thanks to all the staff and singled out a handful of people for special recognition. "Hank is working wonders with Onion Audio," I wrote. "Jim Franklin is doing a wonderful and heroic job with the Ritz."

And even though it was really impossible to completely suppress my irritation over the bad vibes that had been roiled by my Cadillac—and whatever else some of my colleagues wanted to bitch about behind my back—the process of writing about the good things made it easier for me to resist fighting back just then. Despite the struggles and heartaches of the past five years, especially 1975, I still felt lucky as hell to have this job, and although Dale Carnegie would have bitterly disapproved of my casual style, I signed off with a big old hippie hug.

No shit, I like it here.
Thanks, I love you.

Eddie Wilson

Artwork by Micael Priest, 1975.

ROUGH WATERS

★

When you're head honcho, the people who call you in the middle of the night are not calling to tell you to have a nice day. As I used to say, "As head honcho, I don't have the liberty of unplugging the phone. I'm the one they call when the place is burning down."

On January 10, 1975, I got a call about M. K. Hage III, whom we called "Three." He had died in his bedroom at his parents' home. His mother had found him. He had died with his head wedged between the mattress and box spring, in a desperate attempt to silence the noise in his head after ingesting an excessive amount of pharmaceutical cocaine.

Three was there during the summer of 1971, when we tore out the offices in the building to renovate and enlarge the music hall without asking his father's permission. If his father freaked out, Three would handle it, he had said.

Whenever I floated a new scheme, Three was often more enthusiastic about it than anyone else. His faith in my wild fantasies helped keep me going.

Just two days before he died, he had been at my house, talking about helping me steer the Armadillo into the future. He was going to work hard to win his father's confidence. When I walked with him to his car, he even said he was going to get straight, stop getting high, and take responsibility for things. "It's time to grow up," he said.

The cause of death was apparently an allergic reaction to pharmaceutical cocaine. The news left me discombobulated. I bounced between raw acceptance and denial. *It was inevitable . . . No, maybe it wasn't true . . .*

Three's death spelled bad news for the Armadillo. Without him, there would be no way to talk his father into agreeing to a long-term lease.

★ ★ ★

Bobby Hedderman was doing a fine job booking the hall at a time when we were increasingly vulnerable to competition, not only from other live venues but from that new scourge of the day, disco. At the same time, bands and promoters were charging higher fees. Sometimes, though, one of the heavy hitters would offer us easier-than-usual terms. Zappa was one of them. In the spring, Frank Zappa played a two-night stand with Captain Beefheart. Live tracks from that weekend formed the bulk of the Zappa-Beefheart album *Bongo Fury*. The faithful were thrilled by the show, but the critic for *Rolling Stone* called it "a disjointed, jarring package of seemingly off-the-wall musings . . . so conceptually jumbled that it seems impossible for it to sustain listener interest for anything but the briefest periods of time."[1] Even with songs like "Man with the Woman Head" and "Muffin Man," the reviewer posited that Lou Reed's *Metal Machine Music*, also released that year, was probably the only thing standing between *Bongo Fury* and the title of worst LP of 1975.

Roky Erickson made a tentative return to live performance that summer. Roky had a new band called Bleib Alien and a raft of new songs with monster movie titles: "I Walked with a Zombie," "Creature with the Atom Brain," and "Cold Night for Alligators." The songs had chilling, acid-drenched, nightmare lyrics, but with Roky's gift for poetry and tight pop arrangements, they were at least the equal of Phil Spector's best work. Our favorite was the Doug Sahm–produced single "Two-Headed Dog (Red Temple Prayer)," a three-chord classic for all time.

The venue formerly known as the Texas Opry House reared its head again under the name Austin Opry House. The man in charge there was one Tim O'Connor, one of Willie Nelson's people, and Willie himself had a piece of the club. O'Connor had run several smaller clubs already and had produced Willie's second picnic. Tough as a rhino hide and persistent as the sun in late August, Tim had survived in the business long enough to earn a reputation as Austin's Bill Graham. He was skilled in making money while dealing with the best talent in the business, huge crowds, and all the Damon Runyon characters running with Willie.

One of the Austin rock bands that proved a reliable draw for the Armadillo was Too Smooth. They were a slick rock band from the cover band scene, though they played original music. Everybody in the band was a top-notch player. Hank Alrich liked them a lot, and although they inked some deals with major labels, everything fizzled out for them and they never broke nationally.

Another house favorite originated as a live-in jam session. Since Jim Finney had the keys to the studio and the front door, he was a de facto jam organizer. One afternoon, Finney was jamming with Hank Alrich, Jack Jacobs, Fletcher Clark, and Tony Laier from Greezy Wheels. As I walked through the Cabaret, they were sawing their way through "Elvira," the popular tune about a street in East Nashville, and the music put a happy twitch in my butt.

Did they want a job, I asked, as in that night? And did they have a name? The answer to the first question was yes, to the second, no. Fletcher Clark asked if the Five Dollar Name Corporation had anything for sale.

"The only inventory I've got right now are Sleaze-O Demeanor and Balcones Fault," I said. The latter is the name of the fault line that stretches between Del Rio and Dallas and whose tossing and turning over the millennia created the buckled and broken landscape west of Austin known as the Hill Country.

After a quick meeting, they went for Balcones Fault. They played that night and from then on, and even though they never gave me my five bucks, Balcones Fault was our house band.

Clark and Jacobs had more musical energy and produced more frontal lobe stimulation than ten average funky white bands. Fletcher had been a bank vice president in Boston, and Jacob's brother ran the biggest bank on the Texas-Mexico border, which made their defection to the hippie lifestyle seem only natural. The drummer was Michael McGeary, who formerly played with Jerry Jeff Walker and Michael Murphey.

Their repertoire evolved to include ranchera, cumbia, swing, and R&B. Sometimes they were joined onstage by magicians (among them, the future television star Harry Anderson), a belly dancer, dog acts, and jugglers. Eventually, the band left Austin for San Francisco in an attempt to play in the major leagues, but again, it didn't work out.

More racially mixed bands were cropping up in town, appearing regularly on the Armadillo stage. Forty-Seven Times Its Own Weight, Starcrost, and Steam Heat were the cream of the crop. Jazz- and R&B-influenced, all three developed substantial followings.

Van Wilks, one of Austin's many guitar wizards, fronted a band called the Fools. Van played hard Texas boogie in the style of ZZ Top's Billy Gibbons, and on a good night, you'd have to toss a coin to say who was better. With Tommy Shannon providing the thundering foundation on his Fender bass, the Fools were one of the hardest rocking, most dependable local draws at the Armadillo.

Another Austin guitar genius, Eric Johnson, played in a jazz fusion ensemble called the Electromagnets. Everybody in the band was exceptional. The music had a fiery and severe intensity, but it wasn't for everyone. The songs were all instrumental jams, similar to those of Jeff Beck's fusion rock period.

One night the Electromagnets were playing, and there was an incident with a tear gas canister. People went running from the hall to escape. Some of them jumped over the new fence next to the Marimont Cafeteria. As they landed on the cars in the parking lot, the sound made a thunderous roar. The band never stopped playing.

In my opinion, the best homegrown talent with the most potential was D. K. Little, a surly Lubbock character with a voice that was richer than Waylon's and a curled-lip pout that made Springsteen look like an altar boy. Mary Martin of Warner Bros. financed a demo but wanted him to do country, and he wouldn't hear of it. Jerry Wexler didn't have any better luck with him. We had introduced the two of them at the Dillo, and Wexler sat with D. K. on a flight to Los Angeles, talking to him about a career in the music business. Upon landing, D. K. caught the next flight home. He never even left the airport. He later quit playing, went to air-conditioning school, got married, had kids, and died surly.

Smack dab in the middle of July 1975, Clifford Antone opened a blues club at the corner of Sixth and Brazos downtown. Originally called Pecan Street, Sixth Street had once been a thriving commercial district of great ethnic variety. By the 1970s, however, the legacy of discrimination, white flight, and other symptoms of urban rot had left Sixth Street a

D.K. Little onstage at AWHQ.
Photograph by Van Brooks.

ramshackle, seedy area that, nonetheless, had a few good bars. The south side of Sixth was mostly Mexican American clubs, shops, and bars; African American businesses dominated the north side of the street. Few college students were brave enough to go there after dark.

It took an urban pioneer with vision and guts to put his money on a big venue at that location. I wasn't the only person in town who thought he was crazy, and not just because of the address. The Armadillo had presented blues for five years. There were a few exceptions, such as Mance Lipscomb, Freddie King, and maybe one or two others, but as a rule, blues musicians—like bluegrass and jazz musicians—had a limited audience. But here came this kid from Port Arthur with big plans to showcase blues seven nights a week. I gave him six months, tops. At least the young, white blues bands would have someplace to play more regularly than our joint, and maybe they'd quit bitching to me about it. Plus, I would have another place to go.

As it turned out, Clifford was on to something, even though he was better at being a visionary and patron than a businessman. Inside the old joint, which had the acoustic character of a cafeteria, the old masters and their attentive, loving disciples bonded and burned the midnight oil. The torch was passed to a new generation. As Clifford soon learned, running a blues club was no way to get rich, but there was always a sense that something important was happening at his club.

Flocking to Antone's school of the blues were stellar students like Bill Campbell, Jimmie Vaughan, Stevie Ray Vaughan, Denny Freeman, Angela Strehli, Lou Ann Barton, Derek O'Brien, and many others who, over the years, helped establish Austin's reputation as a music capital. Clifford Antone would generously pay headliners like Muddy Waters, Jimmy Reed, Luther Tucker, Hubert Sumlin, and Clifton Chenier, making arrangements for them to hang around for a while before and after their dates, which allowed the young gun guitar players to sit in and learn through observation and immersion. What Austin blues player wouldn't want a chance to jam with Hubert Sumlin or eat catfish with Jimmy Reed?

One thing about the blues scene got on my nerves: hearing people say there had been no place for blues in Austin until Antone's. It kept getting said and printed in the media over and over, even though it was wrong the first time some misinformed person said it.

Denny Freeman remembers it differently. Denny said:

For the first couple of years that I played in Austin with Jimmie Vaughan and Doyle Bramhall in Storm, the only gigs [we] got were the IL Club, the One Knite, the Armadillo, and shows the Armadillo promoted at the University of Texas, Fort Hood, and [in] Victoria. We had the loyalty of the Dillo's Dallasites, Bobby Hedderman and Mike Tolleson. We played there and got paid for playing a lot of times when hardly anybody showed up.[2]

★ ★ ★

The worst late-night call ever came ten months after the one about M. K. III. It was November 9, the second of two nights of the Pointer Sisters. Both shows had sold out. I'd gone home early because I had a big day ahead.

The phone rang, rousing me from a deep sleep. Dub Rose was on the other end. "Yeah, what do you want?" I answered, using my no-you-didn't-wake-me voice.

I heard him sob. "Boss," he said, "Ken Featherston's dead."

"What?"

"He got shot in the parking lot, Boss. He died immediately."

Ken Featherston was twenty-three years old. One of our rising house poster artists, Ken had been gaining a reputation as an equal to Jim Franklin, Danny Garrett, and Micael Priest. He had whipped up a fine-styled, multicolored classic for the Pointer Sisters show. For the Marshall Tucker Band's June 30, 1974, show, Ken did a beautiful rendition of a cowpoke on a bucking bronco in the middle of a dark sky, a golden sun breaking through. The band liked it so much they used it on the cover of their album *Searchin' for a Rainbow*.

Ken was a broad-shouldered, handsome guy. He was part Filipino, with a dark complexion and a thick mane of dark-brown hair flowing down his back. He was athletic, unselfish, cool, and gung ho. His charisma was infectious. One of the most popular people at the Armadillo had been murdered.

Earlier that day, I had called a meeting to remind the staff that the TABC was cracking down; we had to make damn sure no one left the building with a beer in their hand or any other alcoholic beverage (it was legal to bring in your own bottle of liquor, as long as it wasn't beer). After the show ended, Dub Rose was at the exit, collecting empty pitchers with both hands as the crowd filed out. One guy was toting an open whiskey bottle as he walked out.

Dub hollered at him to get his attention. Obviously high and drunk, the whiskey drinker came up to Dub and shoved him. Dub fell back and the pitchers shattered. Henry Gonzalez walked up to the assailant and bear-hugged him to the ground. Other staff came to assist.

"Buddy, we're not going to hurt you," Henry said. "We just can't let you take that bottle out of here." Henry released his hold, and as he stood up, the guy jerked himself upright, went a few steps toward the parking lot, then turned around and said, "I'm gonna come back and kill you."

"Go home, man," Henry said. "You've had too much to drink."

Most of the staff had already gone home. After a long load-out, Henry Gonzalez and Ken Featherston walked out together, ready to head home. There was a car parked under the big tree. From there, Henry and Ken probably looked alike—two tall guys with long hair and dark complexions.

A pistol shot rang out. Ken fell. The bullet entered just above his left eyebrow. He died in Henry's arms.

On a recent Saturday afternoon, I talked about that night with Robert Gower, going over the details of an event that none of us will ever forget.

Doyne Bailey and Jerry Spain were the APD detectives who came in and questioned everyone. They were good policemen, and we'd always gotten along well with them. Bailey and Spain questioned the security staff until long after daylight. Henry Gonzalez and Dub Rose were able to describe the whiskey drinker, but nobody knew his name. It seemed probable that this wasn't the first time he'd had an altercation with a bouncer, which meant there was a good chance that APD had his mug shot. But with nothing else to go on, it might be like searching for a needle in a haystack.

After answering all their questions, Dub said good night and walked back to the security office. He looked up at the wall and saw a picture of himself wearing a new cowboy hat, taken by Burton Wilson. That picture was the key to identifying the whiskey drinker.

Dub recalled that only a minute or two after Burton had snapped the photo, he'd had to lay the hat down to eject a troublemaker. He was certain that this was the same guy, the whiskey drinker.

Burton had just moved to Santa Barbara. When I called to give him the news about Ken, he hadn't even unpacked his stuff. I told him I needed the date of the hat photo. Burton said it might take several days to find it. He was really sorry about that, he said. But two hours later, he called me with the information.

Dub went down to APD headquarters, where he was shown mug shots from the three-day period that Burton had provided, and he picked out the face of the whiskey drinker. The man's name was John Randolph Bingham. An Austin native, Bingham lived with his mother on Hippie Row, which was Thirty-Third Street just north of UT. At one time, the houses on that block constituted the entire Austin counterculture community. When the police pulled up, Bingham slipped out the back door and escaped. Henry Gonzalez drew a sketch of Bingham and gave it to the police to aid in their search.

Ken Featherston's funeral was held in Corpus Christi, and we held a memorial service at the Armadillo. After the services, Jim Franklin went to the Bingham home and talked to Mrs. Bingham, who worked at Dairy Queen on the Drag. At one point, she told Jim that after her husband died, a nice family had offered to raise their son. Now she regretted not saying yes.

After further probing, she said the family now lived in Waco. After leaving Thirty-Third Street, Jim Franklin called directory assistance and learned that the Waco phone directory had three listings under the last name Bingham. Jim called the first and second numbers. No answer. On number three, someone said hello.

"Hello, is John there?" Jim asked. The pause on the other end told him all he needed to know.

Jim called the Waco police, and by the end of the day, John Bingham was in jail. He was sent to the Rusk State Hospital in the small East Texas town of Rusk, the same place Roky Erickson was incarcerated after his 1969 drug bust.

The state released John Bingham sixteen months later. His troubles with the law resumed, and he died in prison.

None of us knew how to cope with the reality that one of our dear friends had been murdered at our hippie music emporium. What did we know about grief counseling in 1975? Nothing.

Henry Gonzalez had been standing next to Ken when the shooting happened. In all likelihood, the bullet had been intended for Henry, not Ken. Henry knew it. The burden of grief was almost too much for him, or anyone, to bear.

Leea Mechling says Henry never really got over it.

Here we were, promoting a song called "The Nights Never Get Lonely" for Lone Star Beer, and we all felt lonely as hell.

★ ★ ★

TYNA/TACI took a lot of hits in 1975. Despite throwing some pretty smart counterpunches, the partners were starting to feel punch-drunk. We pitched some great ideas and sold at least one of them. *Armadillo Radio Headquarters* was our concept for a weekly radio show in the tradition of the *King Biscuit Flour Hour*: a series of live concerts at the Armadillo broadcast on syndicated FM stations across the country. Radio Shack's in-house advertising agency arranged for the company to come on board as a sponsor. But then Radio Shack learned that staff members at the agency had been taking kickbacks. Everyone was fired. That put the quietus on *Armadillo Radio Headquarters*.

Freddie King's Lone Star Beer music commercial had tested stronger than anything else Dr. Turicchi had ever tested on his lab rats. It had "hit" written all over it, if only RSO Records, Freddie's new record label, would release it. Instead, the people in charge of artistic direction at the label got the bright idea to release a song that would cash in on the "bump" dance craze in the disco scene, so they dumped a song called "Boogie Bump" on the innocent public in 1975. Sure, Freddie's stinging lead guitar and great gravelly vocals were present on the track, but it was also awash with wah-wah rhythm guitar, disco bass, and drums. The tune was as sincere as a Malibu sunset printed on a polyester shirt.

We had a plan for a big-budget television commercial that would feature the Pointer Sisters singing the Lost Gonzo Band's "The Nights Never Get Lonely" to a disco beat. Lone Star Beer goes disco? Why not? It was a fact that they needed to reach a bigger demographic. The two-steppers in their Manny Gammage Hi-Roller hats and Charlie Dunn boots were already sold on Lone Star. We needed people in platform shoes, too.

We wanted to take the Lone Star ad campaign into new markets beyond the cosmic cowboy set. We wanted black music and Mexican music. We wanted to make Lone Star the brand of all the people, not just the young bubbas.

We shot the commercial, as scheduled, on Tuesday, the tenth of November. The fact that Ken Featherston had been killed the day before was never far from our thoughts. For the location, we rented Magic Time

Machine, a new theme restaurant on the south shore of Town Lake on Riverside Drive. The place needed very little extra dressing to double as a glamorous disco club. We recruited all the best-looking people we could find for the extras.

The Pointer Sisters were hotter than a handful of raw jalapeño peppers. Beautiful, talented, and savvy, they had worked in various configurations as backup singers since the 1960s. Their sound reeked of a heavy jazz and bebop influence.[3] In 1974, after they had notched several Top 40 hits, their single "Fairytale" crossed over to the country charts. The Pointers took home a Grammy the following year for best country vocal performance by a group.

The Pointer Sisters also happened to be the first black female singers invited to sing at the Grand Ole Opry. We thought they were the perfect act to bring Lone Star Beer into the mainstream. Lone Star disagreed.

Sitting across the table from the Lone Star people, I felt the hairs on the back of my neck rise. No, they told us, this commercial isn't right for us, our distributors would have problems with it. Black faces had raised Lone Star's redneck card.

The big hats at Lone Star wanted to stick with progressive country exclusively. Their advertising gurus felt the same way. The commercial never ran.

We ended up being so pissed off at Lone Star that we went to Pearl Beer, their rival in San Antonio. "We're ready to jump ship," we told them. "We've been screwed by Lone Star." Intrigued and excited, the Pearl boys asked us what we wanted to do next.

I said, "Whatever it takes to get a $10,000 check."

"Let's start with a bumper sticker," they said.

I went home and got high with Woody Roberts. We were drinking Pearl, which was actually a mighty fine brew. At some point I said, "Wow, that's the best 'neck in Texas." I'd heard the expression being used by African Americans.

Woody liked the sound of it. Lone Star had tried to register the term "longneck," but we had beat them to it.

Woody called the guy who printed the "Long Live Longnecks" bumper stickers and ordered a big batch of stickers that called Pearl the "Best Neck in Texas." I drove down to San Antonio and picked up our check for $10,000.

Poster for the Pointer Sisters show at AWHQ,
November 10, 1974. Artwork by Ken Featherston.

Lone Star had screwed up a good thing. We could've made them cool. Other brands were already tapping into the same market they were so focused on. Instead of hiring us to help expand their appeal, Lone Star gave all their business back to their Dallas agency, Glenn, Bozell & Jacobs—the people who had always bitterly coveted our itty-bitty piece of the action and had always tried to take credit for things that we had done.

Ironically, Lone Star sales enjoyed a boost from the Pearl longneck campaign, since most beer drinkers still associated the tall brown bottle with Lone Star instead of Pearl. Within five years, however, both Lone Star and Pearl would be purchased by bigger beer companies who would move the local brewing operations out of town. If Lone Star had listened to us, it might still be made in San Antonio, enjoying the kind of hip cachet that Shiner Beer has today.

Meanwhile, Randy McCall and Mike Tolleson, two former fraternity brothers at SMU who constituted one half of TYNA/TACI, had become like oil and water. Randy didn't like company resources being channeled into videotaping experiments that were not immediately reaping revenue.

Randy also wanted out of TYNA/TACI and insisted that we buy him out of the partnership. He wanted $5,500, plus a percentage of future earnings. We felt that was unreasonable. He suggested we bring the matter to Hank Alrich. We all respected Hank and agreed to abide by his decision. Hank heard us out, then said, "I think Randy's right." Mike Tolleson, Woody Roberts, and I were stunned. We paid Randy. When you think about it, it was crazy. He didn't think the Armadillo should have an in-house agency, and he wanted out of it, even though he didn't need the money—he had another position coming up with Manor Downs, which he expected to be quite lucrative. Yet he wanted a percentage of our future income, even though the hemorrhage of that much cash from a struggling partnership seemed likely to cause its collapse.

Which it did.

Ever since we got a permit to sell it, beer had been keeping the Armadillo ark afloat. We sold lots of beer, but we wouldn't sell just any old beer, even if selling that brand might help improve our bottom line. The brand I'm referring to is Coors, the Colorado export we called "Colorado Kool-Aid" because it was bland to the point of being tasteless. Coors had gained some kind of reputation for being cool, particularly in our baby boom set. Its cachet was something between a scam and an illusion, however, because the Coors family were huge donors to noxious right-wing causes. One of their favorite people was Phyllis Schlafly, the right-wing activist who had almost single-handedly halted the ratification of the Equal Rights Amendment and who had also railed against integration, the UN, globalization, so-called activist judges, and abortion rights.

Ann Richards was one of several local politicos who had already sought my assurance that the Dillo would support the boycott against Coors. Even though she held no elective office at the time, Richards was already a political power hitter, having helped at least two liberal women win seats in the state legislature. I wasn't about to tell her no. But here came Roy Butler, trying to force us to sell Coors. Butler was the former mayor of Austin, a big-time car salesman, country radio station owner, highly competitive hustler, and all-pro asshole. Oh yeah, he was also a beer distributor, and he had acquired the rights to distribute Coors in our area.

Butler's beer distribution manager kept telephoning my bar manager to make an appointment so he could make a presentation that would inform us of all the reasons that Coors should be added to the brands sold at the Armadillo. I kept stonewalling him. One day I got a call from M. K. Hage. "I don't know how Roy Butler knows you're behind on your rent," he said, "but he's really pressuring me to get you to make an appointment with him. Couldn't you please meet with him so he'll quit bothering me?"

I agreed to see Roy, but I didn't say I'd go along with him. When he showed up for our meeting, he came rolling into the office like a velvet steamroller. I told him that I was repulsed by the politics of the Coors family. His counterargument was that the Busch family, who owned Budweiser, were a bunch of former Nazis and hadn't exactly become liberals since the war.

I listened until he finally talked himself out.

"Roy," I said finally, "Ann Richards is a close friend of mine and you're not. She says no."

The Armadillo didn't sell Coors Beer until after I left. How much revenue was lost in the interim? It's hard to say. But I do know that in the late 1980s and 1990s, Whole Foods Market (founded in Austin in the fall of 1980, three months before the Armadillo closed for good) supported the boycott against certain species of tuna to help call attention to the mass slaughter of dolphins by boats harvesting tuna for sandwiches and cat food. Whole Foods might have lost some money on that gambit as well, but taking a moral stand made the company look good, and in the long run, they did pretty well.

Looking back, between the terrible traumas of 1975, we had an over-abundance of great shows. For our fifth birthday that August, Commander Cody brought in a full house, heat be damned. We did bang-up business with Charlie Daniels, as usual. Unfortunately, Bruce Springsteen's manager, Mike Appel, decided that the Armadillo was now too small for Springsteen, so they played across the street at the Municipal Auditorium.

Bobby Hedderman had booked a lineup through the end of the year that was as strong as cowboy coffee. Marcia Ball of Freda and the Firedogs went off to front a group under her own name, Marcia Ball and the Misery Brothers. Starting in the fall, we paired them with compatible road shows at every opportunity to help them grow their audience.

Stellar road shows I remember best were the Flying Burrito Brothers, the Pointer Sisters, Billy Cobham with George Duke (Tomas Ramirez's band Jazzmanian Devil opened the show), Jimmy Cliff, Toots and the Maytals, Chuck Mangione, Commander Cody (twice), Marshall Tucker Band (also twice), Amazing Rhythm Aces, Billy Swan (still hot with his refried rockabilly hit "I Can Help"), Detroit rocker Bob Seger and the Silver Bullet Band, Quicksilver Messenger Service, Mighty Clouds of Joy, Sonny Terry and Brownie McGhee, and a New Year's Eve blowout with Asleep at the Wheel.

As for the numbers, we grossed about $1.3 million in 1975, and after costs, we broke even for the second year in a row. Numbers, of course, have no feelings, and we did—thus the divergent accounts of profit and loss.

Mance Lipscomb and wife, Elnora, at home in Navasota,
Texas, March 15, 1967. Photograph by Burton Wilson.

ONE LAST SWING FOR
THE FENCES

Roy Buchanan came back to the Armadillo at the beginning of 1976 to remind us of all the magic that can be wrung from a Fender Telecaster. In mid-January we hosted yet another benefit for an Austin music club on its last legs. This time it was the Alliance Wagon Yard, with B. W. Stevenson topping the bill.

The year of the US Bicentennial found many of us under a dark cloud. Ken Featherston's death was heavy on our minds. Mance Lipscomb died in January. He was eighty years old and weakened by a stroke. A good many Austin musicians had visited him at his home in Navasota. Others sat at his bedside when he was in the hospital here. Although not unexpected, Mance's death left another hole in our lives.

A few moneybags wandered in and out of the picture. Tom McCamey, the original investor in the kitchen, was followed by Hugh Lawrence, Cleve Howard of Budget Tapes and Records in Houston, and Tom Glasscock. Glasscock was a backer of a band called the Point, which had been formed by Sid Page, former violinist for Dan Hicks and His Hot Licks. There were always too many strings attached to the deals proposed, however, or at least that was how we saw it.

The one real investor in the Armadillo World Headquarters was Hank Alrich. Oddly, I didn't have a lot of day-to-day contact with Hank, who kept busy with the studio, recording shows, recording sessions, and making constant improvements to the facility. Those were his priorities, along with playing music. Hank was first and foremost a musician, and he knew I was there for the musicians.

Various people were always warning Hank that I was going to rip him off. He talked about it many years afterward. "There were many Eddie Wilson haters out there, even people close to me," he said. "I don't know why, but it was out there."[1]

Whatever anonymous animosity and paranoia existed never got in the way of my relationship with Hank. My priorities were keeping the Armadillo running. Sometimes I'd address the troops, channeling the spirit of my favorite football coach at McCallum High and giving them a rousing pep talk that would, temporarily at least, boost morale and quiet the naysayers.

Jan Beeman, the Kitchen Queen, said my speeches were "uplifting and inspiring, no matter how hot and sweaty and tired or cold and freezing you were." Sometimes, she said, "I'd hate Eddie, and then he'd come back and give a State of the Union address, and I'd love him again."[2]

As time went on, I became increasingly obsessed with finding the Big Idea, the scheme that would finally put us over the top, making us financially successful to the point where we could stop constantly worrying about going under from one month to the next. We burrowed down like so many underground critters, cozy in our rooms, daydreaming about what we could do if and when the Big Idea came to fruition and succeeded.

On a day-to-day basis, as with any bureaucracy, turf protection could be an issue. But the space was so big and the number of rooms so plentiful that we grew comfortable with the digs and the way in which it was divided up. It helped that we ran several of the building's original tenants off, which freed up additional space.

Accounting always got first consideration for new space. People in the accounting section always kept their heads down, working more like beavers than the stoned dreamers in the rest of the building.

Mike Tolleson's goals were peace, quiet, and solitude. He was interested in keeping us out of legal trouble and up to speed with the particulars of the music business, and he achieved his goals with little drama.

As ever, the joint was in constant need of upgrading. Even though we lacked a long-term building lease, we had no choice but to invest in improvements. If we didn't, we'd be eating the dust of all the new club hustlers in town.

New office space became available downstairs after a tenant moved out of the offices that sat between the hall and Barton Springs Road. Armadillo people moved in, everyone scuffling for their own piece of the new real estate. Much to our surprise, we discovered that the downstairs complex was air-conditioned by a primitive, water-cooled gas system run by a wooden rooftop cooling tower—a structure that had always been there but whose true purpose had been unknown to us. The effect wasn't arctic frigid, but the evaporative cool feeling on the skin beat the hell out of tropical mugginess.

Our efforts to air-condition the rest of the building continued. Negotiations with Southern Union Gas over leasing portable AC units dragged on almost as long as the Paris peace talks with North Korea, and in the end, we did a Nixon and just pulled out.

Henry Gonzalez started focusing on posters more than security, taking over Jim Franklin's former space, and he became the Armadillo's official art director by acclamation. Henry cleaned out Jim's old space and transformed it into a community art gallery. The shows featured Micael Priest, Sam Yeates, and the space's former tenant, Jim Franklin, along with groups from Mexico and Japan. The gallery also hosted a females-only art exhibition, the first one in Austin history.

The Bicentennial year was still young when I decided to put a moratorium on benefits for political campaigns. Raymond Frank ran for county sheriff on a "No More Pot Busts" platform in 1972, but once he was in office, he proved to be a disappointment and was often a source of embarrassment. We'd also done fundraisers to help elect Jeff Friedman mayor. Friedman had made a name for himself as a student activist leader at UT. He had the support of young voters and a left-of-center coalition. Now thirty years old, with long hair and a mustache, he was called "Austin's hippie mayor," but he always struck me as a charmless bully.

Frank came back to the Armadillo in early February to lend his name to a benefit for the People's Free Community Clinic. Fortunately, the bill was stacked with some talented and interesting characters. Sex, satire, magic, hippie values, and music—we had them covered. For music, we

Poster for a Peoples Community Clinic benefit concert
at AWHQ, February 8, 1976. Artwork by Kerry Awn.

had Ramon, Ramon and the Four Daddyos, Balcones Fault, and a new local hippie satire band called the Savages. The front man for the Savages was Kerry Awn, a visual artist and performer who had more talent and charm in his little finger than the mayor had in his whole body. Our magician was Harry Anderson, and Jim Franklin was our emcee. Balcones Fault had recently added a new attraction, Chastity Fox, who performed her burlesque routine with the band.

Chastity was a sweet person in addition to being beautiful, sexy, and a head taller than me. Besides being great to look at, she'd been an eyewitness to history, having schooled many of the professional dancers who worked at Abe Weinstein's Colony Club and Jack Ruby's Carousel Club in Dallas. Jack Ruby, of course, was gone by the time I met Chastity, but Abe Weinstein and Candy Barr were still very much alive, and thanks to Chastity, I had the pleasure of meeting both of them at Abe's eightieth birthday party.

"It takes a lot to dress up a Tuesday night" was an expression I had coined regarding booking a place with live entertainment. Chastity laughed when she heard me say it, then showed me a large "binder full of women," as Mitt Romney would say, with photos of all the strippers she had trained over the years. She showed me an eight-by-ten of her star pupil, Tuesday Night, onstage in her minimalist costume. Sure enough, it hardly took anything to dress up Tuesday Night.

One night, after the benefit, I was hiding out in one of my favorite places, a back corner booth at El Rancho. Suddenly, the light dimmed. The shadow looming over me belonged to Mayor Friedman, who, by the way, was not related to the Kinkster. I was in a bad mood, and seeing him didn't lighten things a bit. So when he asked how I was doing, my answer wasn't exactly sugar-coated.

"What are you whining for?" he said. His tone sounded insulting. "You're doing more business than anybody in town!"

Since when was the mayor of Austin entitled to deny a citizen's right to be depressed? I went back to the office and announced that the Armadillo wouldn't be holding any more benefits for politicians.

Predictably, our old colleague Ronnie Earle, then a state legislator and attorney, decided to run for the office of district attorney. Previously, Earle had written a letter for us that got a three-day TABC suspension

Poster for a Balcones Fault show at AWHQ,
January 30, 1976. Artwork by Sam Yeates.

dismissed. It had taken him all of ten minutes to write the letter. After turning down his request for a fundraiser, we immediately received a $1,100 bill for legal services.

That made me so mad that I rescinded my apolitical proclamation and put up a large "Ann Richards for County Commissioner" sign on the side of the Dillo. From now on, it wasn't enough to support a politician's views; they had to be someone I liked and respected. Ann Richards not only fit the bill, she was in a class of her own.

★ ★ ★

In February of 1976, the year before punk rock broke out, English art rockers Roxy Music brought out Austin's glam rock aficionados to the Armadillo. Bryan Ferry took the stage wearing a Clark Gable mustache and riding boots, crooning like a cross between Elvis Presley and Edith Piaf. Author and musician Jesse Sublett remembered it as one of his favorite shows at AWHQ.

One of the most hyped shows that spring was a San Francisco band called the Tubes. They were preceded by a reputation for putting on a wild, theatrical show, and for catchy songs like "White Punks on Dope." During that song, the singer Fee Waybill would come out wearing giant platform boots and huge sunglasses. Turk Pipkin opened with his one-man show, performing a mime act, doing magic tricks, and juggling.

That night is a blur to me now, but fortunately Dub Rose, who was working that night, remembers it well. Because their show required so many costumes and props, the Tubes showed up with giant rolling racks for their wardrobe and accessories, the first time Dub had ever seen that. Henry Gonzalez represented the venue in the negotiations with the band as per their requirements, and one thing at the top of the list was a working chain saw. The cutting chain had to be removed, and the chain saw had to start on the first pull.

"That was my job," Dub said. "We had an old chain saw and I cleaned it up, put in a new spark plug, mixed up a new batch of fuel, and took the chain off. I tested it a bunch of times, and it would start on the first pull. But the night of the show I was real nervous. Fee Waybill bent down, picked it up, and it started on the first pull. The chain saw's screaming and smoking, and he jumps into the audience, and the people loved it."

Dub pointed out that, although the Tubes were unusual, they were far from the first band with a gimmick or two to play the Armadillo. One of Dub's favorites was a bluegrass band from Arizona called Goose Creek Symphony.

"They had a roadie they called Zorok from the Planet Zorok," Dub said. "He was a typical nerdy guitar tech, but also a unicyclist. So during the show, when everybody was singing harmonies, Zorok came out, buck naked, riding a six-foot-tall unicycle. He zipped across the stage, going in between each singer and their microphone. Each one of them stepped back to let him pass, never missed a note, and then Zorok rolled back across the stage in the other direction. It was a great gimmick."

I booked Shiva's Headband for the Armadillo's July Fourth Bicentennial show out of pure sentimentality and personal sympathy. Their "Song for Peace" had been our favorite hymn during the antiwar protests in Austin in the 1960s, and having them play was a nod toward celebrating the end of American involvement in the Vietnam War. But hippies were no longer as numerous as they once were, and those who were still around must not have remembered, because attendance was as paltry as Bobby Hedderman had assured me it would be. I decided to force myself to seek a spiritual reckoning by taking LSD one last time, along with a large mescaline chaser.

I was sitting on the steps to the stage as Spencer Perskin cranked up the band for the scattered gathering as multicolored swirls of psychedelic patterns fought for my attention. My effort to contemplate wrestled with the temptation to relax and enjoy. Then the power went off. The sound system, the amps onstage, the lights, everything went dead except the acoustic sound of Spencer's violin and the cellular activity in my brain.

In the enormous blackness and otherwise silent hall, the fiddle sounded tiny and mournful, like a small, lost kitten. Abruptly, the lights and sound returned, bright and loud. *My God, what a trip!* I thought. My heart soared for a few seconds, and then the darkness and silence again fell over the auditorium.

Spencer yelled at the band, "Don't stop!" He kept sawing away, forcing the band to keep plowing through "Kaleidoscopic." Once again, the power came back on, accompanied by sputtering, crackling sounds. One of the staff tapped me on the shoulder and said, "Boss, you'd better come out front and look at this."

After following him through the offices and outdoors, I found myself on Barton Springs Road, facing an automobile wheel spinning at eye level, which made me wonder if this was the weirdest acid trip I'd ever experienced.

There was a crowd of people in the street, and a city policeman was warning people to stand back. The automobile wheel was on the axle of an upside-down pickup truck that had come to rest on the curb. A downed utility pole lay across the sidewalk.

Loud voices overhead snagged my attention. Perhaps they were angels and I was dead. Looking up, I saw Micael Priest and a gang of others on the roof with Bobby Hedderman.

"We thought it was a bomb!" yelled Micael.

My scrambled brain assessed the situation. There'd been an accident. A blown transformer had caused the power outage. The police officer needed assistance with crowd control. The broken power line lying in the street was a hazard to human safety.

The electrical cable was undulating and twitching crazily, like a giant water moccasin on speed. Courageously stepping forward, I navigated around the power line using a combination of hopping and skipping motions. The cop was startled when I touched him on the shoulder, assuring him in my best hippie-boss voice, *I'M HERE TO HELP YOU, MAN.*

Later on, the people who were on the roof with Bobby said they had doubled over with laughter at the sight of my bizarre gymnastic display. Contrary to what I thought I'd seen, the cable had been perfectly motionless, but I had given them a shockingly good time.

★ ★ ★

It was no accident that there was a gang of Armadillo people on the roof that night. The pressure to do something really big had been mounting since the first of the year. I was thirty-three and burnt to a crisp. TYNA/ TACI had fallen apart and I was too numb to try and count the pieces. The betrayal by Lone Star stung badly. My desire to repay Hank Alrich the $50,000 he had put into the joint—never far from my mind—had become the drumbeat of a migraine.

So many of my creative ideas for bringing in revenue had failed.

Other people had ideas. We discussed them, even the ones that annoyed me. I had already rejected an idea to run a Christmas bazaar inside the concert hall in December as a way to generate income. That idea had come from Bruce Willenzik, who had come to us in 1974 from a well-to-do family in New Orleans. He worked his way up from cooking vegetarian beans in the kitchen to handling merchandise sales and advising security. The Armadillo Christmas Bazaar would finally be approved after I left the Armadillo, and the annual event would eventually outlive the hall itself.

But in the summer of 1976, I was still scrambling, banging my head against the wall to see if any worthwhile notions would fall out. Dianne McCall, Randy McCall's ex-wife, suggested holding a hundred-dollar-a-ticket fundraiser. Foundations do it all the time, she said. Get one thousand people to contribute one hundred dollars each, and you have $100,000. That sum of money would relieve a lot of pressure on all of us.

It was a tough call. Tempers flared as we discussed it, trying to decide if it was a good move or not. Hundred dollar tickets seemed the antithesis of everything Armadillo stood for. Yet asking for a lot of help just once seemed better than whining about our deteriorating situation and doing nothing at all about it. Nobody argued that it would be a bad thing if it worked. It was just very hard to swallow that we could really sell many tickets at that price.

Momentum began to mount behind the idea. As people kept coming up with ideas to complement the big-ticket extravaganza, it gained an aroma of inevitability. Some sort of convergence seemed to be at work. Bobby Hedderman felt it, too. One day he announced that he was moving to the roof for the summer. There was an old Superior Dairies billboard up there with an expired lease. Bobby proposed building a platform on top where he would live and work. He planned to keep doing promotion and booking while creating PR buzz just for being high up there, so to speak, on the roof.

Logistics dictated the need for a pup tent, a telephone, food, a portable potty, and a whole lot of suntan lotion. Bobby's goal was to stay up there for sixty-nine days and nights, coming down ceremoniously for the Dillo's sixth birthday party. He had hoped to get into *The Guinness Book of World Records*, but it turned out that they didn't have a category for billboard sitting. Mitch Green assured him, however, that this amazing feat of endurance would be recognized in *The Tomlinson Lone Star Book of Texas Records*, which is published in Fort Worth—and it did, in fact, come to pass.[3]

Poster for the first Armadillo Christmas Bazaar,
December 22–24, 1976. Artwork by Micael Priest.

In any event, we were all confident that Bobby's rooftop stunt would raise the Armadillo's profile and help put us in the black. As a bonus, the outdoor exile would also allow Bobby to escape increasingly tense and bitter office politics.

Henry Gonzalez transformed the Superior Dairies sign into a billboard on top of a billboard, adding flying armadillos to it. He also brought up a kiddie pool for heat relief.

Truck drivers and other travelers equipped with CB radios detoured off of Interstate 35 to witness the spectacle. (In that era, long before we were all connected via the Internet, the popularity of CB radios could sometimes lead to similar crowd phenomena.) By day Bobby worked the telephone, calling everyone in the business that might help with the birthday show, booking acts, and spreading the word while the sun turned his skin browner than Henry Gonzalez's. State representative Gonzalo Barrientos read a proclamation declaring the living billboard an official state treasure. A karate class moved their practice sessions to the roof. Bands climbed the rickety ladder to visit Bobby after sound check and participated in call-in radio promotions. More than once, Bobby hosted chefs who prepared flambé dishes that cast dramatic shadows on the setting. One thing was for certain: if we failed to sell enough tickets, it would not be for lack of promotion.

The Armadillo World Headquarters's sixth-birthday-party, hundred-dollar-a-ticket fundraiser steamrolled ahead and became my big obsession. We divvied up chores, added volunteer sales staff, wrote letters, and made telephone calls. An extravagant stage show was sketched out, built around our most popular house band at the time, Balcones Fault.

Jim Franklin put together a stage production with a troupe of actors, singers, a juggler, and a mime. Pran Productions, our talented friends in New Braunfels, began plotting out a multimedia show that used sixteen projectors, several thousand slides, and a thirty-two-foot-wide rear projection screen.

We hired Mitch Green to work on publicity. He made calls to local and state government officials, rounding up proclamations declaring "Armadillo Week" in Austin and around the state. We got pats on the back from the mayors of Houston and Dallas and feature stories in the major daily newspapers in Texas. As we received verbal assurances of ticket sales from various corners of the city and the music industry, it looked as though the harebrained idea might actually work.

Somewhere in the midst of preparations for the fundraiser birthday show, I had a long overdue powwow and smoke-out with the Mad Dogs. Jerry Jeff Walker and his wife, Susan, were part of the bunch who came down to the Armadillo to hear my pitch about the party. Jerry Jeff was on his best behavior. I gave each one of them a personalized, laminated free pass to the show. The following day, a bum showed up in the beer garden with a pocketful of the laminated tickets. He was trying to trade them in on beer. When questioned about it, he said he'd found them on the South First Street Bridge.

I immediately called Bud Shrake. After an awkward silence, he said that Susan Walker had thrown some of the laminated tickets out their car window. Bud swore he still had his and would treasure it forever. I went home sick.

The TYNA/TACI team had recorded a radio commercial. The content of the ad attempted to distill the Armadillo to its essence. It drew heavily on a press release written by publicist Ramsey Wiggins earlier in the year. The copy spoke of the AWHQ being "a concert hall, a restaurant, a beer garden; on occasion, a ballet theater, art gallery, [and] center for the performing arts." The finale swung for the fences: "We are a community within ourselves. We are something that has never happened before. We are the Armadillo."

Jim Franklin, the "nuclear physicist," and Bobby "the Living Billboard" Hedderman were singled out in the commercial. So were the performers Freddie King, Willie Nelson, Waylon Jennings, Commander Cody, Loudon Wainwright III, Ravi Shankar, Michael Murphey, Chuck Mangione, Bruce Springsteen, Leo Kottke, Van Morrison, Bette Midler, the New Riders of the Purple Sage, Kinky Friedman, Frank Zappa, Toots and the Maytals, Charlie Daniels, Maria Muldaur, Gary P. Nunn, Jerry Lee Lewis, the Mahavishnu Orchestra, Sunny and the Sunliners, the Pointer Sisters, and Kenneth Threadgill.

In a cameo appearance, I tried to explain, in cryptic fashion, who we were. "The crew at Armadillo is kind of like a giant, Technicolor amoeba," I said. "It multiplies and divides and has litters about four times a year.... In other words, if everybody that was responsible for Armadillo and its still being open were to come down at the same time, they'd pack it to the rafters."

Armadillo Appreciation Week started out with the Charlie Daniels Band, always a house favorite. Tuesday night we had the British blues revivalists Savoy Brown and blues shredder Bugs Henderson. Wednesday was a country rocking night, with Rusty Wier and Steve Fromholz. Thursday was fiddle night, with ex-Zappa sideman Jean-Luc Ponty and Vassar Clements, the father of hillbilly jazz; Micael Priest's poster showed a violin covered with armadillo scales. Southern rock ruled on Friday with Atlanta Rhythm Section and Wet Willie. Saturday was the big show with Balcones Fault and all the specially conceived shows with all the trimmings for a one-hundred-dollar admission.

In two of the nonmusical highlights of the evening, Chastity Fox popped up out of a six-foot-wide, two-layer cake lovingly constructed by Dub Rose, and Bobby Hedderman, clad in a white tuxedo, made a dramatic descent from his billboard aerie, flying down a zip line to the floor of the music hall. As with all the festivities, a video crew was supposed to capture the big moment, but they somehow missed the shot.

Although he's tried to forget that night, Bobby remembers it well. "The video people were out to lunch," he said. "They missed a lot of stuff. After all the preparations and the buildup, they got there late and they were just off. Actually, everything was off that night. We were trying to outdo ourselves, and we ended up doing all this stuff that just wasn't us."[4]

Bobby hit the nail on the head. The whole event was a disaster, an artistic bomb, a financial flop. A total of 250 of the hundred-dollar tickets were sold. An equal number of pledges to buy tickets were broken. Among the latter were half a dozen to sheriff Raymond Frank. Other public figures and important folks from various walks of life broke their ticket pledges—all of them allegedly big supporters of ours. We papered the house as best we could with media, tastemakers, and various friends of the joint. Our efforts netted a sum total of $9,300 after we paid all our party expenses and bills. It wasn't a tenth of what we needed to retire our debt.

★ ★ ★

Despite our financial troubles, the Armadillo had passed audits by the TABC and the tax people with flying colors. Our accounting books were things of beauty. That shouldn't have been surprising, after all, since our CPA, Randy McCall, had audited the Panamanian government, Ford, and AT&T before coming to our den of rock 'n' roll and nachos.

Randy had also gained the confidence and support of Hank Alrich and certain other members of the staff. Bobby Hedderman, Mike Tolleson,

Poster for Armadillo Appreciation Week, August 1–7, 1976.
Artwork by Micael Priest.

We learned how to beg for attention. We just never learned how to beg for money. Armadillo Appreciation Week, 1976. From left to right: Genie Wilson, Eddie Wilson, unknown, Jim Franklin, Texas State Representative Gonzalo Barrientos, Jr., and Bobby Hedderman. Photograph by Burton Wilson.

and I were starting to butt heads with Randy over management issues. Serious disagreements festered over financial issues, particularly where money should be spent versus cutting back. One of the most heated arguments arose over our indebtedness to KLBJ. As our concert and promotions business had expanded, we had become KLBJ-FM's biggest advertising account. When the big slowdown of 1976 hit, our account with the radio station was overdue in the amount of $4,300. They were very unhappy about that.

At one point, we had a sufficient amount of cash to pay off our debt to KLBJ. I wanted to use the funds to pay the radio station, but we were also in arrears on sales tax. Randy wanted to pay the sales tax instead. So we paid the sales tax.

Because Hank Alrich's money was at stake, I felt at a disadvantage. Randy was the CPA, and when things were tight, it was his job to decide where the money should be spent. Randy seemed to see every crisis as a chance to throw his weight around and bring himself closer to Hank. At least that's how the guys in my foxhole felt about it. Randy seemed to want to run the place himself.

It was almost as if the Armadillo was a romper room, and Randy McCall thought he was the only adult in the place. He came in and started waggling his finger, insisting that Bobby and I had played around with Hank's money and the Armadillo's toys long enough, and it was time for the grown-ups to take over.

"I objected because Randy wanted to cut some expenditures that I saw as essential to operating the place day to day," said Bobby. "It seemed like Randy wanted to pull a coup."[5]

Maybe Randy was right about some things, but the fact that Bobby felt the same way about the situation told me that the invisible bruises on my body weren't my imagination after all. Some sharp elbows were trying to edge us out of the building.

If we had put off paying our sales tax a little longer, we would have been levied a small fine, which we could have paid off at a later date when business picked up. The consequences of Randy McCall's decision were dire. KLBJ filed suit to get their money. It was only a matter of time before the Armadillo either folded or filed for Chapter 11.

Poster for Armadillo Appreciation Week,
August 1–7, 1976. Artwork by Jim Franklin.

EDDIE HAS LEFT THE BUILDING

★

Weeks went by. Tom Waits played the joint, John Hammond did two nights, and other unforgettable shows happened, but my memories of the fall of 1976 are all blurred; I mostly remember the feelings of frustration and weariness. Being the constant bearer of bad news was physically and mentally debilitating. The financial picture just kept getting uglier.

Before the big anniversary fundraiser folly, we were about $140,000 in debt. We owed $25,000 on thirty accounts payable, $86,000 on bank notes and loans to individuals, and about $5,000 for rent. In June we had lost $8,000 because of cancellations, and there was more of the same in July.[1]

In August we had the fundraiser that raised no funds, and the light at the end of the tunnel turned out to be an oncoming train. We lost $60,000 over the next eleven weeks.

In hindsight, the cost-cutting measures we imposed during that period should probably have been done much sooner. When the slowdown hit—and ours wasn't the only venue in Austin to suffer—and attendance fell off by roughly two-thirds, it was like trying to make a fast U-turn with an aircraft carrier. Among other things, changing tastes had hurt us. Discos were taking a lot of our business. At a disco, you could get mindlessly drunk for the amount of money we charged for admission to see a live band, and most discos didn't charge a cover.

In September we laid off forty-two part-time employees. The cost savings were supposed to enable us to give raises to all of our full-time employees. A story in the *Daily Texan* carried the official line, which was that the belt-tightening had not affected the morale of the staff at all. I was quoted as saying that, in fact, "morale is higher than it's been for the past three years," which wasn't exactly true.[2]

Most of the forty-two terminated employees were friends of ours, people who'd been working less than twelve hours a week. A lot of them never really left, or at least it seemed that way. You could still see them in the beer garden, hanging out, drinking beer, and smoking pot.

John Bevis, who had succeeded Ramsey Wiggins as publicist, was released and replaced by Woody Roberts. I tried to soften the blow by telling the *Daily Texan* reporter that John had been planning to resume his studies at UT anyway.

John admitted having made some mistakes on the job, but he felt that his firing had been an overreaction and that the move had come as a complete surprise: "Eddie said to me, 'It's a nice day outside—you're a free man.'"[3]

Unfortunately, the layoffs had no impact whatsoever on the bottom line. The kitchen, which was doing a paltry one hundred dollars a day in business, was temporarily shut down and its operations moved over to the Rome Inn.

It was a lousy year in other respects, too. A lawsuit was filed by one Sam Kindrick, a club owner and music rag publisher in San Antonio, after we informed him that the armadillo was our trademark and that his use of it in advertising his own club was an infringement. The $350,000 petition would've been merely annoying, but at the same time, Lone Star Beer had gone full-tilt armadillo with its own marketing, despite the fact that we were no longer doing marketing work for them. Lone Star went around us to contract Jim Franklin for more poster art featuring armadillos. They also sponsored armadillo races, which we believed to be inhumane. Despite our written entreaties to Lone Star, in which we pointed out that armadillo racing is cruel and inhumane, the brewery sponsored a race in March at the Hemisfair grounds in San Antonio. With 16,000 people and 300 contestants, the event was a big success. It also meant that at least 300 armadillos were caught in the wild and kept in cages. So we pulled out all of the Lone Star taps and kegs at AWHQ. That's right: we boycotted Lone Star Beer.[4]

One night during the second week in October, Genie and I were waiting at a stoplight next to the capitol when we saw Hank Alrich in his truck next to us.

His characteristic grin was there, as ever. "Hey, how are you?" he said.

"Fine," I said, as glum as I could remember ever feeling. "I'm gonna have to talk to you about that."

I revved the engine and peeled away.

Hank knew what was coming, that the Armadillo had reached a "crisis situation," as was noted in the November 4, 1976, edition of the *Texas Observer*.[5] Two days earlier, at the board of directors meeting, I announced that I had tried my best, but I was through. The only thing that made sense, I said, was to give Hank a shot at running the place. He was the one with money invested in the joint, and therefore he was the most qualified person to steer the ship toward getting a return on it. Maybe the best idea was for me to call it quits, walk away, and cut his losses.

After announcing my resignation and giving my reasons, I officially nominated Hank Alrich for president. A vote was taken, and Hank became the new commander in chief.

Later on, Henry Gonzalez described the mood at the meeting, how there wasn't a word of objection when I passed the baton to Hank.

"We all knew, if it wasn't for Hank, the Armadillo would have folded a long time ago," Henry said. "Everybody realized we were facing some huge problems. They just didn't realize how huge. There was no choice."[6]

Bobby Hedderman also tendered his resignation at the meeting. He had seen the writing on the wall, the pointed elbows at his back.

For too long, it had been a lot like a boxing match, where you have the black hat versus the white hat. Too many people on the staff thought of me as the black hat, the bad guy, that lying son of a bitch, while Hank was the white hat, the good guy, a lovable, down-to-earth, open, honest musician.

"People could not put their minds in the right place," Hank said years later. One big source of what he referred to as "negative energy" directed toward me was my Cadillac. Hank knew how I'd gotten the car and had no real problem with it. "The only thing stupid about it was its gas mileage," he said.

And then there was TYNA/TACI. "To some core souls," Hank said, "[it] looked like an attempt to leverage what had been granted in religious spirit to crass commercialism, if you will. That created a lot of ill will."[7]

In other words, some of our colleagues never accepted the fact that TYNA/TACI had to be a separate entity from the Armadillo in order for us to legally do promotional work for Lone Star, Pearl, or any other brewer or distributor. It seemed really strange to me, since they worked in a huge beer joint and they seemed to be able to grasp all the other TABC regulations that we had to operate under. Why was this particular one so hard to accept?

It was painful for me. Despite the poisonous atmosphere, I was still full of "religious spirit" about AWHQ and everything it represented, so much so that when reporters sought my comments, I continued to sound like the Armadillo's number one booster.

"This is a very healthy time to incorporate some change," I told the *Texas Observer*. "Giving up the leadership was the most creative thing I could've done as a leader. . . . It was just a way to make a point that Armadillo is more than just one person. I don't think anybody could doubt my motivation."

I admitted that enduring "the year of the bad review" had shaken me up. "It's made me less of the jolly person that I used to be."[8]

Despite comments like these, I hit the Armadillo exit door without looking back—no last speech, no farewell party. Some people were bothered by that. It might have been undiplomatic, but it sure lifted a giant load off my shoulders.

Jack Calmes quickly hired Bobby Hedderman at Showco. Bobby's first assignment was to be Freddie King's tour manager. Bobby stayed on at Armadillo for the remainder of 1976 to help with the transition. Right after the New Year, he'd be leaving with Freddie on a tour of Japan.

The timing seemed perfect, but Fate played a wild card: Freddie passed away on December 28 at the age of forty-two. The official cause of death was complications of pancreatitis and ulcers. He had toured three hundred days a year and played his heart out every time. His death left a giant void in the music world, not just at the Armadillo or in Texas, but every place where authentic, soulful music is appreciated.[9]

THE RAW DEAL AND
A WHITE RABBIT

★

Once I left the Dillo, I never went back inside, except once, to see my fellow native Mississippian, Mose Allison, the jazz singer and pianist who'd managed to carve out a regular touring stop at the Armadillo.

My aim was to give Hank Alrich free rein to do whatever he felt he needed to do, without me hanging around or dropping by to ask how things were going. Even if Hank had wanted my advice, I knew that Randy McCall and Bruce Willenzik, who were helping him run the show now, didn't want me looking over their shoulders. Or was I just being self-righteous and bitter? That probably figured into my avoiding the old joint, too.

In my last months at the Dillo, to escape the pressure and depression, I'd begun spending a good deal of time hiding. My first option, the Number One Bar behind the Night Hawk, Austin's most storied coffee shop restaurant, had become too popular. My next place was the back room at Matt's El Rancho on East First Street, now East Cesar Chavez Street.

During my rambles down Sixth Street, I had noticed a little place on Sabine Street. It was a half block off East Sixth and a half block from police headquarters. The rent was $125 a month. The place had my name on it. In fact, the day I resigned at the Armadillo, I knew exactly where I was going next, what kind of dive it was going to be, what the name would

Poster for Mose Allison and Alex Moore show
at AWHQ, 1974. Artwork by Micael Priest.

be, and everything. It was going to be the greasiest spoon in town. All this happened the day after I turned in my badge at the Armadillo.

The name of the joint was the Raw Deal. The modest-to-the-point-of-crude concept was that it would be a beer bar that also sold some stuff to eat. Even with that bare-bones aesthetic in mind, getting the property ready to open presented enough of a challenge that I didn't think about the Armadillo very much. A lot of it was hard labor that I did myself. I scraped the linoleum off the floor, tore down the wall between the kitchen and the dining area, moved in the big refrigerator that my mother, Beulah, had let me take to the Dillo, and smeared a little paint around. The thirtieth day of my work fell on December 7, 1976, Pearl Harbor Day, and I threw myself a little surprise party.

Much to Beulah's dismay, I did not paint over the mural that covered the dining room wall. One-half of the wall depicted Mexican revolutionaries storming out of a landscape that continued across the other half of the room, while in the foreground, white women whose naked chests were pierced with arrows were being scalped by Indians.

Looking out on the street from one of the four front windows was the face of Adlai Stevenson II, the late Democratic politician, in a gigantic blowup of the cover of Life magazine from 1952. Even though he was bald and bland-looking in a rumpled gray suit, the magazine's red logo on the top and the red banner on the bottom made the image reminiscent of the communist Chinese propaganda posters of Chairman Mao.

I have no recollection of where I found the poster, but I thought it sent an appropriate message to potential customers, a message that was also expressed on a big sign by the cash register: "Remember, you found the Raw Deal, the Raw Deal didn't go looking for you."

I filled up a jukebox with instrumental records. It was Woody Roberts's idea and a great one. If one of the records had a vocal on the other side, on the selection label for that track I wrote "Scratched/Do Not Play." On the rare occasions that one of those songs got played, I'd reach behind the box and hit the reject button. If I could easily ID the culprit, I'd growl something like, "Damn it, can't you read?"

The Raw Deal opened on Christmas Day, less than two months after I left the Armadillo in Hank's hands. New Year's Day 1977 was the city's official swearing-in day. Ann Richards came down to the joint to be sworn in as a Travis County commissioner, Frank Ivy was sworn in as

Artwork by Micael Priest.

The Raw Deal was my version of home school.
Photograph by Dub Rose.

justice of the peace for Precinct 1, and I was sworn in as president of the Musicians Union Local No. 433. Heading up the union was my way of avoiding complete presidential withdrawal after leaving the Armadillo. Charlotte McDaniel, longtime secretary of the union, had nominated me. Six months later I resigned, forever cured of political aspirations.

Micael Priest was the first person from the Armadillo to pop in and visit. He also did a few artistic things for me. He made the sign by the cash register ("Remember, the Raw Deal didn't come looking for you…") and repainted the sign outside so that it read: "The Raw Deal #1."

I fed Micael pork chops and hash browns. The menu was very, very simple. There would be no live music. The dining room could accommodate thirty-two people. The bar separated the dining room from the kitchen. A heater/AC unit from a mobile home was set up next to the jukebox in front of a little window blocking a view of Waller Creek, the downtown stream that was in those days permanently trashed. The only place in the Raw Deal where I could hide was up against the double-door refrigerator in the middle of the kitchen. I'd stand with my shoulder blades against it, suck on a joint, and blow toward the window next to the stove. The stove's grease-encased exhaust fan took my exhaled toke toward the police station just down the creek.

East Sixth Street was seedy and run-down in the late seventies. The Two Nickel Cab Company and the Stallion Adult Book Store right around the corner provided a lot of human interest stories for entertainment, along with contributing to the generally bad reputation of the neighborhood. The Two Nickel had a shine stand out front and a pay telephone. The phone was used primarily by people calling their local bookie.

More often than not, there were two or three unmarked delivery cars at the curb. There was a Humpty Dumpty grocery store on Sixth, and the drivers took a lot of delivery orders from customers who didn't have a car. The drivers also did a brisk business selling little brown bags of Mexican heroin to local junkies.

The Raw Deal's one-room layout was a lot easier to manage than an armory complex. When I was asked why this specific place suited me, I said it was the smallest place I could find. I could run it by myself. Galen Barber, my favorite sanitation engineer at the Armadillo, joined me as cook, waiter, and cashier, the same jobs I performed. He had a shift, and I had a shift.

I was very familiar with a few other joints in town where the owner, not the customer, was always right, and I wanted the Raw Deal to be that way, too. One of the classic gruff eateries in town was Virginia's Café on South First Street. Virginia had the best plate-lunch operation in town. The Dry Creek Inn near Mount Bonnell was another. The bartender/proprietor there was the notoriously surly Sarah Ransom. The Hamby brothers ran the Hoffbrau, a stripped-down steak house on West Sixth Street where steaks were pan-fried and cheap. Bag O' Chicken on South Lamar Boulevard was run by Chicken Dick Jennings, a guy whose nickname gave him a license to be cranky.

The rough, almost grouchy comportment of the people who ran these places was part of the atmosphere and attraction. There was something to it. Each place had something special to offer, and in place of being treated like royalty, you got theater.

At Virginia's, you had to follow strict rules or risk getting chewed out. At her café, the procedure was to choose from her handwritten menu, write your order of one entrée and three vegetables on a small pad using a stubby pencil, after which you placed the pad on the corner of the table and sat quietly until she found time to pick up your order and walk it back to the counter.

I remember the first time Mike Tolleson came to a business lunch there and made the mistake of arriving late. Virginia briefed him on procedure and assigned him a table next to the rest of the party. Several minutes later, he noticed that he was being ignored. After she'd swept past his table several times, Mike made the near fatal error of attempting to hand his order to her. She stopped on a dime, snatched it from his fingers, and slammed it down so hard that his water glass nearly fell over. "Mister," she said through clenched teeth, "all these people are before you, and I don't think you've got time to wait."

Chicken Dick was famous for only serving his deep-fried, stuffed jalapeños to his favorite customers. Sarah Ransom was known to scream at people at the top of her lungs if they ordered a beer brand that wasn't written in pencil or crayon on the refrigerator. Customers who left tips on the bar got chastised for ignoring the porcelain piggy bank on the bar. "Money goes in the goddamn pig," she'd say. If you'd gotten thrown out of her place twenty-five years ago, she'd spot you in a minute and toss your ass out the door again.

Eddie Wilson, 1976. Photographer unknown.

Once, I was at the Hoffbrau with my friend Monty Quick, a regular patron of the steak house, when he was served a bad steak. He felt bad about presenting a plate of chewed gristle to old Tommy Hamby, who owned the joint, but he did. "Mr. Hamby," Monty said, "I've been eating here for twenty-five years and this is the first time I've had a steak like this."

Hamby took the plate and scraped it into the trash. "It'll be better next time," he said.

From the Hoffbrau, I went straight to the Raw Deal, a new motto in hand. Fletcher Boone, a painter and sculptor who had smoothly transitioned from customer to owner, liked the sound of it so much, he immediately began working on a scrape of cardboard with a felt marker. Two beers later, he was done and the sign appeared above the door, reading, "It'll be Betty next time." It stayed up a couple weeks. I thought it was a tribute to one of our regulars who worked down the street at *Texas Monthly* magazine. Her name was Betty Moore, and she could've had me without much effort at all.

My first regular at the Raw Deal was James Bailey, the straightest-looking customer ever, who stepped through the screen door and ordered the first of many bottles of Pabst Blue Ribbon Beer. Bailey always wore a blue pinstripe suit. His necktie had a perfect Windsor knot. He wore shiny cuff links and wingtip shoes.

Most impressive of all was the badge he carried reading "Texas State Board of Pharmacy, Agent 01." Bailey was gregarious, theatrical, and almost impractically smart. A graduate of the first class at the LBJ School of Public Affairs at UT, he had taught Russian for the CIA. He had a frontal lobe like a supercomputer. He was also, I learned, a lonely person. As unlikely as it might seem, James Bailey and I became friends, and he adopted the Raw Deal as his living room. He could talk for hours on end without stopping, and only rarely did I ever see him sit down.

One day when the Raw Deal was closed, which could have been a Tuesday, Wednesday, or Thursday, Bailey came banging on the door. I unlocked it and he came inside with something hidden inside his jacket that turned out to be a large brown pharmacy bottle. The bottle was a vintage beauty with a two-and-a-half-inch cork stopper instead of a lid. The label had a skull and crossbones and underneath, antique lettering that said "cocaine."

The bottle, he explained, had been mailed to the Board of Pharmacy from a college somewhere in the state, where it had been discovered by someone cleaning out an old safe. No doubt the college officials just wanted to do the right thing. Bailey and I certainly appreciated it.

He was in a hurry. "Get me a box of Sweeta," he said.

I understood his urgency. Wasting no time, I grabbed a box of the artificial sweetener, and he began tearing open packets two and three at a time.

"Empty that thing into something clean," he said, meaning the antique bottle. "I've got to get back to the office and lord over the ritual flushing of this Sweeta down the toilet."

He came over to my house that night. Using a triple beam scale I had borrowed from Oat Willie's, we weighed the contents. We were a little surprised that it weighed out to be less than we had anticipated, but the coke was so fluffy, you worried that it might fly away when you weren't looking.

★ ★ ★

Among my regular customers, Ann Richards was one of my favorite people to talk to. She and another well-known and powerful Texas politician, Bob Bullock, were very close to each other before they became non-friends. Bullock was state comptroller when I had the Raw Deal and was later elected lieutenant governor and served two terms. With the knowledge that, on occasion, I had special T-shirts printed, one day Ann came to me and asked if I might have some made to honor her friend Bob.

Bullock was in the middle of a campaign, and Ann wanted a T-shirt that would pay tribute to his notorious raging temper and mean-spiritedness. What about something that incorporated an image of the Ugandan dictator Idi Amin? The more we talked about it, the more perfect it sounded.

I called Micael Priest and asked him to create a drawing of Idi Amin wearing his military cap, standing tall behind an old-fashioned cash register, ringing up sales tax. I specified that the words "Idi Amin for Comptroller" should appear in large lettering. I sold dozens of the shirts to Bullock's friends and enemies both—even to members of his staff. Once he found out about the T-shirts, sales immediately stopped. On election day, Bullock sailed to victory, but that was no surprise.

In 1973, when Bullock was still the Texas secretary of state, he had been a regular at the beer garden. He was politically ambitious, and it was known that he was thinking about running for either state comptroller or treasurer. Bullock's daily companion was Ed Wendler, a significant political operator on a more local scale. Wendler was a lawyer who represented developers, a yellow dog Democrat street activist who favored pressed blue jeans. Feeling ballsy one afternoon, I stopped by their table to ask Bob if he'd made up his mind which office he planned to seek.

"Yup, just now, and you'll be the first to know," he said. "I've learned that my liberal friends don't trust me enough to want me as treasurer. I've also learned that they don't know what comptroller means, so I'm going to take that one and shove it up their asses."

Later that day, as Ed and Bob were visibly approaching their limit, Bullock waved me over again. He wanted to know if I saw Willie Nelson regularly. At the time I did, and I told him so.

Bullock wanted me to ask Willie to play a fundraiser for his campaign. Then he went on to remind me that he had grown up in Hillsboro, Texas, the town next door to Abbott, where Willie had grown up. Willie would come into Hillsboro on the interurban bus, and when he got off the bus, toting his guitar, Bullock and his buddies would give Willie a hard time. They'd make Willie take his guitar out of the case and sing a few songs under the implied threat that if he refused, they'd beat him up. Bullock seemed to think it was hilarious. Apparently, no one had told him that Willie was generally pleased to sing and play guitar for anyone, anywhere, at the drop of a hat.

I said I'd be glad to pass along the request.

I saw Willie a few days later and relayed Bullock's request. Willie wanted to know what I thought of Bullock's politics. I told him that Bullock had a future in whatever political arena he chose. Then Willie asked if there was anything else I thought he should know. The only thing I had to add was what Bullock had told me about when they were growing up, which I told him. Willie listened thoughtfully, scratched his chin, cocked his head, and said, "Would you mind telling Mr. Bullock from me to go fuck himself?"

"No, I don't mind at all," I said.

★ ★ ★

The location of the Raw Deal came with its share of winos and drunks. It felt like déjà vu when the first badass I had to deal with was Bill Campbell, the best guitar player and the surliest drunk in town. One day, Campbell was there at the Raw Deal drinking with Mike Mays, my banker friend from the Armadillo days. I was exhausted and wanted to close down, clean up, and go home. Bill kept ragging me about the Armadillo and other assorted pimples on my profile, doing it well enough to really piss me off. He cackled and grew increasingly abusive until I finally whipped out the old framing hammer I kept under the bar and whistled it past him in a big, 180-degree arc. I must have unconsciously held back, because the blow missed by no more than a quarter inch.

Bill closed one eyelid halfway, his cheek twitching. "Eddie, you wouldn't hurt me," he said in a soft, boyish voice. "You love me."

Maybe in a twisted sort of way I did, but he could really piss me off.

Some time later, one morning before daylight, I was out taking a fitness walk on Sixth Street and almost tripped over Bill. He was lying half in, half out of an alley, his socks in the gutter and his shoes closer to his head, filled with vomit. Another derelict lay next to him, with an empty Robitussin bottle in between them. They had probably played a gig a few hours before but never made it home from downtown.

I meant to keep going, not wanting him to know I'd seen him in such a pathetic state, but even before he had both eyes open, he was tearing into me.

"Wilson," he snarled, "what in the fuck are you doing out this time of day, walking around in your underwear?"

"What've you been doing, Bill?" I said.

"Oh, just working and going to school," he said nonchalantly.

Before I could say anything else, he was out again, snoring.

It didn't take long for the Raw Deal's innocent charm to wear off. Less than a year after I opened it, I sold it to a couple of my first regulars, Fletcher Boone and Jim "Lopez" Smitham. Actually, I gave it to them, mainly because by that time, they were enjoying the place more than I was.

As part of the transaction, I handed over a half page of one-line instructions that I believed to be the simplest but most important things for them to abide by in order to avoid failure, including making a deposit every day, no matter how small it was, and "honoring thy format," or, "Don't mess with the simplicity of the menu." Right away, they added a chicken breast dish to the menu. They used a recipe that Frank Bailey had developed specially for them. Besides being a chef, Bailey was the brother of senator Kay Bailey Hutchison. The dish proved to be wildly popular.

★ ★ ★

Once again, quitting made me feel better, but a pattern of walking away from things is no way to get ahead in life. My next move was something that was probably a surprise to everyone, including me, but I took the job for several reasons: it was a challenge, there were principles involved, the money was good, someone I liked and respected had asked me to do it as a favor to him, and I knew it would be temporary—I couldn't see myself running a disco for very long.

Gordy Ham had called me from Lubbock, asking for my help. He was working for a group of vending machine operators who had branched out into the club business. They had a disco in Austin called the White Rabbit, and they needed someone who could turn the place around. Being a six-hour drive from Austin, Gordy couldn't do it himself.

The vending machine people also owned discos in Corpus Christi and Lubbock, all of them named the White Rabbit. The Austin location, which was right around the corner from Kenneth Threadgill's joint, was getting an awful reputation due to a fairly blatant race discrimination policy. Several bad brawls had attracted the attention of police. Bergstrom Air Force Base was about to put the White Rabbit "off limits" to service personnel, which might have ended up being unnecessary, since the TABC was considering pulling the club's liquor license.

The White Rabbit had all the things that discos in the seventies had: a deafening sound system, dark corners, and a light system with the requisite mirrored ball. Skimpy bunny costumes were worn by the waitresses. The security guys and bartenders were rednecks. They hovered protectively around the waitresses, treating customers like intruders into their private harem. And they were plainly prejudiced. They routinely turned away African Americans, including well-dressed African American officers from the air force base, using variations of the old tried-and-true "dress code" excuse.

The first time I went there, I made a mental list of problems that needed addressing immediately. I also counted several instances of despicable behavior by the bouncers that could've turned into fights or a discrimination suit. The overall atmosphere was horny-ugly.

I took the job and rehabilitated the place, starting by calling up Jose Cerna and Monty Quick, veteran Armadillo bouncers, to do a makeover on security. I got new outfits for the security staff. Dressing them up in suits made them look more respectable and served as a constant reminder that they were supposed to conduct themselves in a respectful, nondiscriminatory manner. I also called in Woody, my stepfather, to retrofit the front entrance with a guardrail to separate the in and out traffic and to redo the automatic entry door so that it swung inward. The first time I went there, I had watched in dismay as customers walked up the steps and just as they reached the top, the heavy wooden door would swing violently open, nearly knocking them over. I never saw anyone get hurt that way, but the awkwardness created a bottleneck at the entry. It was stupid. And it only took Woody a few hours' labor to make it right.

A few months later, the *Austin Sun* ran a feature story with a picture of me and the security staff dressed in our tuxes. John Moore, editor of the *Sun*, did a good job on the story. I guess he felt invested in the subject, just as I did.

He quoted me making some very harsh comments, but I meant every word of them. I didn't only want to address the African American community, but the vending machine guys as well; I wanted everybody to know that I meant business:

> *There's not a leg to stand on, to defend the old Rabbit. In my opinion, the people of East Austin would have been perfectly justified if they had burned it down a year ago. The legal file weighs about a pound; there's a public accommodations suit by a black woman who was turned away because she was wearing a turban.*
>
> *It's our fault in the whitest sense of the word. The law says you have to accommodate the public, and you've got to accommodate all the public. Especially if a person pays a cover charge to get in a place, they have got no obligation to do anything but behave. The racist mind has a rule of thumb that you'll never get these two crowds to get along together. Well, that's hogwash.*

The Armadillo and the ongoing struggle there to stay in business was still very much in the news, so I answered questions about it, even though I was no longer its official spokesperson, and I also expounded on the subject of disco and the Austin music scene in general. I sure wasn't the only person in town who wondered if the disco trend meant the imminent extinction of live music, but, being a perennial contrarian, I tried to sound a hopeful note or two. I suggested that disco fever might be cooling off a bit in the near future. If that happened and I was still in charge at the White Rabbit, we might start alternating between disco and live music.

I pointed out that when Mother Earth first opened in 1971, it was a disco featuring a live drummer who played along with records. That format was a big success for a while, but very soon the format changed to focus on live music most nights of the week.

"People talk about the music scene dying, and it's not even out of the crib yet," I said, before moving on to praise the local print media, the film community, and photographers. "I'm a crazed optimist. It's the only thing that gets me up in the morning."

THE ARMADILLO EMERGES

If the picture for the Armadillo was grim when I left, it got steadily worse in the last two months of 1976. Even when Hank Alrich and the skeleton crew that remained threw everything but the kitchen sink at the problem, a spate of pure bad luck would hit. No one was getting paid. About three weeks into December, KLBJ dropped an early Christmas present, filing a suit against Armadillo for their $4,300 debt. Other creditors were threatening to do the same.

Hank Alrich and Randy McCall took a meeting. The bass-playing CPA told Hank, "We had eight weeks here to try something, and we're not going to make it. Bankruptcy is the only thing."[1]

Hank and Randy went to see a bankruptcy attorney named David Cooperman. For several hours Cooperman grilled them, throwing out one tough question after another. Hank said they felt like criminal suspects getting the third degree. Finally, Cooperman lightened up a bit. "There's a possibility you could save this business," he said. "It's called Chapter 11."

"I didn't know much about management, business, bankruptcy, any of that stuff," said Hank. "Bankruptcy to me meant that you were out of business." But, as Cooperman explained, Chapter 11 could possibly offer the Armadillo ark a lifeline, as opposed to scuttling it. Agreements would have to be reached with creditors approving a plan that would allow the Armadillo to pool all its debts, forming an escrow account. Legal action would be forestalled, giving the business a chance to recover and pay off the debt. This would necessitate obtaining additional financing for operating expenses through the next two quarters. Expenses that couldn't be frozen in Chapter 11 included rent, taxes, insurance, and many other basics.

One major obstacle to making the plan work was the huge debt owed to Hank. The solution was brutal, but in Hank's words, it sounded relatively simple and bloodless: "We would have to restructure the corporation to relieve it of my note, which was transferred [i.e., converted] to stock."[2]

What Hank was saying was that he now owned 87 percent of Armadillo Productions Incorporated. To be more precise, that 87 percent was split between Hank and his brother William Alrich, who came to the rescue with another sizable loan. A cynical observer might say that, instead of the Armadillo's assets being seized by one of its creditors, it had been taken over by Hank and his brother. For the most part, however, the change in ownership was viewed benignly. The other stockholders, who had previously owned 8 percent of Armadillo Productions, were left with 1 percent. The alternative to the restructuring was to let the Armadillo fail completely.

According to federal law, more than 50 percent of the creditors would have to agree to the Chapter 11 plan before it could be approved. When presented with the plan drawn up by Randy McCall, Hank Alrich, the attorneys, and US district court judge Bert W. Thompson, the Armadillo's creditors were hit in the face by the same big fact that had haunted me for the past several years: most of the $150,000 owed by the corporation (adjusted for inflation, that would be $626,989 in 2015)[3] was owed to Hank and William Alrich. And for such a large debt, the Armadillo itself had very few assets.

As Hank put it, "Part of the pitch of the bankruptcy pleading was this: look at this comparatively astronomical figure that is owed from an organization whose saleable assets are worth . . . a pittance. It was a few cents on the dollar. We just didn't own much compared to what we owed."

In other words, Armadillo World Headquarters, one of the most famous music halls in the world, wasn't worth suing.

Agreements were secured with an impressive 80 percent of the creditors, and the Chapter 11 plan proceeded. Hank and Randy continued implementing cost-cutting, revenue-enhancing measures, including a forced march of thirteen weeks of no pay for the employees. There were also new renovations to the hall and the beer garden. Leea Mechling was promoted to the front office after she and Henry Gonzalez were given a short time to recover from the birth of their son, Ben. Sadly, one of her first duties on the job was to inform another fifty-five employees that they had gotten the axe.

Dave "Killer" Mabry was promoted from the cleanup crew to assume some of Bobby Hedderman's responsibilities. Randy McCall, who had been on his way out the door to work at Manor Downs before I left, spun on his heels and stayed on. He and Fletcher Clark helped Hank run the joint.

Hank was a jazz fiend, and with his passion, credibility, and contacts, he and Killer Mabry pulled in a bevy of astounding jazz acts. Even during the austerity clampdown, Hank was determined to book shows for jazz fiends that blew their minds, even if they weren't big box office draws. "Some of the serious music shows that drew the smallest audiences," he said, "were actually shocking in the power of their musical, emotional delivery."[4] Jazz aficionados were treated to performances by Sam Rivers with Dave Holland and Barry Altschul, Sonny Rollins, the Carla Bley Band, and Old and New Dreams, to name a few. Old and New Dreams was made up of saxophonists Don Cherry and Dewey Redman, bassist Charlie Haden, and drummer Ed Blackwell, all former sidemen and protégés of avant-jazz guru Ornette Coleman.

"Old and New Dreams hit as hard as a medium dose of a good psychedelic drug," said Hank, "as if Mother Nature herself had instructed the trees to take gentle hold of your skull and open it to the Light."[5] With a review like that, I'm really sorry I missed the show, but Hank's praise was enough to leave me with a contact high.

In the four years after I left the Armadillo, changes and growth in the Austin musical landscape continued at the hectic and half-crazy pace that we had experienced from 1970–1976. Hank and his happy henchmen were sometimes befuddled, sometimes bemused, but in general, the Armadillo embraced musical revolution like a hungry amoeba. But the stage that in 1970–1971 had nurtured East Texas blues songsters, psychedelic folk rock,

Texas guitar boogie, and long-haired country music aficionados now also welcomed spiky-haired punk bands, experimental jazz, heavy metal, and other genres and subgenres.

Managing the Armadillo was, as Hank Alrich said, "something in excess of two full-time jobs," which didn't leave a lot of time to venture outside the joint's mural-covered walls to check the pulse of the local music scene. Hank wasn't the kind of guy you saw putting in an appearance at various places in the name of schmoozing and being cool. Hank relied on trusted sources, including "the community of radio folks, Inner Sanctum [record store] heads, musicians, and the Armadillo staff, who kept me pretty close to the musical heartbeat of the city."[6]

With these resources, Hank said, he felt like he had "a giant musical stethoscope hooked up to [his] skull." Input from the staff was essential. What bands did they like to see? Who was creating a buzz out there? Members of the kitchen staff and other employees were going down to Raul's to see the Skunks, the first of Austin's new punk-oriented rock bands. The scene had arisen overnight, starting with the debut of the Skunks and the Violators in January of 1978. The employees reported back that the Skunks, the Explosives, and a few others were their favorites. By that summer, the Skunks were recording with Joe Gracey in his basement studio at KOKE-FM. The trio of hard, fast rockers scored the opening slot for the New York proto-punk rockers the Dictators in August. The Skunks' half dozen or so gigs at the Dillo in its late period included opening slots for the Clash and Joe Ely as well as the top of the bill for a special benefit show on Thanksgiving Day 1978 called the ThanksGracey Show. Organized with a lot of input from Micael Priest, it was a musical extravaganza and fundraiser for Joe Gracey, who was undergoing treatment for cancer of the throat. Nowhere else but in Austin would you find a top-shelf, extremely varied lineup like the one that played that night: Asleep at the Wheel, Alvin Crow, the Fabulous Thunderbirds, and the Skunks.[7]

The Armadillo continued its policy of pairing road shows with local bands to help fill the room for the former and increase awareness of the latter. The Skunks and other promising bands from the Raul's scene were tapped to open for the Ramones, the Talking Heads, John Cale, Devo, and others. As Jesse Sublett said, "Playing at the Armadillo was a big deal. It helped authenticate your band. People saw that you were professional, that you were for real."[8]

Poster for the Violators and the Skunks show
at Raul's, 1978. Artwork by Jesse Sublett.

Poster for a Talking Heads show at AWHQ,
November 21, 1980. Artwork by Guy Juke.

I've said it before, and I'll say it again: Hank and I had a lot more in common than most people realized, especially when it came to his passion for the artists who played the hall. It also took a lot of guts to ask the staff to sacrifice even more than they had previously, but he did it, and they had his back, a fact that was powerfully illustrated during that thirteen-week moratorium on payroll. Work went on as usual; employees kept showing up, food and beer were served, and the music hall kept rocking. The only difference was that no one got a paycheck. Not a single employee quit. Because of Hank's inspired leadership and radical measures like those, which I could never bring myself to do, the Armadillo started seeing the light at the end of the tunnel of debt.

To the astonishment of the law firm that handled the Chapter 11 deal, as well as the jaded critics who saw us as the old hippie crowd, AWHQ began digging its way out of debt. In the last two years of the Armadillo's existence, red ink turned to black, and the South Austin music and culture emporium actually turned a profit.

One revenue-generating idea that proved successful was the Armadillo Christmas Bazaar. When Bruce Willenzik had originally suggested the idea to use the hall as a staging place for a market where locally produced, handcrafted items would be sold during the Christmas shopping season, the proposal had been debated vigorously, and I had been the skeptic who repeatedly said no. The same month I opened the Raw Deal, Bruce organized the inaugural Christmas Bazaar in the hall. A skeleton crew worked the bar, the kitchen, and security. The crowd wasn't huge, but everyone who worked got paid, and it brought in sufficient revenue to justify making it an annual event. As of this writing, the annual Armadillo Christmas Bazaar has outlasted AWHQ by well over three decades.

Bruce Willenzik moved up the ladder to become one of the major players at the Armadillo. Jan Beeman, who had brought Bruce into the kitchen operation, was confident that Bruce would work out. "I knew right away that he was mean enough to push the kitchen to start making money," she said. "He had a great head for figures and profit and loss. . . . He made me write down all the recipes." Later, she also brought Bruce's brother Allen into the kitchen operation.[9]

Bruce bought the existing kitchen equipment from Hank and purchased additional equipment using his own money. Later, when it appeared that the Armadillo wasn't going to remain open beyond 1980, he moved all the equipment over to the Rome Inn, where he also operated the kitchen. His intent was to have a single kitchen serving both establishments. Various complications ensued, the Rome Inn went out of business, and then Bruce brought the kitchen back to the Dillo.

The additional funding from Hank's brother William Alrich helped finance various improvements in the music hall, including upgrades to the PA and Onion Audio. The financial situation began to improve in early 1978, and Armadillo Productions began turning the corner, emerging from Chapter 11 and showing a profit.

In 1980, which turned out to be the Dillo's last year, Hank approved a proposal for building a new stage in the beer garden. Recently, Hank said he couldn't remember who originally suggested it. Dub Rose thought it was Hank's idea. In any event, an idea was all that Dub needed to hear. "You put Dub Rose in charge of something like that," said Hank, "and you can quit worrying about it right there."

With Dub and his hippie carpenters handling the renovation, the new stage scaled up the beer garden experience and allowed the charging of a cover on ordinary weeknights. "My friend on the custodial staff, Gordon Cole, did a lot of the work with me," said Dub. "He was also in the band Cool Breeze, and as it turned out, they played the opening night for the new stage and it became a regular gig." Randy McCall, the bass-playing CPA, handled the bottom line for the band.[10]

The Charlie Daniels Band, who had been lured away to the Austin Opry House and other venues, returned to the Dillo at the behest of Killer Mabry. On their first date back at the Dillo, the CDB crew arrived on time, as always. The load-in, setup, and sound check all proceeded smoothly. After sound check, Charlie went back to the office to speak with Hank. "This is about the slickest loading and sound check they've ever had here," he said. "You're running a really tight ship. You must have picked up a few more people."

Hank thanked Charlie for the compliment and said he looked forward to a great night, as usual. In reality, the hall was getting by with a smaller staff those days, but Hank saw no reason to explain that to Charlie.

★ ★ ★

The site of Armadillo World Headquarters had been for sale pretty much ever since we moved in. Over the years, we had made renovations, improvements, and repairs and performed general maintenance. We had installed risers, new stages, insulation, heaters, the Cabaret bar, the beer garden, and countless other examples of money and labor invested in the physical property and its operations. It had all been done with no long-term lease from the owner.

Typically, a business such as ours would have secured a long-term lease at the beginning, affording the business operator certain advantages, not the least of which would be the ability to amortize depreciation costs and other tax advantages. In my defense, I could offer that our year-by-year verbal agreement kept our rent low. As a critic, you could say that all that money spent on improvements was poured down a bottomless hole.

In the spring of 1980, M. K. Hage had a series of fateful conferences with his close advisers, the most important of whom was his brother-in-law, Houston attorney Joe Jamail. The son of a prosperous Lebanese grocer from Houston, Joseph Dahr Jamail Jr. was renowned for winning billions in judgments for his clients in more than five hundred jury trials. His nickname, "the $13 Billion Man," was the sum of the $10.53 billion he won for Pennzoil against Texaco in 1985 and the winnings from hundreds of other jury trials. He was Texas's richest lawyer and a longtime friend of Willie Nelson.[11]

Joe Jamail had finally found a buyer for the 7.6 acres of land occupied by the Armadillo. Hage had repeatedly promised the Armadillo folks the right of first refusal, but he never picked up the phone and followed through. For a number of years, the whole 7.6 acres and all the buildings had been on the block for $1 million. We had repeatedly dreamed and schemed to put together deals for raising the money, but it never worked out. The final selling price was $1.4 million.

The fact that the place was finally running a profit when it was sold and slated for demolition was an ironic twist of the knife. With an annual gross income of $1.3 million, the Armadillo was generating a net profit of $80,000, and Hank Alrich was taking home $200 a week. Not a lot of money, but the Armadillo gang wasn't about the money and never had been. The operation was working, the joint was rocking, and to be honest about it, they were performing a public service.

As he added up the figures, Hank saw an even deeper irony: the rental expenditure from the three tenants on the property—Armadillo World Headquarters, Doug Scales Body Shop, and Pounds Photo Lab—could have been used to purchase the corner on a standard thirty-year real estate note.

Once notified that Hage had found a buyer, Hank and the new regime scrambled to find another location. The alternative was to fold up the tents and call it a day. Several locations were scouted out. Negotiations were started with the city over the possibility of leasing the nearby City Coliseum, a modified, no-frills, World War II–era Quonset hut on Riverside Drive, barely two blocks west of the Armadillo. With a capacity of 3,500, the Coliseum was a multiuse facility with an impressive history all its own, having hosted everything from Elvis in 1956 to high school proms, Golden Gloves tournaments, livestock auctions, political conventions, and the Austin City-Wide Garage Sale. Music historians may find it either noteworthy or comical that the band Kiss made their Austin debut there in 1975. The city proved unwilling to relinquish a piece of the concessions, which was a sticking point in the negotiations for the Armadillo franchise.

Back in the summer of 1970, when I had "found" Hage's building looming over my head as I pissed on the side of its wall, it had seemed like a small miracle that I'd discovered such a place waiting to become a music emporium, cultural center, and everything else the Armadillo eventually became. Ten years later, there were no such miracles left in Austin to be found. Indeed, there was no facility that even came close to meeting the Armadillo's needs. The harder Hank and his crew searched, the more unique, weird, unlikely, and even magical the old armory proved to be.

"We couldn't come up with a combination of facility, a reasonable amount of rent, and someplace you could walk to from UT if you missed the bus," said Hank. "There was nowhere else in Austin on January 1, 1981, that you could do that."

Or, as Hank saw it, "the Dallasification of Austin was already happening." Austin had grown considerably in the past decade, from 251,808 in 1970 to 345,890 in 1980. It wasn't exactly a population explosion, but it wasn't hard to see the direction in which the city was headed. The high-tech boom was gaining strength, downtown property values were escalating, and people were cashing in on the boom.[12] Hank had his finger on the pulse of the times.

When the end appeared inevitable, the next decision was a fairly easy one. As Hank put it, "We decided to go out with a bang and try to make as much money as possible."

Booking acts for the big blowout was a job for a veteran booking agent, but Killer Mabry had left the Armadillo to devote more time to his family.

He was burned out, weary of working nights, and anxious to spend quality time with a three-year-old daughter who had seen far too little of him.

Still, it only took a whisper of the impending closure to lure Killer back. He phoned Hank as soon as he heard the news. "I definitely wanted to be there," Mabry said. "Hank welcomed me with open arms." Killer's "retirement" had lasted all of two weeks.

As the last months drew near, the people who had invested so much of their lives in the Armadillo were determined that the legacy of the place would be preserved and perpetuated. Jan Beeman and Allen Willenzik hatched an ambitious recording project: a multidisk compilation of tracks by artists who had played the Dillo over the years. Armadillo Productions agreed to split the recording costs.

More bad luck struck on November 15, 1980, six weeks before the Armadillo was scheduled to close. Hank's brother Bill, his only surviving sibling, died under mysterious circumstances. Some years earlier, Hank's other brother had died in a freak electrical accident. Hank wanted to go comfort his mother, but Armadillo business kept him in Austin.

Despite his grief, Hank pressed on. Efforts on the tribute record continued briefly, but a combination of factors led to the project's demise. One of them was a phone call from Willie Nelson's manager, Mark Rothbaum. Rothbaum called to tell Hank that he was sorry to hear that his brother had died and that Willie didn't want to do a song for an Armadillo tribute album. "Willie says he can't see any reason to do it," said Rothbaum. "He can't figure out anything in it for him."

Randy McCall advised Hank to concentrate solely on working toward the Dillo's last day, to drop the legacy thing and recording projects, and once all the bills were paid, pack all the corporation records away in boxes, put them in storage, and forget about the Armadillo World Headquarters.

"I didn't take his advice," Hank said.

Onion Audio had always been close to Hank's heart. After all, he and Jerry Barnett had started the place with their own handmade mixing console. Armadillo Records had built up a roster of singles from the Austin rock band Too Smooth and a band called the Almost Brothers, in addition to albums by blues guitarist Bugs Henderson, the Cobras, and Balcones Fault. Too Smooth was a big draw at the hall and elsewhere in the state, and their mainstream, Doobie Brothers–style, commercial rock impressed the suits at major labels as well. The band inked one deal after another, and also ran into more roadblocks than a convoy of escapees from the striped-pajama house. Long story short: they gave up and became a Top 40 frat party band again.

If you have a hankering to get kicked when you're down, you can always depend on record distributors, as Hank can verify from experience. "We pressed 1,000 copies of Bugs [Henderson]," he said. "In the first week, the copies were gone, but we had no money back." Hank's late brother had paid the $3,000 for the second pressing. "Six weeks later, those are gone and we have only a third of the money back. Eventually, we got 10,000 pressed, but the distributor went under, owing us for 2,200 copies."

Armadillo Records eventually ran into more bad luck with the Cobras (singer Paul Ray and guitarist Stevie Ray Vaughan had left the band by this time). Titled *The Cobras, Live and Deadly*, the album was recorded live at the Armadillo in November of 1979. Hank put up $10,000 for the project. The band had become a sort of revolving door for personnel, with the original singer, guitarist, and bassist all leaving. Then some of the replacements were replaced, but Hank persisted even during the last weeks before the Armadillo closed. A mere twelve months after the album was recorded, attorneys for the band notified Hank of their intention to file an injunction. The reason cited was damage to the band's career by the label's failure to release the record on a timely basis. Hank was so pissed off that he took the master tapes into the studio and erased them.

Armadillo Records released *The Cobras, Live and Deadly* in 2011, using a safety copy of the master tapes.

After the Armadillo received its eviction notice, Henry Gonzalez made some last-minute changes to a mural he had painted in collaboration with Sam Yeates, recreating Ken Featherston's cowboy-in-the-clouds *Searchin' for a Rainbow* piece. Previously, Henry had added Charlie Daniels to the mural, and now he added the face of Q. S. "Pee Wee" Franks, the wrecking crew chief who would be demolishing everything on the property. Franks was a veteran of Austin construction *and* destruction, having torn down numerous Austin landmarks in years past, including some on the corner of Barton Springs and Riverside. In fact, in one of several interviews with *Statesman* reporters, he remembered being at the same address in 1946, before the armory and skating rink were built.

"There was a furniture store where the Armadillo is," he said. "It burned out and I tore down what was left. Then they built the armory." Franks had even worked on the construction of the skating rink.[13]

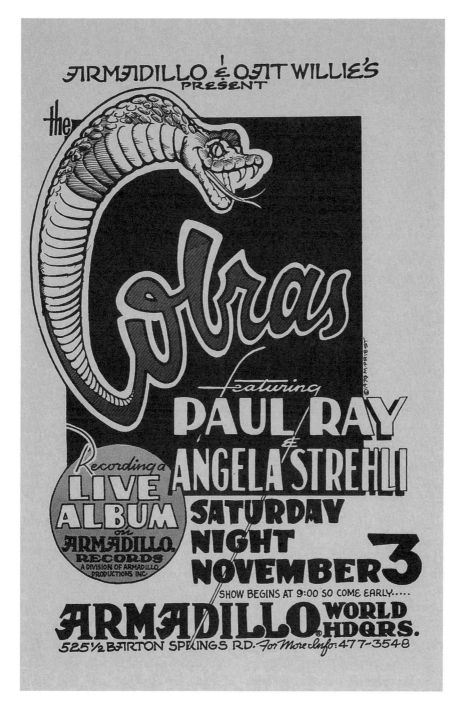

Poster for a Cobras show at AWHQ, 1979.
Artwork by Micael Priest.

In all his decades of experience in erection and destruction, however, this would be first time that Pee Wee Franks ever had to ram a wrecking ball into his own face.

An awful lot of people said they would miss the Armadillo and remarked on what a tragedy the whole situation was. But there was surprisingly little in the way of a great hue and cry. "We had the sympathy of the whole town," said Henry Gonzalez, "but no follow-through."[14]

As the last day approached, there were signs that the sleeping giant of Austin's love affair with its musical community had finally awoken. A group of concerned citizens presented a petition to the Austin Planning Commission, requesting historic landmark status for AWHQ, but the petition fell on deaf ears. Like a well-fed giant, Austin rolled over and went back to sleep, despite all the racket and dust as jackhammers, bulldozers, and cement trucks resumed their inevitable work.

LAST CALL

★

Roy Buchanan played the Dillo for the last time on a two-night staånd in the spring of 1980, just after Hank and company learned that the place was being sold. The supremely gifted guitarist was an emotional fellow, and the idea that he'd never play there again depressed the hell out of him. He'd always wanted to do a live album there, but it had never worked out. He'd always gotten a lot of love from our audiences. After Roy's last show, he and Henry Gonzalez were the last two people in the building. The guitarist pleaded with Henry to go somewhere and party, to do something. Roy just wanted to stay there by himself for a few more hours.

The Dillo went out with a bang. Devo and Roy Orbison played separate nights in August; Leon Redbone and Asleep at the Wheel in September; and James Cotton, Frank Zappa, and Doc and Merle Watson in October. Talking Heads played the week before Thanksgiving; Arlo Guthrie on Thanksgiving night; and on the last night of the month, Robert Shaw, the great Austin barrelhouse pianist, played a farewell boogie-woogie. John Hartford kicked off the first weekend of December, followed by Rockpile on Friday, and Taj Mahal and Townes Van Zandt on Saturday.

Poster for Devo show at AWHQ, 1979.
Artwork by Randy Turner.

The last few weeks saw an abundance of riches: a night with Maria Muldaur and Dan Del Santo; an all-Lubbock show with Joe Ely, Jimmie Dale Gilmore, and Tommy Hancock and the Supernatural Family Band; a redneck rock triple bill with Jerry Jeff Walker, Gary P. Nunn, and Steve Fromholz; and a night revisiting the old Dallas–Fort Worth Turnpike, with Delbert McClinton from the Fort Worth end and Bugs Henderson from the Big D.

With three weeks to go, the Armadillo had a full house on a Monday night for the Charlie Daniels Band. Charlie had long been a big draw at the Dillo but was best known to the music world at large for his recording of the duel-with-the-devil bluegrass hit, "The Devil Went Down to Georgia." During Charlie's set, word spread backstage that John Lennon had been shot. Charlie was informed at some point, but he kept the news to himself and kept the show going. Observant audience members likely noticed several last-second changes in the set list. The set ended with the gospel hymn "How Great Thou Art."

The house lights came up, and instead of an encore, Charlie spoke somberly into the microphone. "Ya'll sit down," he told the crowd. "We gotta go to church here for a minute." After announcing Lennon's death, he called for a moment of silence.

Unfortunately, not everyone had gotten the message. Silent words with the Almighty were interrupted by the clang of metal folding chairs at the back of the hall and a voice yelling, "Clear the hall! Clear the hall! We have to get ready for the Christmas Bazaar!" It may have been Bruce Willenzik's most off-key night.

New Year's Eve, the last night of the Armadillo World Headquarters, featured Commander Cody and His Lost Planet Airmen, Asleep at the Wheel, and Maria Muldaur. A total of 1,500 tickets were sold at twenty-five dollars apiece. Austin mime and magician Turk Pipkin started the proceedings, performing one of his most popular mime routines—rolling a joint. For this occasion, Pipkin rolled the biggest virtual joint in the world. After lighting it and taking a giant hit, he passed it around for everyone to virtually inhale. It was even too big for Doug Sahm to bogart.

Cody's guitar player, Bill Kirchen, was recovering from a broken back. He showed up at the gig wearing a heavy back brace, but by showtime, he'd decided it was too inhibiting. Kirchen's lead playing was as incendiary as ever, but as he launched into his usual onstage antics, people became concerned about him.

Poster for the last show at AWHQ, 1980.
Artwork by Micael Priest.

"During one song he rolled around on the floor, but he couldn't get up," said Jan Beeman. "Someone had to lift him."[1]

After Cody's set, Ray Benson of Asleep at the Wheel introduced Kenneth Threadgill and the Velvet Cowpasture. Benson reminded the crowd that "long before most any of us were here in Austin, and definitely before the Armadillo was even a dream, up on North Lamar a fellow ran a little beer joint, and we're all real happy he did. Besides that, he sings his ass off, and he's one of the greatest yodelers left in Texas today for sure." With that, Benson welcomed the man he called "the granddaddy of Austin, Texas, music."[2]

Kenneth lived up to the billing, taking over the microphone to warble an inspired rendition of "Waiting for a Train," his yodels echoing off the walls one last time. National Public Radio beamed the concert live nationwide, and *Rolling Stone* and *New York Times* reporters were in the room rocking and taking notes.

Jim Franklin was on hand, of course, reminding people of the wisdom of armadillos and the continuity of hippie culture in Austin. After all, he had become almost as much a local icon as the nine-banded creature he had done so much to popularize through his artwork. Jim also called attention to the wrecking ball he had incorporated into a mural in the beer garden.

"This place made me," Cody told a *Statesman* reporter. "We played a gig here with Waylon Jennings when he still had his hair greased back," he said. "A lot of things changed that night, and I don't think anybody's gonna forget it. The spirit of this place will live on. It's too strong to stop."[3]

People laughed. People danced. They boogied and they cried. Unexpected things happened.

Leea Mechling went back to the kitchen to get something and realized a stranger was following her, "talking about how much he'd enjoyed coming to the shows all these years." In the kitchen, the stranger admitted that he was an undercover narcotics agent.

"But then he makes clear that he's totally off duty," said Leea. "The staff liked to smoke joints in the cold vault; you knew it was time whenever someone threw open the door and yelled, 'Fire in the cold vault!' So we took him in there with us, and he smoked a joint with us."[4]

The midnight hour came and went, and the 1980s were four hours old by the time Ray Benson sang the very last song. Ray did his best tallman croon on "Goodnight, Irene," the old, old ballad that Lead Belly had carried with him on his journey down a road of hard knocks, oppression, prison, and eventually, international fame.

I was seven years old when Lead Belly died in 1949, and the following year, "Goodnight, Irene" topped the charts with cover versions by the Weavers and Frank Sinatra. When I was little, I would change the chorus to "Goodnight, Ione" as a tribute to Aunt Ione, the one I loved to cuddle with the most when I was little: "Goodnight, Ione, Goodnight, Ione, I'll see you in my dreams." And it bears mentioning that the last word of the very last song sung at Armadillo World Headquarters was "dreams."

And then Micael Priest got up one last time to bid the crowd good night at the end of the show that also marked the end of an era. "This was the headquarters, but y'all were the armadillos," he said, fighting back tears. "I want you to continue to carry this throughout the country, to teach people how to have fun. And we will do this again."

Although it had always been hard to get every last person to leave the music hall, on that night it was especially difficult, particularly for people on the staff who had literally—in some cases for years at a time—lived there.

"I left about five in the morning," Jan Beeman said. "As I was walking out, I saw Micael Priest, Jim Franklin, and two gals out in the parking lot, crying in their car. They were sisters who'd waitressed for a long, long time. Priest said, '*Hasta luego*.'"[5]

Some of the staff stayed there until the sun came up.

Then there were the staff members who had to go back the next day to clean out their desks and tend to other final chores. A representative from the Texas Employment Commission came down to get everyone sorted out for unemployment benefits. As it turned out, the representative also had a booth at the Christmas Bazaar.

★ ★ ★

How do you say good-bye to a place that's been the center of your life for so long? A place that alternated, sometimes hour by hour, between joyous and maddening, exhilarating and soul crushing, super cool and black-hole depressing? And when you heard the news that it was closing for good, you didn't know whether to cry or laugh or say, "Damn, what a fucking relief!"

I had gotten into the habit of going to the beer garden in the afternoon, especially during the last summer, when the wisteria finally bloomed. But except for the Mose Allison show, I never went inside the music hall, and I wasn't there for the last show.

On the night the Armadillo closed for good, I was crawling around on the floor of a beer joint on the other side of town. Let me rephrase that: I was working on the hardwood floors of Kenneth Threadgill's old gas station and beer joint on North Lamar. I had purchased the place in 1979, then spent two years getting the place ready to open again.

Talk about continuity. I was doing pretty much what I'd been doing the night before the Armadillo opened to the public: hammering, hauling, lifting, screwing, shouting out orders, getting twisted up inside out of fear that the revitalized, fancy, upscale, down-home revival of Threadgill's would not be ready for the public on the first day of 1981.

The hardwood floors, which came out of an old school building in the town of Bartlett, needed a coat or two of stain, but the old planks had just enough varnish left on them that it was hell getting the stain to stick. I was hell-bound to have the place open for business the next day.

The idea of reopening the joint had been on my mind ever since 1974. That was the year that Kenneth Threadgill, faced with the choice of having extensive repairs made to the place or shutting it down, chose the latter option. Subsequently, city council member Lowell Lebermann suggested that Threadgill's deserved consideration for historical preservation. Lebermann had recently replaced Roy Butler as the rich guy on the dais, and I respected his sentiment, although, in a foreshadowing of the city's ho-hum attitude toward the demolition of the Armadillo, no effort was expended toward saving this hallowed Austin music landmark.

By the end of 1974, the old gas station/roadhouse was not only defunct but decrepit. That was the year that the fire department was called out because of a small electrical fire in the attic. In the process of attacking the fire, the responders had chopped a massive hole in the roof. Did they make the hole larger than necessary as payback for all the irritation Kenneth Threadgill had caused the fire marshal over the years by exceeding the crowd limit? Some of us wondered about that. The building had already been overdue for structural repairs before the fire happened. Kenneth had been putting it off for years.

Now the building needed extensive repairs, which Kenneth could not afford. Mildred, his beloved wife of forty-five years, also died that year. The old yodeler shut the place down and told me he was relieved. Not being a business owner gave him more time to play music. He had

Kenneth and Mildred Threadgill. Photographer unknown.
Photo courtesy of the *Houston Chronicle*.

a Sunday night residency gig at the Split Rail and played as much as he could during the rest of the week. Kenneth was a regular at the Armadillo; few artists played there as often as he did.

Then, in 1979, just a few days before I was ready to sign the papers to buy the place, there was another fire, this one started by a transient. I'm pretty sure the culprit was the ghost of the infamous Hobo Bill.

By then the building had been vacant with a big hole in the roof for five years, and it was so thoroughly soaked, it's a wonder that it burned, but the fire pretty much gutted it. It looked as though someone had bundled up the piles of scrap papers and tried to light things up but lost control. One of my favorite souvenirs was found lying facedown under Kenneth's old butcher case: a charred-black, quarter-folded *American-Statesman* page with Janis Joplin's death notice on the side facing down on the wet concrete floor, which saved it. It's now framed on my wall, a reminder of Austin music legacies that live on even after their physical structures have succumbed to natural disaster, arson, or the fickle march of fashion.

The people in charge of preserving Austin landmarks didn't come rushing to the aid of the Armadillo in 1980, nor did their hearts beat in sympathy for Threadgill's place in the 1970s. But some soul with a heart for history and a can of spray paint had written the words "Janis sang here" on the side of the derelict building. By then I had been fantasizing off and on for a long time about reopening the joint, if only as a means of escaping from the daily, angst-inducing grind of running the Armadillo. Once the "for sale" sign appeared, I knew I had to make a move.

As far as I was concerned, the building's historic significance was reason enough to save it, but I didn't want it to be a museum. Austin music history was a hard sell. I couldn't have started another Armadillo even if I'd wanted to, and I didn't. What I had in mind was a place that was steeped in Austin music history: a restaurant with a bar, a collection of local music artifacts, and a kitchen that served the comfort food my mother, Beulah, made and fed to me and several generations of other kids at her nursery school, with a little acoustic music on the side now and then. That was my idea, and I was ready to run with it.

★ ★ ★

On Saturday, January 15, 1981, two weeks after the Armadillo's last night, I finally went back and took a stroll around the place, inside and out. J. C.

Harper Auctioneers was conducting an auction. People were bidding on all sorts of things, but wherever I looked, my eyes met teary eyes. Leea Mechling was having a rough day. "A bunch of the staff wanted to dig out the big wisteria plant in the back," she said. "We went out back and some bastard had come in there with a truck and a front-end loader and put the whole thing in the back of his truck. Wouldn't even let us take cuttings off of it."[6]

Just when the wisteria had finally managed to completely cover the overhead trellis, providing shade in the middle of a summer day, and just when the beer garden had finally matured into an honest beer garden in the great tradition of Scholz Garten, Austin's oldest business, the Dillo was going down before the wrecking ball. Someone eventually tracked down the wisteria to a backyard in South Austin's Bouldin Creek neighborhood, a few blocks away.

About $45,000 of stuff was auctioned off. Over five hundred people registered to bid on items. Mike Harkins spent $75 for the curtains hanging from the rafters. When Harkins was asked how he planned to get the curtains down, a nearby hippie suggested he scrape them off and smoke the residue. Bricks were selling for $4.95 apiece. Lot no. 487 was a garbage can and contents. Another item was a skillet from the kitchen, complete with authentic grease and hamburger scraps. The piano sold for $2,000. George Nash Jr. bought it for a bar on the San Antonio River Walk called the Landing, where Nash's business partner, Jim Cullum, led a Dixieland band. Beer mugs went for as high as $15 each. John Worsham, who bought the "Fast Beer" sign for $75, said he and his wife had moved from Beaumont to Austin years ago precisely because of the Armadillo.

I didn't buy anything, but I did shed a tear or two. Somebody commented that the place looked like an abandoned theme park, which was either clueless or very ironic, since that's precisely what it was. Of course I thought about the night ten years earlier when I had walked out behind the Cactus Club to take a leak, and had looked up and seen my future.

Pee Wee Franks came back later and oversaw the operators of the wrecking ball, bulldozers, dump trucks, and other machines of deconstruction until the lot had been scraped clean. Then the corner sat empty for a long time. Long enough to become an eyesore, as well as a symbol of greediness and a few other unflattering character traits.

The demolition of AWHQ was as fast as ripping off a Band-Aid, January 1981. Photographs from the collection of Dub Rose.

A year after the property was sold, the buyer flipped it, selling it for $2 million, the kind of classic land deal that powered Austin's first major real estate boom in the 1980s and forever ended the city's reputation as a cheap place to live. So many plans were announced for the high-rise building to come that some of us stopped keeping track of them: it was to be a resort hotel, an IBM office building, a bank . . . The property was flipped again twice before a nondescript, bland, ten-story office building was erected on the site. Then the building owner went broke. Today, the city of Austin has offices there in what is called One Texas Center.

People drive by there every day now—tourists, seekers, veterans of back in the day—pausing at what their GPS tells them is the right place. You can see them staring at the intersection, the parking lot, the high-rise, Threadgill's restaurant, and the other structures that have taken the Armadillo's place on the chessboard of the Weird City in the past three and a half decades. Some of them find the commemorative plaque erected by the city in 2006, with its photo collage showing the exterior with the Skating Palace facade, the interior, and the beer garden, accompanied by a thoughtful distillation of the history and legacy of the place.[7] Still, most of these pilgrims look puzzled, as if they just can't fit together the puzzle pieces of what used to be. Even though the vision is still pretty well fixed in my own mind, I can't blame them.

FULL CIRCLE

Threadgill's opened for business on New Year's Day 1981, just in time to serve old friends with new hangovers from the final blowout of the Armadillo's candle. The new joint offered delicious, Southern-style comfort food, with generous portions, low prices, and great service. The interior was decorated with samples from my growing collection of Texas music and roadhouse artifacts. As John Morthland put it, "Threadgill's was Austin's first theme restaurant, and the theme was Austin."[1]

We had instant success. There were long lines to get in, and we won so many awards, it became embarrassing. Finally, I approached Louis Black, editor of the *Austin Chronicle*, and pleaded with him, only half-jokingly, to retire our jersey.

Kenneth Threadgill sang every Wednesday night, just like in the old days. Our customers spanned many generations. The eldest remembered Prohibition days, when they would fill up their gas tank in front, then swing around back to buy an ass-pocket bottle of hooch. We had sixties veterans who'd been regulars on open-mic nights and who proudly told of rubbing elbows with Janis Joplin. Some of them had grown up at the Armadillo. Many others were new in town, migrants feeding Austin's 1980s tech boom.

To accommodate the overflowing demand, we added a retro cool stainless steel diner a few months after opening. Things were going gangbusters when the hairy hand of fate struck. On August 16, 1982, the same day that Elvis had died in 1977 and the same day that Delta blues legend Robert Johnson died in 1938, there was another damned fire at 6416 North Lamar. The investigation found residue of flammable liquids on the office floor, meaning it was either a case of outright arson or a fire set by a burglar to cover his or her tracks.

An employee who lived down the street came knocking on our door at four in the morning. Genie and I only had to go outside to catch our first glimpse of the horrific sight. Flames were leaping high above the buildings between our house and the restaurant.

We lost everything but the outside walls, and if not for the quick action of the firefighters, we would've lost the walls, too. Quite a crowd gathered to watch. As the flames were extinguished and slowly began to cool, an idea began to take shape in our minds. The floor drains in the kitchen of the joint had been incorrectly placed. The grading was wrong as well. Now we had to rebuild. In the big picture, jackhammering out the proper drain lines would be a minor task. The fire had given us a golden opportunity to do the kitchen right. We were so pleased with ourselves, we high-fived and cheered.

One of the guys in raincoats and galoshes on the site turned out to be a fire inspector. Our cheerful outburst made him suspicious. One of the first steps of the investigation was a lie detector test for yours truly. I was so pissed off when they hooked me up to the machine. I thought it was a wonder they didn't pinch me for the Lindbergh kidnapping.

George Majewski was the first person I knew to come around after the fire. I was standing in the ashes when I looked up and saw George. He commiserated with me about the loss of not only the restaurant but my collection of antique beer signs, some of which were still smoking. He'd brought me an old Grand Prize Beer clock and handed it to me through a gap in the window. "Here," he said, "I know you'll have to start collecting these again." George has always been one of my heroes.

We started rebuilding as soon as possible, and during the interim, we served our faithful patrons under tents in the parking lot next door. My slogan for the rebuild and reopening was something I'd stolen from the infamous Austin blues dive on Red River called the One Knite: "This is one joint that won't go out."

Threadgill's after the fire. Personal snapshots.

Just before we started building, I changed the plans and added a second story to the commissary building in back. Obviously, it would be cheaper to build at that moment than later on. I had no idea what we'd use the second floor for, but I'd figure it out somewhere down the line. The sudden, seemingly random change surprised no one who knew me well.

In just ninety-seven days, we were open for business and also had a brand-new commissary at the back of the parking lot. The building was designed to provide the prepared vegetables and gravies for as many new Threadgill's as I could ever want to open. There was an upstairs space in back that I called the "Upstairs Store," primarily devoted to my addiction to collecting old stuff: vintage beer signs, posters, country store furnishings, and other items you could generally file under the category of Americana.

For me, stuff—historical pieces, relics, ephemera, or whatever term applies—has a magical aura. You often find many more stories attached to an object than you could ever glean from a scholarly book on the subject. Not that I don't love old books, too. I even love my antique bookshelves.

Threadgill's had opened at a good time. By the mideighties, there was a big resurgence of diners across the country, and every time you picked up a magazine, there we were. Threadgill's was featured in *Newsweek*, *Rolling Stone*, *Smithsonian*, *National Geographic*, and *Vogue*, to name a few.

Beulah Wilson passed away on September 1, 1986, four years after she and Woody helped me build the restaurant, and the following March, Kenneth Threadgill died. Although we were doing great business, I couldn't help feeling like something was missing, and it didn't take long to realize that that something was music. Jimmie Dale Gilmore inaugurated a revival of Threadgill's Wednesday night music tradition. The choice was a no-brainer. Jimmie Dale's music had been spinning on my mental jukebox for twenty years. I'd been a fan of the Hub City Movers, the Flatlanders, and Jimmie Dale's solo work, too. Unless one of us kicks off fairly soon, it looks like I'll have been one of his most ardent supporters for at least half a century.

As the end of the decade approached, the joint was still going strong, but my marriage to Genie had passed its expiration date. In the divorce settlement I gave her the house, the adjacent lot, and a monthly stipend for two years. Her lawyer jokingly complained that I was making her job look too easy.

Butch Hancock, Jimmie Dale Gilmore, Rich Brotherton, Champ Hood, and Joe Ely play Threadgill's. Photograph by Maria Camillo.

When I ran away from home in those days, New Orleans was invariably my destination. I started spending more time there than in Austin. My birthplace, Lumberton, Mississippi, is a mere ninety miles from the Crescent City, so it was more like communing with my roots than being on the lam. One weekend, I flew back to Austin on a Friday to sign the payroll checks and then jumped on the first flight back to New Orleans. I wasn't just partying, either; I was letting my antiquity addiction run wild. I visited the building on Decatur Street that had served as the consulate for the Republic of Texas. William Joel Bryan, our agent in New Orleans, went there to raise money and logistical support for the Texas Republic before the siege of the Alamo even began, and remained our man in New Orleans up until 1846, when Texas became part of the Union. And I spent hours and hours digging around in other historic places, libraries, and rare book stores.

I looked up the building that had once housed the Jacobs Candy Company factory. The company only existed from 1910–1920, but it made a big impression on the locals, and not just because of the high quality of its chocolate confections. Jacobs really knew how to market its products effectively for the times. The chocolates were sold in ornate tin boxes that often bore the company slogan "Made last night," a phrase that not only assured customers of freshness but also worked as a double entendre for the women of Storyville, New Orleans's red-light district—as in, "Jacobs candies are just like the girls in Storyville: they were *made* last night."[2]

Oftentimes, everything in the Big Easy seems tied in with food, music, sex, and revelry, and Jacobs's marketing was no exception. Local musicians were employed to serve as official Jacobs Candy Men. The Candy Men would make the rounds of the city's ice cream parlors (which, owing to recent advances in commercial refrigeration, were quite numerous at the time), where they would perform song-and-dance routines, passing out free samples in between numbers. There was a special gift for the ladies, too: a lapel pin bearing the slogan "Made last night." Billy Price Augustin pulled a stint as a Candy Man, and so did Al Bernard, the man who wrote "Shake, Rattle and Roll," an early precursor to the famously sexual rock 'n roll song of the same name.[3]

Two of my favorite pieces in the "Upstairs Store" above Threadgill's, the Jacobs Candy glass display counter and Jacobs Candy globe, also had the best stories to tell. I had bought them as a commemoration of a date at Jazz Fest with my future wife, Sandra.

The first time I laid eyes on Sandra was over twenty-five years ago, but I remember it like it was yesterday. It was a cold but sunny day in mid-December. I was in my office, talking on the phone to my Pal with a capital *P*, Billy Gammon. Billy had held my hand through the Threadgill's fire of August 16, 1982, the flooding of my home in the Memorial Day flood of 1981, and countless other traumatic episodes. His friendship was tested and true. A regular dose of his smarmy wisecracks helped alleviate my occasional bouts of melancholy.

Our conversation was interrupted by a light tapping sound on the office door. I made a cranky grunting sound, and the door opened just enough to reveal the face of an angel. With a bit of encouragement, she stepped into the office. She wore a long, black winter coat with the collar turned up. Leaning back in my chair, I had my boots propped on the desktop in the precise manner from which Beulah had labored uselessly to wean me. The angel's pretty face had a mischievous grin. Her whisper made me think of a little crystal jigger. "Are you Mr. Threadgill?" she asked.

"Billy, I've got to go," I said. "I'm in serious trouble."

"No, ma'am," I said to her, quickly rising to my feet. With my boots on the floor, I summoned a self-image remarkably similar to that of John Wayne.

Her name was Sandra. I told her mine. She said we'd talked recently on the phone about my frozen food company possibly leasing a delivery truck. Sure, I remembered that. She was currently living in Los Angeles, having recently moved there to be with her daughter, the actress Renée O'Connor. At the moment, however, Sandra was back in Texas to visit her mother in Houston.

Clear thinking and coherent speech came with difficulty, but somehow I managed to give her a leisurely tour of the commissary and restaurant, which I tried to drag out as long as possible. Sandra was due to pick up her son in Fort Hood. He was being discharged that day from the army, just in time for Christmas. She didn't have long. He was waiting.

How was I going to see her again? I'd lease a truck! Hey, I'd lease several trucks. As she got into her car, I blurted out, "Would you consider going with me to Jazz Fest this spring?" I hadn't gotten her to take off her coat, but I could see we had matching ring fingers—both were unadorned.

I didn't even know exactly when Jazz Fest was, but I knew the date was far enough off that I'd have time to figure something out.

"Yes," she said, blushing.

Eddie and Sandra. Photograph by Burton Wilson.

My life suddenly revolved around a date. On a subsequent telephone call, she stammered that she'd never done such a thing before. She hinted that separate rooms would be a relief, to which I responded with bluster: "Why, of course! What kind of guy do you think I am?"

In reality, I didn't even have one room reserved. "Maybe I should come to LA for our first date," I suggested and, with further lack of forethought, added, "I need to come study the massive produce market there for possible deals for my vegetable sources, if I'm ever going to expand my frozen casserole business."

Which was a crock, but subtleties such as this could be resolved at a later date.

"That'd be wonderful," she said. "You can stay in our guest room."

They didn't have a guest room.

Sandra and Renée picked me up at LAX. I was wearing my best boots—but my favorite boots, an old, broken-in pair, were in a bag slung over my shoulder, an arrangement that helped bolster my confidence.

Clifford Antone happened to be in LA at the time. I'd called him before leaving Austin and arranged for him to meet us for dinner at the Musso and Frank Grill that night, which helped lay the foundation for a cool, interesting evening. Mother and daughter were thrilled to meet the colorful club owner who, as always, exuded the air of a Mafia don. I had already told Clifford that I was going to marry the beautiful brunette. Later in the evening, he told me that he approved. It would be a few more months before I told Sandra.

Our second date, to Jazz Fest, was a placeholder. By the fall I couldn't stand it anymore, and so one mid-October night when she was in Austin, just as we were leaving Conans Pizza on Twenty-Ninth Street, I asked her to marry me on New Year's Eve. She asked if New Year's Day would be better for tax purposes. We decided on midnight so it could go either way by a minute when the tax accountant ruled on the question.

We tied the knot at Threadgill's at the stroke of midnight on New Year's Eve 1991, with seventy-five friends wailing "You Are My Sunshine" on kazoos. On what was an otherwise slow news night, Fred Cantu of Channel 7 TV covered the ceremony as a special broadcast.

★ ★ ★

Another clear-as-yesterday memory is the day in 1995 when I drove past the former Marimont Cafeteria on the corner of Riverside and Barton Springs and saw the new "for lease" sign. The building had been taken over by the Dallas-based Wyatt's chain, but it wasn't a big success. When I saw the sign, I pulled to the curb, rested my head on the steering wheel, and did some serious thinking, flashing back over the last few years.

For at least two years, I'd been looking all over South Austin for another Threadgill's location. The coincidence of finding the answer to my quest right next door to the former site of the AWHQ felt like a cosmic convergence. I thought about 1973, about sitting in the beer garden under the trees, watching the cafeteria being built. Passing a joint back and forth, we had shaken our shaggy heads and muttered, "Those people are the enemy." More important than being a station from which to broadcast my memory of youthful vigor and numerous close calls, the old cafeteria had a kitchen in place as big as the commissary on North Lamar. Now I had the ability to service quite a number of additional locations, in case I wanted to expand further at some point.

My first goal was to get the new restaurant open and both restaurants running smoothly, then build out the magnificent outdoor space at Threadgill's World Headquarters, TWHQ, into the beer garden of my dreams. After all, the location lay less than the distance of a flubbed punt from the Armadillo's magical "Beer Garden of Eden," remembered by all the people who hug me today, thanking me for building the breeding ground of their youthful memories of love and lust, their early contact with Austin music, art, tolerance, and joy.

I sought advice from Mike Mays, my old pal and banker buddy, who had been trying to help me figure out how to grow my latest venture, Threadgill's Frozen Foods. I also got a lot of help from my cousin Physina Miller, the one with all the brains in our gene pool. Not satisfied with being a CPA, Physina had returned to college to obtain more advanced degrees, which eventually helped her trade the bean-counting profession for head and neck surgery. Team Threadgill's put together a fundraiser to form two limited partnerships: one to fund the capture of the new location, and another to shore up the old number-one priority, the beer garden. At one point, an inquisitive newspaper reporter called me after hearing a rumor of our doings. Shortly after I answered the reporter's questions, a feature story was published. The story explained all the reasons why advertising for investors is illegal. OK, so who said that discretion was one of my outstanding character traits?

The phone rang off the hook for several days with people begging to be allowed to invest $50,000 in twenty-five limited partnerships. I left a lot of money on the table, as I was more accustomed to scraping by on the bare minimum. Thanks to Physina's guidance, the deal was put together so that the big store downtown could help support the original restaurant. We were seeing a slowdown in business due to the fact that the location was increasingly isolated, as real estate buzz increased in other parts of town. A failed partnership and an awful fire in 1982 had also left us with huge debts.

Through an extensive renovation, TWHQ began to take shape. I contracted Jim Franklin to create the most elaborate, detailed, three-dimensional rendering of *Dasypus novemcinctus* he had ever attempted. Guy Juke collaborated with Jim in the carving of seventy-two galloping, nine-banded armadillos, each one several times life-size. The whole herd was coated with white stucco and attached to the exterior wall above window level. They look as if they're leaping through the walls, heading out to conquer the world.

The jukebox in the foyer was stocked with one hundred albums by artists who had played the Dillo. The Mason & Hamlin baby grand that I used to take lessons on and that had once been the house piano at the Armadillo was suspended from the ceiling, with a plaque reminding everyone that its black and white ivories had been caressed by artists as diverse as Count Basie, Commander Cody, Jerry Lee Lewis, Ray Charles, Leon Russell, and Captain Beefheart.

We opened Threadgill's World Headquarters in 1996 with a grand party attended by a who's who of the Austin Hippie World—poster artists, South Austin characters, leftists, writers, and other unclassifiable individuals who left their impression on Austin before, during, and after the Vulcan/Armadillo era.

The new location was designed to function as a pretty great restaurant and bar, and also as Austin's unofficial music museum. The joint was packed with Austin and Armadillo memorabilia. Just like AWHQ, TWHQ was also conceived as a community center for liberals, leftists, hippies, and other freethinking, creative spirits. We've hosted speeches by Nobel Prize–winning economist and *New York Times* columnist Paul

Krugman. After the passing of Ed Wendler, the last of the fighting yellow dog Democrats, we held a huge, raucous wake that ran long and loud. Jim Hightower broadcast his liberal populist radio show from there for several years. Some of the grouchier right-wingers in Austin have been known to refer to Threadgill's as "the Kremlin." It makes me proud.

In purely financial terms, TWHQ was a far bigger success in a shorter time than AWHQ ever was. We paid off the investors and earned them over 25 percent before boomtown economics caught up with us. As for participating in Austin's ever-expanding reputation as a music mecca, Live Music Capital of the World, icon of the "Keep it Weird" movement, and one of the coolest places in the world, period, we've been proud to play a continuing role in that boom, too.

A whole lot happened in Austin between 1980 and 1995, the decade and a half between the demise of AWHQ and the opening of TWHQ. One of the biggest things was the South by Southwest (SXSW) Music, Film, and Interactive Festival, which originated as a music festival in March 1987. When 700 attendees showed up at the inaugural festival to see 177 bands in 15 venues, it was considered a wild success—only 150 people had been expected to attend. Film and interactive components were added in 1994. By 2015, the number of SXSW registrants and single-admission ticket holders exceeded 139,000. And many more thousands come to attend non-SXSW-sponsored events, or just to party. In 2015, SXSW was directly responsible for injecting over $315.2 million into the local economy.[4]

Threadgill's World Headquarters is proud to play a role in the festival. During SXSW music week, we host over one hundred bands on the outdoor stage for free.

SXSW Music Festival is the biggest of its kind in the world, and SXSW Interactive can make the same claim. SXSW Film is one of the most prestigious film festivals in the world. It makes me proud to know that great directors like Richard Linklater, Robert Rodriguez, and Mike Judge have roots here and work here. Today, Austin has so many skilled production people and so much logistical support in the city that four major motion pictures can be filmed in the area simultaneously. The seeds of that infrastructure were being planted in the early 1970s, when Mike Tolleson and Bill Narum were shooting live shows at the Armadillo, city council meetings, surrealistic scenes like Mance Lipscomb sitting on the edge of his bed, the inside of Ramblin' Jack Elliott's hat . . . and then they would upload the video late at night to Taylorvision. I also remember heading out to meetings with Mike Tolleson and Woody Roberts, brimming with optimism and enthusiasm as we pitched our film and commercial television concepts to clients like Lone Star, Pearl, and KLRN.

Members of the Armadillo Art Squad always have a huge presence at the American Poster Institute and SXSW's Flatstock, one of the most important exhibitions of music poster art in the country.[5] The Art Squad's work was also the subject of an early 2015 exhibition at the Wittliff Collections at Texas State University, *Homegrown: Austin Music Posters 1967–1982*. At the opening of the exhibition, the hardcover printing of the catalog sold out in two hours.[6]

When the calendar turns to spring every year, it's a happy reminder that Roky Erickson, a true rock 'n' roll superhero, is still here with us. In 2001, after more than two decades of being lost in a wilderness of legal tangles and mental health issues, his problems in both areas were addressed and he was able to reclaim his career. Year after year, Roky's Ice Cream Social show at Threadgill's, inaugurated in 2003 on our outdoor stage, has been one of the must-see events of SXSW.

Speaking of festivals, every fall since 2002, the lush greenbelt between Lady Bird Lake and Barton Springs is taken over by the Austin City Limits Music Festival, popularly known as ACL, an annual series of concerts attended by over 100,000 people. ACL was conceived as a spin-off of *Austin City Limits*, the TV series that passed the forty-year mark in 2014. Naturally, I like to remind people that if they want to dig up the real story on the history of the show, they'll find that *Austin City Limits* came after the KLRN (now KLRU) broadcast of Armadillo Country Music Review in the summer of 1973. *Austin City Limits* came in late 1974 and 1975, after years of pioneering efforts based at Armadillo World Headquarters to get Austin music on television and cable. Armadillo people blazed the trail that others followed.

The official histories of *Austin City Limits* usually mangle or ignore the facts, partially because most of the people who write about it weren't around in 1973, just as most of the people who attend SXSW shows are a decade or more younger than the festival itself. But just think, if things had worked out—that is, if AWHQ and KLRN hadn't gone their separate ways—today, you'd be watching *Armadillo Music Television* every week.

You'd be talking up Armadillo Live Fest or Dillopalooza every fall. And Jim Franklin might be a world-famous master of ceremonies.

Perhaps I'm overly sensitive about the Armadillo's legacy, but I feel fairly confident that diligent researchers will eventually get it right. The facts never change, only the legend.

Austin is cool. It's a matter of civic pride here. We're not the "Number One Producer of Crankshafts" or "Home of the World's Largest Emu Farm." Austin is cool, it's weird, and like the bumper stickers say, we want to keep it that way.

Signs boasting that we're the "Live Music Capital of the World" greet visitors stepping off the jetway at the airport. Another one says, "I wanna go home with the Armadillo." That's where we live.

In Austin, cool plus weird equals a magnet for creative minds. Maybe it's the other way around. No matter, but if not for our city's diverse, tolerant, alternative environment, recruiters would not have been able to attract bright young talent to build the city's high-tech sector, which has been a key factor in keeping things humming here even when the economy hits a speed bump in the red parts of the state.

★ ★ ★

After I had raised the money to build the Threadgill's location on Riverside, I called Hank Alrich and asked what he'd charge for the AWHQ stock. Although I knew he'd lost more than twice the amount he'd given me back in 1972, he answered without hesitation: "I guess what I paid for it, $50,000." I was so confident that I fired back, "Deal!" Then he called back a few minutes later. "I've been thinking it over," he said. "I'd like to keep Armadillo Records and the music publishing, so make it $45,000." "Deal!"

Here's a guy who doesn't know any more about business than I do. He loans $50,000, then, thirty years later, gets $45,000 back and feels good about it. Hank and I talked about how we had refused to let money be so important for a long enough period that a lot of good shit got stitched together.

More amazing deals were made on a sunny Saturday in the middle of January 2015. It was an auction of AWHQ poster art and other artifacts, but this time the mood was a great deal cheerier than it had been thirty-five years before. The event was run by Burley Auction Group in their gallery in New Braunfels, which is about fifty miles down the interstate from Austin. Blame a convergence of bad weather, structural failures, a cash crunch, and other factors from a few months earlier. After getting the go-ahead from the insurance company to repair the leaky roof in the Upstairs Store, I realized that the only way to have the repairs done was to move my now incredibly over-the-top collection to another place. The thought of all that work was frightening. At the same time, there was a pressing need to raise capital for various endeavors—not the least of which was building at least one new Threadgill's location to make up for the possibly inevitable closing of the south location due to skyrocketing rent and property taxes.

In the meantime, funds were sorely needed to finance a facelift of TWHQ. Installing hardwood floors with the auction sales upgraded the joint considerably. No more concrete floors like those in the Dillo! It was satisfying to make these capital improvements without enlisting assistance from my partners. Even better was the validation I got from customers who thanked me with tears in their eyes for beautifying the restaurant.

Once I got used to it, the idea of drastically paring down my collection of stuff made me almost giggly with joy. I love my stuff, but if Sandra and I are ever going to move to New Zealand (a pet idea of ours), we've got to unload everything that doesn't float.

The auctioneer and head honcho was Rob Burley, a lanky former Army Ranger and combat veteran of our recent wars. Dressed in black with a matching felt cowboy hat, he reminded me of an Ace Reid *Cowpokes* character, but wired on thirty cups of coffee. With Sandra and me sitting in the front row, Rob got things off to a lightning start, juggling bids effortlessly, no matter if they came from the gallery, online, or via telephone. It was a dazzling performance. I nudged Jesse Sublett, who was sitting to my right, and said, "It's like rap!" He said, "No, it's like opera!"

We had a lot of success promoting the event, but still, I was humbled by the size of the crowd—standing room only—and their enthusiasm.[7] I couldn't say how many white-haired people (like myself) thanked me for the opportunity to pay hundreds, in some cases thousands, of dollars for an Armadillo gig poster, a painting by one of the Art Squad, or one of the neon beer signs, clocks, country store counters, hat blocks, et cetera.

As things got under way and the prices shot up so fast, the first thing I thought of was that I couldn't believe people were paying these prices for this stuff. I couldn't help worrying once again that I was going to lose my hippie card. Sandra and I were just breathless. A few things didn't sell for as much as I paid for them, but for the most part, it was beyond our expectations.

The first Willie Nelson poster that sold was the one by Micael Priest for Willie's first show at the Dillo, and it sold for $700. A 1954 photo of the Grand Prize Beer football squad, with young Howard Hughes on the team, sold for $1,000. A Lone Star Beer airplane propeller neon sign fetched $8,000. The only thing in the collection I'd stolen instead of buying—from a shuttered old shop in Rosenberg, Texas—sold for $3,500.

There, at center stage, was the baby grand piano, which sold for $22,500. It was less than one might have expected, considering how many gifted hands had played it over the years, but at least it appeared to be going to a good home, a new Cooper's barbecue joint in downtown Austin.

A huge Micael Priest painting that had been commissioned by Jerry Jeff Walker for an album cover sold for $8,000, and as Rob Burley explained to the room, every penny of it was going straight to Micael, who needed some help. A separate auction was also held in May at TWHQ, in which the Armadillo artists sold their own wares and received all the proceeds.

Emotions ran high, as did the bidding for Jim Franklin's masterful Freddie King painting. The winning bids for both sections of the work (top and bottom), which had hung in TWHQ since it opened, were submitted by Steve Wertheimer, owner of the Continental Club and C-Boy's on South Congress. Besides being a very successful Austin club owner, Steve is a cool cat, and I think everyone who wasn't bidding on the piece themselves was relieved that it ended up with him.

For days after the auction, even after we settled with Burley and deposited the proceeds in the bank, Sandra and I were walking around dazed, asking ourselves, "Did that really happen? Is it true?"

And it wasn't just the money, which truly helped us repair a leaky hole in the ship of our lives. Too many positive things happened to tell them all, so I'll just relate my favorite.

The third Willie Nelson poster that came up for auction sold for $3,500. But on the Monday after the auction, Rob Burley called me in a panic, saying there'd been a mistake. He'd taken a photo of one of the posters that was inside a framed collection of posters, which meant that although he had sold three posters, there were only two in the collection. Somebody had paid $3,500 for a poster that Rob didn't have.

By an odd coincidence, our friend Carol Finsrud had been sitting next to Sandra during the auction, and she had whispered to Sandra during the bidding that years ago I had given her one of the Willie posters and that it was framed in their living room. Carol is a member of the old Hyde Park Gym/Texas Athletic Club gang and the wife of my buddy Mike Graham. Mike, a lifelong athlete as well as a scholar of the history of physical culture and strength training, used to own those gyms. In fact, Carol, also a lifelong athlete, had met Mike at Texas Athletic Club when she started training there and doing power lifting. She turned a few heads back in the 1970s, as it was unusual for a female to be lifting heavy weights, but Mike wasn't put off at all, and the two ended up getting married.

Carol's particular passion is throwing heavy shit—that is, discus, javelin, shot put, weight, and hammer. Sandra and I were hoping that she would also be willing to throw us a bone, so to speak. Sandra called Carol, explained the situation, and asked how much she would take for her poster. Carol said, "Well, I can't charge Eddie for that. Eddie gave it to me. I'll just give it back." We told her she couldn't do that. She knew what they sold for, and we were willing to pay top dollar. We said, "How much do you want for it? What would make you feel really, really good?"

She said she had to think about it. She called back a few minutes later and said, "I'm going to Lyon, France, in August to compete in the World Masters Athletic Championship. The fare is $1,700, so if Eddie gave me $1,700, I'd just be in heaven."

We knew about Carol's involvement in the Masters and how much it meant to her. After all, in the last World Masters she had competed in, in 2013, she had won the gold medal in discus for the tenth straight time. So we raced to Lockhart and gave her a check for $1,700. In August, she flew to Lyon and won three gold medals—one for discus, one for weight, and one for the throwing pentathlon (discus, shot put, weight, javelin, and hammer, all in one day).

All in all, our memories of the auction are stupefying. All the people hugging things, embracing objects that were precious to them, or just looking at all the items in the room and telling stories, tears in their eyes, thanking me over and over. It reminded me a little of a trip to Mexico thirty years before. The occasion was a wedding for one of our employees.

I learned that forty-two people from a tiny Mexican village had worked at Threadgill's. Their salaries had supported extended families and put kids and grandchildren through college. The pride and joy I felt was a rare privilege for me.

★ ★ ★

So, here we are, at the place where it all began, the same corner in South Austin. The old shack bars that once surrounded Armadillo World Headquarters are long gone, but the neighborhood still has soul. That's not just my opinion, after all; it's the epicenter of Austin's reputation for being laid-back, cool, and weird. Our neighbors around the corner on South Congress Avenue, once a honky-tonk strip of dive bars and motels with hourly rates, have had their street rebranded as "SoCo." It's the trendiest place for a stroll in town. Meanwhile, the high-rises sprouting like Johnson grass downtown are steadily creeping across the river, and everyone wants to know just how much longer Threadgill's can hold out against the tide.

I ask myself that question. Every few minutes or so. In the last few years, the property taxes on TWHQ have increased by multiples of 100 percent. You don't have to know the specific numbers to know that before long, something's got to give.

The prospect of return of the bulldozers to our quirky corner of town has always been a nightmare. Sometimes, I feel as if I've been haunted by them ever since I left my childhood ghosts behind. But if we're victims of our own success, we also have a lot of good company. Musicians, for example. The unhappy fact is that most local players still struggle to get by in the Live Music Capital of the World. Small businesses and a lot of people whose last name isn't Trump are also feeling the squeeze.

What's going to happen down the road? Who knows? But I'm still in there pitching every day, dreaming up new schemes and projects, and if things work out the way I hope . . . Well, we'll see how it goes and report back soon.

All in all, I have to say that my life has been a pretty good movie.

APPENDIX

A SELECTION OF GIG POSTERS FROM AWHQ

Fats Domino, February 28, 1971.
Artwork by Jim Franklin.

Lightnin' Hopkins and T. Tellonious Troll,
November 13–14, 1970. Artwork by Jim Franklin.

Freddie King backed by Storm & Wildfire, October 2–3, 1970. Mance Lipscomb, Ginger Valley & Storm, October 9–10, 1970. Artwork by Jim Franklin.

Shiva's Headband, T. T. Troll, Rockinhorse, Tiger Balm & Skyrocket, January 15–16, 1971. Artwork by Jim Franklin.

The Incredible String Band with Shiva's Headband,
November 20–21, 1970. Artwork by Jim Franklin.

Ramon, Ramon, and the Four Daddyos and T. Thelonious Troll,
August 21–22, 1970. Artwork by Jim Franklin.

Dan Hicks and His Hot Licks, September 18–19, 1972.
Artwork by Micael Priest.

Freddie King and Freda and the Firedogs,
May 19, 1972. Artwork by Jim Franklin.

Joy of Cooking, November 5, 1972.
Artwork by Jim Franklin.

Greezy Wheels, August 8–11, 1973.
Artwork by Ken Featherston.

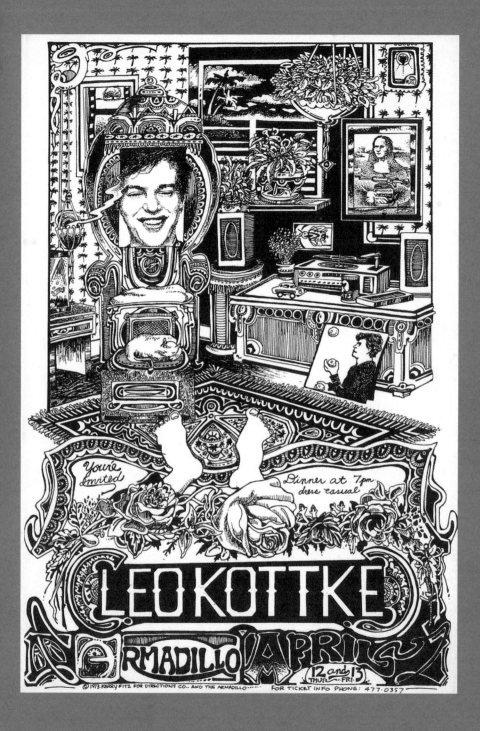

Leo Kottke, April 12–13, 1973.
Artwork by Kerry Awn.

Boz Scaggs with Whistler, May 2–3, 1973.
Artwork by Tom Hansen.

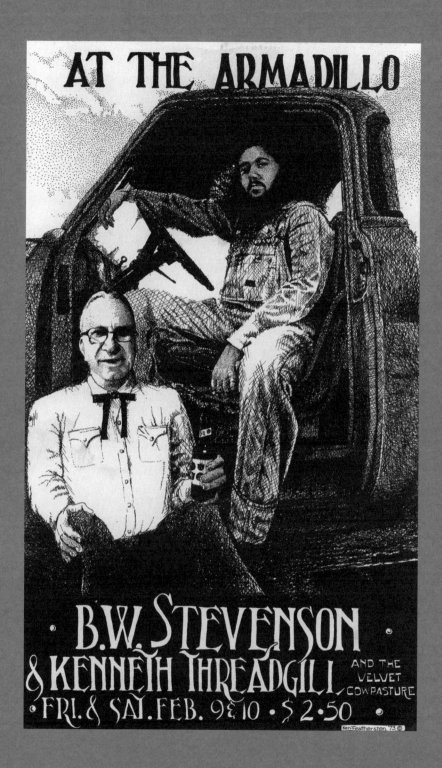

B.W. Stevenson & Kenneth Threadgill, February 9–10, 1973.
Artwork by Ken Featherston.

Tom T. Hall and Chip Taylor, November 14–17, 1973.
Artwork by Jim Franklin.

Bill Monroe and His Bluegrass Boys with Greezy Wheels,
November 22–23, 1974. Artwork by Guy Juke.

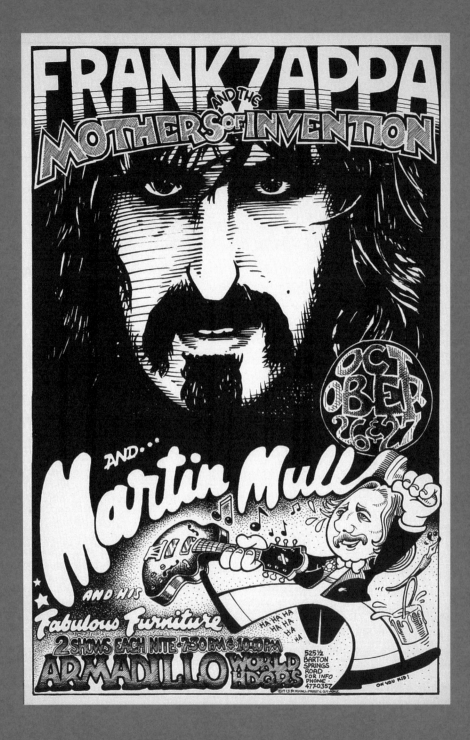

Frank Zappa and the Mothers of Invention and Martin Mull and His Fabulous Furniture,
October 26–27, 1973. Artwork by Micael Priest and Guy Juke.

Bruce Springsteen, November 6–7, 1974.
Artwork by Micael Priest.

Merl Saunders and Jerry Garcia, December
21–22, 1974. Artwork by Guy Juke.

David Bromberg, September 29, 1974.
Artwork by Guy Juke.

The Marshall Tucker Band and the Charlie Daniels
Band, December 31, 1974–January 1, 1975. Artwork
by Micael Priest.

Michael Murphey, March 22–23, 1974.
Artwork by Jim Franklin.

New Riders of the Purple Sage and the Doak Snead Band,
February 4–5, 1975. Artwork by Guy Juke.

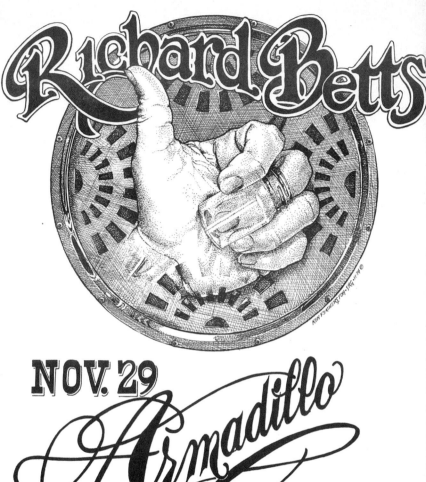

Richard Betts, November 29, 1974.
Artwork by Ken Featherston.

Trapeze and Too Smooth, December 4, 1974.
Artwork by Micael Priest.

Billy Swan & Cate Bros., December 13, 1975.
Artwork by Monica White.

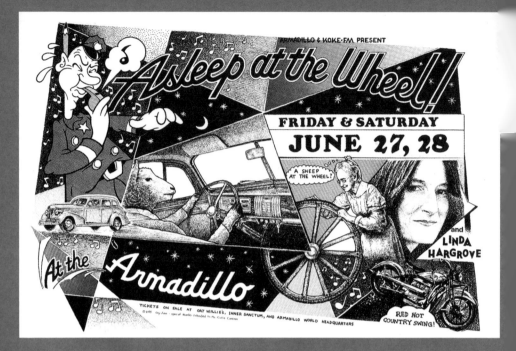

Asleep at the Wheel and Linda Hargrove,
June 27–28, 1975. Artwork by Guy Juke.

Greezy Wheels and Doak Snead Band,
May 30–31, 1975. Artwork by Sam Yeates.

AWHQ Fifth Birthday Party with the Charlie Daniels Band,
August 7, 1975. Artwork by Jim Franklin.

© 1975 JFKLN

HALLOWEEN · ARMADILLO
GREEZY · WHEELS
TOO SMOOTH
OCT. 31 · NOV. 1
ARMADILLO WORLD HEADQUARTERS ~ 3⁰⁰

Halloween at the Armadillo with Greezy Wheels and Too Smooth,
October 31–November 1, 1975. Artwork by Jim Franklin.

Jimmy Cliff and Balcones Fault, November 12–13, 1975.
Artwork by Jim Franklin.

Savoy Brown, October 22, 1975.
Artwork by Ken Featherston.

Shawn Phillips and Daryl Hall and John Oates,
October 20–21, 1975. Artwork by Guy Juke.

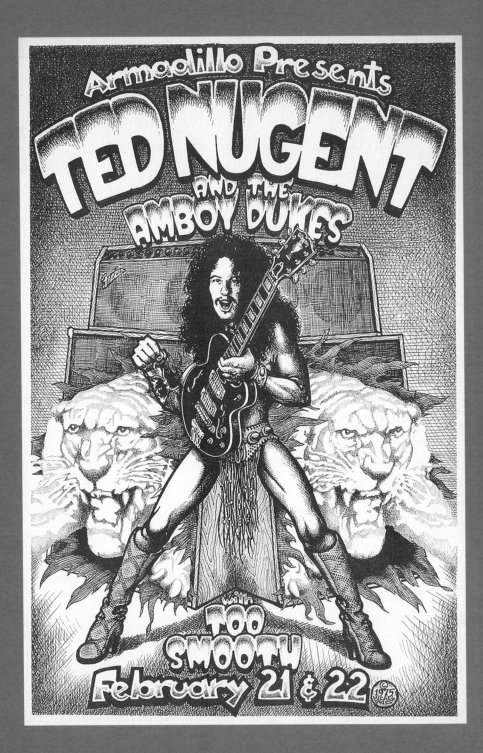

Ted Nugent and the Amboy Dukes with Too Smooth,
February 21–22, 1975. Artwork by Micael Priest.

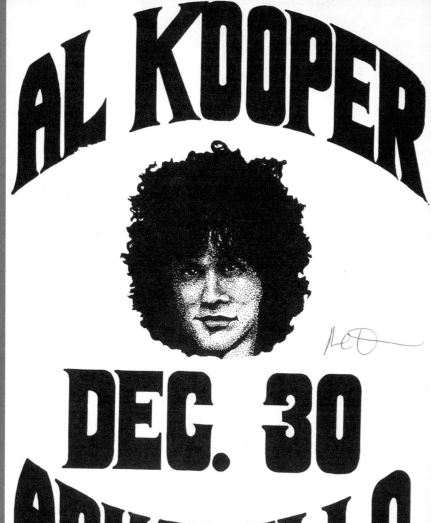

Al Kooper, December 30, 1976.
Artwork by Cliff Carter.

Balcones Fault and the Uranium Savages, February 8, 1976.
Artwork by Kerry Awn and Micael Priest.

John Mayall, September 20, 1976.
Artwork by Micael Priest.

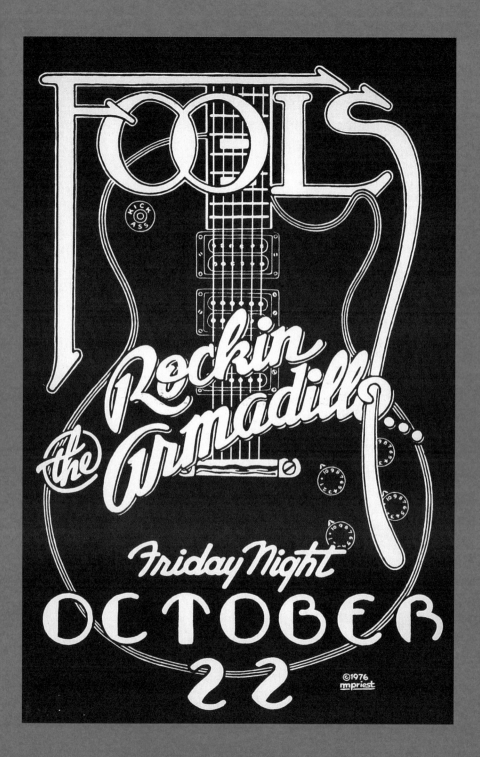

Fools, October 22, 1976.
Artwork by Micael Priest.

Leo Kottke, April 7–8, 1976.
Artwork by Danny Garrett.

Roy Buchanan, November 16, 1976.
Artwork by Guy Juke.

Todd Rundren's Utopia, July 19, 1976.
Artwork by Micael Priest.

Tower of Power and Steam Heat, January 28–29, 1976.
Artwork by Micael Priest.

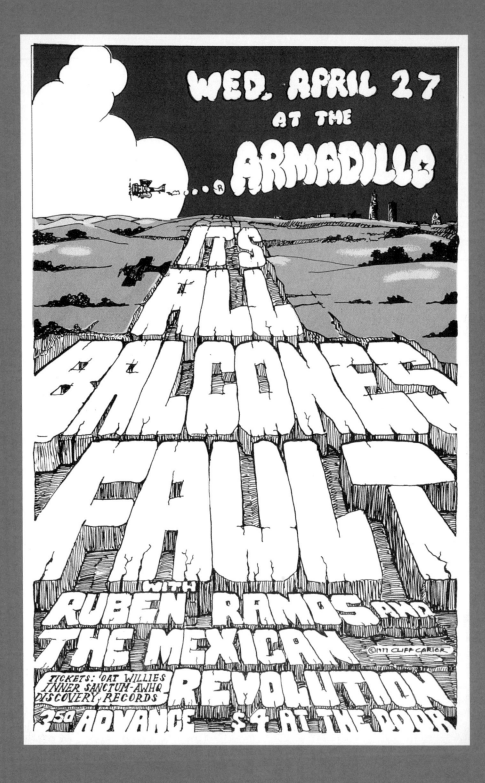

Balcones Fault with Ruben Ramos and the Mexican Revolution,
April 27, 1977. Artwork by Cliff Carter.

Balcones Fault & the Ha Havishnu Orchestra, featuring Boo-Ray
and the Bivalves, May 20–21, 1977. Artwork by Micael Priest.

The Bugs Henderson Group, March 19, 1977.
Artwork by Micael Priest.

Dee Moeller, April 2, 1977.
Artwork by Guy Juke.

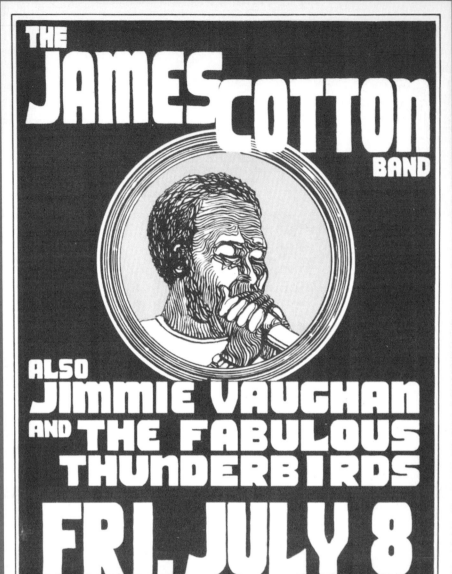

The James Cotton Band and Jimmie Vaughan and the Fabulous
Thunderbirds, July 8, 1977. Artwork by Cliff Carter.

Jimmy Spheeris with Cheezmo Shmaltz,
February 5, 1977. Artwork by Guy Juke.

Kinky Friedman and the Howlers, August 28, 1977.
Artwork by Guy Juke.

LARRY CORYELL

ALSO **AURORA**
AT THE
ARMADILLO
SAT. JULY 9 $ 3.00 ADVANCE
$ 4.00 AT DOOR
ARMADILLO STORE, OAT WILLIE'S, INNER SANCTUM, DISCOVERY RECORDS, YOU SCREAM ICE CREAM

Larry Coryell and Aurora, July 9, 1977.
Artwork by Guy Juke.

Ray Campi and his Rockabilly Rebels with Jon Emory and the
Missouri Valley Boys, August 27, 1977. Artwork by Micael Priest.

Frank Zappa, September 13, 1977.
Artwork by Guy Juke.

Arlo Guthrie, February 26, 1978.
Artwork by Cliff Carter.

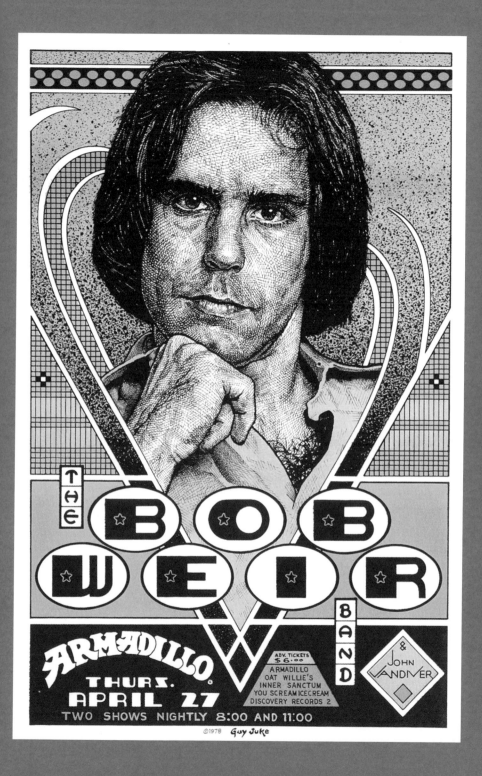

The Bob Weir Band & John Vandiver, April 27, 1978.
Artwork by Guy Juke.

An Evening of Thanks to Joe Gracey featuring Alvin Crow and the Pleasant Valley Boys,
Asleep at the Wheel, Jimmie Vaughan and the Fabulous Thunderbirds, and the Skunks,
November 23, 1978. Artwork by Micael Priest.

Edgar Winter's White Trash, February 25, 1978.
Artwork by Jim Franklin.

Papa John Creach, Kenny Acosta and the Jets,
June 18, 1978. Artwork by Guy Juke.

Parliament Funkadelic and the Brides of Funkenstein,
October 17, 1978. Artist unknown.

PRESENTS

VAN HALEN

PLUS

THE
BUGS HENDERSON
GROUP

featuring
LYNN GROOM

MON. JULY 3

© 1978 Armadillo Productions, Inc

Advance Tickets: $4.50/Zebra Records/Discovery Records/Inner Santum Records/You Scream Ice Cream/Oat Willie's/Armadillo

Van Halen and the Bugs Henderson Group, featuring
Lynn Groom, July 3, 1978. Artist unknown.

Fools with Ruby Starr & the Grey Band, January 13, 1979.
Artwork by Micael Priest.

GROK BOOKS
PRESENTS
AN EVENING WITH

"THE SOLUTIONS TO OUR PREDICAMENT ARE NEUROLOGICAL. WE MUST ALL ASSUME RESPONSIBILITY FOR OUR NERVOUS SYSTEMS..."

TIMOTHY LEARY

Armadillo World Headquarters
(sunday) October 7
8 p.m.

tickets at Grok
503 W 17th
476-0116

Grok Books presents an evening with Timothy Leary,
October 7, 1979. Artwork by B. Goodrich.

Dogs at Play, Tuesdays in June, 1980.
Artwork by Guy Juke.

Dire Straits, November 3, 1980.
Artwork by Guy Juke.

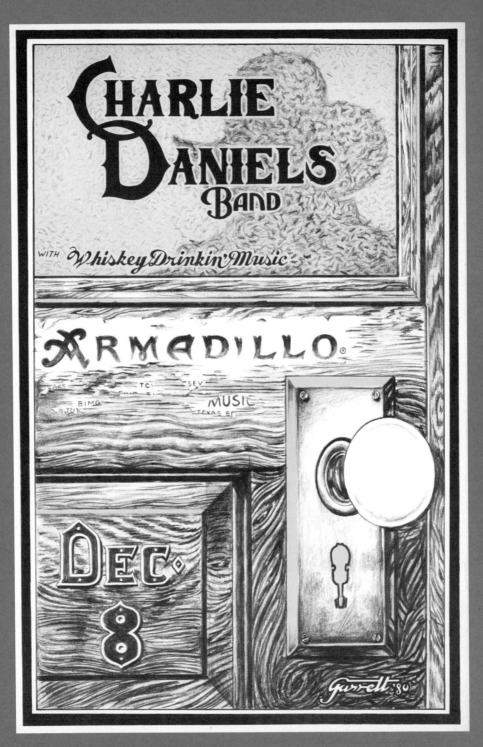

Charlie Daniels Band with Whiskey Drinkin' Music,
December 8, 1980. Artwork by Danny Garrett.

Kenny Acosta's Gumbo Boil & Jelly Roll,
June 15, 1980. Artwork by Micael Priest.

Gary P. Nunn and the Sons of the Bunkhouse Band,
September 12, 1980. Artwork by Danny Garrett.

Maria Muldaur, December 26, 1980.
Artwork by Micael Priest.

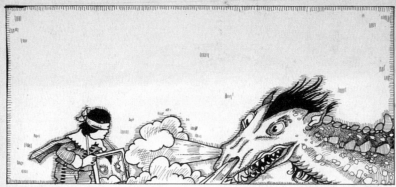

A NOTE ON SOURCES

Sources? I have lots of sources. If there was a way to hook my brain up to a printer or some kind of books-on-demand machine, this book would have been published years ago. Sources? I've got 'em. I'm surrounded by a personal library of books, photos, and ephemera, storerooms stacked with more stuff, and a house crammed with overstuffed binders, filing cabinets, bookshelves, records, and outdated memory storage formats. I had more than enough information to rely on for a bibliography for this book and a few hundred more. Having said that, the reader might be surprised to see endnotes that occasionally cite Wikipedia, a source that isn't always the best (and besides, it was created many years after the last night at the Armadillo). We wanted the book to be useful for general readers and researchers as well, but in some cases, the endnotes are there to point you in the direction of other sources that go deeper on the subject. If you're interested and you've got the notion, take it from there.

I lived this story. It felt a little awkward sometimes, inserting quotes about things that happened thirty or forty or fifty years ago and wanting the reader to be able to look up information on what we did and what we said. In a lot of cases, the people who were there are still around and we discuss these stories amongst ourselves from time to time. You know how we old-timers talk about the glory days.

Jesse Sublett, who came on board to help me get this manuscript put together, cleaned up, and sourced, among other things, conducted interviews to get facts, dates, and other details documented. Other writers helped me at other times, but the interviews Jesse did are the ones most frequently cited.

It's a grand thing that Armadillo World Headquarters was so well-documented by the press. Almost every development of any significance at AWHQ was reported in the local media, and as soon as we shed our diapers, we were being written up in national and international media: *Rolling Stone, Time, Newsweek, Playboy…* even *Sports Illustrated.* In the case of the local press, we had, in addition to special features and reviews, two different music critics (Townsend Miller and Joe Gracey) who had weekly columns in the *Austin American Statesman* and invariably reported on what was happening at the Dillo. On top of that, we got considerable attention in the *Rag*, one of the premiere alternative newspapers in the country, the *Austin Sun*, and the *Daily Texan.*

With all this coverage in print media, we were able to go back and verify details, such as the first time Bruce Springsteen, Willie Nelson, or ZZ Top played the Dillo.

We compiled a day-to-day gig book as well, listing every concert at the hall between August 1970 and December 31, 1980. A few artists probably got left out, such as last-minute opening acts, shows in the beer garden, etc., but probably nothing major. Many of the gig flyers and posters still exist, too, whether original, counterfeit reprint, or digital, and those help give verification as well.

More resources were consulted at the Austin History Center, the Dolph Briscoe Center for American History at the University of Texas, and the Wittliff Collection at Texas State University in San Marcos.

We also have hundreds of hours of videotapes, audio recordings, business files, memos, and even transcripts of my State of the Dillo addresses. Stay tuned, as some of these will be made available in the future.

If there are errors of fact in these pages, I apologize. I'm only human, or so I'm told.

Once again, all I've tried to do with this book is tell the story of the Armadillo World Headquarters as I lived it, plus a bit before and after. I appreciate your indulgence.

NOTES

PREFACE

1. Dave Richards, *Once Upon a Time in Texas: A Liberal in the Lone Star State* (Austin: University of Texas Press, 2002), 179–181.
2. Cecile Richards, interview with Jesse Sublett, April 9, 2016.

INTRODUCTION

1. Mike Tolleson, interview with Jesse Sublett, August 27, 2015.

EARNING MY HIPPIE CARD

1. Thorne Dreyer, interview with Jesse Sublett, 2014; Jack Madigan, "Five Charged Here in Dope Possession," *Austin American-Statesman*, January 28, 1966.

COSMIC JUSTICE

1. Mike Cox, "Wrecker Poised at Armadillo," *Austin American-Statesman*, January 6, 1981.
2. Ibid.
3. "The Sportcenter: Owen Davis, Producer, Proudly Presents—Horace Logan and His Louisiana Hayride, Starring Elvis Presley," August 25, 1955, collection of the author; "Sportcenter, Austin, TX," Scotty Moore official website,

accessed November 20, 2015, http://scottymoore.net/austinSportcenter.html; Ed Ward, "An Armadillo, So Survival-Minded, Succumbs," *Austin American-Statesman*, August 26, 1980.

4. "The Sportcenter: Owen Davis, Producer, Proudly Presents—Horace Logan and His Louisiana Hayride, Starring Elvis Presley," August 25, 1955, collection of the author.

5. *Daily Texan*, October 26, 1976; "M. K. Hage, Jr., Leader in Education, Real Estate, Dies at 82," *Austin American-Statesman*, December 27, 2007.

6. Wikipedia, s.v., "Draft Lottery," last modified February 23, 2016, https://en.wikipedia.org/wiki/Draft_lottery_(1969).

7. Gary Cartwright, *The Best I Recall: A Memoir* (Austin: University of Texas Press, 2015).

8. Chet Flippo, "Uncle Zeke's Rock Emporium," *Rolling Stone*, October 12, 1972.

9. Bobby Hedderman, interview with Joe Nick Patoski, 2003.

10. Ibid.

11. Ibid.

12. Ibid.

13. Mike Tolleson, interview with Jesse Sublett, August 27, 2015.

14. Kaye Northcott, "The Life and Death of the Cosmic Cowboy: From Austin to Amarillo and Abilene, the Sound Moves On," *Mother Jones*, June 16, 1981.

15. *Rag*, August 3, 1970.

HEAD HONCHO

1. Mike Tolleson, interview with Jesse Sublett, August 27, 2015.

2. Thorne Dreyer and Victoria Smith, "The Movement and the New Media," originally published March 1, 1969, http://www.lns-archive.org/histories/1969RagArticle-by-ThorneDreyer-and-VictoriaSmith-LNS-and-NewMedia.htm.

3. Bobby Hedderman, interview with Jesse Sublett, September 3, 2015.

THE ARMADILLO ART SQUAD

1. Marc Savlov, "Violators Will Be Punished," *Austin Chronicle*, September 12, 1997; Alan Schaefer, *Homegrown: Austin Music Posters 1967 to 1982* (Austin: University of Texas Press, 2015).

A KING, A DOMINO, A CAPTAIN, AND A LEO

1. "Earl of Ruston," C. C. Courtney official website, accessed September 23, 2015, http://www.cccourtney.com/Earl%20of%20Ruston.htm; "Earl of Ruston (1970–1971)," Internet Theatre Database, accessed September 23, 2015, http://www.theatredb.com/QShow.php?sid=s2326.

2. Jim Franklin, interview with Joe Nick Patoski, 2003.

LIVING THE DREAM

1. Charles H. Sauer bio, Technologists.com, accessed September 23, 2015, http:// technologists.com/sauer.

A CULTURAL REFINERY

1. Bud Shrake, "An Armored Force on the March," *Sports Illustrated*, January 24, 1972, 1.
2. Sam Wood, "Mini-View," *Austin American-Statesman*, March 24, 1971.

THINGS WERE LOOKING UP

1. Mike Tolleson, interview with Jesse Sublett, August 27, 2015.
2. Marc Crichton, "Armadillo Headquarters: C-W Music Center," *Daily Texan*, August 11, 1972.
3. Ibid.
4. Ben King, "Austin Music Scene Varied," *Daily Texan*, August 11, 1972.
5. Jim Farber, "Early All-Female Rock Band Fanny, Consisting of Sisters June and Jean Millington, Big on Girl Power," *New York Daily News*, August 12, 2011, http://www.nydailynews.com/entertainment/music-arts/early-all-female-rock-band-fanny-consisting-sisters-june-jean-millington-big-girl-power-article-1.950414.
6. Townsend Miller, "A Big Night at Armadillo HQ," *Austin American-Statesman*, July 22, 1972.

THE GREAT REDNECK-HIPPIE MERGER

1. Joe Gracey, "Rock Beat: Willie and Mike Get Together," *Austin American-Statesman*, August 19, 1972.
2. Townsend Miller, "Encore at Dripping Springs?," *Austin American-Statesman*, August 19, 1972.
3. Ed Ward, "An Armadillo, So Survival-Minded, Succumbs," *Austin American-Statesman*, August 26, 1980.
4. Chet Flippo, "Uncle Zeke's Rock Emporium," *Rolling Stone*, October 12, 1972.
5. Ibid.
6. Bobby Hedderman, interview with Jesse Sublett, September 3, 2015.
7. Ibid.
8. Display ad, *Austin American-Statesman*, March 26, 1973.
9. "James Atlee Phillips, 77," *Chicago Tribune*, June 3, 1991, http://articles.chicago-tribune.com/1991-06-03/news/9102190460_1_mr-phillips-novels-edgar-award; Wikipedia, s.v. "Shawn Phillips," last modified February 26, 2016, https:// en.wikipedia.org/wiki/Shawn_Phillips.

10. "Thunder Road (1958)," Internet Movie Database, accessed July 5, 2015, http://www.imdb.com/title/tt0052293.

11. Billy Joe Shaver, *Honky Tonk Hero* (Austin: University of Texas Press, 2005).

A BREED APART

1. Bobby Hedderman, interview with Jesse Sublett, September 3, 2015.

2. Robert Gower, interview with Eddie Wilson and Jesse Sublett, 2015.

BEING THANKFUL FOR WHAT WE'VE GOT

1. Jim Franklin, interview with Joe Nick Patoski, 2004.

2. Ibid.

NOT YOUR DADDY'S BEER JOINT

1. Sid Griffin, *Gram Parsons: A Music Biography* (Etiwands, California: Sierra Records & Books, 1985), 158.

2. Peter Doggett, *Are You Ready for the Country: Elvis, Dylan, Parsons and the Roots of Country Rock* (New York: Penguin, 2000); Wikipedia, "Luckenbach, Texas," last modified January 15, 2016, https://en.wikipedia.org/wiki/Luckenbach,_Texas.

THE FIRST WILLIE NELSON PICNIC

1. Mike Tolleson, interview with Jesse Sublett, August 27, 2015.

2. Eddie Wilson, Bobby Hedderman, Woody Roberts, and Mike Tolleson, interview with Jesse Sublett, September 4, 2015.

3. Mike Tolleson, interview with Jesse Sublett, August 27, 2015.

ARMADILLO TV, OR WHAT MIGHT HAVE BEEN

1. Joe Gracey, "Rock Beat," *Austin American-Statesman*, July 7, 1973.

2. Ibid.

3. Jan Reid, *The Improbable Rise of Redneck Rock* (Austin: University of Texas Press, 2004).

4. Eddie Wilson, Bobby Hedderman, Woody Roberts, and Mike Tolleson, interview with Jesse Sublett, September 4, 2015; Mike Tolleson, interview with Jesse Sublett, August 27, 2015.

5. Townsend Miller, "Country Music," *Austin American-Statesman*, July 21, 1973.

6. "History of ACL on Austin City Limits." Austin City Limits. Accessed November 28, 2016. http://acltv.com/history-of-acl.

7. Ibid.

8. Ibid.

9. Jan Reid, *The Improbable Rise of Redneck Rock* (Austin: University of Texas Press, 2004).

10. Sam Roberts, "Bill Arhos, Founder of 'Austin City Limits,' Dies at 80," *New York Times*, April 14, 2015, http://www.nytimes.com/2015/04/15/arts/television/bill-arhos-founder-of-austin-city-limits-dies-at-80.html.

11. Jason Mellard, *Progressive Country: How the 1970s Transformed the Texan in Popular Culture* (Austin: University of Texas Press, 2013), 2.

HOME WITH THE ARMADILLO

1. Joe Gracey, "Rock Beat," *Austin American-Statesman*, November 1973.

2. Jan Reid and Don Roth, "The Coming of Redneck Hip," *Texas Monthly*, November 1973, http://www.texasmonthly.com/the-culture/the-coming-of-redneck-hip.

3. Ibid.

4. Chet Flippo, "Uncle Zeke's Rock Emporium," *Rolling Stone*, October 12, 1972.

5. A. B. Gunter, "Musical 'Boundaries' Disappearing," *Daily Texan*, December 7, 1972

6. A. B. Gunter, "Country-Rock Stirs Social Mix," *Daily Texan*, December 8, 1972.

7. Jan Reid, *The Improbable Rise of Redneck Rock* (Austin: University of Texas Press, 2004).

8. Jason Dean Mellard, "Home with the Armadillo: Public Memory and Performance in the 1970s Austin Music Scene," *Journal of Texas Music History*, vol. 10 (2010): 1–14.

9. Gary P. Nunn, "London Homesick Blues."

LONG LIVE LONGNECKS

1. Eddie Wilson, Bobby Hedderman, Woody Roberts, and Mike Tolleson, interview with Jesse Sublett, September 4, 2015.

2. Ibid.

3. Ibid.

4. Ibid.

5. Douglas Martin, "Hank Thompson Is Dead; Country Singer Was 82," *New York Times*, November 8, 2007, http://www.nytimes.com/2007/11/08/arts/08thompson.html?_r=0.

6. Michael Ennis, "The Beer That Made Armadillos Famous," *Texas Monthly*, February 1982, http://www.texasmonthly.com/articles/the-beer-that-made-armadillos-famous/; John Spong, "Bottle Rocket," *Texas Monthly*, November 2014, http://www.texasmonthly.com/food/bottle-rocket.

POT, BIG RED, ACID, COKE, AND PUMPKINS

1. Roy Butler obituary, *Houston Chronicle*, November 16, 2009, http://www.leg-acy.com/obituaries/houstonchronicle/obituary.aspx?pid=135946886.

FEEDING THE LEGEND

1. Gordon Rayner, "Queen's Birthday Honours: Van Morrison Knighted," *Telegraph*, June 12, 2015, http://www.telegraph.co.uk/news/uknews/honours-list/11671979/Queens-Birthday-Honours-Van-Morrison-knighted.html.
2. Cory Graves, "Songs About Dallas: The Rolling Stones' 'Rip This Joint,'" Central Track, February 7, 2014, http://centraltrack.com/Music/4860/Songs-About-Dallas/The-Rolling-Stones-Rip-This-Joint.

CROSSTOWN COMPETITION

1. Michael Ventura bio, accessed November 11, 2015, http://michaelventura.org.
2. Dub Rose, interview with Jesse Sublett, July 15, 2015.
3. Wikipedia, s.v. "Asleep at the Wheel," last modified January 8, 2016, https://en.wikipedia.org/wiki/Asleep_at_the_Wheel.
4. Leea Mechling, interview with Joe Nick Patoski, 2003.
5. The cover stories were, respectively, Maureen Orth, "The Making of a Rock Star," *Newsweek*, October 27, 1975, and Jay Cocks, "Rock's New Sensation," *Time*, October 27, 1975; for more background, see Dave Lifton, "The Story of Bruce Springsteen's Historic 'Time' and 'Newsweek' Covers," Ultimate Classic Rock, October 27, 2015, http://ultimateclassicrock.com/bruce-springsteen-time-newsweek.
6. "Music: Groover's Paradise," *Time*, September 9, 1974.
7. Ibid.

TRAVELING ARMADILLO BLUES

1. "The John Hammond Years: Interview with John Hammond and Leonard Cohen, BBC, September 20, 1986," Leonard Cohen Files, accessed July 22, 2015, http://www.leonardcohenfiles.com/jhammond.html.

DEAR LONE STAR

1. Information in the header of the letter-styled report is official TYNA/TACI letterhead, designed by Micael Priest.
2. American National Theatre and Academy (ANTA) Washington Square Theatre.

ROUGH WATERS

1. Gordon Fletcher, "Bongo Fury," *Rolling Stone*, January 1, 1976, http://www.rollingstone.com/music/albumreviews/bongo-fury-19760101.
2. Denny Freeman, interview with Joe Nick Patoski, 2004.
3. Wikipedia, s.v. "The Pointer Sisters," last modified March 1, 2016, https://en.wikipedia.org/wiki/The_Pointer_Sisters.

ONE LAST SWING FOR THE FENCES

1. Hank Alrich, interview with Joe Nick Patoski, 2004.
2. Jan Beeman, interview with Joe Nick Patoski 2004.
3. *The Tomlinson Lone Star Book of Texas Records*, 4th ed. (Fort Worth: Lone Star Book of Texas Records, 1980).
4. Bobby Hedderman, interview with Jesse Sublett, November 18, 2015.
5. Bobby Hedderman, interview with Jesse Sublett and Eddie Wilson, August 4, 2015.

EDDIE HAS LEFT THE BUILDING

1. "Dillo in Debt," *Texas Monthly*, August 1976.
2. Betsy Stevens, "Armadillo Terminates 42," *Daily Texan*, September 24, 1976.
3. Ibid.
4. Joe Nick Patoski, "Whose Armadillo?," *Texas Monthly*, May 1976.
5. "Dillo Still Afloat—Wilson," *Texas Observer*, November 4, 1976.
6. Henry Gonzalez, interview with Joe Nick Patoski, 2004.
7. Hank Alrich, e-mail to Eddie Wilson and Jesse Sublett, July 21, 2015.
8. "Dillo Still Afloat—Wilson," *Texas Observer*, November 4, 1976; "Stormy Weather for the Armadillo," *Austin Sun*, November 12, 1976.
9. Freddie King bio, Rock and Roll Hall of Fame, accessed December 1, 2015, https://rockhall.com/inductees/freddie-king/bio/; Amy Van Beveren and Laurie E. Jasinski, "King, Freddie," Handbook of Texas Online, accessed December 1, 2015, https://tshaonline.org/handbook/online/articles/fkimt.

THE ARMADILLO EMERGES

1. Several sources covered details of Armadillo Productions' Chapter 11 and restructuring: Hank Alrich, interview with Joe Nick Patoski, 2004; "Austin Notes Interviews Hank Alrich," *Austin Notes*, August 1977; Joe Frolick, "Armadillo Keeps Faith in Austin Music," *Austin American-Statesman*, August 11, 1978; Brad Stribling, "Armadillo Refinances to Continue Operating," *Daily Texan*, February 9, 1977.
2. Ed Miller, "Austin Notes Interviews Hank Alrich," *Austin Notes*, August 1977.

3. US Inflation Calculator, accessed November 28, 2015, http://www.usinflation-calculator.com.

4. Hank Alrich, e-mail to Eddie Wilson and Jesse Sublett, July 21, 2015.

5. Ibid.

6. Ibid.

7. Vikki Barnhart, *Daily Texan*, November 27, 1978.

8. For an authoritative inside view of the Austin punk/new wave scene in the late 1970s, see Jesse Sublett, *Never the Same Again: A Rock 'n' Roll Gothic* (Austin: Boaz/Tenspeed, 2004); Jeff Whittington, "New Wave Groups Rock Austin: Dictators, Skunks Punk Out Dillo," *Daily Texan*, August 29, 1978.

9. Jan Beeman, interview with Joe Nick Patoski, 2004.

10. Dub Rose, interview with Jesse Sublett, 2015.

11. Erin Geiger Smith, "Joe Jamail, Pennzoil's $13 Billion Man, Makes 80 Over 80 List," *Business Insider*, October 22, 2009, http://www.businessinsider.com/joe-jamail-pennzoils-3-billion-man-makes-80-over-80-list-2009-10#ixzz34FdTDDW0; Wikipedia, s.v. "Joe Jamail," last modified February 20, 2016; https://en.wikipedia.org/wiki/Joe_Jamail; Joe Nick Patoski, "The Armadillo's Last Waltz," *Texas Monthly*, August 1980, 163.

12. "City of Austin Population History 1840 to 2015," City of Austin, accessed August 24, 2015, http://www.austintexas.gov/sites/default/files/files/Planning/Demographics/population_history_pub.pdf.

13. "Wrecker Poised at Armadillo," *Austin American-Statesman*, January 6, 1981.

14. Henry Gonzalez, interview with Joe Nick Patoski, 2003.

LAST CALL

1. Jan Beeman, interview with Joe Nick Patoski, 2004.

2. Ed Ward, "Thanks for the Memories," *Austin American-Statesman*, January 1, 1981.

3. Ed Ward, "Thanks for the Memories," *Austin American-Statesman*, January 2, 1981.

4. Leea Mechling, interview with Joe Nick Patoski, 2004.

5. Jan Beeman, interview with Joe Nick Patoski, 2004.

6. Leea Mechling, interview with Joe Nick Patoski, 2004.

7. Wikipedia, s.v. "Armadillo World Headquarters," last modified February 12, 2016, https://en.wikipedia.org/wiki/Armadillo_World_Headquarters.

FULL CIRCLE

1. John Morthland made the statement in a story for the *Los Angeles Times*, and although we haven't been able to find the article, John Morthland assured me via e-mail in 2015 that he did write that line and can't remember the subject or title of the article, either.

2. Al Rose, *I Remember Jazz: Six Decades Among the Great Jazzmen* (Baton Rouge: Louisiana State University Press, 1987).

3. Ibid.; Wikipedia, s.v. "Shake, Rattle and Roll," last modified January 21, 2016, https://en.wikipedia.org/wiki/Shake,_Rattle_and_Roll.

4. Rory Burbeck, "SXSW 2015 Economic Impact Report," September 15, 2015, http://www.sxsw.com/news/2015/economic-impact-report.

5. Wikipedia, "American Poster Institute," last modified November 24, 2014, https://en.wikipedia.org/wiki/American_Poster_Institute.

6. Alan Schaefer, *Homegrown: Austin Music Posters 1967 to 1982* (Austin: University of Texas Press, 2015).

7. Omar Gallega, "New Braunfels Event Sold Pieces of Threadgill's Owner Eddie Wilson's Austin Treasures," *Austin American-Statesman*, January 17, 2015, http://www.mystatesman.com/news/news/local/nostalgia-big-bids-send-off-armadillo-world-headqu/njqsf; Kevin Curtin, "Armadillos to the Highest Bidder," *Austin Chronicle*, January 19, 2015.

INDEX

Page numbers in italics refer to illustrations.

Abelard String Quartet, 141
Abel Moses, 283
AC/DC, 7
ACL. *See* Austin City Limits (festival);
    Austin City Limits (TV show)
Airoldi, Tony, *156*
Alexander, Charles B. "Alex," 42, 43
Alexander, Stan, 54, 59, 62
Ali, Muhammad, 162
Allen, Carolyn, 255
Alliance Wagon Yard, 282, 333
Allison, Mose, 201, 355, 356, 389
Allman, Duane, 176
Allred, Sammy, 51, 127
Almost Brothers, 379
Alrich, Hank, 3, 89, 174, 210; and AWHQ
    bankruptcy, 369–371; as AWHQ
    shareholder, 149, 315, 370, 408; and
    Eddie's departure from AWHQ, 5,
    353–354, 355, 357; and final days of
AWHQ, 378, 379, 380; and loans to
AWHQ, 148–149, 168, 313, 334, 341,
349; and management of AWHQ,
371–372, 375, 376, 377; as musician, 87,
215, 319; and Onion Audio, 238, 315,
379; and Randy McCall, 329, 346, 349
Alrich, William, 370, 376, 379, 380
Altschul, Barry, 371
Amazing Rhythm Aces, 331
Anderson, Harry, 319, 337
Antone, Clifford, 320, 322, 403
Antone's, 96, 320, 322
Appel, Mike, 287, 331
Arhoolie Records, 81
Arhos, Bill, 228, 229, 230–231
Armadillo Appreciation Week, 342,
    344–346, 347, 348, 350
Armadillo Art Squad, 92, 93–94, 96,
    100–101, 143, 297, 407. *See also specific
    artists*
Armadillo Christmas Bazaar, 341–342,
    343, 375, 385, 388
Armadillo Confab, 215–216

Armadillo Country Music Review, 5, 97, 166, *167*, 168, 215, *226*; and KLRN-TV taping, 227–229, 230, 231, 407

Armadillo Productions, 3, 64, 76, 149, 315, 370

Armadillo Pumpkin Stomp, 263, *264*, 265

Armadillo Radio Headquarters, 326

Armadillo Records, 379, 380, 408

armadillos, 7, 53, 135, 215, 352–353

Armadillo World Headquarters: and auctions of memorabilia, 391–392, 408–412; and bankruptcy, 349, 369–371, 375, 376; beer sales at, 5, 27, 52, 117–118, 121, *236*, 251, 261, 329–330; closing night of, 3, 385, 386, 387–389; and competition from other venues, 275, 282–283, 284, 295, 297, 298, 318; demolition of, 377, 380, 389, 392, *393*, 394; diversity of offerings at, 53–54, 75, 140–143, 245–246, *316*; and early history of site, 48–49, 51; Eddie's departure from, 353–354, 357; and financial troubles, 127, 148–149, 168, 333–334, 341–342, 346, 351–352; game room at, 132, 199, 234–235; house piano at, *33*, *34*, 109, 175, 195, 405, 410; and HVAC troubles, 9, 118, 291, 314, 335; interior photos of, 69, *72*, *104*, *119*, *120*; kitchen at, 266, 269–270, 272, 273–274, 287; legacy of, 5, 7, 9, 379, 394; murals at, *23*, *74*, *88*, *90*, *97*, *271*, 380, 387; opening of, 1–3, 64, 65, 66–68, *73*; prime location of, 376–378, 394, 412; and redneck/hippie merger, 159, 165, 166, 184, 244–245; renovations to, 118, *120*, 121, 127, *144*, 145–146, *147*, 148, 283–284; security team at, 185–189, 207, 213, 225, 231; and short-term lease, 52, 283, 313, 314, 315, 318, 335, 377; staff of, 2–3, 6, 132, *133*, 134, 150, 237, 272

Armadillo World Series, The, 142

Ashley, Elizabeth, 140, 301, 304, 307

Asleep at the Wheel, 201, 284–285, 312, 331, 372, 383, 385. *See also* Benson, Ray

Astrodome, 5, 247

Atlanta Rhythm Section, 346

Atlantic Records, 210, 306, 307

Auger, Brian, 292

Augustin, Billy Price, 400

Austin, 10, 172, 378, 394; counterculture in, 22, 64, 140, 257; development of scene in, 5, 9, 59, 100, 171, 282, 314–315; flooding in, 47–48, 233–234; as Live Music Capital of the World, 27, 406, 408, 412

Austin American-Statesman, 140, 152, 165, 175–176, 227, 244, 276, 380; and Vulcan Gas Company, 25, 52

Austin Ballet Theatre, 141, 201, 284, 292

Austin City Limits (festival), 5, 407

Austin City Limits (TV show), 5, 7, 229–231, 407

Austin Community College, 51

Austin Consultants. *See* TYNA/TACI

Austin Country Club, 38

Austin Freak Merchants Guild, 141

Austin Opry House. *See* Texas Opry House

Austin Police Department, 22, 27, 28, 155, 262–263; and murder of Ken Feather-ston, 324, 325

Austin Sun, 282, 367–368

Avalon, 100

Awn, Kerry, 94, 95, 100, 337; gig posters by, *336*, *423*, *444*, *475*

Axton, Hoyt, 292, *310*

Bag O' Chicken, 360

Bailey, Doyne, 324

Bailey, Frank, 366

Bailey, James, 362–363

Baker, LaVern, 155

Balcones Fault, 150, 190, 319–320, 337, 344, 346, 379; gig posters for, *338*, *439*, *444*, *450*, *451*

Ball, Marcia, 152, *153. See also* Freda and the Firedogs
Barber, Galen, *119*, 234, 359
Barnett, Jerry, 89, 132, *194*, 197, 379
Barr, Candy, 337
Barrientos, Gonzalo, Jr., 344, *348*
Barton, Lou Ann, 322
Barton Springs, 51, 96, 257, 273, 407
Basie, Count, 405
Beach Boys, 274
Beatles, 160, 175
Beeman, Jan, 270, 334, 375, 379, 387, 388; and food for musicians, 206, 269, 273–274
beer garden, 9, *144*, 146, *147*, *148*, 237, 269, 291; renovations to, 371, 376, 392
Bell, Rusty, 239
Bell, Tony, 27, 291
Benson, Ray, 284–285, *286*, 287, 387
Bentley, Bill, 282
Bergstrom Air Force Base, 174, 282, 366
Bernard, Al, 400
Berry, Chuck, 175
Bevis, John, 352
Big Brother and the Holding Company, 62, 137
Big G Club, 178, 181
Bingham, John Randolph, 325
Black, Louis, 395
Black Queen, 282
Blackwell, Ed, 371
Bland, Bobby "Blue," 37
Bleib Alien, 318
Bley, Carla, 371
Bloodrock, 121
"Blueberry Hill" (Boone), 37–38
blues, 85, 184, 186, 320, 322; at Vulcan Gas Company, 25, 27
Blume, Augie, 307, 308
Bongo Fury (Zappa and Beefheart), 206, 318
Boone, Fletcher, 362, 365–366
Boone, Pat: "Blueberry Hill," 37–38

Bosner, Paul, 230
Bouldin Creek, 234, 392
Bowland, Bruce, 85
Braggs, Al "TNT," 201
Bramhall, Doyle, *86*, 323
Brewer and Shipley, 159
Brewers Association, 27–28, 41–43, 52, 117, 247, 259, 263
Broken Spoke, 152, 282
Brown, Bill, 187–188
Brown, George, 39
Brown, Joe, 160
Bryan, William Joel, 400
Bryson, Joe, 175
Bubble Puppy, 13
Buchanan, Roy, 7, 279, 280, *281*, 333, 383, *447*
Bullock, Bob, 363–364
Burke, Solomon, 155
Burley, Rob, 409, 410–411
Bush, Johnny, 160
Butler, Roy, 263, 330, 389
Byram, John D., 312, 313
Byram, Sally, 311–313
Byrds, 183, 199

Cactus Club, 1, 28–29, 52, 392
Caldwell, Toy, 261
Cale, J. J., 297
Cale, John, 372
Calmes, Jack, 121–122, 124, 299, 306, 311, 354
Campbell, Bill, 186, 215, 322, 365
Canned Heat, 25
Cantu, Fred, 403
Capitol Records, 11, 54, 76, 148
Captain Beefheart, 107, *108*, 143, 155, 206, 405; Bongo Fury, 206, 318
Carousel Club, 337
Carr, Frances, 193
Carter, Cliff: gig posters by, *208*, *443*, *450*, *454*, *460*
Cartwright, Gary, 54, 166

Cash, Johnny, 51, 259

Castle Creek, 298

Cat on a Hot Tin Roof (Williams), 140, 301, 304

Caught in the Act, 238

Causey, John, 238

C-Boy's, 410

Cerna, Jose, 187, 188–189, 367

Chapparal, 282

Charles, Ray, 155, 294, 295, 296, 405

Charlie Daniels Band, 7, 273, 292, 331, 345, 376, 380, 385; gig posters for, *430, 437, 470*

Charlie's Playhouse, 186

Chavez, Cesar, 96

Chenier, Clifton, 295, 322

Chequered Flag, 66, 282

Cherry, Don, 371

Chessmen, 85

Chip and Dale, 35–36, 37–38

Chuck Wagon, 78

Cibulka, Danny, 265

City Coliseum, 51, 378

Clark, Fletcher, 319, 371

Clark, Gary, Jr., 186

Clark, Guy, 159

Clash, 372

Clay, John, 141

Clearlight acid. *See* LSD

Clements, Vassar, *126*, 346, 347

Cliff, Jimmy, 331, *439*

Cline, Patsy, 164

Cobham, Billy, 331

Cobras, 379, *381*; *The Cobras, Live and Deadly,* 380

cocaine, 260–262, 273, 299, 300, 317, 318, 362–363

Cocker, Joe, 124

Coe, David Allen, 294–295

Cohen, Leonard, 301

Cole, Gordon, 376

Coleman, Ornette, 371

Collins, Judy, 301

Colony Club, 337

Colorado River, 47–48, 234. *See also* Lady Bird Lake

Columbia Records, 13, 25, 287

"Coming of Redneck Hip, The" (Reid and Roth), 243–244, 245, 293

Commander Cody and His Lost Planet Airmen, 183–184, 201, 239, 284, 292, 331, 345; and AWHQ kitchen, 274, 285, 287; and AWHQ's final night, 385, 387; gig posters for, *180, 310, 386*; and Linda Ronstadt, 276, 279; *Live from Deep in the Heart of Texas,* 241, 276

Conans Pizza, 403

Conqueroo, 13, 74, 282

Continental Club, 118, 410

Cooder, Ry, 107, *108*

Coolidge, Rita, *217, 218*

Cooper, Alice, 284

Cooper, Billy, 216, 225

Cooper, Mike, *12*

Cooperman, David, 369–370

Coors Beer, 247, 329–330

Cope, Barbara, 270

Copeland, Sam, 122, 124

Cordell, Denny, 124

Cornelius, Wayne, 39, 41, 42

cosmic cowboy. *See* progressive country

Cotton, James, *18, 19,* 383, 454

Country Dinner Playhouse, 282

country rock. *See* progressive country

Courtney, C. C., 105

Courtney, Ragan, 105

Cowtown Jamboree, 160

Cricket Club, 282

Crow, Alvin, 152, 282, 285, 287, 290, 372, 462

Cullum, Jim, 392

Cutler, Sam, 193

Daily Bread Bakery, *128*, 129–130
Daily Texan, 57, 105, 150, 244, 245, 353
Dan Hicks and His Hot Licks, 152, 333, *419*
Daniel, Tom, 222
Daniels, Charlie, 287. *See also* Charlie Daniels Band
Darcy, Joe, 25, 27
Darvin, Karen, 290
Davis, David, 57
Davis, George, 52
Davis, Owen, 49
Deep in the Heart of Texas (Franklin), *90*, *91*, 124, 410
Delaney and Bonnie, 124
Del Santo, Dan, 385
DeMaine, Jess, 285
Deshannon, Jackie, 240
Dessau Hall, 51, 283
Devo, 372, 383, *384*
De White. *See* Juke, Guy
Diamond Rio, 215, 227
Dictators, 372
Diddley, Bo, 122
Directions Agency, 93, 239
Dire Straits, *469*
Doggett, Lloyd, 152
Domino, Fats, 33, 37, 109, *110*, *111*, 112, *414*
Domino, Floyd, 285, *286*, 287
Donovan, 175
Doris Miller Auditorium, 25
draft lottery, 53
Dreyer, Thorne, 76
Dr. Hepcat, 36–37
Dr. Hook and the Medicine Show, 292
Drifters, 155
Dripping Springs, TX, *214*, 216, *217*, 218
Dr. John, the Night Tripper, 152, *154*
drug use, 22, 27, 100, 178, 187, 206–207. *See also* cocaine; heroin; LSD; marijuana
Dry Creek Inn, 360

Duke, George, 331
Dyer, Doug, 139, 142
Dylan, Bob, 121–122, 124, 164, 219, 301; "I Feel a Change Comin' On," 183

Eagles, 284, 294
Earle, Ronnie, 337, 339
Earl of Ruston, 105, *106*
Egan, Sweet Mary, 155, *156*, 189, *194*, 197
Electric Grandmother, 25
Electromagnets, 320
Elliott, Annie C., 112
Elliott, Ramblin' Jack, 193, 407
Elliott, Tim, 134
El Paso Cattle Company, 282
Ely, Joe, 150, 372, 385, *399*; *Live Shots*, 96
English, Paul, 162, 164, 165, 222
Entertainers Information Guild, 143
Erickson, Roky, 13, 22, 318, 325, 407
Ernie's Chicken Shack, 186
Erwin, Frank, 7
Eskatrol, 260
Estes, Sleepy John, *21*, 25
Esther's Follies, 142
Explosives, 372

Fabulous Furry Freak Brothers, 22, 23, 160
Fabulous Thunderbirds, 372, *454*, *462*. *See also* Vaughan, Jimmie
Falstaff Beer, 43, 250
Family Dog, 100, 137
Fanny, 152
Faulk, John Henry, 139
Featherston, Ken, 94, 96, 100, 273, 380; gig posters by, *280*, *328*, *422*, *425*, *433*, *440*; murder of, 323–326, 333
Feed Lot, 282
Ferry, Bryan, 339
Fillmore, 100, 137, 291
Finney, Jim, 195, *196*, 197, 237–238, 319
Finsrud, Carol, 411

Fitzgerald, Kerry. *See* Awn, Kerry

Flatlanders, 150, *151*, 152, 398. *See also* Gilmore, Jimmie Dale

Flippo, Chet, 254–255, 303, 305; "Uncle Zeke's Rock Emporium," 169, 171–172, 244

Flying Burrito Brothers, *158*, 159, 183, 199, 331

Fools, 320, *445*, *466*

Fortenberry, Lloyd, 219

Forty-Seven Times Its Own Weight, 320

Fourth of July Picnic, Willie Nelson's, 216, *217*, 218–219, 221–222, 224, 244; photos of, *214*, *220*, *223*

Fox, Chastity, 337, *338*, 346

Frank, Raymond, 262, 335, 346

Franklin, Aretha, 155

Franklin, Jim, 4, 53, 93, 172, 191, 222, 269, 270; and Armadillo Appreciation Week, 344, 345, 348, *350*; and armadillo art, 7, *8*, 9, 22, 387, 405; and Armadillo Pumpkin Stomp, 263, *264*, 265; as AWHQ shareholder, 149, 315; and Bobby Hedderman, 3, 54, 56; and closing of AWHQ, 387, 388; *Deep in the Heart of Texas*, 90, 91, 124, 410; and emcee duties, 68, 115, 337, 408; gig posters by, *xviii*, 65, 86, *108*, *114*, *125*, *158*, *173*, *217*, 288, *414–418*, *420*, *421*, *426*, *431*, *437–439*, *463*, *474*; and Lone Star Beer work, 100, 251–252, 255, 256, 304, 352; murals at AWHQ by, *74*, *87*, *88*, *90*, *91*, 124; and murder of Ken Featherston, 323, 325; other artwork by, *77*, *106*, *107*, *113*, *128*, 219, 241; and Ritz Theater, 297, 315; and studio/living quarters at AWHQ, 91, *92*, *95*, 136, 150, 335; and Vulcan Gas Company, 24, 27, 28. *See also* Ramon, Ramon and the Four Daddyos

Franks, Q. S. "Pee Wee," 49, 380, 382, 392

Freda and the Firedogs, 150, 152, *153*, 155, 218, 285, *420*

Frederick, Tracy, 70

Freeman, Denny, 85, 322–323

Friedman, Jeff, 335, 337

Friedman, Kinky, 201, 207, 209–210, 284, 337, 345; gig posters for, *208*, *456*

Fromholz, Steven, 9, 94, 346, 385

Fugs, 20, 25, 27

Gammon, Billy, 401

Gann, Harvey, 22, 155

Garcia, Jerry, 127, *194*, 195, *196*, 207, 269, 429

Garnier, Tony, 285

Garrett, Danny, 96, 323; gig posters by, *446*, *470*, *472*

Geezinslaws, 127

Gent, Pete, 135, 136

George, Lowell, 276, 279

Georgetown Medical Band, 13

Gerding, Burt, 22

Gibbons, Billy, 81, 320

Gilmore, Jimmie Dale, *1*, *2*, 67, 150, 385, 398, 399

Glasscock, Tom, 333

Goat Leg, 105

Goering, Lloyd, 132

Go-Go's, 152

Gonzalez, Henry, 96, 253, 335, 339, 344, 371; and closing of AWHQ, 380, 382, 383; and murder of Ken Featherston, 324, 325–326

"Goodnight, Irene" (Lead Belly), 387–388

Goodrich, B., *467*

Goose Creek Symphony, 159, 340

Gower, Robert, 189–190, 234, 324

Gracey, Joe, 165, 210, 227, 231, 239, 244, 372

Graham, Bill, 137, *138*, 139–140

Graham, Mike, 411

Grand Ole Opry, 160, 282, 327

Granny Risher. *See* Risher, Granny

Grant, Peter, 300

Grateful Dead, 22, 127, 137, 160, 193, 197, 201, 239, 274, 305; *Wake of the Flood*, 233. *See also* Garcia, Jerry

Green, Mitch, 342, 344

Greenbriar School, 141

Greezy Wheels, 150, 155, *156*, 157, 215, 227, 244; gig posters for, *86*, *114*, *163*, *422*, *427*, *436*, *438*; and Willie's first AWHQ show, 164, 165. *See also* Egan, Sweet Mary

Guinness Book of World Records, The, 342

Gunter, A. B., 245

Guthrie, Arlo, 383, *460*

Guy, Buddy, 260

Haden, Charlie, 371

Hage, M. K., 48, 51

Hage, M. K., Jr., 48, 51–52, 117, 134, 314, 317, 330; and sale of AWHQ property, 377, 378

Hage, M. K., III, 52, 134, 317–318

Haggard, Merle, 259

Hall, Stanley, 141

Hall, Tommy, 13

Hall, Tom T., *217*, 240–241, *426*

Hall and Oates, *441*

Ham, Bill, 81, 82, 225

Ham, Gordy, 255, 301, 366

Hamby, Tommy, 362

Hammond, John, 301, 351

Hancock, Butch, 96, 150, *399*

Hancock, Tommy, 385

Hancock Recreation Center, 38

Haney, Betsy, 270

Hansel and Gretel, 282

Hansen, Tom, *424*

Harkins, Mike, 392

Harms, John, 82

Harr, Mike, 3, 70, 149, 315

Harris, Emmylou, *198*, 199, 200

Harrison, George, 124

Harter, Jim, *158*

Hartford, John, 383

Hattersley, Cleve, 155, *156*

Hattersley, Craig, 189

Hattersley, Lissa, 155, *156*

Hedderman, Bobby, 56–57, 89, 103, 105, 132, 136, 174, 287, 346; and AWHQ security staff, 188, 189; as AWHQ shareholder, 149, 315; and booking at AWHQ, 76, 82, 149, 172, 318, 323, 331, 340; and departure from AWHQ, 353, 354, 371; and friction with Willie's posse, 225, 231–232; and game room flood, 234, 235; and living billboard, 341, 342, 344, 345, 346, 348; photos of, *55*, *144*, *348*; and Vulcan Gas Company, 3, 28, 54; and Willie Nelson's picnic, 218, 222

Hee Haw, 282

Helms, Chet, 137

Henderson, Bugs, 346, 379, 385, *452*, *465*, *474*

Hendrix, Jimi, 78, 81, 85, 240

Herman High School (Van Vleck, TX), 39, 41

heroin, 78, 81, 200, 259, 263, 359

Hicks, Dan. See Dan Hicks and His Hot Licks

Highland Lakes, 48

"High Noon" (Ritter), 37

Hightower, Jim, 406

Hoffbrau Steakhouse, 360, 362

Holder, Noddy, 213

Holland, Dave, 371

Holliday, Billie, 301

Holly, Buddy, 181

Homegrown, 238

Hood, Champ, *399*

Hooker, John Lee, 25

Hopkins, Lightnin', 13, 25, 82, *84*, 122, *415*

Hopper, Dennis, 139

Horton, Johnny, 297

Hot Tuna, 284

Howard, Cleve, 333

Howlin' Wolf, 51

Hub City Movers, 64, 66–67, 132, 134, 150, 398; and Eddie's discovery of AWHQ site, 1, 28–29
Huddleston, Diane, 222
Hume, Martha, 254, 255
Hurlbut Ranch, 216
Hutchison, Kay Bailey, 222, 366
Hyde, Don, 25, 26, 27, 28, 71
Hyde Park, 33, 38

"I Feel a Change Comin' On" (Dylan), 183
IL Club, 186, 323
Improbable Rise of Redneck Rock, The (Reid), 224, 228, 230, 245, 293, 308
Incredible String Band (ISB), 87, 417
Inmon, Mike, 195
Inner Sanctum, 175, 372
Ivy, Frank, 357, 359

Jackson, Bobby, 42
Jackson, Jack, 100
Jacobs, Jack, 319
Jacobs Candy Company, 400
Jamail, Joe, 216, 222, 377
James, Etta, 37
Jazzmanian Devil, 331
Jefferson Airplane, 22, 137
Jennings, Chicken Dick, 360
Jennings, Waylon, 174, 178, 179, 180, 181, 184, 244, 246, 345, 387; "Luckenbach, Texas," 209; and Texas Opry House, 275, 284, 294; and Willie Nelson's picnic, 216, 217, 218, 224
Jersig, Harry, 250–251, 256, 301
J. Geils Band, 284
John, Little Willie, 37
Johnson, Eric, 186, 320
Johnson, Robert, 396
Jo Jo Gunne, 190
Joplin, Janis, 62, 63, 64, 79, 134, 137; death of, 78, 259, 391; and Threadgill's place, 243, 391, 395
Joyce, Chuck, 62

Joy of Cooking, 152, *421*
Judge, Mike, 406
Juke, Guy, 96, 405; gig posters by, *310, 374, 427–430, 432, 436, 441, 447, 453, 455–457, 459, 461, 463, 468, 469*

Kennedy, Rod, 66, 282
Kent State University, 53, 78
Kerr, Joe, 285
Kershaw, Doug, 87, 88, 89
Kindred, Mike, 85
Kindrick, Sam, 352
King, Freddie, 103, 105, 122, 124, 136, 150, 201, 284, 322; artwork featuring, *90, 91, 124, 410, 416, 420*; and "The Nights Never Get Lonely," 255, 305, 306, 307, 308, 326; photos of, *102, 104, 123*; and touring, 94, 226, 354
Kirchen, Bill, 276, 279, 385
Kiss, 378
KLBJ-FM, 349, 369
KLRN-TV. *See* KLRU-TV
KLRU-TV, 5, 7, 227, 229, 230, 407
KOKE-FM, 100, 228, 238–239, 240, 282, 372
Kottke, Leo, 112, *113*, 115, 246, 284, 287, 345; gig posters for, *114, 423, 448*
Krackerjack, 85
Kristofferson, Kris, 216, 217, 218, 224; "Me and Bobby McGee," 62; "Sunday Morning Coming Down," 62, 64
KRMH-FM, 195, 227, 298
Krugman, Paul, 405
KTAE-AM, 37
KTBC-TV, 35
KT Jamboree, 59, 62, 64
KTSA-FM, 250
KVET-AM, 36–37

Lady Bird Lake, 48, 107, 407
La Fuentes, 29
Laier, Tony, 155, 319
LA Weekly, 282
Lawrence, Hugh, 333

Lead Belly: "Goodnight, Irene," 387–388
Leanne and the Bizarros, 282
Leary, Timothy, 11, 39, 142, *467*
Lebermann, Lowell, 389
Led Zeppelin, 299, 300
Lennon, John, 385
Leonard, Homer, 42
Lesh, Phil, *194*, 195
Lewis, Jerry Lee, 51, 172, *173*, 174–175, 345, 405
Liberal Outlet, 35, 38
Liberty Hall, 200, 276
Link, Peter, 105
Linklater, Richard, 406
Lipscomb, Mance, 13, 81, 122, 150, 322, 333, 406–407; gig posters for, *99*, *416*; photos of, *18*, *80*, *98*, *332*
Little, D. K., 215, 227, 320, *321*
Little Feat, 276, *277*, 279
Live from Armadillo World Headquarters, 228
Live from Deep in the Heart of Texas (Cody), 241, 276
Live Shots (Ely), 96
living billboard, 342, 344, 346, *348*
Livingood, Bill, 297
Livingston, Bob, 254
Lockett, Sandy, 25
Logan, Horace, 49
"London Homesick Blues" (Nunn), 7, 231, 246
London Records, 82
Lone Star Beer, 5, 43, 229, 247, 341; and armadillo marketing, 352–353; and Eddie's New York trip, 301, 303–309; and Pearl Beer, 292, 327, 329; and progressive country, 255, 327; and TYNA/TACI work, 248–256, 326–327. *See also* "Long Live Longnecks"; "Nights Never Get Lonely, The" (Nunn)
"Long Live Longnecks," 9, 140, 251–253, 255, 256, 304
Lost Gonzo Band, 169, 254, 305, 326

Louisiana Hayride, 49, *50*, 51
Lovin' Spoonful, 127
Lower Colorado River Authority (LCRA), 48
LSD, 27, 45, 67, 70–71, 87, 100, 259, 340–341
"Luckenbach, Texas" (Jennings), 209
Lynn, Janet, 285
Lyon, Genie. *See* Wilson, Genie
Lyon, Johnny, 285

Mabry, Dave "Killer," 371, 376, 378–379
Mad Dog, Inc., 54, 222, 345. *See also* Shrake, Edwin "Bud"
Magic Time Machine, 326–327
Mahal, Taj, 7, *98*, *99*, 383
Mahavishnu Orchestra, 246, 284, 345
Majer, Carlyne, 295, 297
Majewski, George, 295, 296, 396
Mamas and the Papas, 127
Mangione, Chuck, 331, 345
Manilow, Barry, 201, 210
Man Mountain and the Green Slime Boys, 200, 215, 244, 285
Manor Downs, 329, 371
marijuana, 39, 70, 118, 121, 160, 257, 259, 261–262
Marshall Tucker Band, 261, 323, 331, *430*
Martin, Mary, 301, 304, 320
Matt's El Rancho, 273, 337, 355
Maxwell, Gary, 25
Mays, Mike, 143, 365, 404
Mays, Prissy, 143
McCall, Dianne, 342
McCall, Randy, 346, 349, 355, 376, 379; and AWHQ bankruptcy, 369, 371; and TYNA/TACI, 248, 250, 329
McCamey, Tom, 333
McCarthy, Joseph, 139
McClain, Blind George, 201, 202, *204*, 205
McClinton, Delbert, 295, 385
McCormick, Mack, 81
McCoslin, Geno, 219, 221

McDaniel, Charlotte, 359
McDaniel, Steve, *153*
McDowell, Fred, 25
McElhenney, Ada, 311–312, *313*
McElhenney, Tom R., 312, *313*
McFarland, Tiny, 215
McGeary, Michael, 319
McGhee, Brownie, 246, 331
McLaughlin, John, 152, 201, 246, 284
"Me and Bobby McGee" (Kristofferson), 62
Mechling, Leea, 290, 326, 371, 387, 392
Medlin, James "Big Boy," 282
Mellard, Jason, 245–246
Memorial Stadium, 82
Mercer, Mincemeat, 107
Meredith, Don, 135, 136–137
Metal Machine Music (Reed), 318
Meyers, Augie, 235
Meyers, Lloyd, 33
Midler, Bette, 7, 201, 210, *211*, *212*, 246, 345
Mighty Clouds of Joy, 331
Miller, Physina, 404, 405
Miller, Roger, 259
Miller, Townsend, 152, 165, 228–229, 244, 292
Millikin, Chesley, 193
Moby Grape, 22, 25
Monday Night Football, 135
Monfrey, John, 43
Monroe, Bill, 241, 242, 243, 292, 427
Moods of Country Music, 176
Moon-Hill Management, 94
Moore, Betty, 362
Moore, John, 367
MoPac Expressway, 148
Morrison, Sterling, 282
Morrison, Van, 267, *268*, 269, 274, 275, 301, 345
Morthland, John, 276
Mother Earth, 282, 368
Moursund, Big Rikke, 270, *271*

Moving Sidewalks, 81
Moyer, Ken, 239
Mueller Airport, 155, 174
Muldaur, Maria, 345, 385, *473*
Mull, Martin, 246
Municipal Auditorium, 121, 274, 331
Murphey, Michael, 9, 94, 171, 218, 239, 244, 345, *431*; and Armadillo Country Music Review, 166, *167*, 168–169, 227; and *Redneck Rock* lawsuit, 308, 311; and Texas Opry House, 284, 292–294
Muscle Shoals Rhythm Section, 176
Myrick, Gary, 85

Narum, Bill, 94, 96, 227, 228, 301, 406
Narum, Paula, 301
Nash, George, Jr., 392
National Lawyers Guild, 141
National Public Radio, 387
Nealy, Bill, *98*
Nelson, Willie, 155, *161*, 162, 171, 181, 229, 364, 379; and Armadillo Country Music Review, 166, *167*, 168, 215, 226, 227, 231; and first AWHQ show, 149, 159–160, 162, *163*, 164–166; and Leon Russell, 191, 193, 282; and rise of progressive country, 7, 9, 239, 244, 246; and tension with AWHQ, 224–225, 231–232; and Texas Opry House, 283, 318. *See also* Fourth of July Picnic, Willie Nelson's
New Deal, 48
Newman, Randy, 305
New Orleans, 400; Jazz Fest, 401, 403
New Riders of the Purple Sage, 183, 239, 282, 345, *432*
New York Times, 387
Night Hawk, 355
"Nights Never Get Lonely, The" (Nunn), 254–255, 305, 306, 307, 308–309, 326–327
Nitty Gritty Dirt Band, 159
Northcott, Bob, *144*

North Texas State Teachers College, 38

North Texas State University, 54

Now Dig This, 35–36, 37–38

Now the Revolution, 142

Nugent, Ted, *442*

Number One Bar, 355

Nunn, Gary P., 345, 385, *472*; "London Homesick Blues," 7, 231, 246; "The Nights Never Get Lonely," 254–255, 305, 306, 307, 308–309, 326–327

Oakes, Bill, 306

Oasis, 282

Oat Willie's, 100, 363

O'Brien, Derek, 322

Oceans, Lucky, 284, 285

O'Connell, Chris, 285

O'Connor, Renée, 401, 403

O'Connor, Tim, 318–319

Old and New Dreams, 371

Oleo Strut, 141

One Knite, 323, 396

One Texas Center, 394

Onion Audio, 89, 238, 313, 315, 376, 379

Orbison, Roy, 51, 383

Osborne, Edwin, 31–32

Osborne, Michael, 93, 94, 239

Overton, Timmy, 186

Page, Sid, 333

Palmer Auditorium, 193

Pankratz, Carlotta, 3, 149, 221, 231, 232, 315

Pankratz, Chickie, 157, 195

Pankratz, Lucky, 157, 195, 200

Pankratz, Pat, 155, *156*

Panther A-Go-Go, 160

Panther Hall, 160

Paramount Theater, 38

Parellis, Marty, 205

Parliament Funkadelic, *464*

Parsons, Gram, 159, *198*, 199–200

Party Barn, 59, 62

Paul, Julie, 62

Pearl Beer, 43, 291, 292, 327, 329, 354

Pemberton Heights, 132

People's Free Community Clinic, 76, 141, 335, *336*

Pepper, Allan, 306

Perez, Fermin "Speedy," 239

Perkins, Carl, 51

Perskin, Pete, 132

Perskin, Spencer, 66, 68, 76, 93, 132, 148, 149, 215, 340; and AWHQ financing, 54, 64; and Eddie Wilson, 11, 27, 28–29, 43, 45; photos of, *12*, *44*

Phillips, David, 176

Phillips, James Atlee, 175, 176

Phillips, Shawn, 152, 175–176, 246, *441*

Pickett, Wilson, 155

Pipkin, Turk, 339, 385

Plant, Robert, 300

Pointer Sisters, 255, 292, 323, 326–327, *328*, 331, 345

Ponty, Jean-Luc, 189, 201, 346, *347*

Port Arthur, TX, 62, 78, 93

poster artists, 22, 91, 100, 101. *See also* Armadillo Art Squad; *specific artists*

Presley, Elvis, 49, *50*, 51, *83*, 378, 396

Preston, Leroy, 285

Pretty Things, 297

Priest, Micael, 96, 97, 162, 239, 323, 335, 359, 410; design work by, 94, 100, 142, 224, 363; and emcee duties, 297–298, 388; gig posters by, *158*, *163*, *167*, *180*, *277*, *347*, *356*, *381*, *386*, *419*, *428–430*, *434*, *442*, *444*, *445*, *448*, *449*, *451*, *452*, *458*, *462*, *466*, *471*, *473*

Prine, John, 152, 223, 224

Professor Longhair, 295

progressive country, 7, 9, 150, 159, 184, 238–239, 243–246; and Lone Star Beer, 255, 327. *See also* "Coming of Redneck Hip, The" (Reid and Roth); *Improbable Rise of Redneck Rock, The* (Reid)

Prohibition, 59

Pryor, Cactus, 37

psychedelic rock, 13, 22, 193

Pugh, Mike, 155, *156*

Putnam, Sarah, 303

Quick, Monty, 362, 367

Quicksilver Messenger Service, 331

Radio Shack, 326

Rag, 64, 73, 76, 77, 94, 107, 263, 282

Rainbow Pavilion, 306, 311

Raitt, Bonnie, 282

Rakha, Alla, 124

Ramirez, Tomas, 331

Ramon, Ramon and the Four Daddyos, 64, 66, 68, 107, 265, 337, *418*

Ramones, 7, 372

Ramsey, Willis Alan, 234–235, 239

Ranger, 7, 243

Ransom, Sarah, 360

Rat Creek, *158*

Raul's, 372, 373

Rauschenberg, Robert, 93

Raw Deal, 357, *358*, 359–360, 362, 365–366, 375

Ray, Paul, 380, *381*

Ray, Wade, 160

Redbone, Leon, 383

Redman, Dewey, 371

redneck rock. *See* progressive country

Reed, Jimmy, *17*, 25, 122, 322

Reed, John X., 1, 2, 67, *153*, 258

Reed, Lou: *Metal Machine Music*, 318

Reid, Jan, 54; "The Coming of Redneck Hip," 243–244, 245, 293; *The Improbable Rise of Redneck Rock*, 224, 228, 230, 245, 293, 308

Reshen, Neil, 232

Retzloff, Jerry, 248–249, 255, 301

Richards, Ann, 54, 117, 162, 330, 339, 357, 363, *xii*

Richards, David, 54, 64

Righteous Scrub Company, 70

Risher, Granny, 31, 33, 36, 37, 109, 112, 146

Risher, Ione, 32, 388

Ritter, Ike, *12*, 67, *271*

Ritter, Tex, 216; "High Noon," 37

Ritz Theater, 38, 297, 315

Rivera, Bert, 285

Rivers, Sam, 371

Roberts, Woody, 228, 352, 357, 407; and Lone Star Beer work, 252–256, 327; and TYNA/TACI, 248–251, 307, 329; and Willie Nelson's picnic, 216, 218–219

Rockpile, 383

Rodgers, Jimmie, 59, 62

Rodriguez, Leon, 207

Rodriguez, Robert, 406

Rolling Stone, 169, 172, 244, 304, 318, 387

Rolling Stones, 284

Rollins, Sonny, 371

Rome Inn, 352, 376

Ronstadt, Linda, 200, 276, 278, 279

Rose, Dub, 185–186, 283–284, 323–324, 325, 339–340, 346, 376

Rose, Ron, 200

Roth, Don: "The Coming of Redneck Hip," 243–244, 245, 293

Rothbaum, Mark, 379

Roxy Music, 339

Royal, Darrell K, 165–166

RSO Records, 306, 307, 326

Ruby, Jack, 337

Runaways, 152

Rundgren, Todd, 290, *448*

Rusk State Hospital, 22, 325

Russell, Leon, 33, *123*, 124, 192, 229, 282, 405; and friendship with Willie, 191, 193; and Jim Franklin, 93, 124, 191; and Thanksgiving jam session, *194*, 195, *196*, 197; and Willie Nelson's picnic, 218–219, 224

Russell, Steve, 213

Rusty Nail, 282

Saddle Club, 282

Sahm, Doug, 191, *194*, 197, 239, *258*, 259, 318; and Austin/Dillo hype, 291, 292; bogarting ways of, 193, 195, 257, 385; and game room flood, 234, 235; and Jerry Wexler, 152, 155; and Soap Creek Saloon, 295, 297; and Willie Nelson's picnic, *217*, *218*, *219*

Salvation, 105

Sam's Showcase, 186

San Francisco, 7, 22, 27, 62, 76, 100, 137, 160, 319

San Francisco Mime Troupe, 137, 141

Sauer, Charlie, 134

Savages, 337

Savoy Brown, 346, *440*

Saxon Pub, 283

Scafe, Bruce, 228, 230

Scaggs, Boz, 176, *177*, 178, 284, 294, *424*

Scales, Doug, *144*, 146, 148, 171

Scanlon, Gary, 71

Scarbrough's, 35

Scat Records, 82

Schaefer Beer, 304

Schlafly, Phyllis, 330

Schlotzsky's, 118

Scholz Garten, 392

Scorpio, 282

Scruggs, Earl, *126*, 127, *158*, 159

Seaholm, J. T., 265

Sebastian, John, *126*, 127, 169

Sedwick, Shannon, 142

Seger, Bob, 331

segregation, racial, 33, 35, 39, 41

Selman, Wallace, 283, 293, 294

Seton Hospital, 52

Shankar, Ravi, 124, *125*, 345

Shannon, Tommy, 13, *15*, 85, 320

Shaver, Billy Joe, 9, 181, *182*, 183, 218, 227, 275

Shaver, Eddy, 183

Shaw, Robert, 383

Shelter Records, 124, 229

Shelton, Gilbert, 7, *14*, 22, 23, 27, 66–67, 100, 160, 291

Shelton, Michael, 142

Sheriff's Posse Arena, 282

Sherrod, Blackie, 54

Shiner Beer, 43, 329

Shiva's Headband, *12*, 13, 57, 62, *77*, 81, 160, 215, 340; and AWHQ's opening night, 64, 66, 68; and AWHQ's original purpose, 28, 75, 76, 148, 149; and Eddie Wilson, 11, 29, 56, 132, 141; gig posters for, *14*, *416*, *417*

Showco Productions, 121, 254, 299

Shrake, Edwin "Bud," 28, 53, 54, 127, 135, 136, 139, 345

Siegel, Shawn, *12*

Sinatra, Frank, 81, 388

Sixth Street, 320, 322, 355, 359

Skating Palace, 29, *46*, 48, 49

Skunks, 213, *372*, *373*, *462*

Skyline Club, 51, 283, 297

Slade, 213, 246

Smith, Al, 25, *26*

Smith, Bessie, 78

Smith, Bobby Earl, *153*

Smitham, Jim "Lopez," 365–366

Soap Creek Saloon, 94, 152, 261, 295, 297

South by Southwest (SXSW), 5, 406–407

Space City!, 94

Space City Video, 94

Spain, Jerry, 27, 262–263, 324

Spann, Otis, *86*

Spears, Bee, 164

Split Rail, 152, 282, 391

Spong, John, 255

Sportcenter, 49, *50*, 51

Sports Illustrated, 135

Springfield, Dusty, 155

Springsteen, Bruce, 7, 287, *288*, 289, 290, 292, 331, 345, *429*

Squirrel's Inn, 29

Staehely, John, 85

"Stand By Your Man" (Wynette), 152
Starcrost, 320
Steam Heat, 320, *449*
Stein, Andy, 276
Steppenwolf, 76, 260
Steve Miller Band, 25, 176
Stevenson, B. W., 94, 229, 239, 244, 333, 425
Stigwood, Robert, 306
Storm, 85, *86*, 103, 323, *416*
Strachwitz, Chris, 81
Strehli, Angela, 322, *381*
Stromquist, Big Gil, 186
Sublett, Jesse, 213, 248, 339, 372, *373*, 409
Sullivan, Barry, 248–249, 250, 251, 253, 256, 301
Sumlin, Hubert, 322
"Sunday Morning Coming Down" (Kristofferson), 62, 64
Sunny and the Sunliners, 208, 255, 305, 345
Sun Records, 51
Swan, Billy, 331, *435*
Sweet Home, TX, 43
SXSW. *See* South By Southwest (SXSW)
Sylar, Robin, 85

Talking Heads, 372, *374*, 383
Tarrytown, 132
Taylor, Chip, 240, *426*
Taylor, Jesse, 85
Taylor, TX, 37, 94
Taylorvision, 94, 228, 407
Terrace Motor Hotel, 283, 297
Terry, Sonny, 246, 331
Texas Alcoholic Beverage Commission (TABC), 136, 137, 265, 292, 323, 337, 346, 366; and TYNA/TACI, 249, 354
Texas Brewers' Institute, 42
Texas City, TX, 32–33
Texas Flatlanders. *See* Flatlanders
Texas Instruments, 201

Texas Monthly, 243, 255, 293, 362
Texas Observer, 105, 353, 354
Texas Opry House, 9, 178, 283, 284, 292–294, 297, 318, 376
ThanksGracey benefit, 372, *462*
13th Floor Elevators, 13, *14*, 22, 25, 81, 197
Thomas, Rufus, 51
Thompson, Bert W., 370
Thompson, Hank, 250, 285
Thornton, Big Mama, *21*, 25, 78
Threadgill, Dotty, 59
Threadgill, Kenneth, 155, 218, 282, 290, 387, 389, 391, 398; and Janis Joplin, 62, 64; legacy of, 57, 150, 243; photos of, *60*, *61*, *63*, *302*, *390*, *425*; and Wednesday music nights, 54, 59, 60, 78, 395
Threadgill, Mildred, 389, *390*
Threadgill's Restaurant, 389, 391, 395–396, 399, 412; fire at, 396, 397, 398, 401; and "Upstairs Store," 398, 400, 409; World Headquarters, 404–406, 408, 409, 412
Thurman, Benny, 197
Tiger Balm, 87, *416*
Time, 290, 291–292
Tolleson, Mike, 3, 57, *58*, 132, 207, 323, 346, 360, 407; as AWHQ shareholder, 149, 315; as house attorney, 164, 334; on Spencer Perskin, 76, 149; and TV music show, 227, 228, 229, 230–231, 406; and TYNA/TACI, 247–248, 249, 250, 329; and Willie Nelson's picnic, 216, 218, 221–222, 224
Tomlinson Lone Star Book of Texas Records, The, 342
Too Smooth, 319, 379–380, *434*, *438*, *442*
Toots and the Maytals, 331, 345
Town Lake. *See* Lady Bird Lake
Trader, Larry, 216, 218, 221
Troggs, 240
Troll, T. T., *415*, *416*, *418*
Tubb, Ernest, 216
Tubes, 339–340

Tucker, Luther, 322
Turicchi, Tom, 253–254, 306, 307, 326
Turner, John, 13, *15*, 85
Turner, Randy, *384*
TYNA/TACI, 247–250, 313, 345, 354; breakup of, 326–327, 329, 341; and New York trip, 301, 303–309, 311. *See also* "Long Live Longnecks"; "Nights Never Get Lonely, The" (Nunn)

"Uncle Zeke's Rock Emporium" (Flippo), 169, 171–172, 244
Underground Press Syndicate, 140–141
University of Texas at Austin, 7, 10, 39, 78, 137, 139, 210

Van Halen, *465*
Van Vleck, TX, 39
Van Vliet, Don. *See* Captain Beefheart
Van Zandt, Townes, 239, 383
Vaughan, Charles, 228
Vaughan, Jimmie, 85, *86*, 322, 323, *454*, *462*
Vaughan, Stevie Ray, 85, 186, 322, 380
Velvet Cowpasture, 62, 387
Velvet Underground, 25, 27, 282
Ventura, Michael, 282
Victoria, TX, 215–216
Vietnam War, 45, 53, 340
Violators, 372, *373*
Virginia's Café, 360
Vizard, Ed, 67
Von, Tony, 37
Vulcan Gas Company, 3, 7, 13, *14*, 25, 81, 263; and comparisons to AWHQ, 22, 52, 53, 73; and drug busts, 27–28, 56; photos of, *15, 16, 17, 18, 19, 20, 21, 24*

Wagner, Cyrus, 284
Wainwright, Loudon, III, 201, 345
Waits, Tom, 351
Wake of the Flood (Grateful Dead), 233

Walker, Jerry Jeff, 169, *170*, 171, 218, 239, 244, 291, 345, 385
Walker, Susan, 345
Waller Creek Boys, 243
Ward, Ed, 166, 276
Warner Bros. Records, 140, 301, 304, 320
Watergate hearings, 228–229, 231
Waters, Muddy, 13, *16*, 25, 322
Watkins, Larry, 292–293
Watson, Doc, 383
Watson, Merle, 383
Waybill, Fee, 339
Waylors, 181, 224
Weddell, Wray, 52
Weddle, Vernon, 32–33
Weinstein, Abe, 337
Weir, Bob, *194*, *461*
Wendler, Ed, 364, 406
Wertheimer, Steve, 410
Wet Willie, 346
Wexler, Jerry, 152, 155, 320
Wharton County Junior College, 38
Whistler, 64, *424*
White, Blackie. *See* Juke, Guy
White, Houston, *24*, 25, 27, 28
White, James, 152
White, Monica, *435*
White Rabbit, 366–368
White's Pharmacy, 35
Whitten, Sam, 101
Whole Foods Market, 330–331
Wier, Rusty, 94, 346
Wiggins, Lanny, 243
Wiggins, Ramsey, 243, 345, 352
Wilks, Van, 320
Willenzik, Allen, 375, 379
Willenzik, Bruce, 342, 355, 375–376, 385
Williams, Big Joe, 25
Williams, Hank, 297
Williams, Tennessee, 304; *Cat on a Hot Tin Roof*, 140, 301, 304
Wills, Bob, 164, 285

Wilson, Beulah, 10, 30, 31–32, 148, 157, 357, 391, 398; and AWHQ house piano, 33, 109, 112

Wilson, Burton, 79, 98, 130, *131*, 132, *153*, 164; and murder of Ken Featherston, 324–325

Wilson, Eddie, 4, 30, 74, *116*, 194, *348*, 361, *402*; as AWHQ shareholder, 3, 149, 315; and childhood in Austin, 31–33, 35–38; and departure from AWHQ, 353–354, 355, 357, 359; and discovery of AWHQ site, 1–3, 28–29, 391; and postcollege wandering, 38–40, 41–43; and tensions with AWHQ staff, 256, 311, 313–315, 334; and vision for AWHQ, 56–57, 76, 149, 245, 313–315; Woody Roberts on, 249–250. *See also* Armadillo World Headquarters; Raw Deal; Threadgill's Restaurant; TYNA/TACI

Wilson, Frank, 30, 195

Wilson, Genie, 3, 39, 40, 56, *348*, 353, 396, 398; as AWHQ shareholder, 149, 315; and houseguests, 132, 267

Wilson, Sandra, 400–401, *402*, 403, 409, 410–411

Wilson, Woody, 30, 32–33, 38, 195, 367, 398; and AWHQ improvements, 56, *147*, 148

Winter, Johnny, 13, *15*, 25, 74, 78, 81, 85, 259

Winterland, 76, 137, 260

Wonder Wart-Hog, 22, 291

Wood, Sam, *140*

Woolworth's, 35

World War II, 31, 32, 49

Worsham, John, 392

Wuenche, Linda, 185

Wynette, Tammy: "Stand By Your Man," 152

Wynne, Angus, III, 121, 124

Xeno Sound, 238

Yeates, Sam, 96, 335, 380; gig posters by, *338*, *436*

Young, Neil, 200

Zappa, Frank, 7, 189, 201–202, 205–207, 246, 284, 345, 383; *Bongo Fury*, 206, 318; gig posters for, 287, *428*, *459*; photos of, *203*, *204*

Zihuatanejo, Mexico, 12, 38–39

ZZ Top, 82, 83, 94, 96, 320